What others are saying about this b

"Seven Choices is one of the best books e
mourning."
— *Value & Visions*, Cultural Information Service, voi. 25, No. 4

"This is the best book I have ever read on grieving; and I have read many. This is the most empowering book I have ever used in working with grieving people; and I have worked with many."
— Bill Moore, National Trainer, AARP, Widowed Persons Services

"Seven Choices is an affirmation of the power of the grieving process, a source of hope and validation. Dr. Neeld clearly goes well beyond a focus on coping (which is necessary) and acceptance to the importance of integration and self-empowerment. This is a book that is easy to recommend to a friend or loved one struggling with a loss, needing validation of their own process. It provides ways to heal and offers hope during the darkest times." — Dr. John Schneider, author, *Stress, Loss and Grief*

"Thirty-five years as a pastor has convinced me that a person in grief needs a friend. *Seven Choices* is a friend indeed. It is encouraging, honest, and intimate. Through reading it, one emerges from isolation by making the connection with all who sorrow." — Rev. William Youngkin, Pastor, David's United Church of Christ, Dayton, OH

"Seven Choices is a profound book in many ways because the author really cares about people; her subtle suggestions bear the mark of someone who has been there herself and knows exactly how gut-wrenching a sudden loss can be. Deeply compassionate and very wise. This is a fine, sensitive book written by a very intelligent person. Extremely well done."
— *The Coast Book Review Service*, Fullerton, CA

"This is the best work on mourning since Judith Viorst's *Necessary Losses*. What makes *Seven Choices* such an extraordinary work is Neeld's thought-provoking diary entries and her skillful use of a wide variety of quotations about change, self-discovery, emotional renewal, reminiscence, and making meaning out of memories. This is the kind of book which both professionals and lay people in the process of grieving can use to replenish the spirit."
— *Living Room Learning*, Cultural Information Service

"Men and women who live in the abyss of grief report the discovery of grace and, ultimately, joy as they study and appropriate *Seven Choices*."
— Dr. Betty Youngkin, Assistant Professor of English, University of Dayton

"My son was killed on his motorcycle eleven years ago, and, yes, there has been tremendous healing. *Seven Choices* is still very helpful to me, however, after all this time. Thank you."
— SM, Maryland, letter to author

"I am deeply impressed with *Seven Choices* and feel it will be most helpful for many of the grieving persons in the Grief Work Group."
— Dorothy Smith, Chaplain, Miami Valley Hospital, OH

"Our support group has used *Seven Choices* several times for intensive, small-group series. Your wisdom, honesty and shared experience have equipped us with the necessary tools to move forward—as an informed choice!"
— Pam Walker, Co-Founder, Young Widows' Support Group, Dayton, OH

"*Seven Choices* celebrates the power within each of us to choose a path through the grieving process and shows us how not to lose ourselves to the helplessness and hopelessness of loss."
— Paula Whitson, Houston, Texas

"By the use of personal stories and the account of others, Dr. Neeld describes the journeys of the newly bereaved. She suggests that a person who is in fragments, broken into pieces by the impact of the circumstances, has choices to make in order to gather the pieces into "one whole" again. Leading the reader gently to the focus of each chapter, she directly offers a clear description of The Choice in each of the seven choices."
— Bucky Poppleton, Book Reviewer, *Hospice Journal*

"Anyone who has experienced loss through death or divorce needs education and support. An excellent reference book on grieving is the book *Seven Choices* by Elizabeth Harper Neeld, Ph.D.."
— Vivian Kotler-Haas, therapist, *Farmington Connecticut News*

Seven Choices

By Elizabeth Harper Neeld

Writing, 1, 2, 3 Editions
Writing Brief, 1, 2, 3 Editions
Readings for Writing
The Way a Writer Reads
Writing: A Short Course
Options for the Teaching of English:
The Undergraduate Curriculum (ed.)
Either Way Will Hurt & Other Essays on English (ed.)
Harper & Row Studies in Language and Literature (ed.)
Fairy Tales of the Sea (ed.)
From the Plow to the Pulpit (ed.)
Yes! You Can Write (audio)
Sister Bernadette: Cowboy
Nun from Texas
A Sacred Primer: The Essential Guide to Quiet Time and Prayer

Seven Choices

TAKING THE STEPS TO
NEW LIFE AFTER LOSS
SHATTERS YOUR WORLD

Elizabeth Harper Neeld, Ph.D.

Centerpoint Press

Published by
Centerpoint Press
a division of
MBI Publishing
6706 Beauford Drive
Austin, Texas, 78750
512-342-2890
www.centerpointpress.com
e-mail: cppaustin@aol.com

1990 Clarkson N. Potter, Inc. (Hardbound)
1992 Bantam Doubleday Dell (Paperback)
1997 Centerpoint Press (Third Edition, Revised)
Fourth Printing

The stories told in *Seven Choices* are true. In order to honor the privacy of the more than sixty generous and kind individuals who were willing to discuss with me their grieving process, I have altered names and other distinguishing features of the accounts. In addition, in the telling of my own story, I have looked backward with eyes that can now see pattern, order, significance, and progression in what was at the time often only random, unconnected events. I have told the *truth* of my story at the same time that I have, on occasion, telescoped events, consolidated meanings, and altered strict chronological sequence in order to provide lucidity and precision in the discussion of the mourning process. I have also changed some names and details in order to respect the privacy of individuals with whom I interacted during those years.

LIBRARY OF CONGRESS CATALOGING-IN-PUBLICATION DATA
Neeld, Elizabeth Harper, 1940-
Seven choices: taking the steps to new life after loss shatters your world/
Elizabeth Harper Neeld.--3rd ed., rev.
p.   cm.
Includes bibliographical references and index.
ISBN 0-937897-90-6
1. Bereavement--Psychological aspects. 2. Death--Psychological aspects. 3. Grief.
I. Title.
BF575.G7N44 1997

155.9'37—dc21   96-48252

CIP
ISBN: 0-937897-90-6
SAN: 659-4352

Cover Art: Sandi Jackson
Cover Design: Luis Gonzales

For All Past and Future Readers

CONTENTS

ACKNOWLEDGMENTS

It was at the Stanford Professional Publishing Course, directed by the wise and ebullient Della van Heyst, that I met three individuals, visiting faculty for the SPPC, who were key in my following through on the idea to write this book: Martin Levin and Robert Baensch, who reviewed my previous publications and urged me to build on that success by writing for the trade; and Lawrence Ashmead, who read an early excerpt from *Seven Choices* and encouraged me to seek publication. I am appreciative of these men, not only for their engagement with my work, but also for their obvious commitment to books and for their humane concern for the people who write them.

To Elizabeth Backman, my agent, who saw possibilities in the original ideas I had for this book that I had not seen, I owe a debt of thanks. I also appreciate the enthusiasm with which she represented my work.

The poet William Stafford once told me that an editor is a friend who keeps you from looking foolish. Carol Southern, my editor, has been that kind of friend. For that and her many other contributions, I thank her.

To Harry Lipscomb, M.D., and John Talmadge, M.D., who read the book in manuscript and assured me of its soundness, I am deeply indebted. And, likewise, to Julia Poppy, whose careful, critical reading allowed me to know that the book was finished. Charles Anderson offered the counsel both of a friend and a writer, and I was greatly benefited. Arthur Egendorf gave advice about ways to strengthen the book that I found valuable. And the other individuals who read the book in draft form, each a representative of some segment of the broad audience for whom I was writing, I thank: Lyn Fraser, Russell Duesterhoft, Beth Mercer, Jane Adkins, Martha Faulkner, Lil Jackson, Lynne Sims, Carol Estes, Sandra Linton, and Rick Smith.

Eliot Lippman provided impeccable research service; the materials he gathered inform every section of *Seven Choices*. Virginia Bass generously gave of her time to locate hard-to-find references, and Jeanette Rychlik checked and rechecked the accuracy of the book's documentation. Gerald Vinson refined the visual map of the grieving process. Rachel Harper gave personal support, without which the book would not have been written. David Rosen, M.D., gave professional support during the time I was writing this book that enabled me to understand more clearly my own grieving. And Jerele Don Neeld, my husband, made everything possible.

ACKNOWLEDGMENTS TO THIRD REVISED EDITION

I wish to acknowledge these persons who gave so much assistance to this new edition of *Seven Choices*. Thanks to: Ryanto Putra for his expert computer skills and attention to administration; Kathleen Sauvé for her impeccable manuscript preparation; Cynthia Ludnecky for her gift of support which let me know how much new editions of *Seven Choices* were desired; Jerele Neeld whose sharp eye helped me bring the right staff together for the preparation of this edition; Sandi Jackson for the cover art; and Luis Gonzales for his design of the cover.

INTRODUCTION TO
THIRD REVISED EDITION

*S*even Choices was first published by Clarkson Potter, a subsidiary of Random House, in hardback in 1990. In 1992 Bantum Doubleday Dell Publishing Group made *Seven Choices* available as a Delta quality paperback. *Seven Choices* and Dr. Neeld were also the subject of an hour-long Public Television documentary entitled "The Challenge of Grief" which was shown on PBS stations throughout the United States. It is with pleasure that Centerpoint Press carries forward the publishing record of this book by making it available now in this Third Revised Edition.

What old friends of *Seven Choices* will find here is the same account of Elizabeth Neeld's story as she worked to integrate into her life the sudden death of a young husband; the same in-depth research of doctors, scientists, philosophers, thinkers on the subject of grief and life; the same narratives of more than sixty people who shared their experiences of finding new life after losing someone they loved.

What previous and new readers of *Seven Choices* will find, in addition, is an epilogue in which Dr. Neeld writes of her life since the initial publishing of *Seven Choices*; research and literary sections revised for conciseness and more direct applicability; an updated resources guide.

Seven Choices has proven to be a lifeline, a hope, an ongoing reference, a guide to thousands and thousands of individuals. This Third Edition, Revised is offered as a commitment to continue and to extend that contribution.

PROLOGUE

What is happening to me?
How can I live through this?
How can I get over my loss?

These are questions that haunt us when we lose someone we love.

We do not understand the mercurial emotions that heave inside us. We are not prepared for the ever-present pain and the unrelenting reminders. We do not know what to do with ourselves once the event is over. We see nothing that we can do to make things any better. Our loss is like an envelope we live in. Always there. Always on our minds. Always pressing.

Then, as the days and months, even years, progress, we ask ourselves, "Wasn't the passage of time supposed to be the answer? Why are there so many touchy spots that remain—places I can't go, things I can't do, thoughts I can't entertain, objects I can't look at?" We wonder if we will always be so upset. If we will always be hostages to our pain.

Perhaps as time goes on, we find ourselves becoming ill more often than we used to: "I seem to have one cold after another.... The pains in my chest are getting worse.... I worry about my health." Or having more accidents: "Can you believe it? A man who's been skiing for twenty years without a fall, and *now* I break my leg."

Or it could be that we finally arrive at the place where we think we are over the loss. We don't cry anymore. We don't feel a lot of pain. Yet we don't want to go anywhere or do anything. Nothing around us interests us. The things we enjoyed in the past now give us no pleasure. We have no energy, no enthusiasm. We do not feel alive. Life has no meaning.

What we do not know is that each of these experiences—the intense emotion, the stress that can cause sickness and accidents, the apathy and ennui—are all a natural response to our loss. We are unaware that a complex process was started the moment we perceived the first hint of the intrusion of loss into our lives, and that everything we are feeling—the sadness, the pain, the imbalance, the emptiness— is a part of that process. We also do not know, because what we are experiencing now is so upsetting, that the process that has begun can culminate in our regaining our equilibrium. As Dr. George Pollock, a psychiatrist who has done important work in grief research, puts it, if we choose to move through the complete grieving process, we can achieve a creative outcome wherein the suffocating domination of grief lightens and we find ourselves feeling new energies. These ener- gies may take many forms: a quickened verve for living; a new rela- tionship; a creative product; the ability to feel happy or peaceful or well again; the desire to get back to work; the stirring of ideas and plans; a sense of release; a new calm.

To learn as much as we can, then, about this mourning process is one of the most valuable things we can do for ourselves when we are grieving. Not only so that we can anticipate the different kinds of experiences we can expect to have—the experiences that are normal — but, much more important, so that we can be aware that we our- selves play the critical role in determining the outcome of our mourn- ing.

Of course, there is an extremely wide range of what is considered "normal" in grieving. According to recent research, some people re- ported that they did not experience intense distress or depression after the loss of a loved one. Such individuals were able, in the word of one psychologist, to bear their grief "lightly." Resilience, a belief system that allows the loss to be put into a larger context, a spiritual outlook that gives hope and perspective—such conditions and circum- stances, researchers suggest, explain why some people are able to respond to a loss without intense upset, depression, and distress.

On the other hand, millions of us have not found the means to bear our grief lightly. Even when we hold a spiritual outlook deeply impor- tant to us, or work to find a source of resiliency soon after our loss, or attempt to put what has happened into a context of understanding and acceptance, we are still jolted off our feet, pained beyond expres- sion, and mercilessly confused and confounded by the chaos wrought in our lives. We need information that will enable us to understand our responses and reactions and to make the choices that will result in a new sense of equilibrium in our lives. For us, learning about the complex process of grieving can, literally and figuratively, save our lives.

For the sad truth is that not everybody makes it. At least one researcher tells us that it is possible that as high a percentage as one out of every three individuals who grieve do not experience a positive resolution to their mourning. These individuals, instead, remain caught in a cycle of unfinished grieving that can result in ill health and ill temper (and even in death); in perpetual disquiet and unease; in apathy and boredom; in distrust and anger; in lonely, unfulfilled searches for comfort and companionship; in frantic flailings for purpose and meaning; in permanent loss of visions and dreams.

Fortunately, the chapters that follow show how to avoid such a sad end to mourning. This is a guidebook that you can use to make your way through the unfamiliar, upsetting, life-threatening experience of loss. A guidebook that teaches how to make a successful passage through the complex grieving process so that you can complete mourning and reach a constructive outcome.

In earlier days, the rituals followed by clan or community greatly facilitated passage through the grieving process. These rituals gave direction; they promoted the release of emotion; they helped make the absence of the person real; they assisted those grieving to plan a new life in which the lost person would be absent. These rituals directed the thinking and actions of a person who had experienced loss so that mourning could be completed.

Imagine, for instance, an East African man of the last century who had just become a widower. For twelve months the entire community participated with this man and his family in the rituals of mourning.

First, there was the funeral. Then, when the funeral was over, an extended period of mourning began. For one full year the widower and his family kept the dead woman alive in everyone's mind by talking about her endlessly and by continuing to display intense grief in public.

At the same time the community was preparing for a second funeral to be held on the anniversary of the woman's death. This second funeral would be a major event in the lives of friends, family, and clan members who would come from long distances to participate.

At the second funeral the woman's grave was opened slightly, and those attending lamented and grieved loudly. Then the wailing would cease, for the dead woman was believed to have now left the living world and to have joined her ancestors in the spirit world. The funeral now turned into a celebration.

The Alaskan Tlingit Indian tribe, in earlier times, participated in an even longer rite of mourning. Let's follow the experience of a woman of the nineteenth century whose husband had just died.

The widow first sat mute for three days by her dead husband, who was propped up in front of a brightly decorated wall. Following these three days of vigil, the clan performed the cremation ceremony with wailing, singing, dancing with branches, and clipping of hair—both theirs and the widow's—clippings they subsequently threw into the funeral fire.

After the cremation the widow entered an eight-day period of silence and solitude, during which time she slept with a rock under her pillow, ensuring long life for her next husband, and with a cord around her waist, ensuring long life for all members of her family. Her bedding and clothing were burned, and she received new items. She used no knife when she ate, symbolizing that her life would not be shortened. On the last day of her solitude, the widow and the deceased's sisters washed their hair in the juice of blueberries to prevent their hair from turning gray in old age.

But the mourning would have just begun. Emerging from her days of silence, the widow entered an extended period of mourning during which three things happened: Members of the tribe built a grave house for her husband's bones and ashes; they built a new house for her or remodeled the old one; and the widow and her kin collected large numbers of gifts to be distributed at the ceremony that would be held when the building and remodeling were completed. During this extended period of mourning—which could be from several months to several years in length—the widow had a special role. She was a part of the tribe but did not participate in communal life in her usual way.

Then, when the grave house and the widow's house were ready and the gifts had been gathered, the tribe held a celebration. People came from far places to eat and to receive gifts. Food was placed on the fire for all who had died, including the widow's late husband. There was dancing and singing. The conclusion of the ceremony marked the end of the widow's mourning. She was then free to remarry and to resume her regular place in tribal life.

But we don't have such rituals today to tell us what to do and how to think about our losses. Instead, mourning now takes place in what Nor Hall refers to as our "interior terrain." Our grieving is a mental process, as Anthony Storr points out. A private, not a public, ritual. Therefore, we are forced to direct our own grief process; we must be aware of and responsible for our own thinking and actions, which makes mourning even harder.

Is it possible to have a map of this interior terrain where we are obligated to carry out our private grieving? A map that identifies the different phases or sets of experiences that could be part of our mourning? It has been my intention, in writing this book, to provide just such a map to guide the way (see page 7).

Any map, of course, at best can be only a representation of the locale to be traversed. And every traveler makes the journey through any mapped terrain in a personal way. A map is invaluable, nonetheless, when we want to locate ourselves, to check our options, or to mark our route. Such is the value we can find in a map of the grieving process.

In my study of grief, I have identified seven sets or clusters of experience—seven phases—that mark the grieving process. Not everyone experiences all seven of these phases—certainly not in the same intensity or proportion—and not everyone moves through the seven phases in the order in which they appear on the map. The pacing is personal, with much back-and-forth movement and much overlapping or simultaneity in our experiences. Yet the experiences that I have isolated and mapped are familiar enough to be identified, are true for most of us, and can lead to a new state of balance and a new sense of equilibrium when we choose to do the work that results in integration.

First, there is Impact, that moment when we are assaulted by the news of our loss and after which we will not be the same. Impact is often followed by the Second Crisis, a period of bleak emptiness, loneliness, sadness, and depression, during which our lives have no familiar form or structure. At some point we have the opportunity to move into Observation, a time when we make a distinction between the event that has happened and our reaction to that event, and a time when we take stock of how we are behaving and of the options that lie before us. From Observation we make the Turn, a private moment of commitment and decision that asserts that we do have a future, even if that future is as yet blank and unknown. The experiences of Reconstruction follow, when we begin the actual building of a new life at the same time that we attend to our continuing connection to the past. Working Through is that difficult period when the problems and challenges of the life we are now building intersect with the problems and challenges related to our life from the past, and we are forced to deal creatively and simultaneously with both. We understand the value of this hard work, however, when we experience Integration, a release from feeling dominated by our mourning that brings with it a new sense of freedom. Our world has regained its equilibrium, and we recognize that we have grieved.

Movement through this grieving process is not a function of the passage of time. Rather, it is our own decisions that determine whether or not we reach Integration. For at critical junctures in the process, we do make particular choices that move us forward toward a constructive outcome. Or we fail to make those choices and remain stuck, unable to finish our grieving and move on.

Without a doubt the private ritual of mourning we must conduct is confusing and almost always lonely (regardless of the kindnesses of our family and friends). But to know that it is within our own power —by virtue of the choices we make—to determine the outcome of our grieving is to see at least some kind of opening ahead. Even though we can do nothing about the loss itself, we can, through the choices we make now, create for ourselves a new future.

Having experienced a series of losses—a divorce, the suicide of one grandfather and the natural death of another, the deaths of two grandmothers, and, then, the sudden death of my young husband, I have reflected much on the mourning process. I've had much opportunity to halt and to bungle my own progress, because for so long I didn't understand how to grieve. I've had much opportunity to learn, often by trial and error, what works to bring mourning to a constructive conclusion. It has taken me a long time to make sense of my own mourning—it's been more than ten years since my husband died—

Map of the Complete Grieving Process

**LIFE
AS IT WAS**

The Event

IMPACT

*To Choose to Experience
and Express Grief Fully*

THE SECOND CRISIS

*To Choose to Suffer
and to Endure*

OBSERVATION

To Choose to Look Honestly

**LIFE
BACK IN BALANCE**

Freedom from the Domination of Grief

INTEGRATION

*To Choose to Continue
to Make Choices*

WORKING THROUGH

*To Choose to Engage
in the Conflicts*

RECONSTRUCTION

To Choose to Take Action

THE TURN

To Choose to Make an Assertion

but I am now much clearer about what I did that hindered and helped the process.

My purpose in the pages that follow is to pass on what I have learned from my own experience as well as from both the practical and theoretical research I have subsequently conducted. I have taken pains to match my personal experience against the findings of medical and scientific research. I have talked with doctors and therapists, read books and studies, interviewed people who had experienced mourning. To test and refine my findings, I have worked with several hundred people in classes, workshops, and lectures. The result, which you will find in this book, is a delineation of the complete grieving process—with a focus on the choices we can make that will allow us to reach a constructive outcome in our mourning.

Each section of the book that follows begins with a narrative of my own experience of that particular phase of the mourning process. Agreeing with the British social scientist Peter Marris that "the grieving of widowhood [provides] the clearest model of an internal struggle which appears again and again, in transmuted form, in response to many kinds of loss," I have focused these narratives on the loss of my husband.

You will find, however, that my story merely serves as a mirror to reflect the disasters and the triumphs we all experience during the process of grieving for many kinds of losses—divorce, the death of (or separation from) our parents, children, partners, brothers and sisters, friends. The stories of the more than sixty individuals whom I have interviewed, as well as the facts and figures, observations and findings from medical and scientific research that I have included throughout the commentary, further demonstrate the universality of the grieving process. Moreover, the stories and information serve another very important function: they provide incontrovertible evidence that those of us who have experienced a traumatic loss do not have to be doomed to the deadness and sadness and hopelessness that come from unfinished grieving.

But enough framing of the tale.

It is now time to begin....

1

Impact

Well, everyone can master grief

'cept he that has it.

WILLIAM SHAKESPEARE

I looked at my watch: 8:17 P.M.

"He really should be back," I thought. "I know it's harder to jog here than back home. But, even so, he's had enough time to finish his run by now."

Every summer, as soon as the spring term ended at Texas A&M, Greg and I came to our cabin in the Tennessee hills. We had bought the place four years earlier, just after we had gotten married. We could hardly believe our good fortune: the cabin cost us almost nothing because it was so old and run-down (a condition Greg found most appealing—he loved to wield a saw and a hammer) and the location reminded us so much of the beautiful spot where we were married.

In fact, the mountains around our cabin were part of the same range that sheltered Cade's Cove, the site of our wedding. When we were dating, we had come upon the tiny cove that appears so unexpectedly and incongruously among the rugged and steep mountain peaks. Here a few families of pioneers, trekking in the early nineteenth century toward a new life, had found a haven among the cove's meadows. The barrier of mountains surrounding them required the settlers to rely on their own ingenuity. Their cabins, water mill, barns, churches, and pasture fences are still standing, now preserved as a national treasure, a testimony to the pioneer's self-sufficiency. When we decided to get married, it was the oldest cabin in the cove, the John Oliver place, that Greg and I chose as the wedding site. That cabin, with its hand-hewn timbers, its doors fastened with carved wooden hinges, its floors worn smooth by generations of living, was a symbol for us of the way we wanted to live our new life together: simple, strong, in harmony with the environment.

Our own cabin had been built only 40 years ago, not over 150, but it and the surroundings had the same sense of timelessness and peace as Cade's Cove and John Oliver's cabin. Whether it was down at the feed store listening to the farmers guess about rain or on my parents' front porch, our chairs tilted back against the wall, listening to night talk, we felt our spirits renewed when we came here.

My seventy-two-year-old daddy, a Holiness preacher retired from pastoring but not from preaching, as he was quick to tell you, had settled himself and Mother a few years before in a little wood-framed house on Possum Creek in Soddy-Daisy, which was right nearby. Greg and I loved to walk up the road at the end of the day and visit with my parents on their front porch.

"Got two bushels of butter beans out of the garden today," Daddy would report. "And if we get rain, there'll be more the day after tomorrow.... Here, Elizabeth, take this dishpan and see if your thumbs still know how to open a bean."

And then there'd be discussion about the progress of Mother's fourteen-day cucumber pickles and whether or not there were enough tomatoes to begin to can. Most nights there'd be homemade peach ice cream about bedtime; and then Daddy would say, "Time to turn in." Greg and I would start for the cabin.

We always seemed to be able to see the moon and at least one bright star in front of us as we walked down the country road. I would look up at the sky and chant a rhyme from my childhood:

> I see the moon;
> The moon sees me;
> God bless the moon
> And God bless . . .

Instead of "God bless me," I always said, "And God bless us."
Greg would answer:

> Star light, star bright,
> First star I see tonight;
> I wish I may, I wish I might,
> Have the wish I wish tonight.

"But," he'd say, pulling me close, "I've already got my wish. I've got you!" No matter how predictable this ritual, we still laughed every time he said those words.

Greg and I were both professors, and we used the summer months to do our writing. We had come to the cabin this summer to finish a book we were writing together, and our work was going well. In the five days since we arrived we had opened up the cabin, unpacked our books and supplies, and decided where each of us would work.

Greg's spot was at a small table on the tiny screened-in front porch. "Let's me see who's going up and down the road," he joked, as if any more than one or two neighbors were likely to pass in a whole day's time. I worked inside at the table we had placed beside a long wall of windows. I could watch the chameleons that scampered along the old stone foundation where, in some earlier time, another part of the cabin had stood. And if I looked up, I could almost see the tops of the pine trees that grew all around the cabin. "Virgin pines. Hundreds of years old," Greg explained. "They've never been cut; that's why they're so tall."

Work had gone well today, and after supper Greg had said, "Want to join me for a six-mile run?"

"No, sir, offer declined," I said. "I'll do the two-mile route and see you back here when you're finished."

So I had run to the Possum Creek bridge and back, and it was now time—past time—for Greg to be home. Minutes passed. "I bet these hills *did* get to him," I said to myself. "He's probably walking the last miles. I'll take the car and go pick him up; he'll appreciate a ride back home."

I started the car and guided it carefully over the big roots of the trees that grew all the way up to the edge of the cabin. I turned onto the paved road from the cabin lane. It was that time between daylight and dark that makes one feel lonesome and melancholy. Reaching the bridge at Possum Creek, I noticed how still and deep the water looked. Everything was covered with that kind of gray-green light left in the mountains when the sun has almost gone down. I crossed the bridge and rounded a curve.

There I came upon a scene of confusion. Large groups of people were standing on both sides of the road and spilling out into it. Carefully, I threaded my way through the crowd. I drove past the black-and-white car that belonged to the sheriff's patrol. I drove past the orange-and-white ambulance parked in the gravel on the left-hand side of the road. What held my attention was getting back onto the open road.

The trees and bushes were thick and grew close to the pavement. "It'll be easy to miss him if you aren't careful," I reminded myself as I left the crowd behind. So I drove slowly, looking carefully to the right and to the left.

There he is! I see him! It was a glimpse of Greg's orange running shorts. I had known I would find him taking it slow and easy up and down these hills! I accelerated the car and exhaled a sigh of relief. How long, I wondered, had I been holding my breath?

But when I got to the spot where Greg was, the orange was a cylinder that had been mounted on a post, meant to hold a newspaper.

By now I had reached the country store that I knew was Greg's three-mile turnaround point. "I've just missed him somewhere on the road," I said, speaking aloud to no one but myself. "I'll turn around here. I know I'll see him on the way back. I've just managed somehow to miss him."

When I got to the curve above Possum Creek, the large crowd was still there. So was the black-and-white car that belonged to the sheriff's patrol. And so was the orange-and-white ambulance.

I noticed a man standing in the middle of the road. He seemed to be directing traffic.

"What happened?" I asked, rolling down the window when I got abreast of him.

"Lady, move on. You're blocking traffic," was the man's reply.

I eased the car on down toward another man who was also standing in the middle of the road. This man appeared to be in charge.

"Sir, what happened?" I asked again.

"We found a man in the ditch," he answered.

"Well, I'm looking for my husband," I said. "My husband went for a six-mile run, and he hasn't come home yet."

For a few seconds the man said nothing. Then he spoke in a voice so low that I could hardly hear him. "Ma'am, I think you should pull your car over to the side of the road." I felt no emotion. I asked no additional questions. If there was any connection between what was happening beside that road and my life, it still was not apparent to me. But I did what I was told. I pulled over to the side of the road.

There was a place I could park on the gravel. I pulled in beyond the ambulance and turned off the motor. By the time I put my feet on the ground outside the car, that man and another were there by my open door. They were waiting for me to get out of the car.

From my seat, I looked up at the two strange men. It was only then that I realized that the man they had found in the ditch and the man I was looking for were probably one and the same.

"Is he dead?" I asked.

There was a long silence. One of the men finally answered.

"Yes, ma'am. He is."

I got out of the car. One man stood on my right side and one on my left. We began to walk, not touching, toward the ambulance. Greg, my husband, was dead.

We reached the back door of the orange-and-white ambulance. The crowd standing there quickly moved aside. No one was talking. I stepped up to get into the ambulance. The wire-mesh grate under my feet did not seem stable. I held on to the railing to keep from falling.

A shiny chrome bench ran the length of the ambulance; it was cold when I sat down on it. In front of me a body lay on a stretcher, covered by a white sheet. A pair of jogging shoes rested on top of the body's stomach. Blue Adidas. I knew they were Greg's before I ever saw him.

When the man pulled down the sheet, I felt no emotion. How can you cry when you know it is not possible that your husband is dead? "Look at him," I thought. "There's nothing wrong with him. He looks exactly the way he did taking a nap on the front porch swing this afternoon. He couldn't have died from those gravel burns on his cheek. There's just been some mistake; I know he's not dead." Nevertheless, when the man standing at the door of the ambulance said he needed to ask me some questions, I covered the body up again.

"Is this your husband? . . . What was his address? . . . What is his date of birth? . . . What is your name? . . . Does he have any children?

. . . Are his parents living? . . . What was his occupation? . . ." I felt
so competent, knowing all the answers. There was not a single one I
stumbled over.

My mother and father arrived at the ambulance. I heard my
father crying and calling out before I ever saw him. "I don't believe
it's Greg," he was saying as he pushed his way through the crowd.
"Let me through. I've got to see if it's him."

When he got to the door, I said, "Yes, Daddy, it's Greg." I got
out of the ambulance so he could see. Then I saw my mother running through the crowd. She was crying, but there was no sound.
Mother did not go to the ambulance; she came straight to me. We
got into my car, and I drove back to the cabin.

I spent the next hours being efficient. People must be called:
make a list. Find the telephone numbers. Sit down and dial. Greg's
two sons, his ex-wife, his mother. My family. Our friends. People
we worked with. When one is emotionally frozen, one can deliver
even devastating news without cracking.

My sister arrived from Chattanooga. She, my brother-in-law, and
I went to the hospital to release the body. I came back and chose the
burial clothes. Neighbor women brought chocolate cupcakes and hot
strong coffee. Neighbor men sat in silence on the front porch with
my father. My friend Felicia arrived from Knoxville. My brother
Frank came from Atlanta. Others were flying, to arrive tomorrow
from more distant places.

Everyone sat in the living room all night. Frank, Barbara, and I
planned the memorial service—I sat on the couch, Barbara on the
floor, and Frank on the fireplace hearth. Frank wrote on memo paper
that Mother brought him from beside the telephone.

Details were decided. We would hold the service down on the
grassy slope by Possum Creek. Frank would be in charge, and we
would ask several of Greg's friends just to stand and talk. We'd put
flowers in big tin buckets and place the casket down by the water.
Mother's and Daddy's minister would give a final prayer. Greg's
body would be buried in the family plot in the country cemetery
nearby.

Only once all night—when Barbara first arrived and came
running through the door calling, "Oh, Sister! Oh, Sister!"—did I
almost feel tears. Only once, as I walked through the empty dining

room and just happened to glance up and see the moon and one star framed by the windowpane, did a deep groan sound from somewhere far, far away, from somewhere outside me.

As I was standing in the lumber yard the next day buying plywood to put down by the creek for the memorial service, I realized this was a strange affair. But all I could think to say was, "Daddy, we never thought we'd be buying plywood for this purpose, did we?"

I went to the memorial service wearing the only dressy thing I had brought to the cabin, the white suit and bright red silk blouse I had bought for Frank's graduation from law school the month before. Two small ceramic stars that Greg had bought for me—one red and one black—were still pinned on the lapel.

When it was time for Frank to begin the service, he stepped up to the rock wall that edged the water and began to talk:

> We are here to celebrate the life of Gregory M. Cowan. We are having this service here by the water because it was one of Greg's favorite places and one he would want us to remember him in. A few of Greg's friends are going to speak of what Greg meant to them and what he contributed to their lives....

I felt pride when I heard the eulogy given by David, Greg's friend and department head at the university....

> We come bringing our garlands of flowers and of words in honor of a man who loved loveliness in all things.... In his presence we all thought better of the world and spoke better about each other. This is why the sad occasion that has brought us here has its affirmative, its joyous side. Where Greg led we shall follow. The memory of his smile, of the twinkle in his eyes, of his patient voice, will disperse and blend into the mystery of each of our lives and life itself. The spirit of affirmation that was the light of Greg's life has rejoined the spirit of affirmation that lights the lives of good men in all times and places and that enables us to find our way.

As David spoke the funeral eulogy, I heard his words; but I was also participating in another ceremony....

The wind is blowing the pages of the marriage book, and the dairy farmer-turned-justice-of-the-peace is having trouble keeping his place. Greg and I stand in front of him, our backs to John Oliver's cabin, Greg with a big white daisy in his lapel, me carrying a bouquet of daisies tied with yellow streamers. The vows . . . *Will you have this man to be your wedded husband ? . . . Will you have this woman to be your wedded wife.... to live together according to God's holy ordinance ... till death do you part? . . . I do, I do.* The prayers . . . *I will lift up my eyes unto these hills from whence cometh my help....* This was my promise. And Greg, turning his head to take in the numinous beauty around us, quoted a prayer he had written in a letter to me several months before: *May we be blessed by the birds, the bark, and the slanted rock.*

I returned to Possum Creek. The service was coming to an end. Frank was speaking:

After hearing what Greg meant to all these people, if you can imagine that a hundredfold, you will begin to understand what he meant to his family. One talent that he had that we can all try to emulate was his ability and willingness to express his feelings toward others. An example of this was just three weeks ago when everyone came to Atlanta for my graduation from law school. That night after Greg and Sister had gotten back to Texas, Greg called to let me know how much the day had meant to him and how much he enjoyed being with me. Here today, before each of you, I pledge for myself that I will try to let each of you know what you mean to my life, and I urge you to make that same commitment.

It was time for the closing hymns. The congregation, gathered on the hillside, began to sing an old spiritual, "I'll Fly Away." I heard the words: "Some glad morning, when this life is o'er, I'll fly away, to that home on God's celestial shore, I'll fly away. I'll fly away, oh, glory, I'll fly away. When I die, hallelujah, by and by, I'll fly away." Again, I suddenly found myself somewhere else....

It's a Sunday morning in Mexico. I'm on a path cut out of the edge of the jungle. The bougainvilleas grow so close to the path that we brush them as we jog past. A yellow-and-green parrot is sitting high up in a plantain tree.
     "Let's sing," I say.

Reaching for my hand, Greg replies, "It's Sunday, so let's sing a hymn."

"How about 'I'll Fly Away'?" I answered.

We sing, jogging along together.

The congregation is now beginning the final hymn: "Amazing Grace, how sweet the sound." I listen, but I am not present at a memorial service on July 4 at noon by the side of Possum Creek in Soddy-Daisy, Tennessee. I am far away....

In a big white room in a house in Texas. The sun shining in through the east windows gives the softest light you have ever seen. It's Sunday, and the *New York Times* covers the floor. The coffee cups are almost empty. Greg says, "Hey, I haven't heard our concert this morning. Isn't it about time?" And I go over to the piano I've had since I was a little girl and begin to play. "Amazing Grace, how sweet the sound . . ."

I come to myself as the audience sings the last refrain. Some friends, carrying big buckets, are moving among the people on the hillside. The buckets are filled with flowers. Everyone is being given a white daisy to take away.

I looked and saw the light sparkling on the water in front of me. As the sounds of the hymn echoed from the mountains across the creek, I noticed that a flock of ducks had swum up to the edge of the water. The ducks were all lined up in a row, as still as they could be.

Then there was the drive to the cemetery and the walk up the hill to the spot where Greg's body would be laid. The minister reads . . . *The fruit of the Spirit is love, joy, peace, long-suffering, gentleness, goodness, faith* . . . My sister, brother, their spouses, and I sing a little song we had made up one summer night when we three couples were vacationing together: *You are my lovely daffodil, that grows upon the yonder hill* . . . Somebody prays. Then the kind funeral director asks if we want to stay or leave as the casket is lowered into the ground. I suggest that we leave. The sun feels excruciatingly hot on my head as I step away from the gravesite, and my feet slip several times on small pebbles as we walk back down the hill.

In the days and weeks following, I must have told the story a thousand times.... *It was Monday afternoon, we were at our cabin, he went for a jog.... He died in stride as he ran along the road ... a congenital heart defect so small the coroner said it would never have been detected.... The doctor said he would have died that night no matter what he was doing.... He had a heart that was going to last forty-three years, and that was it.*

I wrote long letters to all our friends, giving them every detail of the weeks before Greg's death—what he had done, what I noticed and remembered now, the amazing things I could see in hindsight. I answered note after note, acknowledging the kind words people had written: *Hans, I know exactly what you mean when you say you feel as if you've lost your biggest fan.... Dear Amilde, Yes, he was so relaxed; and I, too, always felt he was listening, that he always had time, that I had his full attention when he was with me.* I relived our last day over and over and over again. The way he made a flower out of the butter lettuce for our salad at lunch. The way we worked on the manuscript all day together. The particular book, *Gift from the Sea,* that he left turned down at his work table. How I called out, "Grego, those legs look terrific," as he jogged away from the cabin.

I took little notice of the strange things that were happening to my body—or to my mind. My appetite disappeared. For days I felt no hunger. It was more than two weeks before I remembered that there were good things in the world to eat. One morning I smelled Mother's biscuits baking in the oven and realized that I wanted breakfast. It was the first food I had tasted in days, a plate of gravy and biscuits. The meal made me feel good because it brought back cozy childhood memories.

I lay awake for hours when I went to bed. Every night, when I finally did get to sleep, I would wake up at exactly the same hour, three A.M. I had dreamed that someone had stolen my wedding bracelet. The same dream night after night. The first thing I would do when I woke up was reach frantically for my arm. Was the bracelet still there?

After this, I could never go back to sleep. I would lie there imagining that the insurance company would find something wrong with the policies and I wouldn't have the money to buy a monument for Greg's grave. I would think of my two stepsons and fear that I would not be able to save anything for them. I would think of all the bills piling up and try to figure out how I was going to pay them with only one salary.

My menstrual period started fifteen days early and flooded like a hemorrhage. And when the period finally ended, it began again in only seven days. I couldn't think clearly. I did strange things. I carried gravel around in my coin purse, gravel that was speckled with blood from the scratches on Greg's face when he fell. Every time I got change out, I picked up the pieces of gravel and squeezed them in my hand. Once, when I was washing my hair, I saw a crack in the sink. For a moment I was certain that the crack was blood from one of Greg's scratches.

I had finally cried, on the fourth day after Greg had died. Two friends who had not been able to come to the funeral flew from New York to Tennessee. I said I wanted to drive to the airport to get them. When I sat down behind the wheel of the car, every detail of Monday afternoon came back to me. Leaving the cabin. Looking for Greg. Asking the man what had happened. Stretching high to reach the wire-mesh step at the back of the ambulance. As I remembered, the tears had come like a torrent.

And now I could not stop crying. I cried as I typed letters. I cried when I went to bed at night, and I cried when I woke up in the morning. At times during the day I would feel rushes of grief, like waves, and I would sob convulsively. Often I felt I was choking.

I took a trip to see one of Greg's sons. We talked for hours about his father. I ordered what I knew Greg liked when we went to the restaurant. I was angry that he was not there to see how neatly Fred had cleaned his apartment in preparation for my visit. I was loath to leave because to be with Fred and his brother, David, was the closest I could now get to Greg.

I thought about committing suicide. When my sister, brother, and I went to the Pacific Northwest for a memorial service in Greg's hometown, we made part of the trip on a ferry. This was a ride Greg and I had taken many times. I had always loved the exhilaration of the spray on my face and the wind whipping around me. On this day, however, I only felt dull. My eyes would not focus. Instead of seeing the water, I was seeing only other years and other days. *A cold winter's day on the Oregon coast. Greg coming into the house with wood he had just cut for the fire. Teasing me with his cold hands.* "Remember the Snyder poem you sent me when we first met?" "Yes, I remember: 'Bring in the axe, the rake, / the wood / we'll lean on the wall / against each other / stew simmering on the fire / as it grows dark / drinking wine.'" Suddenly a realization shot through my brain: I could jump! I could jump right into the water. I could go where Greg is. But would I be able to find him? That was the question.

Everywhere I went I looked for Greg. I had to go to New York to discuss the future of the book we had been writing; and when I wasn't working, I roamed. I went to the apartment house where Greg and I had lived before we moved to Texas, to the restaurant where he surprised me with an engagement ring set with jade. I retraced the route we took the day we carried a sheet of plywood on our heads from the lumber store on West Broadway to our apartment on Bleecker Street. I ate cannoli at Ferrarro's and ordered a full plate of antipasto at the Greek restaurant, even though I knew it was too much for one person.

I stood in the entry of the Little Church Around the Corner and imagined the candles being lit on Christmas Eve. I rode the A train to the end of the line and walked up the hill to see the unicorn tapestries hanging in the Cloisters. I ran my hands over the coolness of the stone walls and sat in the opening of the arched walls, watching the shadows move across the courtyard. Everywhere, I tried to find my past. But all I found was incontrovertible evidence, assaulting evidence, that Greg was not present. And that everything—the past, the present, and the future—was irrevocably altered by the fact that he was dead.

I went to see a therapist. "I feel so abandoned," I said to him again and again. "Do you think Greg misses me the way I am missing him? Do you think he cares about me anymore? Does he see me? Does he know I'm still here?"

The kind therapist reassured me that my questions—and my feelings—were normal. "Don't hold anything back," he counseled. "Cry as much as you want to. Don't try to be strong and brave. You have not just lost a husband; you have lost a part of yourself. You are mourning not only for Greg," he reminded me. "You're also mourning yourself. You're mourning your own death."

In the absence of any purpose for life, my mind was constantly swirling with emotions and thoughts that repeated the same message.

Guilt. Was I responsible for Greg's death? If I hadn't been so keen on jogging, would Greg be alive today? Was there some sign of his problem that I ignored or just missed? Why wasn't I kinder to him the last time he had a cold? Did I kill him by thinking ugly thoughts when I was angry? And why did *he* die and not me? He was a much better person than I was, much kinder and more loving. And those times I had enjoyed being by myself, happy he was gone on a trip, even fantasizing about being an independent woman completely on my own again, back in my apartment in New York . . . did God know about those thoughts and punish me by killing Greg?

Regret. Why didn't I run with him that day? At least I would have been with him when he died. Why did I agree to such a tight deadline on the book? If we had not been so rushed, maybe he wouldn't have worked so hard; and then he might not have died. Why hadn't we spent more time with his children?

Resentment. Why didn't it do any good that we took care of ourselves? What did it matter that we ate well and always exercised? And dragged that blender around with us when we went to conventions so that we would not miss that horrible-tasting health milkshake every morning? Who cared now that we took all those vitamins? Why did he have to die before we completed the book? Why did he go off and leave me with all the remaining work?

Anger. In New York the bell captain at the hotel where Greg and I had stayed many times in the past asks when I get out of the cab, "You alone this time, Mrs. Cowan? Where's the boss?" At that moment I hated Greg. I hated him for deserting me. I hated him because I was the one who had to tell this man that he was dead. I hated the empty hotel room. I hated the double bed. It seemed preposterous to me at that moment that a human being could just disappear from the earth! I sat down at the desk in my room and wrote furiously: "I absolutely cannot believe at 10:59 P.M. on Tuesday, July 31, that Greg Cowan is dead. No Greg Cowan. An empty space. No one to fill the Greg Cowan space. There is no Greg Cowan any more on this planet. I hate the world! I hate the world! He was a presence felt. He occupied space. He was. Where are you, Greg? Where, where are you? Can you really have gone away?"

Mystery. There were mysterious happenings. One day while sitting in a fifth-floor office at my publisher's, editing a chapter of the book, I saw for the first time a note in the margin in Greg's hand: "Get butterfly haiku." Just the day before, I had called my graduate assistant in Texas and asked her to find a short poem for the text, and she had given me this Japanese haiku:

> *Spring Scene*
> On the temple bell
>   Has settled, and is fast asleep
>   A butterfly.
>   Anonymous

Reading Greg's note, "Get butterfly haiku," I think, "I've already done that. I did that yesterday!" I was so stunned by this coincidence that I turned in the swivel chair to look outside. There I saw, hovering against the glass, five floors above Third Avenue in New York City, a bright orange butterfly!

Then another kind of mysterious happening.

Returning to Tennessee from New York, as the plane touched down on the runway, I felt as if I were suddenly engulfed in darkness. I could not breathe. I could not stand without holding on to the seat in front of me. When I tried to walk down the aisle, I stumbled from side to side; everything was black in front of me. The same words kept circling: "What am I coming back to? Nothing but more of the same. Nothing but an empty cabin."

And then the unexplainable happened. As if a voice spoke, although I heard no sound, the words came: "Look outside. The sun is shining. Life is good." In that moment, I felt a release from the heaviness that had pressed in on me ever since we landed. Somehow, in that split second, I knew I was going to be all right. It was a genuine moment of grace. And even though the feeling did not last, I never forgot the miracle of its occurring.

Visions. As I was flipping through a magazine back at Possum Creek with my parents, a photograph caught my eye. It was a sepia-tinted photograph of an old town in the West, a town very similar to one Greg and I had stayed in once when we were traveling through South Dakota. As I stared at the picture, I could feel Greg and me pulling into that town in the late afternoon. It was as if we were driving right into the picture. I knew exactly what we would have said. I felt how we would have felt.

Hearing an insect buzz, I looked up from the magazine and out toward the yard. Suddenly, as if slides were being flashed on a screen, I saw three scenes suspended like a mirage in the glare of the hot August sun.

An Irish fisherman's wife was sitting by a fire on a cold, stormy night. The oil lamp on the table beside her cast a warm yellow light. The woman was knitting rapidly and nervously; the rain was beating on the windowpane. As I watched this scene, I knew the woman's husband would never come home. I knew he would be drowned at sea that night during the storm.

A Native American woman was preparing her brave for battle, telling him good-bye as he left to fight. His face was painted with diagonal stripes of blue. A feather attached to a leather band rode high above his head. His short loincloth struck his inner thighs. There was one brief moment when the woman reached up and straightened the band around the warrior's head. As she made that gesture, I knew the brave would die in this battle and never come home again.

The third scene was a lonesome prairie. There was nothing but emptiness as far as the eye could see. The grass was tall and spiky, the kind that hurts your legs when you walk through it. Standing among this wiry grass was a family, their covered wagon behind them. The mother stood motionless, looking down at the ground. Two children huddled near her, their faces buried in her skirts. The father stood a short distance away. He, too, was staring toward the baby's tiny grave.

In the few seconds these three scenes flashed before my eyes, I gained wisdom. I realized that death was impersonal, that women—

and men, too—in all times and the world over had felt the pain of losing a loved one. And millions more would experience it also. I saw that death and grief were a condition of living. Death was not something that had happened only to me. I was not special.

I cried from the depths of my being. I cried for the Irish fisherman's wife, for the Native American woman whose brave did not return from battle, for the pioneer family who left their baby on the lone prairie. I cried for the human condition. I knew that what had happened to me was not a personal thing, that in my grief I was participating in a way that the world was. The way life was set up to be. And even though this wisdom could not shield me from what lay ahead, it nevertheless did allow me to get in contact with and express my deepest pain.

As every day passed, I realized more fully that I had not only lost a husband, I had lost the very purpose and shape of my life. The bulwark I had built against the randomness, the chaos, of existence, that bulwark had been destroyed. My life no longer had any contours; there was nothing into which I could fit. I had no expectations. I had no plans. I dreamed at night of thin crystal vases, broken while being washed. I dreamed of sheets hanging on a clothesline above an ocean, being whipped, whipped, whipped by a very strong wind.

Day after day it was the same. In the twilight period between sleep and waking I would hear the words "Oh, Greg, oh, Greg," except that they sounded like "Oh, sad, oh, sad." When my mother asked one morning, "How are you today?" all I could say was, "I feel so weary. So stretched out and caught. I'm the loser for being alive."

I wrote a friend: "The nothingness of life. Nothing is important. There's no reason to be here; and yet if you kill yourself, you'll have it as bad there as you do here. So you're stuck. Stuck. Stuck. Greg's dying has done more than just leave me alone. It has rocked me to the foundation and shaken all my optimism about life. I feel like running head on into a tree."

That is what it means to grieve. You allow yourself to see the truth — the devastating truth. The continuity of your life is gone.

The connections are broken. The web of human relations that you had with courage reached out to build turns out to be so fragile. So quickly destroyed. And you are impotent. Powerless. The force—the robber —has struck. About this you have no say.

Grief is excruciating pain. You understand why for centuries, in cultures around the world, the wail of grief has sounded. That wordless cry into the night. The lament of life and death. You now know the meaning of those long, mournful wails.

This is Impact. Surprising. Shattering. Gut-wrenching. Debilitating. Overwhelming.

Our lives have changed, but without our permission. We are disoriented, frightened, confused. We reel, stagger, stumble, unable to regain our balance.

This response to the unwanted change that has intruded into our lives is natural. For what we have lost is the very shape of our lives, the structure that told us who we are and what we are about in life. How could we, then, *not* react with such intensity?

But there is also a paradox in our behavior. We may respond to the news of the loss in such a way that people say things like "It hasn't hit her yet" or "He still hasn't let himself realize what has happened." But regardless of appearances, these people are wrong.

It is true that for a period of time—minutes, hours, days, even weeks—we may pay little attention to a reality in which people concern themselves with long-range planning, or with making their way in the world, or with friendly, sociable discourse. But never think for one minute that we are not in touch with reality. We are in touch with the most profound kind of reality there is. The kind of reality that is grounded in our deep interconnectedness to all around us. The kind of reality that centers on the personal world each of us has constructed —the people we love, the work we do, the place we live, the things we enjoy. The kind of reality that we sometimes get in touch with when we stand over our children as they are sleeping or when we gaze out at sea or when we finish planting a garden or painting a picture.

Yes, the grieving person is in touch with reality. It is the most elemental of realities, the ground of realities. To this, attention is being paid.

It may be, as the Institute of Medicine suggests in its study of bereavement, that during this time of stress our brains secrete special neurohormones that allow us to register or recognize things happening around us in a detached, slow-motion way. It may be that some part of us closes down since what has happened to us is so over-whelming.

Yet for the neurohormones and the defenses even to go into action, we had to first know that something terrible had happened. So while we are perhaps protected for a time from realizing the *external* implications of the loss, nothing protects us from the immediate *internal* knowledge that something has threatened our life. That some alien force has intruded. That we are in danger; our survival is at stake. We know *this* immediately—before we even know the facts or details. We register the loss through some frequency that bypasses words and conscious thoughts and at some velocity quicker than sound.

We are never more alert and aroused than when we have experienced a loss. We are in a state of emergency. As with all emergencies, even emergencies of far less significant import (think of our response when pipes burst during a winter's freeze), we devote our entire and immediate attention to reacting.

We may react by becoming numb and detached. We may react by becoming efficient and able. We may react by crying or falling to pieces. But we do react. We are not dumb to what has happened. We know it to the very core of our being.

More than one researcher has remarked on the deep evolutionary roots of this response to loss. We have such terrible pain, they say, because far back in the timeless past we learned, as a species, that we had to bond with others in order to find food and to protect ourselves from enemies. To break those bonds was to die ourselves. Even now, when the bonds we have with others are sundered, at some deep level we fear for our very survival.

This response is so elemental that we even share it with animals. Konrad Lorenz took note of how greylag geese responded when they lost their mates. The first reaction of the goose was to begin to look frantically for the partner and to continue day and night, moving about, searching and sounding a plaintive call. The reactions we have during the experience of Impact, then, have a long evolutionary history. We find ourselves in a state of alarm. We behave as if we are searching for the one who is lost, even though we are not consciously expecting to find this person. The restlessness we experience—going from place to place, from room to room—is one way we search. So is the alteration in our perception that causes us to think we see or hear the person who is absent and the slip in attention that results in our setting the lost person's place at the table or looking for the absent one in a crowd. We are aroused at a deep, evolutionary level, and our actions—shock, crying, anger, pining, searching—are automatic and testify to the connectedness and bonding that has existed among animals and among human beings for millions of years.

What is "normal" behavior during the first days, weeks, and months following a traumatic loss? That is a question we ask ourselves often, for during Impact we behave in erratic ways and even fear that we are going crazy. We are occupied almost every minute with thoughts of what has happened and experience everything— including ourselves —as unfamiliar, unreal, and unpredictable. Conversations I have held with men and women who talked about their early grieving reveal that during Impact any—and perhaps all— of the following reactions can happen....

SPONTANEOUS EMOTION

A young father remembers:

When they called me at work, they said, "Daniel has stopped breathing; he's been taken to the hospital." All the way to the emergency room, I figured it was something bad, but I didn't think he was dead. Maybe it was just because I didn't want to think my three-month-old son was dead. I mean, it was so fast.

When I got to the hospital, I saw my cousin standing outside. He didn't say anything as I ran past, only shook his head. So I ran inside to the desk and asked the nurse, "Where's my son? His name is Daniel. Where's my son?" She pointed me to a door. I ran inside, and Jill said, "Our boy is dead." I fell to the floor, and I cried.

A TEMPORARY SHUTTING OUT OF THE LONG-TERM IMPLICATIONS OF THE LOSS

A widow recalls:

When Jack killed himself, I was so calm and so efficient that my sister-in-law, who had come from Ohio to Pennsylvania to be with me, called her family to say she was coming home early. "Joan is doing so well," I heard her say on the telephone. "You should see her determination! She's got fire in her eyes! She's taking care of everything. She doesn't need anyone here to help her."

If my sister-in-law had only known.

A week later, the reality hit me; and for months I could not function.

PHYSICAL PAIN; DESPERATION

A divorced man tells this story:

The day finally came when I knew it was final. We had talked about splitting up and divorce and all that, but I never thought much about it because we had worked through many things and survived. But one day when she came home finally and said, "Joe, I want out," I had a tremendous physical reaction. I mean, literally— intense pain. Like tremendous—like somebody had run a knife in my stomach. I doubled over with the pain. And then there was uncontrollable emotion. I knew it was over. Done. That was it.

So what followed immediately afterward was a sense of real desperation. Thinking, you know, there's too much history—fifteen years of history—that was worth fighting for, even though at some level I knew it was useless. So we struggled with going to a counselor for a couple of weeks, but it was with a sense of desperation, trying to do and say and think anything to make it better. To resurrect the marriage. Then she said, "Either you're going to leave the house, or I'm going to leave the house." So I took my art supplies with me— she said she'd send my paintings later—and I went to my sister's in Iowa City to figure out what I was going to do next.

IRRATIONAL FEAR

A newly divorced man reports:

The day I rented the apartment I didn't notice that there were no lights in the ceiling. The house Marie and I had lived in for twenty-eight years had lights in the ceiling, so I just didn't think about an apartment being wired only for lamps. So here I was, staying my first night in the apartment, with no light except a photographer's light that I used when I developed pictures. The bed I had bought hadn't come yet either, so I slept on the floor that night. I can tell you I was as scared as a ten-year-old. The dark scared me. The sounds scared me. When the icemaker came on in the refrigerator, the noise frightened me to death. Off and on all night, I got up and walked around the empty apartment. I hardly slept at all.

SEEING THE LOST ONE

A young widow speaks:

I walked past the stairs, and out of the corner of my eye, I saw him sitting on the top step. He was putting his tennis shoes on. The image was so vivid. He was bent over tying his shoe just the way he always did, with his racket up against his knee. The scene startled me so much that I jerked to a stop. But when I looked again, the step was bare.

CONFUSION AND DISORIENTATION

A father tells this story:

That first night, the house seemed so strange and unfamiliar. Penny was still crying after we went to bed, and I was trying to comfort her. Early in the morning I dozed off, only to wake up with Penny shaking me. "I think someone is trying to get into the house," she said. "And something has happened to the lights."

Everything was black. You couldn't see your hand in front of you. The bedside lamps would not turn on. "I smell smoke, too." By now Penny was almost hysterical.

I looked outside and saw that the streetlight was out also. My first thought was, "Maybe I'm dead. Maybe I'm not alive anymore, and this is all a dream." But Penny was talking to me, things about the telephone and the table by the door. I tried to find my way around the room, but I was bumping into everything.

Finally, I got down on my hands and knees and started to crawl. I crawled until I found the table with the telephone on it. Everything was dark, absolutely black. I dialed 0 and told the operator I was in trouble. "I don't know what's happening," I said. "There are no lights. Something is wrong here." I was frantic.

The operator attempted to calm me. "A transformer has blown; the entire town is without power. Do you need help?" It was then that I realized why I was so addled and disoriented. I remembered that this was the day we had lost everything. Robin was dead.

RESTLESSNESS
A mother whose son was killed in an automobile accident recounts:

When I'm home, I roam from room to room. I can't sit still. I hunt for something to occupy my time and can't find anything. When I'm at work, it's no better because Dan worked with us in the family business.

Today was my first day back at work, and all I did was walk from laboratory to laboratory. I suppose, in one sense, I was looking for Dan, although I knew, of course, that I wasn't going to find him. Finally, I started talking to him quietly as I went through the building. "I love you," was the thing I said the most. "Dan, I love you." I also told him how much I miss him. Sometimes, if no one else was around, I'd call out his name.

When the crew sat down for lunch together, as we do every day, Dan's absence was so obvious. I found myself several times looking to the place at the table where he always sat, and I was surprised every time when he wasn't there. You would think I'd realize, after the first time looking for him, that he was gone; but I guess it was such a habit to expect him to be there. During the entire lunch hour, I never stopped expecting to see him at his place at the table, no matter how often I was disappointed when I looked.

FORGETTING THE LOST ONE IS GONE
A widow recalls:

Our son-in-law called from Germany. Beth had had the baby, a girl. I was so happy! As soon as we hung up, I called Frank at the office. It wasn't until the receptionist said, "Hello," that I remembered that Frank was dead.

I put down the phone and just stood, looking around the house. Nothing belonged to me. Nothing was familiar. This could just as easily have been a strange hotel as the home in which I had lived for thirty-five years. There was nowhere now that meant anything to me, nowhere that I cared about or where I belonged. Even the air in the room felt dead.

WAVES AND SPASMS OF UNEXPECTED EMOTION: CRYING, CALLING OUT, SCREAMING, SOBBING

A divorced husband relates this experience:

As I was driving home from work, I could see the United Bank Building in the distance. I always tried to avoid looking that way— that was where she worked—but today the setting sun was so bright on the windows that they looked like mirrors. I couldn't look away. Suddenly I remembered the mirror we bought on our honeymoon— I could see the old man who sold it to us, smell the musty odor in the run-down shop, hear Helen's laugh when she rubbed the dust off and discovered a beautiful cherrywood frame underneath.

Suddenly, I started crying so hard that I could not see to drive. I sobbed from the very bottom of my gut. I remember I kept calling out, "Helen, why did you do it? Why did you leave?" I cried so hard that I began to choke. It was all I could do to maneuver the car across the lanes of traffic and stop on the shoulder of the freeway. I sat there in the car and sobbed for a long time.

ANGER AND RESENTMENT

Hear this story:

I was walking along the streets in New Orleans. Everywhere I looked there was a couple. All I could see was couples. Couples laughing. Couples with their arms around each other. Couples shopping. Couples eating oyster sandwiches at the Desiree Bar. At that moment I hated Joe more than anything else in the world. I hated him; I hated being one-half of a couple. I thought, "If I had a knife in my pocket, I would stab every couple I see." I even fanta-sized about going back to the hotel, putting a knife in my purse, and coming back out on the street to kill every couple I met.

FEELINGS OF GUILT AND BLAME

Listen to this widow:

I knew my husband was sick, but I didn't know how sick. I had to go to a business meeting at four-thirty that afternoon with some disgruntled customers. "I'll be back by seven," I told him as I left.

He must have had the convulsion almost as soon as I was out the door.

I don't think I'll ever be able to forgive myself for going to that meeting. If I had been there, the convulsion wouldn't have been so bad or gone on so long. I could have gotten him to the doctor sooner. I called him from the meeting; but the line was busy, and, of course, I thought he was on the phone. He must have tried to call me because when I found him moaning on the floor—his face as gray as death— the phone was on the floor beside him. If only I hadn't gone, I could have saved him so much suffering.

PHYSICAL DISTURBANCES
A daughter reports:

A few days after my mother died, I was at work and suddenly felt a heaviness in my chest and upper arms. I couldn't get my breath, just sat at my desk gasping. I felt as if I were going to die. The attack lasted for two or three minutes, but the heaviness stayed. For several days I could hardly lift my arms high enough to get them on the steering wheel to drive the car. Finally, when the breathing attacks began to occur more frequently, I went to the doctor. "Stress angina," he said, and prescribed some nitroglycerine patches, which I am now wearing every day. "If the situation gets worse," the doctor said, "we'll have to consider other alternatives." He mentioned angioplasty and bypass surgery.

OBSESSION WITH MEMORIES
A widow recounts being haunted by a recurring image:

Every time I close my eyes, I see the room in the hospital where the attendant met me. "Here is the form you need to sign to release your husband's body." That was all she said. I suppose I expected her to say something else, maybe "I'm sorry" or "How are you?" or "Would you like to sit down?" But she didn't. All she did was hand me the paper and say, "Sign on the line at the bottom of the page."

"But I'd like to talk to someone," I said.

"I'm the person to talk to," she responded.

"Will there be an autopsy?" I asked.

"No need for an autopsy," she replied. "Your husband was a hit and run."

"But I'd like to have an autopsy," I answered.

"The coroner did not request an autopsy," she answered. "We already have your husband ready for the morgue."

As the attendant took the paper and started to leave the room, she handed me a small yellow envelope. I had no idea what it was. I turned the envelope upside down to empty out the contents. My husband's watch and wedding ring fell into my hand.

Nothing has ever hit me harder than sitting in that hospital cubicle, staring down at my husband's watch and ring. Not even the first news of his death. I cannot forget this scene. It flashes before my eyes, I guess, a hundred times a day. Over and over I see the woman giving me the yellow envelope. Over and over I see myself turning the envelope upside down. Over and over I see his wedding ring and watch falling out into my hand.

UNEXPLAINABLE EXPERIENCES
A widow reports:

I was riding in a taxi. Elliott had just died. I was going home from the hospital to get burial clothes to take to the mortuary.

Suddenly the taxi was filled—literally filled—with the smell of violets. I looked out of the taxi window to see who might be carrying flowers or to locate a flower stall. But there was no sign of flowers anywhere on the street.

"The violets must be in the front seat with the driver," I thought. "What a beautiful smell," I said. "Where are the flowers?"

The driver looked startled. "I was about to ask you what perfume you're wearing," he responded. Neither of us could come up with an explanation for the sudden smell of violets. It was one of those weird, unexplainable occurrences. In some strange way, though, that mystery was comforting to me. I was uplifted by the smell of those violets. I felt as though I'd been touched by Elliott or the hand of God.

THE FOCUS DURING IMPACT

It is clear when we hear these stories that during Impact our lives are in upheaval. It does not feel as if we are "of this world"; all is strangeness. Little matters except what is going on in our interior being. We know that nothing can make our situation better except the reversal of the terrible thing that has happened.

Yet even in those dire straits, there are things we can do and ways we can think that will help us.

Taking Care of Ourselves

When we experience a loss, a very ancient reaction is triggered in our brain: the flight-or-fight response. Because we have sensed we are in danger, the body has been mobilized to protect itself from the intruder or, if that is not possible, to escape to safety. But loss is no hostile tribe we can guard the camp against, nor is it an enemy we can run from. Therefore, we are caught in a state of tension. Our brain has stimulated us to take action; but since we cannot undo the loss, there is at this moment no action we can take. We are, therefore, held taut. And this means that our bodies are under enormous stress.

The results of this stress show up immediately. Medical studies report that the chemical regulation of our breathing may become defective. Our vital processes are altered: biological rhythms of sleeping and eating are disturbed. Our immune system becomes impaired. In fact, as the Institute of Medicine reports, the reaction of our bodies to grief are multiple: the autonomic, physiologic, biochemical, and endocrinologic systems are all affected. Hormones go haywire; T cells stop protecting us from infections and viruses as they previously did; our blood flow and cardiac rate increase; our digestion, metabolism, circulation, and respiration change. We experience multiple heartbeats and heart flutters. Our adrenal system is activated. Our ability to concentrate and pay attention is decreased; our anxiety is increased. In response to loss, then, our bodies are out of balance; homeostasis has been disturbed.

What can we do about this?

The most important thing is to understand that we are in a state of emergency. Our very self has been assaulted. Our bodies and minds are reacting intensely to the loss. We need to take as good care of ourselves as we can. This means taking sufficient time off from work. It means eating as well as we can, drinking water and resting in ways that support our well-being. It means going on walks or bike rides, running, swimming—whatever allows us to feel our bodies moving. It means taking special measures, like getting massages or other kinds of bodywork, putting a cold cloth over our eyes, resting, and listening to music.

Does it mean taking medicine, especially drugs such as tranquilizers or antidepressants?

This is a controversial and difficult question.

Of course, we have to be responsible for our physical and mental condition. But where do we draw the line between being duly responsible and using medicine or drugs to blunt our experience, when such blunting is to our detriment? Unfortunately, many physicians interpret the prescribing of barbiturates and tranquilizers for grieving individuals as an automatic "standard of care"; and the majority of the general public, not understanding the grieving process, see mourning as something that "must be suppressed either by use of medicine or alcohol or through sheer determination or exercise of faith."

There are many who are adamantly opposed to the prescribing of tranquilizers, barbiturates, and antidepressants for those who are grieving. My own doctor, when he read an early manuscript of this book, wrote me: "One of the reprehensible practices in medicine in the past fifty or so years has been the pushing of drugs on the bereaved—probably to make sure that they didn't embarrass themselves or the family with their true feelings—screaming rage, gnashing of teeth, pulling of hair, falling on the ground, and so on. Maybe if doctors could encourage patients to 'let it all hang out,' we wouldn't be faced with hidden, prolonged grief (guilt and the like), which is the fodder of contemporary psychiatry." My experience supports my doctor's position. I feel that by never taking barbiturates, tranquilizers, or antidepressants during times of grieving, I allowed a natural evolution of the grieving process to take place. This resulted, I believe, in my experiencing the mourning that had to be done at my own pace and in the appropriate sequence.

One would hope that we and our doctors will make decisions that take our need to grieve into account. If there is a legitimate need for drugs—a situation many professionals feel is rare—the use of these medications should be brief.

There are, as Dr. Glen Davidson points out, alternatives. For instance, changing one's diet to include carbohydrates eaten about ninety minutes before bedtime can often induce sleep most effectively because, as the carbohydrates are digested, the brain releases a natural opiate or barbiturate. And this is only one of many possible alternatives to taking drugs. A good doctor who practices preventive medicine or a professional health practitioner can offer many other suggestions.

The most important thing to say about the subject of our well-being during Impact is that, while these intense experiences are occurring, we need to do everything we can to stay healthy. The unfortunate thing is that at this time we often feel little inclination to care for ourselves. Therefore, it is often only by an act of *sheer intention* that we do what we need to do to stay in good health.

Relying on Others

Over and over people remark, "Without my friends, without my family, I wouldn't have made it." The nurturing given by those who care for us provides a kind of cocoon of comfort, peace, and safety that during the experiences of Impact we need so desperately. I remember hearing Buckminster Fuller say once that love is metaphysical gravity; and we never realize the truth of this statement more than during a loss, when it seems that the presence of our family and friends is all that allows us to hold anything together.

This is the time to rely on those around us in practical matters, to let them do for us completely. To accept their offers and allow their gestures of care and support. Let others take care of the children, run errands, prepare food, assist with arrangements, handle immediate business or legal affairs.

It is also the time to rely on our family and friends for emotional support. To spend as much time with them as possible. Talking about the lost one, even if incessantly; crying unashamedly; wailing and screaming; cleaning house, chopping wood; sitting mute or speaking quietly. Just being in the presence of people who love us sends a message somewhere deep inside us, even if we don't realize it consciously, that we are still connected in that fragile web we call *life* and that, in spite of the rupture caused by the loss, there is still some continuity.

Reserving Judgment About Guilt and Anger

Since no human being is perfect, it will be highly unlikely that we do not feel guilty about something related to the lost person: we wish we hadn't done something that we did do or we didn't do something we could have done; we had thoughts we are now ashamed of; we have mixed feelings about our relationship with the lost person; we hurt the person unnecessarily; we wonder why we are the one still alive and the other person isn't . . . and the list goes on.

The important thing at this point in the grieving process is to withhold final judgment about these matters until we are under less stress and can think more clearly. We should hold out the possibility at least that our judgment of ourselves may be more harsh than is warranted. And if we are at fault in some way, the intense period of Impact is not a good time to try to work out appropriate action to take in response to the situation. It is better deliberately to put the matter of guilt aside for a time and say, "I'll think about that later. I'm not in a frame of mind now to do justice to the matter."

We are also likely to feel anger toward others. We may be angry at the person who is gone: he could have stopped smoking, but he didn't; she abandoned us; he left me with all the responsibility. Perhaps we feel someone else is to blame for what happened: the hospital staff could have done more, and they didn't; his mother egged him into leaving; there was never appropriate attention paid to the children; she drove after drinking and caused the accident. Or we may just be angry in general, over things trivial: how long the clerk takes to sack the groceries; what clothes the children put on in the morning; whether or not the grass is cut first thing on Saturday.

It is true that we are not much in control during Impact; but if we can be aware that anger is a common response to grief and that we may not be angry about exactly what we think we are, we may be able to express our anger in ways that do not tear at our relationships and have us gouging at others.

Asking Questions

It is important to learn as many facts as possible about the circumstances of the loss. If we do not, it is likely that for months, or even years, ahead, we will be obsessed with questions. What kind of heart attack did he have? What literally happened in her body? Where exactly on the road did the collision occur? At what point in the relationship did things go wrong? When such questions can be answered, we should ask for the most minute details about what happened. Accurate information will substitute for fantasies, fears, and haunting mysteries.

A friend told me recently, "I am so sorry we did not ask the details about Dad's death." Her father, whom everyone, including himself, considered to be extremely healthy, had died of a heart attack at age sixty-two just minutes after being stricken. The family was so stunned that no one asked the doctor certain questions, questions that cannot now be asked and answered. "We'll never know some things about my father's condition, things that my brother and I especially would like to know as we get older. So, urge people to get the facts," my friend admonished me. "They will rest so much easier later."

I saw the positive effect of getting all the facts a few months ago when friends whose son had died in an automobile accident spent time learning everything they could about the accident. They examined the car; drove out to the site of the accident to look at the skid marks on the pavement; asked the patrolman all kinds of questions. The end result was that they felt fully informed. This didn't, of course, answer all those painful existential questions—Why did it happen? Why a young man? Why couldn't it have been different?—but the family did have an accurate picture of what had happened. They knew the truth, and it was clear to all of us that, for them, this made an enormous difference.

Giving Attention to Ritual

One of the things people often tell me they regret when they look back on their grieving process is that, when the event happened, they rushed through the good-bye services or ceremonies. Or that they bowed to convention and did not have the kind of service or event they really wanted. (Or, as is usually the case with divorce, they made no acknowledgment at all.)

It is important to listen to one's own wisdom. To return to the community of origin, if that is important, no matter the extra trouble or the distance. To hold the service in an environment that is right, even if it is unconventional. To have the songs sung that you desire, even if they are not funereal. To take some symbolic action in private or with close friends, if the divorce seems incomplete without it.

But even if the loss occurred in the now distant past, there are still other opportunities. Many of the individuals who have spoken to me of their regrets told me, also, of services or ceremonies they held in memorial, often much later: a musical evening in which a string quartet played Mozart concertos; a picnic on a hill; a memorial service held on the anniversary of the event. These were a kind of second acknowledgment that allowed the individuals who were grieving to plan and do things not done initially. (In the notes for Part 1 that appear at the back of this book, I have listed under the heading "Giving Attention to Ritual" an excellent source for obtaining simple but beautiful death and memorial ceremonies.)

Telling the Truth About Our Loss

Again and again during Impact, we discover how much our lives have been changed by our loss. It is important that we deny none of these changes.

But many people want to make things better for us. Loss is an awkward subject. It is hard to be around someone who is grieving. Not only because a friend or acquaintance is in distress, but also because another's loss reminds all individuals of their own vulnerability and their own mortality. And perhaps it reminds these individuals, too, of losses they have already experienced that are painful to remember.

Whatever the reason—whether out of concern for the grieving person or out of concern for themselves—many people have a natural tendency to try to say or do something that will make us feel better: "There's a purpose for what has happened; I know you'll see this later"; "You will have other children"; "You're better off without him"; "She's out of her suffering"; "You'll meet somebody else"; "You'll be so much stronger as a result of this experience"; "He had a good life"; "You're still young"; "He would want you to be happy"; and so on and so forth.

People do not realize that such statements are totally irrelevant. It doesn't matter that, in the whole scheme of things, some of these observations may turn out later to be true, and even useful. Now, however, everything is destroyed, and life is in shambles. Nothing anyone can say can make *that* any different.

We need to remember that these attempts at consolation, which we find so jejune and banal, are the way many people attempt to stave off the harsh realities of loss—both for themselves and for us. We also have to be careful that we do not begin to wonder if we have become hardened or evil or self-indulgent because we not only are unmoved by these "words of comfort," but are perhaps even angered by them. Unfortunately, we often think we *should* believe or act upon the "truths" others remind us of; and when we cannot, we feel small and perhaps even guilty.

However, the period of Impact is no time to force oneself to try to be philosophical or reasonable or logical. It may be that in a few months we *will* see things differently. But none of this matters now as we deal with the loss we are experiencing. So we must keep telling ourselves the truth. We must acknowledge all the ways this loss has changed our life and mourn each one of these changes.

Helping Young Children Deal with Loss

It is extremely difficult to grieve fully oneself during Impact and, at the same time, to facilitate a child's grieving. Yet that is what parents, grandparents, aunts, uncles, and siblings often need to do.

The first step is to recognize that children experience a phased mourning process also, although to different degrees and in different proportions from adults. George Pollock points out that for younger children it is the earliest phases of the mourning process that predominate and that in older children the full process can often be seen. In her excellent book, *Helping Children Cope with Separation and Loss,* Claudia Jewett discusses children's passage through different phases: phase one, early grief—shock/numbing, alarm, and denial and disbelief; phase two, acute grief—yearning/pining, searching, strong feelings of sadness, anger, guilt and shame, disorganization, and despair; and phase three, integration of loss and grief.

In addition to understanding that children, like adults, exhibit their grief in different ways at different times, we can also communicate with them straightforwardly. To help a child understand, death can be described as "what happens when the body stops working"; or the dead person can be described as someone who "no longer eats or talks or breathes," who has been buried "in a special place and cannot return," and who "feels no pain." Important religious beliefs can also be added and explained.

Almost everyone agrees that children should be included in the mourning rituals. Experts vary on the age at which children should attend funerals—the opinions range from age three to five to seven—but all agree that the choice of whether or not to attend should be the child's. For many children, being part of the funeral and burial activities helps them express their sorrow.

Remember, too, that children experience many of the same fears as adults do: that they caused the death or separation; that they are in danger themselves; that they have been personally abandoned and rejected. They may also be angry. These fears and emotions may be present in the case of both death and divorce, but may be even more severe when the loss is from divorce. Adults, therefore, should discuss these issues with the children fully, helping them acknowledge their fears and put them into perspective.

It is critical during Impact, and beyond, that children be encouraged to express their feelings. Adults have told me that often simple things make such a difference with a child who is grieving: deliberately setting aside time and creating an opportunity for the child to talk about the lost person; preparing a scrapbook together that commemorates life with the person who is gone; putting pictures in a photograph album; making sure the child has a picture of the lost person available close by; carrying out a project with the child that is related to one of the interests of the absent person.

In the case of divorce, special things also might include marking a calendar with the child to indicate when the absent parent will return to pick up the child for a visit; giving the child the absent parent's telephone number so calls can be made frequently and easily; preparing envelopes with address and stamp to enable the child to send notes at any time.

Treating with Respect Unexplainable and Mysterious Occurrences

Almost everyone experiences some kind of strange phenomenon following the loss of a loved one. But most people are embarrassed to talk about these unusual events for fear that others will think they are crazy.

There are many theories to explain strange events that occur. Physicists talk about "implicate order" and "morphogenic fields." Philosophers talk about "the Tao" and "first cause." Scientists talk about "laws of seriality" and "object-impact interactions." Analytical psychologists talk about "numinosity" and "the existence of an ordering principle which stands beyond the logical theories of cause and effect." Theologians talk about "grace" and "a higher Being."

The most useful way to hold these mysterious events early in the process of mourning is not to try to understand them but merely to acknowledge and reflect on them. And to realize that a grieving person who sees or hears something unexplainable has not suddenly become infirm or addled. We don't have to be able to explain a phenomenon in order to take comfort from it or to marvel at it. Perhaps the most important thing about experiencing such occurrences is the truth they put before us: that we do not know everything. That life contains mysteries, and that it is possible to be greatly enriched and even strengthened by these mysteries and moments of grace.

THE CHOICE

Since our initial responses following a loss are automatic—rooted far back in time and designed to protect us and keep us connected to others—the idea that we can make a choice seems improbable, if not ludicrous. The loss has occurred. About that it is clear we can do nothing. We are helpless and hopeless. Sick, frightened, hurt, disoriented, left behind. How is it possible that we have any choice in this matter?

But there is a choice during Impact. A critical choice that we are required to make if we are to move through the mourning process and achieve a creative outcome:

We must choose to experience and express our grief fully.

But, someone might say, if the responses during Impact are automatic, how could an individual *not* make the choice to experience grief fully?

That's the paradox. The automatic, natural responses occur, but *we* decide whether to experience these responses or to stifle and suppress them.

And there are many reasons we might choose to suppress our grief instead of express it. The pain might seem unbearable. It may seem more reasonable, since nothing can be done about the loss, to try to forget it—to put it behind us—as quickly as possible. People around us may encourage us "to be brave," "to be strong," "to pull ourselves together." Or we may feel that if we don't rise above the loss, we are denying tenets of faith or a philosophy we have affirmed and lived by. Perhaps people around us may indicate—and we ourselves may believe—that sufficient time has passed for us to be finished with our grieving. We may be embarrassed to express our grief in front of others. We may fear we are going crazy because we think weird thoughts and do weird things. Or perhaps we decide to curtail the expression of our grief because it is interfering with our daily activities.

All of these reasons not to choose to experience and express our grief fully can be found in our own reluctance to feel the pain of grief and in the general attitude toward grieving that is present in our culture. The first, of course, is understandable. We don't want to stare into the emptiness of the black abyss. We don't want to be overcome by rushes of sorrow and lose control. We don't want to open ourselves to hurt. And until we know that there is a natural, normal mourning process that can culminate in a constructive outcome—and that this intense grieving is necessary for the beginning of that process—we have little incentive to choose to experience the pain.

And society gives us little permission to grieve. We know that the better we appear to be coping, the easier it is for people to be around us. We know that what people want to hear are reports such as "He is holding up well"; "She went back to work on Monday." The anthropologist Geoffrey Gorer says it bluntly: "Mourning is treated as if it were a weakness, a self-indulgence, a reprehensible habit instead of a psychological necessity." And Lily Pincus, the noted family therapist, commented that she had recently attended a funeral rite "that lasted altogether seven minutes," illustrating society's attitude toward mourning—a general conspiracy that death has not occurred.

In our culture, the attempts not to know about death, not to be reminded of it, are predominant....Funerals and cremations are "got over" as hurriedly as possible....There seems to be a general conspiracy that death has not occurred....Yet human beings need to mourn in response to loss, and if they are denied this, they will suffer, psychologically, physically, or both.

So, the cards seem to be stacked against us, both within ourselves and in the outside environment. We can understand, then, why the choice to experience and express our grief fully may not be easy. But no matter the difficulty, when we do make the choice, we will have begun the process that can return us to equilibrium.

Anthony Storr points out how dangerous it is not to choose to express grief fully: objective studies show that widows who suppress their emotions have more physical and psychological ailments during the first month, remain disturbed much longer, and, even as long as thirteen months after their husband's death, are still displaying more marked disturbances than widows who were willing to "break down" during the first weeks.

John Bowlby talks too about the positive side: persons who will achieve a healthy outcome to their grieving are people who let themselves "be swept by pangs of grief...[the] tearful expression of yearning and distress will come naturally. If sympathetic friends are available, [they] will find comfort in recalling happier days and reflection on the satisfactions of [the] lost relationship without having to obliterate all of its limitations."

Of course, how each of us expresses our grief will be different. Colin Murray Parkes reminds us that there is an optimal 'level of grieving' which varies from one person to another. Some will cry and sob, others will exhibit their feelings differently. The important thing is for feelings to be expressed. How they are expressed is of secondary importance.

If we do choose to experience and express our grief fully, there will come a time of release. This will not mean, of course, that the grieving process is over; but it will mean that we are free of the constant suffocating crush of emotion.

The following story illustrates the release that can come from expressing grief fully.

A mother told me:

When our son died at age twenty-seven, for weeks I was crushed by the pain of his death.

One night Gray and I were sitting at supper. I was suddenly overwhelmed with the realization that I would never see John again in this life. That this was the end physically of my relationship with this little baby that I had carried. I began to cry, and I cried and cried and cried, uncontrollably.

I went into the bedroom and I took off my clothes and put on my bathing suit. I went out to the pool, jumped into the water and swam and cried and cried. It was maybe fifty laps. Then I got out of the pool; I felt better. I felt I had released it all. The dam had burst. Gray drew me a hot bath. I realized as I took the tub bath that the emotional grief was over. I never cried after that. From that night on, whenever I thought of John, I saw him the way he always came into the house, his long blond hair flying, saying, "Hi, Mom." I would find that when I was doing something that reminded me of John, I would just talk to him. Not with any philosophical or ethical meaning . . . it was always, "Are you there, John?" And that's the sort of relationship we've had ever since.

WHAT WE NEED FROM FAMILY AND FRIENDS DURING IMPACT

One bereaved person after another has told me that hearing family and friends say three simple words has brought them the deepest comfort. Three simple words: *I am sorry.* Spoken with no elaboration. Followed by no awkward attempts at consolation. Just *I am sorry.* Words that reveal the speaker's understanding that a terrible rupture has ripped our life and that we are in torturing pain.

In the days, weeks, and months that follow the event of our loss, what we need most is the love, support, and presence of those who care for us. We should not hesitate to show how much we want to be with our family and friends; to admit how scared, how alone, we feel; to let others take care of us and do everything they can to look after us.

One of the most frustrating things for our friends and family is not knowing how they can help us. If we will say "I'm afraid to be in the house by myself; will you stay with me?" or "All the papers are in the file box; will you handle what has to be handled?" or "I need to talk to someone; may I tell you what happened?" those around us will have an outlet for demonstrating their care and concern. And as time goes on, it will become even more important that we let our friends and family know what we need; for once the immediacy of the event is over, with customary rituals and initial activities completed, loved ones are often at a loss as to what they can do to help us. We should, therefore, ask for what we need: *I know I've talked constantly about Clifford for weeks, but it's so important to me to be able to keep him in my memory.... I'm feeling overwhelmed; could you lend me $2,000? ... May I drop the children off while I go sign the Social Security forms and insurance papers? . . . Will you go with us the first Sunday we return to church? . . . I'm feeling lonely; may I come over and watch TV?* Impact is a difficult time for everyone; our family and friends will deeply appreciate our letting them know what specifically they can do to assist us.

Among our family and friends, we need to spend as much time as possible with at least one person who is completely comfortable in the presence of even our most emotional or persistent grieving. Someone who gives us total permission to grieve, who encourages us to talk as much as we wish, to cry, to show our anger. Someone who does not try to make us feel better or urge us to make the best of what has occurred or attempt to show us all the good that is still present in our lives. But, instead, someone who says "I'd love to look at all the pictures" or "Tell me about him when he was younger" or "What are you feeling today?" Such a person knows that, although it may seem as if we are crying about the same thing again and again, in actuality each experience is different, following a kind of logic consistent only with a bereaved person's heart.

John Bowlby points out how important spending time with such an accepting person can be to the outcome of our grieving. He talks first about the damage done when bereaved persons are told to pull themselves together and control themselves, are reminded that they are "not the only one to suffer, that weeping does no good and that [they] would be wise to face the problems of the future rather than dwell unproductively on the past." Individuals given such advice as this often suffer the debilitating effects of unresolved grief, even years later. "By contrast," Dr. Bowlby writes, "a widow with a good outcome would report how at least one person with whom she had been in contact had made it easy for her to cry and to express the intensity of her feelings; and would describe what a relief it had been to be able to talk freely and at length about past days with her husband and the circumstances of his death." We should, therefore, during Impact spend as much time as possible with such a person, pouring out our sorrow and revealing our pain.

We should also indicate to others that we are not upset by their grieving. Many of our family members and friends are hesitant to let us see them grieving, for fear that their sadness and tears will make us feel worse. But the truth is that we are comforted by knowing that the person we have lost was important to and loved by others. I remember how much I appreciated people telling me about experiences they had had with Greg—events, conversations, communications that meant a lot to them. When they cried or showed their feelings in other ways, it felt to me like an honoring of my husband. If we will let those around us know that we *want* to hear how they, too, miss the lost person, they will feel the permission to join us in our grieving, a situation that will be good for all. (Likewise, if we are angry at the person who is gone, as is often the case in divorce, and do not want to hear about the individual, we should be straightforward in making our wishes known.)

Of course, as Colin Murray Parkes puts it so succinctly, we don't need someone around us who tries to "pluck at the heartstrings" until we have a breakdown, but neither do we need people around us who "connive" with us in endless attempts to avoid the grief work that we absolutely must do. "Both probing and 'jollying along' are unhelpful," Dr. Parkes tells us. We have a painful and difficult task to perform which cannot be avoided and cannot be rushed. Our family and friends who understand Impact will recognize this fact and will help us find the time and the circumstances in which to do this grieving. Just being near those who love and care for us is life-giving during this intense time in our grieving. We should stay close, allowing family and friends to help us, relying on them. Even when there is nothing to say or do, just the presence of those who love us is solace and comfort. At a time when we feel lost and dismayed, we also feel loved.

There is no easy way through the period of Impact. To paraphrase the old prophet Isaiah, "The bed is too short and the covers too narrow." Nothing fits. While one is living this emotional raw experience, you don't know what you are doing or why you are doing it. You move forward by trial and error (mostly error), by default, by the help of family and friends, and by the grace of God. It is only in hindsight that you can see what you have lived through.

2

The Second Crisis

I want to go home, to ride to my village gate.

I want to go back, but there's no road back.

MEI SHÊNG AND FU I

FIRST CENTURY B.C.

It had been almost eight weeks since Greg's death, and I was now making plans to return to Texas. The fall semester would begin soon at the university, and I had students to teach. In many ways I was looking forward to being home—in my house, among my things—getting on with life. But I also dreaded what was next.

As the time to leave drew nearer, I lost ground. All I could think of was how much I missed Greg. Everything seemed edged in black—the lake, the mountains, the meadows. I would stand in the yard and look down toward the water of Possum Creek, and my heart would sink. I felt so desolate, so alone.

The terrible dreams began again: young women, with only one arm and no legs, sitting in wheelchairs; rooms with strange walls, every inch covered with dresses, gowns, robes, scraps of fabric—all black. I began to wake again every morning at 3 A.M., in terror. Again, I thought my wedding bracelet had been stolen.

Life felt stagnant. "I must begin to think, do, be in some way not connected to Greg's death," I told myself. "I must get on with it." Then I'd ask myself, "But what is it! How do I fill the space of Greg?"

A day or two before it was time to leave, my mother showed me an interview in the newspaper. A reporter had asked a widow whose husband had also died suddenly, "Looking back now from a vantage point of four years, what was the wisest thing you did after your husband's death?"

The widow had responded, "Going to his grave a few weeks after he died and telling him everything I wanted to tell him."

As I read the interview, I thought, "This is something that I should do, too. If it helped her, maybe it will help me." So the following afternoon, my last day in Tennessee, I drove myself to the cemetery.

I walked up the hill to the place Greg was buried under the dogwood tree and sat down. I could look across the valley and see the foothills of the Smoky Mountains in the distance.

What had the young widow done that was so valuable?

"I first told his body good-bye," she had said. "I recognized that however I was going to relate to him in the future, it would not be to his body. That was now gone."

So I began.

I imagined Greg's body in the coffin. I started with his head. "Good-bye, curly hair. Good-bye, forehead. Good-bye, eyes. Good-bye, nose. Good-bye, mouth. Good-bye, teeth. Good-bye tongue. Good-bye, beard. Good-bye, tiny scar on cheek. Good-bye ears. Good-bye, neck." I continued until I had said good-bye to every part of his body.

"Then I told him all the things I was sorry for," the young widow had told the reporter.

So I apologized to Greg and asked him to forgive me for all the times I got angry and wouldn't speak; for last winter when he had a cold and I didn't do anything special to take care of him; for being so angry at him at times that I wished we weren't married. The list was long; I tried to remember everything.

"The last thing I did," the young widow had said, "was to thank him for all the things he did that made me happy."

So I began my list: bringing coffee to the bathroom every morning when I was getting ready. Leaving love notes on the entryway floor. Surprising me by putting sausage and biscuits and orange juice in my office while I was teaching an eight o'clock class. Hiding presents all over the house on our anniversary. Cooking veal stew on the days I had to work late. Carving the letters J-O-Y for my office wall. That list was long, too; there were so many things to thank him for.

It was late afternoon when I left the cemetery. When I got back to the house, I walked down to Possum Creek. The sun was about to go down, but there was still enough light to see by. I dragged an old green wooden armchair from the picnic area down to the edge of the water, unfolded the notepaper I had brought with me, and wrote Greg a letter:

Dear Greg,

I've just walked down to the water for the final time before leaving for Texas. I wanted to come to the place where your service was held.
I walked over to the spot where your casket stood and looked out at the water which you would have seen, if you had been able to see that day.
I can hardly believe I'm leaving here without you.

Do you remember the T-shirt you wore on the drive from Texas to the cabin—the one that said "Adios to Summer Races"? Well, it's now Adios to Everything. I think about the days we came down here and played in the water on our floats. I think about all the afternoons we walked down here after work. I've come to say good-bye to everything.

I am saying good-bye to your spirit in the sunset, the rocks, the grass. What does it all mean? I don't know. Where are you? I don't know.

Do you remember that story "The Old People" by William Faulkner? The one where Sam Fathers, one of the ancient ones, speaks to the deer. "Hail, Grandfather," he says, his arm raised in homage to the buck who is bounding across the mountainside.

Well, sweetheart, today I say to the water, the grass, the rocks, the East Tennessee hills, the mist, the view, the cabin, "Hail, Greg." They are all you.
I love you, Greg.

Your wife,
Elizabeth

The next morning it was time to leave. As I got into the car alone at my parents' house, I thought, "How different this is from the way I arrived." I realized that I was closing one chapter in my life and starting another one. And I didn't like it. In fact, I hated it. But there was nothing else I could do.

"What is that ritual when a cavalry officer has been killed in battle?" I asked myself as I drove past the cabin. "Doesn't his horse walk in the parade without a rider?" As I reached the end of the lane and prepared to turn the car onto the highway, I reached over and patted the empty seat.

For weeks after I returned to Texas I lived a vagabond existence. I was afraid to stay in my house alone—the same woman who had lived by herself for three years in New York City, relishing the experience. An ominous dread and chilling fear permeated the rooms of my house, and I could not stand to be there. I slept at one friend's house one night, another friend's house the next.

But roaming from place to place became unacceptable. I was embarrassed that a thirty-seven-year-old professor would be so dependent. I also hated not belonging anywhere. "This is *my* house," I finally said to myself angrily, "and I am going to live in it!" So I mustered up the courage to spend a night alone.

I timed my return home from school in order to arrive as late as possible but still before darkness fell. I turned on the television set as soon as I entered; at least I could hear voices. Then I went through the house, looking under every bed, in the bathtub, in every closet. When it started to get dark, I put a towel over the kitchen window.

I spent the evening sitting down and getting up. I made lists of things to do and then decided not to do them. I skipped supper and instead ate a quart of vanilla ice cream. At bedtime I moved from the upstairs to the downstairs bedroom in case I needed to get out of the house quickly to escape some intruder. I was afraid to undress, so I slept in my clothes. I put a pistol from Greg's ROTC days by the bed, even though I did not know how to load it. I was still awake when the alarm went off in the morning.

So much of every day was taken up with unfamiliar and painful business. The legal and business affairs related to Greg's death seemed unending. Entering the lawyer's office, I would reassure myself, "No need to be concerned; this will be no problem. It's just a piece of legal business." I felt strong and capable. But when I started to tell the man why I was there, I discovered that I was crying.

Every day brought new instructions. The accountant informed me, "The IRS requires that you make an inventory of the items in the house and put a valuation on them. That information will be used in determining the tax you owe the government." A valuation on everything in the house? A train set? An old guitar? Pots and pans? The contents of all the closets? Even though I later realized that the accountant had not expected me to take his words so literally, I still found trying to estimate the value of our possessions an onerous task.

I was frightened by surprise visits from investigators employed by the insurance company. They had written: "Since Mr. Cowan had not held this insurance for the mandatory two-year period, we must investigate this claim. Might there be a chance he had a heart condition prior to his death, a condition about which we were not informed?" I was furious. Didn't they know that if there had been any symptom of a heart condition, our doctor would have found it and Greg would be alive today? The question was an insult. Yet I lived in fear that they would not pay.

I worried constantly about not having enough money. At night I dreamed of dying a shriveled-up old woman in the poorhouse—a scene that always looked like something from a Dickens novel. When I got my first paycheck for the new school year, I realized that the monthly bills amounted to more than my salary. Greg and I had made several long-term financial commitments that I now had to pay for alone, commitments that were as worthless and useless to me now as they were irreversible. The only way I could make ends meet was to dip into the small pot of insurance money each month; I had already figured out how long it would be before that security was gone. I knew I would have to find some second source of income. With Greg, my financial future had been comfortable and secure; now it was bleak and frightening.

Such were the concerns of my daily life. Nothing was the same. Everything was unfamiliar.

My place in the world was also drastically altered. People who had been friendly in the past were now awkward around me. The first time I went into the mailroom at the university, some of my colleagues were gathered around, passing the time and chatting. I walked in, and everything changed. The easy conversation turned to dead silence. The joviality turned to haste to get out of the room. Within seconds everyone was gone. Several people said hello to me as they passed; but no one mentioned Greg, even though some of them had written me notes when he died. One day an acquaintance came to the house to visit and stayed two hours. Not once was anything said that indicated that my husband had died, even though the woman had earlier sent me a lovely note of condolence. I understood this reluctance to talk of death, this awkwardness and avoidance, but I also hated it.

Greg and I had belonged to a gourmet cooking club for three

years. I decided to attend the first meeting in September. Everyone was happy to see me, and I felt genuinely welcomed back into the group. When the list of members was passed around, however, I realized that I was the only person on the list without a spouse. It dawned on me then how naive I had been to imagine I could continue to enjoy being in the club. Not only would I have no one to help me prepare the elaborate and complicated dishes; but, worse than that, I would have no one to go with me to the dinners. I would always be the odd person at the table.

At a professional conference I attended that fall, a colleague from another university said to me, "You must be devastated to be here by yourself. You and Greg were such a golden couple, and you must already be realizing that you will never shine that way alone." Did he mean to be cruel? Did he realize what he was saying? I cannot say. I do know that I lost all interest in attending the conference and left.

I had lost the routine and structure of daily living. I had lost my identity. As the weeks passed, it also became clear to me that an equally devastating loss was the loss of the future I had assumed I would have. I had expected to have Greg's children. Katie Rachel Pearl . . . Jeremiah Cade. Now there would be no babies. At night I dreamed of brown-eyed sons and curly-haired daughters. At thirty-seven, I mourned those never-to-be children.

I had expected always to be a part of Greg's family—a daughter-in-law to his mother, a stepmother to his sons. Now I worried if the four and a half years we had been married had been long enough for me to establish a place in their lives. When they called, I listened to catch every nuance in their voices. Was I still included in the family?

I had also expected to grow old with Greg, retire with him. We were going to polish agates in Oregon and climb mountains in Tennessee. I now had to readjust my entire future.

These new stresses brought repercussions. I began to revive old resentments toward certain people. I took umbrage at the slightest affront, whether real or imagined. I nursed these grudges privately and became more bitter.

It was in reviewing my life with Greg that I took refuge. I found myself fixated on the smallest details of our life together. What he ordered on a hot pastrami sandwich at the Grapevine Restaurant. What camera we used when we took the movies in the Grand Tetons. How cold it was the night we went out in the ice storm to see the frozen crystals that haloed our neighbor's tree. How I always smiled when I saw him coming home from the university on his Yamaha, dressed up in a suit and tie and wearing that silly motorcycle helmet!

I became afraid that I would forget things about him, so I made a list: "Things I Never Want to Forget" . . . the time we went to church in Chimayo; the poems we read in room 222; how he sat in his chair grading papers while I wove at the loom; how he cooked steaks that time in a fireplace and opened champagne with a nail; his request for a bud vase for his birthday one August. I was already beginning to feel that I was forgetting his voice, his image, his words. "Oh, come back, sweet one," I wrote. "Come back and call me Bessa. Be with me. Give joy to my life. Bring purpose to my existence. Give meaning to my days."

Things came to a climax one rainy Sunday in early November. My sister and brother-in-law had been visiting for the weekend, and they had just left to catch the plane for Tennessee. Even a few minutes with nothing to do were intolerable, so as soon as they left I drove to the shopping center to see a movie. Four films were playing, none of them familiar. One title, however, caught my eye: *Starting Over,* a movie starring Burt Reynolds and Jill Clayburgh. I bought my ticket and found a seat.

For two hours I saw my life on the screen. Oh, to be sure, the movie was about a man whose wife had just left him, not a woman whose husband had just died. But this man's life had the same vacancy, the same lack of direction, the same empty, shapeless future as mine did. The man on that screen was me—resenting, hesitating, fighting, pulling back, crying, wandering. The only thing different was that by the end of the movie, he had found the courage to start his life over.

I hated the movie. Hurrying across the parking lot toward my car, I castigated myself: "Why in the world did I go to *that* movie! Just to hurt myself? Isn't it enough to live it; do I also have to go watch my empty life on a stupid screen?" The truth was, I hated the film because I had gotten the message: there is terrible and unavoidable pain and suffering when people lose. There is no way to avoid it. And, in the face of that loss, every person has an inescapable option —to choose to be courageous and make the changes necessary to start life over or not to. Yes, I hated the movie because I had gotten the message.

It was almost dark when I got home, and a light rain was falling. I could see the kitchen from the carport. I had left a light on and through the mist the room looked warm and cheerful. Tall, bright, red chairs clustered around an old circular oak farm table. Red-and-white napkins on the table. Green plants on the shelf. But I knew the scene was a lie. That kitchen was not warm and cheery; it was empty. There was nothing to do in that house, no one to be with. There was nothing in that house but coldness and deathlike stillness.

Something snapped inside me. I was overcome with fury. I found myself running into the house; I headed straight for Greg's study, where everything was the way he had left it. On the wall was a large paper butterfly kite that I had bought him. I jerked the kite off the wall and began to break it into a hundred pieces. I made balls of the crushed paper, scattering them all over the room. I cracked the sticks until they were hardly larger than match stems. I knew Greg had loved that kite, and I could hardly believe I was destroying it. But I hated Greg for what he had done to my life by dying. I had loved my life the way it was; it had been just the way I had dreamed life could be. And now everything had to change, everything was changed. Whether I wanted it or not, a new life lay ahead of me. And I didn't want it. I didn't want to have to change my life. And now I knew I had to, regardless of whether it was a change I had asked for or chosen.

When the kite was destroyed, I tore through the house like a madwoman. I ran from room to room, bumping into corners of hallways, falling against doorjambs as I passed. Then I saw the firewood. I grabbed the largest piece I could manage and began to beat the sofa in the living room. I beat the sofa, and I screamed, *"But I don't want to start my life over. I want my life the way it was. I want my husband.*

I want things to be the same. I want what I had worked so hard for. I want what I had. I hate you, Greg, for dying. I hate you, life, for doing this to me. I hate being alone. I hate not knowing what to do. I hate having no structure for my life, no direction to go in. I hate having to make a new future."

Finally, my fury was spent. I dropped the log and collapsed on the floor by the sofa. With my head in my arms, I first cried quietly and then sat on the floor for a long time in total silence.

For a day or two after this outburst, I was more clear-headed. I talked sensibly to myself. "There is *loss* in the world, and this is what it feels like," I acknowledged. "How you acted Sunday is how people act when they experience loss. And everybody experiences it. Loss, like grief, is impersonal. It is just a given in life; you cannot avoid it."

Something else also became clear to me. I realized that in all my reveries Greg and I never got any older. We never had any new problems; nobody ever got sick; we never changed from how we were. "That," I said to myself, "is totally unrealistic. Maybe things would have always been good, but you don't know. One thing for certain, life would have been different; and you have no way of knowing how it would have turned out." I could see that in my memories and my fantasies I had frozen my life with Greg in time.

But the clear-headedness didn't last. I could not keep my new insights in focus when every day was such a vacuum. I didn't care about anything. Nothing mattered. One morning as I was dressing it came to me that nothing from the past now gave me any pleasure. Not only was my husband gone—so was everything that I valued in the past.

Just the evening before I had gone with friends to hear the Houston Symphony play some of my favorite music. It had meant nothing to me. I never sat down at my loom to weave anymore because now that meant nothing to me. I didn't have enthusiasm for teaching; work was just a place I had to go to make the money I had to make. I hated Sunday mornings because reading the newspaper and drinking coffee were the last things I wanted to do. My house could have fallen down, and I would hardly have noticed. My family was important to me, but it was clear now that they alone couldn't give meaning to my future.

With every minute I was getting closer to a breakdown. Whether I wanted to or not, I was seeing more and more clearly what I was facing. I began to realize that to keep on living I would have to establish whole new habit patterns—how I came into the house, what I did in my spare moments, what I did when I got up. "New paths must be made," I realized, "like new veins for blood to run in." I had seen what I had to do, and I didn't want it.

I knew I was about to go under. I saw some rust on the hinge of the bedroom door, and for a minute I thought it was blood. I got dressed and went to school; but I cried the entire day. I had to dismiss my classes, telling the students I was ill. It was all I could do to keep the tears from flowing down my face as I spoke to them. I cried as I drove home. My head hurt terribly. I felt anger toward everybody. I thought, "I cannot stand to keep on walking into an empty house. I want to just fall apart, go to bed, and have someone come and take care of me. I don't like being stiff and courageous. I don't like coping. Right now I would like to go to the emergency room or go crazy and take pills."

Then I had a comforting thought: "Maybe someone will break into my house tonight and kill me. Then I won't have to commit suicide, and I could go where Greg is. So why get so upset? Why worry?"

———————

It was Thanksgiving. A joke of a holiday. "Would you come to Chicago for the weekend?" my cousin Ernestine had asked me. "Yes," I had said, thinking that perhaps being with family in a new environment would help. I was frightened because I knew I was losing hold on reality. Just the day before, in filling out a form for the department secretary, I found myself writing "The Land of the Dead" under Foreign Travel. I knew I was going crazy. Maybe getting away to Chicago was the answer.

"Let's go into the lounge and get you a doctor's jacket," Ernestine said the first afternoon of my visit. "Then you can do rounds with me." Nine months my junior, Ernestine was a highly respected and well-established surgeon. She was poised, confident, and professional.

As we went through the hospital, I realized for the first time that dying young could be a virtue. At least Greg, by dying at forty-three and in perfect health, had never faced this: illnesses, operations, tubes, oxygen tents, vital signs machines, pain, suffering. This was what the rest of us had to look forward to. What an ending. I was disgusted.

Driving home, I asked Ernestine, "How do you do it every day? How do you stand the responsibility of all those people's lives resting in your hands? How do you live with the fickleness of life—some people living and others dying?"

She took my questions seriously. "I think of each patient as a hand of cards that has been dealt me," she replied. "A hand over which I have no say-so. Patients are in whatever condition they are when I meet them. I treat them the best way I know how, doing my best not to hurt them or make them worse. In other words, I attempt to make the most of the hand that's been dealt me." What my cousin said made sense. But it only showed me how useless it is to pretend we human beings have much to do with anything. I thought, "We're only living some kind of busy charade."

That night I could not sleep. I finally got up and stood looking out the window. Crusts of dirty snow and ice lay everywhere. Grotesque shapes hid in the shadows—shapes I would recognize in the daylight as doorways, garbage cans, concrete embankments—but tonight they looked like specters of the dead. I stared into the darkness.

"Life *is* meaningless," I realized. "You can pretend things matter, but they don't. Finally, you have to admit that there is no meaning in anything we human beings do. We just fool ourselves. We need to think our actions matter. We think the little worlds we make, the purposes we organize our lives around, the things we commit to, matter. But life is nothing. And death is the end of it all. So what is the use of pretending? Why put effort and care and commitment into anything when it finally makes absolutely no difference? When nothing matters? Everything *is* vanity. Emptiness. Nothingness."

With these thoughts I lost my mental footing. For weeks I had been staring into the abyss. Now I fell into it. Everything was blackness. I lost touch with life. I lost touch with the future. I lost touch with any chance of new opportunity.

In the airport on the way home I deliberately tried to hit people with my suitcases. "Get out of my way," I yelled at strangers. When I got to my dark, cold house, I didn't even notice. Because now nothing mattered, not even that Greg had died. I cared about nothing.

For months I lived in this condition. I felt unhinged, unable to judge what I was doing or to think clearly. I denied my values. I tempted danger. I switched from wine coolers to Scotch, tried to learn to smoke, and drove my car fast and recklessly. I dated indiscriminately and spent and lost money foolishly, depleting my already limited resources. I planned ridiculous career changes. Perhaps I'd stop being a professor and become a financial planner in Florida—or an earth mother in California. Or maybe I'd just stay where I was and be neat and cool, defiant of all conventions.

I enjoyed the adrenaline rush that came with taking the high-wire risks. These were the only times I felt alive in what otherwise were days and nights of numbness. But the truth was, I had hit rock bottom. I was desperate for something to give meaning in my life, for something to take the place of Greg. I was trying to find something to do with my life. I didn't know who I was supposed to be. I was trying to avoid being swallowed up by the emptiness. But I was failing on all accounts. Everything I was doing was self-destructive.

Why would someone who drops by all the time—someone who is your best friend—call suddenly and say she's coming over? When Emma arrived, she didn't want to sit down. She said she'd just stand in front of the fireplace.

"Elizabeth," she said, "I've kept quiet as long as I'm going to. I know the loss of Greg has been devastating. That's why over the past few months, when I saw you being so self-destructive, I never criticized. I knew you had lost your footing. And I knew that it would take time, maybe a long time, for you to regain your equilibrium."

She paused. I had no idea what she was going to say next.

"But I have lost my patience," she continued. "I want you to know that I am really angry at you; in fact, I am furious. You are acting as if you want to lose *everything* in your life, not just your husband. You seem to think that, alone, you are nothing.

"But there's something very important I think you've forgotten," Emma went on to say. "You were a whole person before you met Greg, and you can be a whole person after him. It's time for you to remember that. That's all I came to say," she concluded, "except this. We have been best friends for a long time, but I won't have your craziness in my life anymore. I won't support you. If you want to stop trying to destroy your life and start being the terrific person you really are, then I'm your friend forever. But if you don't, then don't count me in on anything you are doing."

Her mission completed, Emma gave me a hug and said good-bye. "I'll call you," I said quietly as she was leaving.

I sat on the couch for several minutes, thinking. I was not angry at anything Emma had said. In fact, I felt relief. It was as if I had just been waiting for someone to tell me I had to set limits. Because when I told the truth to myself, I was sick of the way I was living. For weeks now, I had been waking up every morning with the words from that awful night in Chicago ringing in my ears: *Everything is vanity. Life is empty. Nothing matters.*

I knew Emma was right. I had to do something else. I had to set a new direction.

The next day, in a most mundane situation, I surprised myself by taking action.

A young man servicing my car told me I needed some air in my tires and asked how many pounds the tires were supposed to carry. My first thought was to respond as I had done in other situations like this: *I've never had to take care of the tires before . . . that was always my husband's responsibility ... and he died a few months ago.... I don't know what to tell you.... Perhaps you can help me....*

But this time I did not tell my usual story.

"Just a minute," I told him. "I have to look it up." I opened the glove compartment, took out the owner's manual, and located the information the young man needed. I sat back in my seat as if I had just climbed Mt. Everest. I felt such satisfaction! I felt so capable, so strong! Why, I even felt like a person who might have a future!

As I drove away from the service station, however, the cost of what I had done hit me. By being competent and taking care of the situation, I had lost something very important: I had lost the opportunity to talk about my husband. Now this young man would never know what a wonderful man I had been married to and how much I missed him. Talking about Greg was the only way I now had to keep him present. If I didn't get to talk about him, I would lose him completely.

The dilemma was crystal clear, and I hated it.

Suddenly, a poem I taught in my literature classes flashed into my mind. It was by Robert Frost, called "Home Burial." In the poem a young wife withdraws from her husband, accusing him angrily of being callous about their firstborn's death. She determines not to turn back to life and living people. "She's right," I shouted angrily. "I won't have grief so, either. No matter what anybody says, I won't just turn around, walk back into life, and forget Greg. I won't let love go that easily."

I lashed out at Emma as if she were sitting in the car with me: "I haven't seen a husband of yours die!" I told her. "If you had, you might be able to understand me. What right have you to tell me that I can choose to stop grieving? It's easy for you to say, since you don't have to do it!"

I had made my decision.

"No, no matter what anybody says—I will not betray Greg by turning my back on the beautiful life we had together. I will not dishonor our love by moving ahead to other things. I don't care if it means a lifetime of mourning. I don't care what happens to me. I don't care if I am never happy. No, I won't turn away from Greg. It's the least I can do for his memory."

T his is the Second Crisis. Dark. Bleak. Hopeless. All the structure, shape, focus, and direction of the past gone, with absolutely nothing to take its place in the present. Every assumption one has ever had about how life works and what an individual's role is or can be is assaulted. You are completely knocked off course. You don't know what to believe, what to think, what to hold on to. The underpinnings of your life have been destroyed. The world you had created has been shattered into smithereens. And you have neither the desire nor the resources to rebuild it.

If anything, the Second Crisis is worse than the original loss itself.

By this time you are discovering how totally your life has been changed by the loss. At the beginning, you have no idea how extensive and deep are the patterns: how much milk you buy at the store; what you schedule to do after work; how many holiday cards you order; how the income tax is handled; what you do on birthdays and anniversaries. There's no one to call out, "I'll get it," when the telephone rings and nobody to help bring in the groceries. When I was a child our house burned down, and I can remember that for years my mother kept remembering things she missed or needed that had been lost in the fire. This is how it is when you lose someone or something important to your existence. As every week and month passes, you see new ways your life has been affected. You come to see that this loss cannot be compensated for. It is irreversible. You realize that you are ultimately helpless in how things go in the universe. Nothing you do, in the final analysis, matters. You lose all hope. When all this becomes *inescapably* known, you experience the Second Crisis.

Peter Marris, the British social scientist, talks about it this way: When the lost person has been a "keystone" in our lives, the whole structure of meaning in life collapses when that keystone disappears. A relationship is gone that identified who we were and what we did each day. Our purposes, our satisfactions—even our "important anxieties" and "resentments"—involved this person. So whether we were happy, ambivalent, or unhappy in the relationship (an irony divorced people especially can appreciate), the familiar world we live in has been shattered.

The collected wisdom perhaps would say, "Since that's the way it is and there is nothing you can do about it, you just have to quit looking to the past and build a new structure." Not so easy, says Professor Marris. A person can't just adopt new purposes, because purposes are culminations of a lifetime's experiences. The task we find staring us in the face, then, is nothing short of a "painful retrieval of purpose from the wreck of dead hopes," but during the Second Crisis it is clear that we do not have the wherewithal to accomplish it.

John Bowlby suggests another reason this period is so painful. "In the course of our evolution," he says, "our instinctual equipment has come to be so fashioned that all losses are assumed to be retrievable and are responded to accordingly." But by this time we know undeniably that the loss we have sustained is not retrievable—we will not be able to "restore the bond that has been severed." The loss is permanent. It is undoable. It is forever. And we are undone by this realization.

As I have listened to people tell me about their experience of the Second Crisis, I have heard both pain and strength in their voices. It was clear, in hearing them speak, that the trauma of this period of the grieving process had been devastating. But it was also clear that these individuals—even as they told me their stories—were recognizing what it meant that they had lived through this terrible time in their lives. Their conversations were, for me, a kind of celebration of the resiliency that is part of the gift of being human.

These women and men with whom I talked say that such experiences as these are characteristic of the Second Crisis....

THE LOSS OF IDENTITY
A divorced man recalls:

It was a time of chaos. My life was liquid; it had no form. I didn't know who I was; I didn't know where I was; I didn't know where I was going.

You see, I had been defined before. I was Sandra's husband; I was David's dad; I lived on the corner of Greenwich and Dawson. I had a definition.

And now, I couldn't even tell you my address. Most of the time I gave people the wrong phone number. "I live out by K-Mart," I'd say, and that was about the best I could do on directions.

I was just an unknown quantity. I didn't exist. I wasn't attached to anything. I quit writing. I avoided people wherever possible. And I just . . . sometimes I think I felt like I was, as some people say, drifting. Just floating along, like these wisps that come off cottonwood trees or dandelions; they just float off into space and they drift down and they float up and drift down and they float up; and you don't know where they're going to end up.

THE ALTERATION OF LIFE'S BASIC STRUCTURE

A divorced woman with young children describes the change:

Everything about you changes. You have to do even the normal things differently. You have to get up thirty minutes earlier in the morning because you're the only one to check to be sure the kids get dressed and their teeth are brushed since your husband isn't there now to help you.

Just on a day-to-day basis your life is going to have to change because you're now everything to the children. I mean, you can't cook dinner and clean the dishes and let Daddy bathe them. You have to cook dinner, clean the dishes, bathe them, and listen to them read. You have to be different because you have to fit all that in, and there's still just twenty-four hours in the day.

THE DISAPPEARANCE OF THE FUTURE

A widow tells her story:

It's one thing to remember the past, the good and the bad, and you remember both. But it's another thing to grieve over what's not happening now that would have happened if the person had not died. I think a lot, "If Cam were here now, we'd be doing that or doing this, things would be this way, and the future would look like this."

Cam was the major money-maker. And because his business was construction, we were always looking for a big payoff in the future. He'd say, "It's not good now, but we're going to stick it out; and next year it'll be better, and the next year it'll be even better." Everything in our life was oriented around a future when the economic slump would be over. But now that he's dead, it's irrelevant to me and the kids whether or not the construction business gets better in the future.

I had to let the rental houses go, for instance, because now I don't have the luxury to wait for things to turn around. But it was so hard for me to accept that the future has been wiped out. That now I have to get in a position to earn enough money to meet the responsibilities. That's a weight that's just added to the shock and sadness of Cam's death.

It has taken me many months to get to the point where I can say, "All right, the future is not going to be what you thought it was. It's gone, and you're not going to have it. You just will not have it. Your future went with him. Now you've got to build a new one." That is traumatic. I don't feel sorry for myself anymore for the past; I just miss all the things that are now never going to happen.

FEELINGS OF DESPAIR
A divorced man remembers:

I decided that I would finally unpack. The first thing I took out of the box was a Mr. Coffee. Well, as I unloaded the coffee maker, the glass decanter fell out and broke on the tile floor. I was so heartbroken that I just sat down on the floor, broken glass and all, and I cried. Like a little baby. I had lost control of everything.

I'd cut my finger on the glass, and some combination of things— the broken glass, me sitting there on the floor, completely worn out, completely spent, the blood on my hands, the blood on the floor, the boxes around me, nothing, no good smells, no food cooking, no anything—made me feel total despair. "This is the beginning of death," I said to myself.

For at least a month I shook a lot, my voice trembled, I cried easily, I was angry and short with people without notice. I began behaving erratically—I'm not a drinker, but I'd buy a bottle of wine and drink the whole bottle in one night. I started cooking enormous meals, which I then wouldn't eat because I didn't want them. In fact, I'd go without eating for days, just living on orange juice, coffee, candy. I didn't even know who I was. For thirty days and thirty nights—the nights were separate from the days and doubled the length of the days—I lived a life of nobody-ness. It was a month of being helpless and hopeless. Perhaps it was even longer....

AN AVOIDANCE BY OTHERS OF THE SUBJECT
OF DEATH OR LOSS
A widow remembers:

Four months after he died, I gave my first dinner party. I worked for days preparing a wonderful menu for eight people with whom Claude and I had spent many evenings, weekends, and vacations. When the dinner began, I expected that at least one of the friends at the table would suggest that we do a toast to Claude or at least acknowledge in some way his absence.

But I was wrong. Not once during the entire evening did any of
the eight even mention him. It was as if he had never existed. I was
so hurt by this. I felt like standing up and yelling, "How can you just
sit there? Claude is dead." I should have. But I didn't. During the
course of the evening, one man made reference to death in some
other context; and I felt a bond with him because he would even risk
mentioning the word.

FRANTIC ATTEMPTS TO FILL THE EMPTINESS
A man talks about his reaction to the loss of his partner:

About a month after Ben died, I started doing everything I could
to avoid thinking about it. I went out and bought a Dodge convert-
ible, which I couldn't afford, and all I did was drive that car from
party to party. At one of these parties, I met up with some rich but
questionable characters; and I ended up serving as their confidante
and companion. This meant that my days were almost entirely filled
with conflict as I tried to help my friends extricate themselves from
their legal situations. This, of course, only added to the upset I
already had over Ben's dying. So at night I'd try to forget by going
to more and more parties.

At these parties I began to drink more heavily and started using
cocaine. To try to get away from myself, I even took three trips
abroad in six months—to places like Egypt, the Philippines, London
—and ran up huge bills on my credit cards. That, plus the amount of
money I was spending on drugs, pushed me to the edge of bankruptcy. I was caught in a vicious cycle.

A LOSS OF FAITH
A mother whose daughter died:

You know, when a child dies, in addition to the sense of loss,
there is a sense of outrage because it's unnatural. It's not in the
scheme of things. A parent should go first; a child should learn to
cope with that loss. But when a child dies, that sense of outrage is
keener because there is a sense of a wasted life. You can never know
what the child might have become.

We have not been able to make the loss of our daughter compat-
ible with any scheme of fairness or with any belief in a plan in the
universe. We have lost our faith. We were fairly regular templegoers

before Charlotte died, but Carson has never set foot in the temple again. He can't. He can't reconcile a loving God with the loss of Charlotte. I've been back once or twice only when they have a special ceremony that the family always participated in.

STRAIN IN RELATIONSHIPS
A daughter discusses events after her father's death:

When my father died, that was it on my being part of a family. Three years before, my sister and my mother had died within twelve months of each other. With no immediate family left, I tried to cling to my father's brothers. I had never been close to them, so I don't know why I thought all of a sudden I could be close; but I made advances in that direction. It turned out to be a horrible disaster because what they wanted was my dad's money.

Everything revolved around some property that had been in the family for a long time. Many years before, the family had been getting ready to sell the property; but my father decided he just couldn't let the property go out of the family, so he paid the other members of the family for their shares and bought it himself.

Several years later Dad got a phone call from a land company. "We think there's oil there; will you let us drill?" My father said okay. Well, the minute the oil well hit, all of a sudden, my uncles are saying, "If we had had any idea there was oil on the property, we wouldn't have sold it." It really got ugly.

Then after Dad died, they started pressuring me: "If your father were still alive, he'd give it back." It was horrible for me. A shock. I was devastated. When I did not return the property, my uncles and their families stopped speaking to me. This taught me that just because you're related, all the feelings are not necessarily going to be good.

SYMPATHETIC ILLNESS
A daughter recalls:

My father died on January 19, and on March 12 I came down with an affliction just like his. He was in his eighties when he went into the hospital for excruciating lower back pain. They operated on him, but he never got well. He was in such pain before he died—you could hear him calling out all over the hospital floor.

Well, on March 12 I woke up paralyzed, in excruciating pain. My lower back—which had never bothered me in the past—was in spasms. My husband carried me to the doctor, who said I must have fallen or picked up something heavy, but I hadn't. He gave me tranquilizers. Then I went to another doctor, who said he thought it was stress and gave me muscle relaxant tablets. My husband finally insisted that I go to an orthopedic surgeon, who also could find nothing wrong.

I knew all along that my illness was related to my father's death. I even had a dream the day I woke up in such pain—my father said to me in the dream that I did not have to do what he did. I didn't have to take on his pain. Finally, somewhere in my head I got the message, and the pain went away. I haven't been bothered with it since.

BEHAVIOR THAT IS OUT OF CHARACTER
A widow recalls:

I went with my son and daughter-in-law to Lake Tahoe on vacation. I did a stupid thing there. So embarrassing. We met other couples that I knew there, and we went to one of these lovely places up in the mountains to eat. One of the men in the group knew the type of music I liked, and he had the pianist play those pieces for me. Then the pianist called me over to sit on the piano bench with him, and we all sang the songs. I'd had some wine, so I sang and got louder and louder and weepier and weepier. I just plain made a fool of myself. I sang those songs and I cried; and, of course, all the people I was with thought it was so great for the widow to be coming out of her shell a little bit that they said we just had to go back there the next night.

We went back the next night, and then I realized the pianist was making a come-on and I knew I had set that up—and my husband hadn't been dead more than a few months. Suddenly I wanted to throw up. I got out of that room fast. I felt as if I had done something bad. It was so out of character.

CHRONIC DEPRESSION
A divorced woman says:

Sixteen months ago the divorce was final. Since then I've had only two periods. The doctors say it's too early for menopause, but I think that is what I'm having. I wake up sometimes at night with such a burning feeling that I think I'm going to smother. I've gained all the weight back that I lost, and it's settled in different places. And I think I look old. Look old? Damn, I *am* old, old at forty-one.

I was almost through with my R.N. degree when this happened, and I have no desire now to finish it. I lack only the internship, and I'd have it. But I just don't care about it. I just don't care.

The truth is, I feel pretty much nothing. I stay in the house as much as possible. I guess I'm just trying to pull the walls in around me.

A DECLINE IN HEALTH

A widow remembers:

I ate constantly. I found out later that I was anemic, which might have caused that. I threw up all the time. Physically, I was a wreck. I used up all my physical energy. I'd go by myself and play racquetball, an hour or many times two hours. I just used up everything I had. I lost thirty pounds and became so nauseated I couldn't eat. I would get up at six-thirty or seven, make myself get dressed, make myself go to work—at that time, one neighbor was taking one child to school, and I was taking the other one to a friend's house—so I'd get the kids off and then in the afternoon usually their grandmother or aunt would keep them. So, I'd stay at the office from eight-thirty to maybe five-thirty or six.

AN INCREASE IN ACCIDENTS

A teenage son tells this story:

A few months after my dad's death, I injured my leg. It was on a Saturday, and I was getting ready to go to the locker room to suit up for the game. I ran out of my dorm room in my stocking feet, and when I turned the corner my feet slipped out from under me and I fell. One leg bent way back under me. I went on to the game but didn't get to play.

There was massive internal bleeding in the leg. It swelled up so badly that they had to rip the inside seam of my uniform pants to relieve the pressure. I had to be in the infirmary for a day or two, and after that I developed what the orthopedic surgeon called "cavalryman's disease"— soldiers would ride the horses so long and hard that their muscles would tear and bleed. The blood would clot so that it was too much for the bloodstream to carry away, and the blood would then calcify, causing atrophy to the muscles. That is what happened to my leg, so that even today I have a calcium deposit probably four inches long and an inch thick in that leg that has just completely ruined my mobility. It's never been the same since—that leg is smaller than the other one and not strong. And the injury ended my football career.

In the months after my dad's death and before the accident happened, I would sit by myself in my dorm room, in the dark, and look out at the trees and sky. I have never felt so blue and lonely in my life. I wouldn't be thinking of my father directly, but I'd just be so empty. When the accident happened, it was like it finished off something that began back in those terrible afternoons.

ANGER
A friend talks:

One of my closest friends just died from AIDS, and I am so angry at the reaction of some members of his family. Near the end Cal had spent all his resources on treatment, he had no insurance, and he was still desperately fighting for his life. "I'm going to beat this thing," he kept saying. "I don't care if they say there is no cure, I'm going to beat it." It was inspiring to be in the presence of his commitment to life and his courage.

But the attitude of several members of his family seemed to me to be so callous. When Cal asked them to help him financially, they responded by saying, "Are you really sick, or are you just in trouble with your creditors for overcharging on your accounts?" They reminded him of all the times before he had gotten into trouble with his money and how they had often helped bail him out. This hurt Cal so much that he severed all relationship with his family. When he finally died, not one member of his family was with him. I am so angry about this that I can't even grieve for Cal. Just to think of him having to put up with such reactions, when all the while he was dying. I am so angry. So very, very angry.

GUILT
A daughter recounts these circumstances:

I blame myself. I'm a registered first-aid person. If I had only been home that weekend, I could have personally saved my mother because I would have recognized her symptoms. My father didn't recognize that she had had heart failure because her symptoms were different from his when he had a heart attack. But he had digitalis right there in his pocket, and if I had been there—I'm still not over not being there to help them.

I think a lot, too, of how I could have helped my mother be happier. I'll see a talk show about people who are chronically depressed, and I think of my mother. I remember things from my childhood— like my mother coming home and saying she stood for twenty minutes in front of the green beans trying to decide which brand to buy. I would just look at her sort of quizzically and say, "Mother, that's weird." I really feel guilty about that now. I wish I had known more then and could have helped her. I watch the movie *'Night, Mother,* with Anne Bancroft, over and over. You know, the movie where Anne tries to save her daughter, who is going to commit suicide. I identify with the Bancroft character; I wish I could have saved my mother. Or I'll watch *The Big Chill.* There's this line where—I think it's Jo Beth Williams who says it—something about, "If only I'd known, maybe I could've helped." And one of the other characters snaps back at her, "Oh, do you think you have that kind of power?" Then I realize that I do think I have that kind of power. I think that surely I could have helped if only I'd said the right thing or been there at the right time.

THE FOCUS DURING THE SECOND CRISIS

As we can see from these stories, there is little to relieve the bleakness, the despair, of the Second Crisis. It is a time in our grieving process when things are the blackest. When we are living a no-person's life, caught in a place we can only call limbo.

Why are we having it so hard? What else about life is this loss now uncovering and revealing? And what will be our response after we see this? These are the difficult questions that lie at the heart of the Second Crisis. Never will the way we think and the actions we take be more critical in determining whether and how we finish our grieving.

Understanding that We Are Grieving for Much More than the Lost Person

During the Second Crisis we are dealing with much more than the loss of a person significant in our lives, as central as that loss may be. We are also dealing with the loss of those purposes that determined not only how our life had been but also how we thought our life would be in the future. We've lost the structure that informs our life—our "assumptive world," is the way some writers put it.

I remember reading a father's poignant account of what it is like not to be able to count any longer on one's assumptions. Writing in the *New York Times Magazine* about the death of his only child, a son, he remarked that now there would be no child to inherit the family's antique organ, the glassware blown by his wife's grandfather, the family silverware and china. Nor, he said, would there be children or grandchildren to listen to family stories and pass them on. Near the end of the article, the father said, "I have been surprised by how the assumptions that a man's child will marry and have children— and that they will all outlive him—are his constant companions, molding thought and actions in innumerable subtle ways. Suddenly, my thoughts and actions were inappropriate, because the assumptions on which they were based were no longer valid. Until some new assumptions replace those shattered by Paul's fall, I feel like a ship without engine, sail or rudder, floating helplessly without direction."

This father speaks for all of us. When life has no center that holds, when we can no longer live and plan according to our assumptions, the sense that we have no direction leaves us hopeless. Now we must not only mourn the absent one; we must mourn the loss of the picture of ourselves in the future we thought we were going to have.

There is a second issue that also often makes our grieving during the Second Crisis even harder. We begin to notice a change in some of the people around us. We don't get invited to places we used to go, for instance. Some acquaintances are awkward when we run into them in public places. Even certain old friends now avoid us.

How to account for this behavior which is so hurtful and confusing? Are death and loss so threatening to others—something they will go to such extremes not to acknowledge—that they choose to confuse the griever with the grief and try to ignore us completely? (Colin Murray Parkes puts his finger on this issue when he says that in our society we don't burn our widows; we just pity and avoid them. And we could paraphrase that for divorcees, who are often not so much pitied and avoided as pushed out and marked as threatening.) And if these reactions do occur, they come at a time when we are least able to excuse or even understand them. Therefore, this behavior of others exacerbates what was already an almost unbearable situation.

As if dealing with the loss of our assumptive world and the loss of the comradeship of certain friends and acquaintances were not enough, we have still another issue that increases our hardship. During the Second Crisis many people will not recognize that the thoughts we are having and the behavior we are carrying out are a form of grieving. They will say things like "Now, you've just got to snap out of it." Or "It happens to everybody; you're going to have to stop pitying yourself." Or perhaps they try to cheer us up every time they see us; or maybe they even scold us, pointing out that since there is nothing that can be done about the situation, we just have to do whatever we can to make the best of it.

It may also be that our loss is one for which society gives no allowance for grieving: a miscarriage, the birth of a stillborn baby, an abortion, the death of a friend or companion whom the general public is reluctant to acknowledge as a primary relation.

I remember once standing at a counter in a business establishment and overhearing a young mother talk exuberantly about the sonar pictures that had just been made of her baby. "Can you believe," she said, excitedly, "that even at only twenty weeks, we could see the baby's esophagus! And watch the baby reach down with tiny little hands and grab its feet! The doctor even made a video of the pictures, and at night my husband and I sit in the den and watch the tape, hardly able to believe that this is our baby. My dad keeps asking me if the doctor can't make 8 x 10's for the rest of the family!"

As I listened, I realized how much this mother—and millions like her—knew and loved her baby long before it breathed the oxygen of the outside world, and thought with sorrow of how often that love is not acknowledged and honored by others when a miscarriage occurs or a baby's life is lost.

Similarly, the pain of the loss of a partner or friend can be exacerbated when others do not acknowledge the depth of the relationship and, hence, the depth of the loss. Such responses create still another layer of pain and confusion at a time when we are already deeply burdened.

Recognizing Our Defenses

John Bowlby tells us that it is almost inevitable: we will attempt to defend ourselves against the pain of our loss and all the awareness that comes with it. There is probably no age, he says, when we are not vulnerable to the reactivation of whatever defense mechanisms we established earlier in life to help us cope with those things we did not want to experience. So, we will respond to our loss with certain behaviors that we think, usually at some unconscious level, protected us in the past.

What are some of these defenses? Becoming ill; having accidents; losing ourselves in work or other frenetic activities; giving excessive care to others; copying the mannerisms, behavior, or even the physical condition of the lost person; engaging in destructive behavior; being engulfed by anger, guilt, and blame; becoming depressed or perhaps even euphoric.

During the Second Crisis we will exhibit some of these or other defending behaviors. Such behavior just comes with the territory. But John Bowlby points to what we need to watch out for when he says that defensive behaviors are a regular part of mourning at every age. What makes them dangerous is the forms they take and especially the degree to which the defenses are reversible. Therefore, we need to be aware that during the Second Crisis we will very likely engage in some form(s) of defensive behavior in order to protect ourselves from what we are facing, and that among these defenses are some that can seriously hurt us—or even kill us. Here are a few defenses we need to take special note of.

Illness and death. Dr. Beverley Raphael warns us that bereavement may also be fatal. And there are many statistics to support this assertion. One study showed an increase of almost 40 percent in the death rate of widowers over the age of fifty-four during the first six months of bereavement. Another study looked at the death rate of close relatives of persons who died over a six-year period. Of these close relatives, 4.8 percent died within the first year of bereavement, as compared with only 0.7 percent of a comparable group of non-bereaved people of the same age, living in the same area.

In a study reported by the Institute of Medicine, the mortality rate was at least seven times greater among the young widowed group (under age 45) than for the matched young married control group. The mortality rate for death from cardiovascular disease was 10 times higher for young widowers than for married men of the same age. Another study showed a death rate of 34.3 percent over five years for bereaved individuals, as contrasted with a death rate of 6.9 percent among those not bereaved.

Suicide is also a hazard. Studies show that the suicide rate among a group of 320 widows and widowers was 2.5 times higher in the first six months after bereavement and 1.5 times higher in the first, second, and third years after bereavement than in the fourth and subsequent years. When this group was compared with a control group, the age-standardized suicide rate for widowed men was 3.5 times higher than among married men and for women the rate was twice as high.

We can see from these statistics that it isn't only during the first year of bereavement that we need to be concerned about the increased likelihood of death. The editors of the Institute of Medicine's study discuss evidence that suggests that mortality rates can remain high for certain individuals perhaps into the sixth year after their loss.

What are some of the illnesses that contribute to these high death rates? Numerous diseases have been linked with grief and mourning, especially among those individuals predisposed to such medical problems. Here is only a partial list: cardiovascular disorders, heart disease, cancer, pernicious anemia, ulcerative colitis, leukemia, lymphoma, lupus, hyperthyroidism, pneumonia, rheumatoid arthritis, diabetes, tuberculosis, influenza, cirrhosis of the liver, glaucoma.

As early as 1944, Erich Lindemann; M.D., found that these seven illnesses, in particular, were high risks for mourners: "myocardial infarct (the so-called heart attack), cancers of the gastrointestinal tract, hypertension (high blood pressure), neurodermatitis (chronic itching and eruptions of the skin, particularly in areas of heavy perspiration and in the webbing of the fingers and toes), rheumatoid arthritis, diabetes, and thyrotoxicosis (thyroid malfunction, most frequently seen in women)."

And to these seven, Dr. Glen Davidson adds: "Chronic depression, alcoholism and other drug dependencies, malnutrition (both under- and over-nutrition), and electrolyte disorders in which the blood chemistry, particularly salts, are out of balance." Davidson says that other disorders mourners often cope with include headaches (particularly the migraine variety), lower-back pain, frequent bouts with colds and flu, excessive fatigue, impotence, and significant sleep disturbances.

We must be on the alert for an onset of illness even past the first year of mourning. There is some indication that the number of incidents of illness actually increases in the second and third years following bereavement.

We must also monitor during the Second Crisis the temptation to use the "sick role" to get the attention we want and need, to avoid responsibilities and to be passive rather than active in the face of our grief. It is natural during this bleak time to need desperately the sustenance and nurturing friends and family can provide us. But it is easy to see from the statistics above that the "sick role" is not a good way to ask for this attention.

Destructive behavior. This is another defense that can destroy us. In the face of the harsh realities of mourning, some individuals choose to take on "the derelict role." "All studies," reports the Institute of Medicine, "document increases in alcohol consumption and smoking and greater use of tranquilizers or hypnotic medication (or both) among the bereaved." And Dr. Beverley Raphael points out other types of destructive behavior mourners often engage in: "antisocial, delinquent, and criminal activity (for example, stealing or shoplifting); sexual behaviors including promiscuity leading sometimes to pregnancy; dependency disorders such as alcohol or drug dependence; and eating behavior disorders."

Often we engage in such behaviors not only to block out painful experiences, but also to have some sense of aliveness at a time when, otherwise, we only feel dead. And it is true that destructive behavior can provide its own kind of high. When we engage in dangerous activities, we have a feeling that we're "on a roll," making things happen, living it up. The danger, the risk taking, gives life an edge. But only for so long. There is always the emptiness, the loneliness, the nothingness of grief, to come home to. Therefore, defending behaviors like these can only compound our mourning. Until they finally destroy us.

Relationships. The misuse of personal relationships is another defense we may carry to such an extreme that our grieving does not proceed normally. There are several ways we may relate in an attempt to avoid the pain of grieving: we can become overprotective of others or become an excessive care giver who is always compelled to look for someone weaker to help. We can establish a relationship that is little more than a replacement, hoping that being with this person will allow us to avoid mourning. Or perhaps we may choose to engage only in relationships that require no intimacy, hoping thereby to protect ourselves from future losses; or we may engage in relationships that provide a battleground for the display of our hostility and anger. Whatever form our defensive use of relationships takes, we create for ourselves double heartache. For our mourning is never finished, and we are also denied the satisfaction that can come when we relate to others authentically.

One of the outcomes of excessive defensive behaviors is that we can become pathological mourners. Dr. Beverley Raphael points out that pathological mourning can take many forms: (1) *chronic or prolonged mourning,* a state in which the initial intense grief of the early phases of loss continues unremittingly and the bereaved seems to take on "a new and special role, that of the grief-stricken one"; (2) *absent grief,* a situation in which the bereaved carries on "as though nothing has happened" in order to fend off threatening emotions too painful to bear; (3) *delayed grief,* which entails a long period of absent grief, perhaps months or years, after which grief-like symptoms emerge; (4) *inhibited grief,* a condition in which the expressions of grief are "toned down or shut off"; (5) *distorted bereavement,* which takes several forms: intense pervasive anger in the absence of sadness and mourning and overwhelming guilt linked to intense ambivalence about the relationship between the mourner and the lost person; absorption in caring for others who have been bereaved; denial that the person is permanently lost; and so forth.

How likely are we to continue our defensive behavior until we become pathological mourners? Opinions vary. Glen Davidson says, "The best that can be determined is that between 5-15% of the population have unhealthy grief reactions." But Beverley Raphael suggests a much higher percentage: "The levels of morbid outcome or pathological patterns of grief are known in only a few instances, but they may represent at least one in three bereavements." Whatever the number, it is high enough to alert us: our defending behaviors can become dangerous. Not only can these behaviors destroy all chances that we will be able to finish our grief normally, but, as we have seen, they can also become fatal. The thrush's remark in *Aesop's Fables* should stay in our consciousness: "I am not half so much troubled at the thought of dying as at the fatality of contributing to my own ruin."

Understanding Our Depression

During the Second Crisis we should not be surprised if we experience deep bouts of depression. We now know the permanence of our loss. We realize the extent to which our world is in shambles. We know that there is nothing we can do to make things different, and because of this we feel both hopeless and helpless. Ahead of us is nothing but the empty unknown, and around us there is only chaos.

We do well, therefore, to remind ourselves of the common symptoms of depression so that we can recognize them for what they are if they do occur:

- Feelings of sadness, hopelessness
- Insomnia, early wakening, difficulty getting up
- Thoughts of suicide and death
- Restlessness, irritability
- Low self-esteem or guilt
- Eating disturbance—usually loss of appetite and weight
- Fatigue, weakness, decreased energy
- Diminished ability to think or concentrate
- Loss of interest and pleasure in activities once enjoyed, such as sex
- Chronic pains that fail to respond to typical treatment

Most authorities agree that if we are suffering at least four of these symptoms, including the "inability to experience pleasure, sleep disturbances, and the loss of weight, appetite, and energy," we can be said to be suffering "major depression."

Is there anything we can do to avoid this depression? Perhaps the better question is, "Should we try to avoid depression when it comes?" Beverley Raphael reminds us how important it is to "know, and name, and express the pain that the dead person's absence causes." Many attempt, however, to block their experience of depression through medication, drugs, alcohol, and other means that studies suggest do little to help. It is important to remember, that part of the work of grieving often requires a period of depression and personal reassessment.

Dr. John Bowlby goes so far as to say that depression as a mood which most people occasionally experience is inevitable in a situation in which behaviour has become disorganized, as it is likely to do after a loss. Pre-loss patterns of behaviour cannot be used after a loss, and until they are dismantled, new patterns, organized for new interactions, cannot be built up. Then Dr. Bowlby makes a statement, which I find encouraging: "It is characteristic of the mentally healthy person that he can bear with this phase of depression and disorganization and emerge from it after not too long a time with behaviour, thought, and feeling beginning to be reorganized for interactions of a new sort."

Observations like these enable us to understand the necessity for allowing and experiencing our depression. But Alexander Shand, in his classic study of the emotions, *The Foundations of Character*, asserts that the despair we experience can actually be beneficial: "While we think," he says, "of Despair as the most awful emotion to which the human mind is subject, and vainly hope to elude it for ever, it is, except in extreme cases . . . not awful at all."

How can Alexander Shand make such a startling assertion?

Because, he states, "Despair tends to elicit courage." He then goes on to explain. "Despair tends to evoke an energy in desire and a resolution capable of attempting the most dangerous and uncertain actions." The key word here, I think, is "resolution," which *Webster's New Collegiate Dictionary* defines as "the act of answering." When, in the depth of our depression, we finally abandon all hope—for instance, let ourselves realize the truth that we will never see the lost persons again in the form we knew them or acknowledge that we are going to have to take measures to earn our own livelihood—there is then the possibility for a new desire to form in the place of the old. Perhaps we decide to volunteer time each month to a cause about which the lost person deeply cared, or we resolve to go to school and learn a new skill so that we will never find ourselves in so destitute a condition again. Because we experience the depth of despair and lose all hope of getting what we cannot have, there is an opening. With a sense of the opening comes the opportunity to *resolve* to do something. With strength and courage, we *answer* the despair. We decide to *act*.

There is one caveat to consider before we leave the subject of depression. While it is true that most of us can expect to feel depressed during our grieving, all of our feelings of sadness will not be feelings of depression. Beverley Raphael warns us that sadness and depression are not the same and that we acknowledge the normal emotion of sadness very little in contemporary Western society. We run the risk, then, of allowing ourselves to be treated for the illness, clinical depression, when what we may actually be experiencing is the sadness that accompanies normal grief.

Recognizing What We Can Do

Dodie Smith, the English playwright, once quipped back in the late 1800s: "Noble deeds and hot baths are the best cures for depression." This is the approach I think we have to take to the state of affairs we find ourselves in during the Second Crisis: to look for things to do that will make us feel good about ourselves rather than to think we can do something about or change the root cause of our suffering. For since we have lost irrevocably, there is only truth in what we are experiencing. The emptiness, hopelessness, disorganization, sadness, confusion, and intense psychic pain of the Second Crisis are something we have no alternative but to pass through if we are to be able to move on and complete the other work of our grieving.

But individuals have told me about certain things they did that helped them as they experienced the Second Crisis: setting up and carrying out a regular exercise program; writing in a journal; painting and drawing; sewing and cooking; spending time with friends; seeing a therapist; listening to music; speaking with a priest, rabbi, or minister; going camping or walking in the country; doing hard physical labor; fishing; praying.

From my own experience, I would recommend these two things in particular: slowing down and speaking about one's situation with a professional. Let me talk first about slowing down.

Mourning is hard work. It requires much attention and enormous energy. Therefore, we need to place some kind of moratorium on as many other activities as possible so that we have fewer responsibilities and can attend to our grieving. And when it isn't possible to relieve ourselves of certain duties and obligations, we should do everything we can, otherwise, to take care of ourselves: eating food we like, taking as much time off as possible, maintaining healthy living habits, getting massages, resting and relaxing, asking friends and family for help.

Part of slowing down should be getting a physical examination sometime between the fourth and fifth months of bereavement. "If a mourner is developing an illness," Glen Davidson says, "the symptoms will usually appear during this time and yet be in an early enough phase of development to allow effective medical intervention."

Another form of slowing down should be to delay the making of major decisions. Research shows that we do think differently when we are under stress, when we feel ill. For instance, even with a common illness like a severe case of the flu, people are likely to have mental dysfunction. This dysfunction may take the form of losing perspective and being unable to visualize objects or to form thoughts from more than a single viewpoint. Or there may be the loss of the ability to reason, resulting in a heavy dependency on others. Perception may be altered.

Drs. Sidney Zisook and Stephen Shuchter also warn us that "acute grief frequently creates degrees of mental disorganization, confusion, anxiety, memory disturbances, and distractibility.... Contributing to this dysfunction are intrusive thoughts and images and strong emotional reactions to them." Such dysfunctions as these—and more— may plague us during the Second Crisis without our being able to recognize the alteration in our mental abilities. Therefore, by slowing down and putting off all major decisions, we do ourselves an enormous favor.

Another form of slowing down is having quiet time. Time when we sit, contemplating the Mystery of life, the Whole of which we are a part, the Divine Other that presences in unexpected ways, Life that carries life. Prayer can be part of quiet time, too; occasions when we ask for what we need and want or merely voice the bleakness of the place where we now find ourselves.

My second recommendation for what to do during this extremely stressful period? Speak to a professional. Peter Marris gets at the heart of the value of using professionals to support us in our grieving when he says, "I think a stranger, who understands grief in general, and stands in an acknowledged therapeutic role, can probably give more support to the working out of grief itself. Because this support is, in a sense, impersonal, it does not threaten to pre-empt the personal resolution of the crisis: for the most part, it simply offers reassurance that the crisis is natural, that it will find a resolution in time." My own experience bears out the truth of Professor Marris's statement. I found the objectivity, wisdom, and guidance of the professional I saw at different times during my grieving process a gift of life.

We may have to be courageous to seek professional assistance, however. There may be people around us, in their biased ignorance of the value of counseling and therapy, who would try to dissuade us by their uninformed evaluations that only "sick or weak people" ask for help. However, we are going through probably the most severe physical, mental, emotional, and spiritual crisis of our entire lives. And to have as part of our support team people who have studied grief and loss and who have been guided themselves and have guided others through the grief process is to show a true commitment to our future, not weakness.

THE CHOICE

What is the choice of value during the Second Crisis?

We must choose to suffer and to endure.

In defining the choice of the Second Crisis, I am not using the word *suffer* in its ordinary sense, although we certainly do have pain. But when I say we must choose to suffer, I am using the word in an older sense, in which *suffer* meant "to be willing to be exposed to an experience that may be disturbing." For this is what we have to do during the Second Crisis: let ourselves be exposed to the truth about what we have lost, certainly an experience that is disturbing.

Colin Murray Parkes talks about the choice to suffer and to endure from this perspective: We either choose to fight—to find "an approach to the problems"—or we choose to take flight—to avoid the tasks "of problem-solving." And this decision to fight or take flight is a deliberate commitment. As Dr. Parkes points out, it is a peculiar attribute of the human being that we bring to "this age-old situation, not a terrifying and dangerous set of teeth and claws but a highly efficient decision-making mechanism." That decision-making mechanism, of course, is our ability to choose, our ability to say what we are going to do. It will be our behavior, not our physiology, that determines the outcome of our grieving. Choosing to suffer and to endure the darkness of the Second Crisis, then, is to say, "I am willing to feel. I am willing to tell the truth to myself about what I have lost. I will face whatever I have to face in order to achieve a satisfactory outcome to my grieving."

WHAT WE NEED FROM FAMILY AND FRIENDS DURING THE SECOND CRISIS

For many, the signs of acute grieving that we display during Impact are synonymous with the grieving process. After we go back to work, resume family obligations, or begin to handle daily affairs, these individuals think that we are now okay. Those closest to us may continue to try to be helpful—perhaps by suggesting someone we can date or something we can do with our time—not recognizing that it is much too early for us to be receptive to this kind of assistance.

The kind of assistance we *do* need during the Second Crisis may seem to some like no assistance at all: we need to be allowed to do whatever we do. To feel as bad as we feel. To behave however we behave. To think in whatever ways we think. To make whatever mistakes we make. For we have to find our own way through the Second Crisis, even if it means that we hurt ourselves or flounder or act in ways that our friends and family think unlike us. We are at this time engaged in a struggle which others can do little to resolve. We cannot hear the wisdom of others at this time or see the pitfalls that they are seeing. We are frantically flailing around, trying to find firm ground on which to stand, to find the boundaries of a world we do not know.

At the same time, we do need the companionship of those who love us and who understand that what we are now going through is very private. As much as possible, we need to allow ourselves to be sustained by the continuity of our relationships, for often our family and friends seem to be our only link to life. Perhaps it's a friend we jog with every morning; a family tradition we participate in even though we don't feel like celebrating; a niece or nephew we take shopping or a son or daughter we take to the movies; a wise aunt we feel we can talk to. To know that the presence of these people is always abiding—that is what we need and must ask for from our family and friends during the Second Crisis.

The paradox of this phase of our grieving is that while it is true that we must be left alone to make our own way through this period, at some point we need to listen to—and actually to *hear*—either our own wisdom or the wisdom of someone around us, wisdom that urges us to do something about the quality of our lives. Perhaps it will be an inner voice saying, "Enough is enough; you must stop this destructive behavior, this apathetic way of being." Or perhaps it will be the shock that comes when one day we are hit with the reality of what our thoughts and behavior have cost us. Or perhaps it will be the words of a beloved parent or of a friend; some passage we read; an experience we have outdoors to which we are receptive; the message of a minister; the impact of a traditional ritual; and we are returned to our senses. We are able to turn to ourselves and to those who love us, those we respect, and find an anchor once again.

The choice of the Second Crisis is captured for me in the haunting words of an old folk song that was part of my preschool years spent in the piny woods of South Georgia. I learned this song from Annie. As she tended the fire under the black iron wash pot in the backyard or swished the clothes boiling in the water with a long, shaved stick, she sang, her voice low and moaning: "You gotta walk that lonesome road; gotta take the trip through the long, long vale...." Even a four-year-old could hear the accumulated pain, hardship, sadness—and courage—captured in that song. I loved Annie. All day I would ask, "Annie, when can I go to your house again and see the wallpaper?" Annie had pasted sheets of newspaper over the wooden planks of her cabin; I thought this was the most wonderful thing in the world—to live in a house that had words on all the walls. I learned to read in Annie's cabin. Finally, my dad and I would take Annie home. As we rode in the old Model A, we'd pass many proud black women, in their homemade flour-sack dresses, walking straight and tall down the sandy two-rut roads cut through the broad fields and the stands of trees that dripped the valuable resin their men collected. They walked, with dignity and grace, from their jobs at the big houses where they baked the biscuits and washed the sheets. We would pass them in the car and Annie would hail them.

"You gotta walk that lonesome road....Take a trip down that long, long vale." These women, deep reservoirs of strength and wisdom . . . these women suffered and endured.

Now, thirty-three years later, I knew another Annie; this time, however, her name was Thornell. The granddaughter of slaves and the mother of a daughter who is a computer specialist and a son who is a Ph.D., she too taught me what it meant to suffer and endure. When I was alone, more than a thousand miles away from my family, Thornell held the center of gravity while I whirled and flailed during the Second Crisis. "You go out and do whatever you want to do," she counseled me. "And when you get through, you wipe your mouth and come on home. You're a good person, and a woman's gotta do what a woman's gotta do." I was comforted and I was guided by Thornell. She modeled what it meant to suffer and to endure.

3

Observation

Danger and deliverance make their advances
together, and it is only in the last push that
one or the other takes the lead.

THOMAS PAINE

I'm going to be in the city to meet with my publisher," I told his secretary on the phone. "I'd like to make an appointment to see Mr. DiMele."

Armand DiMele was the therapist I had visited when I was in New York just a few weeks after Greg's death. It had been Armand who had told me about the phonograph album that I played night after night when I could not go to sleep. "Jean Michael Jarre's 'Oxygene,' " he said. "Buy it. Perhaps the sound of that music can give you some sense of what Greg felt when life left his body."

It was Armand who had given me a special present. The last time I had seen him before returning to Tennessee, he held out a small object. "See, Elizabeth," he said as he showed me the tiny glass figurine, "we have to be whatever we are at any given time in our lives, even when we are wounded. We have to live that moment on the way to other moments." Then he handed me a beautiful crystal bird. One wing had been broken.

I suppose I expected something similar from Armand when I saw him this time—wisdom offered with gentleness and indirection. But today he did not speak the way he had in the past. His words were sharp and straight.

I began by speaking of my depression, of loss and tragedy; Armand responded by speaking of the limits of human perception.

"How do you know death is a tragedy?" he asked me. "For people who die, it may not be a tragedy at all. They may be far happier than they were here on earth—who can say? Those of us left here certainly don't know. It may well be," he concluded, "that tragedy is something only the living imagine."

When I spoke of my desperate desire to find something or someone that would make me happy, Armand spoke of the futility of my efforts:

"You will never be so happy again," he warned me. "You will never be so innocent and trusting. You will never know anyone else who will love you the way Greg did. You may," he said, "meet someone to love and be loved by, but you will then be a different person. You will never be able to repeat what you had with Greg. You might as well stop looking. The only place you are going to find happiness is within you."

When I spoke of the impossibility of living without Greg, Armand spoke of actions to be taken:

"Invite a friend to go to dinner tonight. And have this as a rule: Don't mention Greg once during the evening."

I spoke of the emptiness and loneliness of every day, and Armand challenged:

"Well, Elizabeth, what are you going to do about that?"

When I said I wanted my life the way it used to be, he asked:

"Are you going to be like the person I met the other day whose husband has been dead twenty-eight years and she has never taken one item of his clothing from the closet or changed one item in their bedroom? It would be amusing if it weren't so tragic. Because she keeps wondering why she can't get over her sadness. She's such a lonely and unhappy person.

"Oh, I could tell you the stories, Elizabeth," Armand went on to say, "of grieving people who attempted to lose themselves in causes—or in excessive care of others. Of those who have retreated to a safe environment and settled for so much less than they ever dreamed of. People who have given up their zest for living and exist in resignation. Many avoid new relationships; if they don't care for anyone, perhaps they will never be hurt again. Some give up all their ideals and beliefs, some withdraw from life, some—"

"But I can't see that I have done any of those things," I said defensively. "What am I hiding behind in order not to have to get on with living?"

"What do you think?" he asked me.

We sat in silence for several seconds. I knew it was time for an honest appraisal.

"Well," I began tentatively, "I have tried to run away from the loss —to try to find something or someone to substitute for Greg so that my life would have meaning again. I have also tried to become a different person, perhaps so I wouldn't have to solve the problems that plagued the person I used to be."

"But weren't these activities also beneficial?" Armand asked me.

"Well, yes, at the beginning, I suppose, they were a way to stay alive. But later they became walls to hide behind. I wanted people to think I was strong and competent. I wanted to show that I could overcome any loss."

"But you haven't, have you?" Armand asked me.

"No," I answered quietly.

"What is the next step?" I asked after we sat a few moments in silence.

Armand did not answer right away. Then he began to read from a paper in his hand. It was a poem which began, "There is a time to stop traveling...A time to refuel yourself...A time where the only number you dial is your own." He gave me a copy of the poem to take with me back to Texas, and I read it every day for many days.

———

It was one of those nights made for outdoor parties. As I drove onto the grounds, I could see the colored Japanese lanterns in the distance bobbing in the breeze; and as soon as I stepped out of the car, I heard music coming from somewhere across the small lake. I followed the sounds, walking down a winding rock path that had been lined with *farolitos.*

"The party of the year," the gossips billed it. A local real estate agency's open house for the business community, held annually on the country estate of one of the agency's owners. As a professor I had, of course, never come to this big event; but my friend Emma came every year with her businessman husband, and this time she had seen to it that I was invited. So here I was, feeling out of my league but excited.

As I circled the lake and came closer to the central location of the party, I felt more and more as if I were entering a world of magic. Women dressed in gauzy cocktail dresses looked ethereal as they moved among the willow trees that grew along the edge of water. I could now see the musicians playing from the raised platform in the gazebo, their clarinets and saxophones gleaming. The buffet tables, covered in white linen and lighted with tall silver candelabra, were being constantly replenished by waiters in tuxedos. I wandered, looking for my friend Emma.

When I did not see Emma or her husband, I began to chitchat with the strangers who were near me. A lawyer from Dallas and her husband. A horse trainer and his small son from the Rio Grande Valley. Several local people whose faces I recognized from pictures in the newspaper or from having seen them in their places of business. I was having fun. Not once since arriving had I thought of my misery.

It was at the buffet table that I met him. He walked up behind me as I was attempting to extricate a shish kebob stick from the pineapple it was stuck in. "Let me help you with that," he said, deftly pulling the shish kebob out and placing it on the plate he had taken from me. He was a handsome man, with hair that reminded me of Greg's. "You a regular at this shindig?" he asked, smiling the kind of smile that suggests you and he may soon discover you are both imposters or maybe co-conspirators.

"No, it's my first time," I answered. "What about you?"

"Yep. My first time, too. Just came in from Tulsa to visit my mother." We walked away from the buffet table together.

Finding a bench down by the water, we sat down. As I ate, he talked about his job—he was anchorman at a local television station in a small town in Oklahoma—his last vacation in the Bahamas, how he came here as often as he could to see his mother. Then he turned his attention on me. What did I do? Where was I from? And what was an attractive woman like me doing alone at a party? When I told him I was a widow, he patted my arm sympathetically and said he understood, that he had just broken up with his girlfriend. "Let's go somewhere and talk," he said. "I know we've got a lot in common."

I suppose it took me about fifteen minutes into the conversation to come to my senses. I had followed this man into town in my car, and we were now seated in a dingy roadside cafe. He was talking about his misfortunes. The women in his life hadn't understood him . . . they seemed never to be able to realize that it was to their good that he gave first priority to his work . . . always became bitter when he had so little time to give to them . . . oh, it was all such a sad history . . . yes, he knew how awful it was to be alone. "We wounded ones," he said, reaching over to pat my hand, "we wounded ones just have to stick together."

That was when it hit me. I had left an elegant party for this! To sit in a plastic booth in a run-down restaurant, listening to this self-centered, garrulous man tell his boring stories. And I knew where the scenario was headed . . . I had been there before. "Why don't we leave here and go somewhere a little more private?" Loneliness trying to lose itself in loneliness.

I realized now that this was what my decision not to let Greg go would always bring me: weak, whiny men, pandering to my own weakness and whining. It must work something like radar, I thought. Those signals one sends out that say, "I'm living a sad story. Tell me about yours."

But tonight was going to be different. For something had suddenly shifted inside me. I was no longer willing to play the role of a destitute widow, even to keep Greg close. And I was no longer willing to listen sympathetically to a man's pitiful tale just to get to be with him. So without saying a word, and even as the man continued to talk, I picked up my purse, walked out of the restaurant, and drove myself back to the party.

I suppose that waking up in one area tends to make one more observant in others. I found myself, after that party, paying more attention to all of my behavior. It was as if through that event I had come to realize that I was an actor in my own story, that I myself played a significant part in what happened to me and around me.

It became a challenge to question my reactions. To try to understand things about which in the past I would have said "That's just the way it is" or "Such is natural and unavoidable." More and more often I was able to put two and two together to make meaning of something that had just happened.

The graduate faculty meeting had gone badly, the work of a whole year down the drain. The committee and I had been sure our curriculum proposals would be accepted, but they were all returned, marked "Further study needed." I was so hurt and angry that it was all I could do not to cry as I walked down the hall to my office.

As I sat down at my desk, I looked outside and noticed that the grackles were back. Hundreds of them, flying all over the campus. Suddenly, in memory, I saw Greg that first year we were living in Texas, running into the house, excited. "You won't believe the number of birds that are flying over at the university. Come on. You've got to see it."

That was the same day he'd written the verse and left it on the kitchen table:

Partners

You make the salmon loaf.
I make the sandwiches.

As I sat in my office now looking out at the birds, I longed for Greg as if he had died yesterday. I missed him so. I wanted to see him. I sat down, put my head on the desk, and sobbed uncontrollably.

It wasn't until I was on the way home that the question flashed into my mind: Could there be any connection between that faculty meeting and this relapse in my grieving? Did one hurt and disappointment just open up the wound of another? Was I transferring the upset from one thing to another?

We were five for dinner: an elderly couple, a child, and two young women. As the hostess crossed the floor, it was clear that she did not know whom to address. Who in this group was in charge? We weren't in couples. The one male among us was not stepping forward. We did not fit the usual grouping.

Seeing the hostess's awkwardness and embarrassment, I said, "May we have a table for five, please?" The lady was clearly relieved. She smiled her best hostess smile and led us to a table.

As I sat down, something exploded inside me. "Have you ever seen anybody so rude?" I asked the group.

"Who?" they asked, having no idea why I was so angry.

"That hostess," I sputtered. "She let us just stand there looking foolish. If I hadn't spoken to her first, I guess we would still be waiting."

"I didn't notice anything," the older woman said tentatively.

"I didn't, either," said my friend, "but then," she added placatingly, "I also wasn't paying any attention." It was clear that no one except me had noticed anything unusual.

Later that night, while I was brushing my teeth, truth broke through the illusion: "You weren't mad at that hostess at the restaurant," I realized. "You were mad at Greg for deserting you. You don't like being a single woman. You don't like not having a man with you who takes charge, who looks after you. You hate having to change roles and construct a new identity."

I went over to the physical education department to take a special fitness test they were providing for the faculty. My results were excellent, and I should have been happy. However, as I walked back across campus, I felt sad. "What is wrong?" I asked myself. "No one there knew your husband had died," came the answer, "and you didn't tell them. They didn't know, then, that you live such a contrast: though you are healthy in body, your spirit is broken."

When I got back to the office, I sat at my desk and wrote this verse:

Upon Taking a Physical After Her Husband Has Died

It's amazing that the electrocardiogram doesn't
show irregular beats

And the stress test printouts don't show blocked
and partially blocked valves

The water test doesn't reflect the extra weight of
the heart

The pulmonary tests didn't catch the inability on
occasion to breathe.

Imagine that.

What's wrong with those machines?

I was now coming to understand the source of moods to which previously I had felt only a victim.

I was clearing out Greg's desk at home. A file marked "Divorce" caught my attention. The folder contained copies of the divorce decree from his first wife, the property settlement, records of child support payments, and other assorted documents. As I thumbed through, I saw a copy of a letter he had written to a friend during the divorce proceedings. I sat down on the couch and read it. One paragraph touched me deeply. Greg had written:

Sometimes I worry about the boys. What kind of lesson am I giving them? I could define myself as a pillar of the community, an example to my children, a mainstay of my spouse. But the point of life isn't pretense; it's once around, baby, not a single tick more; and damn serious people damn well better see that nice things are nicer than nasty ones and good appetites, good digestion, good spirits, sound sleep all grow out of living life good—not ends in themselves but benefits accruing to the pilgrims who dare. Now, if you were somebody's son, wouldn't you like that for a lesson?

When I read the letter, I felt so guilty. Why had I not realized how painful it must have been for a good man to leave his children? Why had I never appreciated what he had lost? All I could think about was the numerous times I had criticized him for a divorce settlement that I thought was too generous. And the way I had not been big enough to try to include the boys in our lives more centrally. I was ashamed, so ashamed. I knew I had been such a petty person. And that there was no way I could undo my selfish behavior.

One day, however, when it seemed that this guilt would just about suffocate me, a thought came to me: *Human beings are mistake makers.* It wasn't an excuse. It wasn't a rationalization. It wasn't a justification. It was just the truth: *Human beings are mistake makers.*

Yes, I had made mistakes. And I deeply regretted them. There was no making up for those mistakes. Nothing could undo them. But I realized I had become more conscious as a result of recognizing the mistakes. I could not now be so blind about my pettiness in any area, including Greg's children. That, it seemed to me, was something valuable.

There were other realizations: that Greg and I had not had a perfect life, no matter how pretty I painted the picture. We had fought over a lot of things. I had wanted to change his behavior, and he had resisted; he had wanted our personal life to be everything, and I had resisted. We both had tried to build a cocoon together that took us away from the outside world and gave us total safety and security, and life had resisted.

It was interesting to watch what happened as I became more reflective and introspective. I had days when my life seemed to lighten up. Times when I was able to find enjoyment in simple activities. Occasions when I could imagine regaining a sense of humor.

One afternoon I decided to wash the car. I had forgotten how much pleasure it brings to see a car come clean. I polished the headlamps. I scrubbed the tires. I oiled the leather. When I finished, I realized why, when Greg called me out to admire his wash job, he was always so happy. I felt a deep satisfaction.

As I was getting ready for bed one night, I went in to take a shower. Just at the moment that I took off the final piece of my clothing, the light bulb overhead blinked. I laughed and said, "Greg, you rascal. Is that you?" The next morning as I was walking out to get something from the utility room, I hummed a song in my head: "All I Need Is You." For a second I thought the song was about Greg, but then I knew I was singing it to myself!

I found myself spending more time alone, being much quieter. A new friend, Betty, had given me a book to read. My thinking had been stimulated by the book, especially by a chapter called "A Philosophy to Live By."

"I want a personal, workable way of life," a person quoted in that chapter had said. This simple statement resonated deeply within me; for I wanted desperately to make meaning of what had happened in my life, which up until now seemed only senseless and useless. The author had put forth a simple philosophy: *Realize first your relationship to the Creative Forces of the Universe, or God; formulate your ideals and purposes in life; strive to achieve those ideals; be active; be patient; be joyous; leave the results to God; do not seek to evade any problem; be a channel of good to other persons.* I wrote this list in my journal and thought about it often.

It was Betty, too, who introduced me to a new form of prayer: just sitting quietly and thinking of God. Formal prayer had been infrequent in my life since I had given up the strict doctrine of my youth, but I found that this sitting quietly—"in communion with God Who is also within us," was how Betty put it—was calming.

I found that there were times now when I could think about Greg with peace and not pain. For instance, one day I was watching the Joffrey Ballet troupe dance on television and thinking about how much Greg loved to go to the ballet. I felt sad. Then I really looked at the dancers, their grace, the simple beauty of the movements. It seemed as if I were seeing not only the dancers, but also Greg's spirit. I felt his beautiful self in the dance, his gentleness. It was amazing, but in that moment I felt closer to him than at any time since he had died.

On another day I saw an author on a talk show discussing ethics and morality, and I remembered the decision Greg made a few months before he died always to tell the truth, to himself and to others. I had been inspired by that commitment then; but listening to the man on television, I recognized that the commitment continued to inspire me now. I realized that Greg's ideals had lived past him; and, in this very important way, he was still part of my life in the present.

It's amazing how like calls to like. When I was still telling my sad story, I seemed to draw people who also had a sad story. But in the past weeks, things had been different. It seemed the quieter I got, the more people I met who were deep and reflective. Like my new friend Betty, who had given me the book. And my new friend Tommy.

I met him first at a chili cook-off where Emma and I were two of the judges. I sensed something different about him, even just in passing. He was . . . well, it wasn't impersonal . . . I suppose you would say detached. Observing. Standing back, almost as if he and life had a solitary pact. I liked this man and wanted to get to know him.

"Don't get your heart broken," Emma warned me. "Tommy is a very private man. Many women have been attracted to him, only to discover that when they pushed he disappeared." So from the beginning I determined to do something I had not done since Greg's death: Let a friendship develop with a man instead of acting as if I expected him to be my beau.

It was Tommy's relationship to the land that drew me. We spent many a Saturday or Sunday on his family ranch, checking to see if the washes between the bunkhouse and the river were or were not passable, hunting for twisted grapevine sticks to add to his collection, scaring up jackrabbits, deer, and armadillos. We combed the landscape looking for mesquite branches and broken limbs to make a brushpile in front of the bunkhouse.

At night we'd sit on the porch waiting for the moon to rise and the wind to die down. When it was time, he would light a piece of kindling and put it to the mounds of dried grass and leaves at the bottom of the brushpile. The fire caught fast. Flames licked twenty, thirty feet up toward the sky.

We sat on the ground near the fire. Tommy talked about the native Americans who used to live on this land. About the wild boar we had seen that morning. About the stand of trees in the bottom. The scene was almost eerie—nothing but sky and earth enveloping us; familiar constellations of stars distinct and clear above us; dark shadows all around us, except for where the brush was burning. "Like a primitive tribal rite," I thought to myself, "or a fire made by nomads in the desert to ward off danger." I felt out of time, like one of the ancients.

Then Tommy began to call the coyotes, making sounds long and plaintive. We waited in silence. At first there was no echo, only stillness. Then, after a few more calls, the coyotes began to return the sound. Over and over. Again and again. We sat there till long after midnight watching the fire burn and listening as the coyotes

answered. Experiences such as these gave me a sense of connectedness with the earth deeper than any I had ever known. They brought
me great solace.

It must be that the law of compensation works in everything:
when I was feeling the most peaceful I had felt since Greg's death,
news came that threw me off-center. My girlfriend Felicia called
from Tennessee; she and Al were separating after fifteen years of
marriage. I had been friends with Felicia and Al since graduate
school days, they had been our closest companions when I was
married to my first husband. Now she was alone with a young
daughter. "Could you come for a day or two?" she asked. "Just until
I can pull some of the pieces together?" I went, naturally.

We talked long into the night. I lashed out in such hatred: "I
despise him," I said. "How could he do this? How could he leave a
person like you? I'd like to kill him."

And it was true. I felt murder in my soul. I felt rage. In that
moment I knew the meaning of "killing in the heat of passion." The
intensity of the anger and hate that I felt frightened me; it was so out
of proportion.

The morning I left Felicia's house to drive to the airport, I was
feeling sad for her pain and loss, but the country through which I
was driving also made me feel happy. These mountains of East
Tennessee were my home, and I had never seen them look more
beautiful. It was early, and the mist that gives the mountains their
smoky look—and their name—was lifting. A blue haze lined the far
horizon. The road turned back and forth through cuts of granite, and
now and again I could see tiny lines of sparkle where the sun hit the
thin streams of water running down the rocks.

I was thinking about the conversations with Felicia and how
angry I was at Al, how hurt. "Does love always have to cost so
much?" I asked myself. "Does caring always have to bring loss and
pain?" Of course the questions were moot, for I already knew the
answers. "Nothing—no one—can be counted on," I said in bitterness.

Then, suddenly, from somewhere far back in the past, I began to hear the notes of a children's song: *Three blind mice. Three blind mice. See how they run. See how they run....* Where in the world was that song coming from? Then I remembered. How many years had it been since our teacher played that phonograph record in elementary school? "Pick one of these songs," she had said, "and when you get scared, begin to sing it. Whatever you pick will always be your song of courage."

Now the notes of that nursery rhyme were sounding of their own accord. *Three blind mice. Three blind mice.*

And I knew the question they were asking: Would I have the courage to love—to love people, to love life—in spite of the fact that things often turned out rotten? Would I run the risk of caring anyway, even if nothing and no one could be counted on?

It was a moment as critical as the day I decided whether or not to jump into the water off the deck of the *Captain Jack.* Was I willing to forgive life for what had happened to me? Did I have the courage to love?

I heard the sound coming from deep inside me. It was with a wavering and a teary voice, but I *was* singing: "Three blind mice. Three blind mice. See how they run. See how they run...." *Something* was saying, "Yes." Suddenly, waves of love flooded over me. Love for the world. Love for every person in the world. Even love for Felicia's husband. I looked out of the sun roof at the sky, which by now was a midmorning blue, and I shouted aloud, "I yield. I yield. I surrender. I will expand my love for Greg to everyone. Yes, I will love."

T his is Observation. A time of review. Of noticing. Of paying attention. Of attempting to make sense of our actions and responses. A time of coming to terms with guilt and anger; a time of forgiving. A time when the painful missing of the lost person alternates with recognition that in certain ways he or she will always be present. A time of being still and quiet. A time for gaining wisdom.

"Mourning requires that a person review the relationship," says Mardi Horowitz of the University of California at San Francisco Medical School, "mull it over in memories, dreams, fantasies." This review is "at the nub of mourning," for it "allows an update of people's mental map of themselves and their world, to adjust it to the reality of the loss. You scan your memory banks to see what is still relevant to your life, what is not. You want to know, 'What do I have to let go of? What will I have to find in someone else? What can I contain within me?' "

Much of this review involves "a very intense re-experiencing of much of the past development of the relationship, back to its earliest times." The review, of course, has been part of the mourning process from the very beginning, but during the experiences of Observation it becomes a more defined activity. In a way, the past is now more contained. The images are now "not growing and active," so we can review "piece by piece, memories, thoughts, and feelings associated with the image" of the lost person. Beverley Raphael gives this description:

Many powerful feelings well up as memories of the relationship are sifted through: regret that more was not valued when the partner was alive; resentment over those things that were not made right or over being cheated by death of what was hoped for the future; ineffable sadness over what was and can no longer be; sorrow for the lost past and the younger years that are gone with it; anger at life, the dead person, the self for what one did not have and now may never have—perhaps children, perhaps love; guilt for the love that was not perfect, for the hate that was nurtured, the care that failed; release from the suffering of illness, from the suffering of relationship; triumph that one did not die oneself, guilt that such a feeling could appear; depression at the emptiness of self and world; and envy of those who have not lost, who live unscathed by death.

Memories of the relationship are *sifted through*. Those key words from Dr. Raphael's description encapsulate the activity of the period of Observation. We are *sifting through* our feelings and experiences— "studying and investigating thoroughly," as the dictionary defines *sift;*

"separating out as if by putting through a sieve," as the root word for *sift* tells us.

It is during the experiences of Observation that we realize, if we have not before, that "the work of mourning is, by its nature, something which takes place in the watches of the night and in the solitary recesses of the individual mind." Friends and family can help us to confirm or not our initial evaluations, but it is we who make these first evaluations. Therefore, much of the work of Observation must be done in solitude and quietness.

What can we expect during this time of Observation? Men and women who have paid attention to their own process of mourning report such experiences as these....

AN AWKWARDNESS IN LEARNING TO BE ALONE
A young widow recalls:

At first I could not be alone. I stayed busy constantly, even though I didn't know I was doing it when I was doing it. I just stayed real busy, thinking about what my next thing was going to be, that next thing I was going to do *right then*. If some friends came over and said they wanted to take Jeffrey to the Dairy Queen to get an ice cream, I said okay. Then after they left, I left, too. The empty house was just too scary.

But one day I thought, "Okay, you have to wean yourself. You have to sit here and just sit . . . you can't just be doing something, you have to make yourself literally be by yourself." I made myself get in the recliner—it was a Sunday afternoon, which has got to be the worst time in the week to be by yourself. "Just look outside," I told myself. And I just did it. I did it, and I didn't run from it.

Now I enjoy my time alone. My mom took Jeffrey home with her the other night, and I put music on and was just sitting here singing. I would never do that before. I mean, the amazing things that change inside you as a result of your actions . . . it's unbelievable.

AN APPRECIATION OF THE VALUE OF BEING ALONE
A divorcee tells us:

I deliberately took three months after my separation to clam up and discuss this thing with myself. I wish everyone who experiences a loss could do this.

During this time alone I did a lot of standing in front of the mirror and having hour-long discussions about what caused things to go the way they did, what kind of person he was, what kind of person I was. I knew I had to get some perspective on myself if I was going to be able to go out and say to a new employer, "Hire me; I'm a good person." I had to get to know the person I was again. I had married right after college. I never pursued a career—I helped him pursue his career—so it was as if I had graduated yesterday.

By spending time by myself without any interruptions, I got to know a lot about me. In getting to know myself again, I could think about how I saw my life, now that the other part of my life was over. I would let my imagination go, fantasize about what I'd like to see. On the basis of that, I began to build some courage to make at least part of that vision become a reality for myself. I came to realize that it's all there—we're all equipped with everything we need, all of it—we just have to be willing to reach for it.

I also had to be alone to grieve. If you spend twelve years in a relationship with a man, even if it wasn't much of a relationship, that's twelve years of your life. And when that marriage is over, you need to give yourself time to grieve. You have to be able to say good-bye to that. Even if you know the divorce is the best thing. You have to give yourself time to say good-bye. You have to grieve for the hopes that you had in the beginning. You know, you can remember when you first married, what you thought the marriage was going to bring into your life and into his life and to "our lives." That's part of the grieving. I also grieved for the lost time in my life. The time I had given to that marriage long past the point when I knew it was over. I just always kept hoping that we could work it out.

The whole time of being alone was a healing process. I found myself one day saying, "Look, this marriage is a canceled check. It's gone. You have no control over what has already happened, and you don't know what is going to happen tomorrow. But you do have this minute. You can do something with this minute." I also found myself asking for courage to get on with my life.

When people ask me how I have so much gumption, I say, "I ask for it." You know, I wasn't taught that in my religious upbringing—

but we're not all bad, we do have some grace. Courage—I think that's the measuring stick between the people who don't grow from a painful experience and those who do. And if you don't have enough, you can just ask for it!

AN INCREASED CLARITY ABOUT WHAT YOU HAVE LOST
A son who was fourteen when his father died says:

When my father died, I could not figure out why I continued to be so upset for so long after the event. My parents already having been divorced for so many years, I had adjusted myself to that fairly well and reconciled myself. I was an adjusted normal child of a separated household. Therefore, I could not understand the devastating effect the loss had on me.

It's taken a lot of reflecting for me to get a handle on this. But I see now that, even though I did not live with my father, as long as he was alive there was still the possibility of relating with him and going to see him when I did. On Father's Day I could send him a card and things like that. I see now that what I'm mourning is the loss of the opportunity to relate to him and develop and nurture my relationship with him as an adult. When my father died, I felt I was in the most positive relationship I had ever been in with him—it felt like the start of something new. I was growing up, maturing. I could imagine us doing all kinds of father-son things in the future. So the loss of never getting to develop our relationship as two adults is what has continued to gnaw at me. It was been freeing just to realize that.

A GAIN IN UNDERSTANDING ABOUT WHAT IS RIGHT TO DO
A widow with two small sons recalls:

I began to observe the boys and how they were about the death of their daddy. One day, several months after Lee's accidental death, the boys and I were pulling into the driveway, and the four-year-old kept asking me, "Mama, what does *accident* mean? What's an *accident?*"

Before I could answer, Jeremy, who is seven, spoke up and said, "I don't want anybody else to ever talk about Daddy in front of me again. You just don't have to talk about him in front of me."

I stopped right there and said to myself, "It's time for the three

of us to stop trying to avoid what has happened and to face up to it."
So I said, "Jeremy, that is not the way it is. Anybody that wants to
talk about Daddy is going to be able to talk about him anytime he
feels like it. It's a lot better for us to talk about it than it is to just sit
and think about it." Then I told him, "I'm going to be talking about
him from now on; and if your brother has any questions or wants to
talk about his daddy, he is free to do it. From now on that is going to
be a rule of this house. Each person can talk, and nobody will keep
the others from talking."

That probably wasn't very sensitive, but I was being truthful
with him. I went on and told Jeremy, "You're old enough to know
we can't ignore this. We're not going to pretend Daddy never lived,
because we had happy times and we ought to talk about them and
remember them. It will be especially nice if we talk about the good
times, but we'll talk about the bad times, too, when we remember
them. And sometimes when we talk, it will make us sad and we'll
want to cry. You're going to see Mama cry. And it won't be your
fault that Mama is crying, and it won't be Daddy's fault. But if I feel
sad or if you and Danny feel sad about Daddy or anything else, it is
perfectly all right to cry. And we're not going to hide any of these
things in our house. We're not hiding anything that we feel about
Daddy, good or bad."

I guess that really sank in because a few days later we were
putting up the Christmas tree lights—this had always been a job for
Lee and the boys—and they wanted me to hurry and turn the lights
on. So we turned off all the other lights in the house and just had the
tree lights on. The three of us were sitting there in the living room
looking at them, and Jeremy spoke up and said, "Oh, Mama, this is
so nice. This is so nice. If Daddy was here, he'd love it 'cause he
always liked the lights. This would be even happier if Daddy was
here."

And I held him and said, "You're right, Jeremy. We wish he was
here, but he's not. And we'll just have Christmas anyway. And it's
all right for us to remember how happy it used to be."

It's been several months now, and both of the boys talk about
their dad. A month or six weeks ago, Danny, the little one, came
running into his grandmother's kitchen and said, "You know,
Grandma, what I really miss about Daddy is his wrestling with us."

He said this right out of the blue. So I know, though the boys don't seem to dwell on it, they do think about him and miss him.

A DECISION TO STOP AVOIDANCE BEHAVIOR
A mother whose son died in a job-site accident told this story:

I hadn't catered a party in more than two years; and, suddenly, a few weeks after Jack's death, all these people started calling me. Within a week I had five jobs, ranging from a company picnic for five hundred to an intimate dinner for six. I grabbed at all the work. It was much more than a one-person operation could handle, but all I could think was that the jobs would fill my time and keep me from dwelling so much on Jack. And that's the way it was for months and months afterward. People kept calling, and I kept taking the work.

But now, a year later, I'm burned out. I'm tired. And I also think that the purpose of the frenzied work is over. Now, instead of wanting to keep Jack out of my mind, I want to think about him. I want some time now to think about what it means that he is gone. I see now that my antidote to the pain of losing Jack—working in a frenzy night and day—just delayed what I'm going to have to do: get used to life without my son.

AN HONEST ASSESSMENT OF BEHAVIOR THAT IS DAMAGING
A widow tells her story:

Ever since Carter died, I have blamed his business partners. He was a director of the company, and it was in bad shape. Needed a lot of capital. They couldn't get it, so he went out and found two larger companies that would buy them. The stockholders could either get all their money, or they could take stock in the new holding company. Everybody would have made a lot of money. But the board voted against it. It was an awful time. There was a fight. We had a meeting, and people got up and talked . . . said they found an old rule that said it was too late for us to vote . . . etc., etc. It was a bitter, ugly thing. Carter couldn't understand why they didn't see his side. And it just ate him up. All of his physical problems started then—oh, he had a bad back before then, but nothing serious.

I realized something very important the other day when I was watching one of the talk shows and a doctor on there said that depression was anger turned inward and that you couldn't hold a grudge, else it would really hurt you. That's when it snapped for me that it was really Carter's grudge against those company officers that killed him. That's when I decided that I would stop holding a grudge against them—which means, I guess, that I forgive them—because I've seen the damage that kind of thinking can do. It destroyed a man's health, ruined him. Now I try to see where the other person is coming from. But if I'm not able to do that, I let go of the grudge anyway, if only for a selfish reason—so my life won't be damaged by it. I watch myself and my children and try to teach them about grudges. I have done a lot of that since I saw that program.

AN OPPORTUNITY TO UNHOOK FROM ANGER
A divorced man describes an important realization:

For a long time after the divorce it was so easy for me to get angry. All I had to do was see her red pickup truck just parked on the street. One night when I was in my house by myself I realized that my anger toward her was my enemy and that when I didn't have anger, life went on in so much better a fashion. Finally, I realized that my bad feelings toward my ex-wife gave her control of my life. That was the hook she still had in me. It was like a cable running from her house to mine. All the way across town—from Oak Street to Hilton Drive. That cable of anger connected her to me, and I permitted that connection. It even determined whether or not I'd fix anything to eat and how much I accomplished at work. How stupid can you be!

So I began to make a conscious effort; it was not something you do like slice a piece of cake, or at least for me it wasn't. I'd have to repeat over and over again: "Don't let that anger keep you connected." I'd say, "Look, anger is anger; it's an emotion, and it's just stored in a closet in your mind; and you let it out, and it does all kinds of cruel and mean things to you. Anger doesn't necessarily come in kinds— anger toward your wife, anger toward yourself— it's just anger."

When worse comes to worst, and I can't get rid of the anger any other way, I go out to the flower beds and start digging up the weeds. The ground is really dry, and there are lots of clods. I have this brick wall around my backyard. So, if I'm so angry that I can't talk myself out of it, I go out there and pick up those clods and swing them as hard as I can. They just *explode* when they hit that wall. I confess, sometimes I even get to talking to those weeds and clods of dirt. "Okay, you so and so," I'll say, "you're going next—just hold on, you're going next!" I tell you, I am killing weeds! I am breaking clods! And what worked out so well was that when I threw the clods against the brick wall they fell back into the flower beds as soil!

I've also found a category to put my ex-wife in: people that I don't like. I'm not talking about enemies; I'm not talking about people I fear. I'm just talking about people that I don't like. You know, they just don't appeal to you. Well, that's the category my ex-wife is in now, and it works.

A RECOGNITION OF THE FUTILITY OF BLAME
A divorcee relates:

I finally stopped blaming him. The more I thought about it, the more I knew that it takes two to have problems. I faced the truth that I had to take some responsibility, too, for the marriage ending. Oh, it would have been easy to keep on blaming him—the whole town expected me to. It would have been so easy to get caught up in who's right and who's wrong. But that would have gotten me nowhere. If you accept that it takes two to make it end, then your biggest insurance policy is to face what you did and did not do in the marriage that caused it to go under so that you won't repeat that. That's your insurance policy.

A REALIZATION THAT IT IS HEALTHY TO BEGIN TO RELY ON YOURSELF
A woman whose companion had died advises:

You're surprised when you find out that you're going to make it. That there is some kind of ability we all have that just shows up on your front porch, so to speak. You have to have some kind of rationality present, however; and for so long, of course, you don't have it. But there comes a time when you do. I would say there is far too much advice out there on what to do about these matters. One thing I've discovered is that there are a thousand advisers; and I'm sure it's all good advice, but it's also confusing. So, somehow or other, I think you need to take time to sort it out alone. I think all the major decisions after loss have to be made alone. They are made when you're driving the car or standing in the kitchen or mowing the lawn.

I know there's a tendency for people to say, "Don't try to do it alone; turn to your friends for help." And that's good advice for a certain time period. Goodness knows, we need love from others; but I think there's a tendency to turn to other people so much that you forget about your own abilities and forget about the fact that it is only your decisions that are going to carry you through in the long run.

A RECOGNITION THAT WE ARE IN DANGER OF BLINDLY REPEATING THE PAST

A divorced man says:

My wife and I married when we were both eighteen. We grew up together. When she left, I could not stand being alone, so I found another woman to be in my life as quickly as possible. For four years now we have been in a relationship—or, I guess it would be more honest to call it an entanglement. She is married, so we have to be very careful about going out in public. Even though she says she wants a divorce, she is a basket case about losing her security. I didn't see what I was doing for a long time—just trying to hide from the anger and pain of my divorce by loving her.

And I do think I love her. But not long ago something happened that made me realize I needed to take stock of what I was doing. We had just eaten and were sitting on the couch after dinner. Shirlee reached over and kissed me. At that moment something hit me: this was just the way it had been with my ex-wife. The same smell; the same hazy talk; the same insecurity. "Am I just repeating the same pattern? Is this relationship just like the last one?" That's what I asked myself. The realization scared me. I realized that I had to withdraw from the situation and get some perspective. That's what I'm doing now. I'm just considering and thinking.

RECOGNITION THAT GRIEF OVER ONE THING
MAY MASK GRIEF OVER ANOTHER

A widow recalls:

I loved classical music; and when I would play it after Benjamin's death, I would cry so hard that I had to turn the music off. I'd think, "Oh, I'm missing Benjamin so much." And then one day I realized that my crying over "Moonlight Sonata" had nothing to do with Benjamin.

I thought back to when I had first heard it, and it was in a movie when I was a young girl, I think about fourteen. It was during the Depression, and I would go with the other girls in my little country town to the movies. We couldn't get gas or tires, so just to get the fourteen miles into town on a Saturday night was really something.

I would sit there watching John Payne and Betty Grable or Kathryn Grayson and long for the world out there. I can even remember where I was sitting in the theater the night I heard "Moonlight Sonata." I don't remember the name of the movie, but I remember the song so distinctly. I sat there and dreamed of singing and dancing the way they did. I dreamed of being in their world, which looked so wonderful; I longed to have that.

So when I thought I was crying over Benjamin as I listened to "Moonlight Sonata," I was actually crying over my lost youth, over the fantasy world I had thought existed out there. I was crying for that little girl back during the Depression.

COMING TO TERMS WITH GUILT

A young man reports:

I did wrong, and my best friend paid for it. I drank too much at a party and then drove home recklessly. I lost control going around a curve and turned the car over in a field. I wasn't injured, but my buddy was killed.

This is something I will always live with. Right now, I am doing retribution. The judge said, "In addition to giving you a probated prison sentence, I am going to require you to pay retribution." I work construction; so each week when I get paid, I send my friend's parents a certain amount of money that the judge said I must pay them. I know this can do nothing about the loss of my buddy, but it's

a way that I can say I'm sorry. The thing that matters most to me—
and something I will never forget in my whole life—happened at the
trial when Jim's mother came up, put her arms around me, and said,
"Jacky, I forgive you."

AN ABILITY TO SEE WHERE ONE IS STUCK
A widow recalls:

It was almost a year after Donald had died. A man came to the
back door—he worked for the telephone company—and asked if
he could check some wires on the back of the property. When he
came back, he rang the doorbell to tell me he was through, and he
said "This is a beautiful home. It's so lovely." And I said, "Thank
you; my husband built most of it himself." But I didn't stop there. I
went on to tell him that the house was Donald's dream and that I
couldn't get rid of it now that he was dead.

The lineman said, "Oh, I'm sorry he's dead." I said yes, and then
told him the whole story. I told him Donald committed suicide. I
showed him where he did it. I told him how awful it was to find
him. I just told this stranger every tiny detail. It was awful. I'd cry
and talk to him and talk to him and cry. Just sat there wallowing in
my loss and stirring up his.

After he left, I went back in and thought, "This is the pits. This
is the worst. I cannot believe anyone in the world would do this.
Stop a stranger to tell him about your problems. I am down to the
last person, I guess; I've told everyone until they are tired of hearing
it. So I grabbed at somebody that I could tell that story to."

I haven't done that since. I realize that I have told many people
how Donald died when it was completely unnecessary. I know it's
healthy to be truthful when someone has committed suicide, but
you don't have to use the method of death to get more sympathy.
That is what I saw I was doing. So now if I need to remind myself,
I sit down and I try to think, "Why do I do that? Do I try to shock
people? Am I trying to make someone else as shocked as I still
am that it happened? Or is it that I have to tell it to think, 'Don't
you feel sorry for me that he took his life? That he chose not to be
with us anymore?'" I see that it is very important to question why
you are continuing to do what you are doing. Whether you can quit
doing it right away or not, there's value in the questioning.

ACKNOWLEDGING AMBIVALENT FEELINGS
A young widow discloses:

I don't know if we would have made it or not. He died in December, and in October we had talked about getting a divorce. I told him I could not stand the way he tried to dominate me. He had to be the macho husband, and he wanted me to be the sweet little wife. I wanted to finish high school, and he didn't want me to. I wanted to have a career; and he said, by damn, he was the breadwinner. We were headed for some change—either through counseling or divorcing—and I doubt that it would have been counseling.

So now that he is dead I feel two ways. I'm sad and lonely; I miss him more than I would have ever thought I would. But sometimes I'm also relieved and, I guess you would say, even grateful. In some ways I am lucky that he died because now I am my own person. I can live my life to the fullest. But, you know, even saying that makes me think something bad will happen to me. You aren't supposed to feel that way about the death of your husband!

EXPERIENCE OF EXISTENTIAL LONELINESS
A widow talked:

Now that I am spending more time in solitude, I have recurring feelings of being alone in the universe. You may laugh when I tell you; but as early as age six or seven, I would be lying on the bed before I went to sleep at night, looking out the window to see if I could see the stars. I would find one star and think about going up into the sky.... I would get such a peculiar feeling. The star was so way out there . . . and where was I? I would keep thinking about that. I would get a little afraid. Out there would seem like such a void. And, though that young, I would wonder, "How do I fit into life?" Even then I knew there was something called reality and that was the earth, me, things around me. But what were those stars up there? And what is the earth in relation to those stars? How do I fit in?

I would feel so lonely then. And that's the kind of loneliness I feel now. I feel alone in the universe. I wonder often how I fit into everything. It's the kind of loneliness that sometimes also feels like fear.

AWARENESS THAT THERE ARE THINGS
STILL TO BE HANDLED

A widow discusses the situation in her family:

Don has been dead two years now; and my three sons, all in their forties, are still awkward when their dad is mentioned. The other day Don's brother, who looks so much like Don that they could have been twins, came to visit. The boys kept asking me if it didn't bother me to see Uncle Gene sitting in Don's chair, looking just the way Don did. The truth is, it hadn't bothered me at all; I hadn't even thought about it until they mentioned it.

One of my sons, I think, is trying to live his life as if he doesn't have grieving to do for his father; and, of course, he does. So he's upset most of the time about other things—his work, our relationship, his health—and I think a lot of this is because he is avoiding grieving.

I've noticed something else. Every time I step out some and do something on my own—like drive myself to the dentist or say I'm going to take ceramics classes—my sons get upset. It's as if they want me to stay the way I was when their father was alive; any changes I make seem to be threatening. I haven't figured this out yet, but I certainly notice it.

But I notice things about myself, too. I bought a new stereo a few weeks ago; and when Don's brother came to visit, I found myself embarrassed to mention the stereo or to show it to him. It was as if I was embarrassed that I had stepped out this way. I think I was afraid he would think I had spent too much money. Of course, he already knew about the stereo before he even got here and was thrilled when I showed it to him.

So, there's "east" to go, as I've heard some people put it. There's grieving yet to be worked out and completed, and there's a whole set of family dynamics enmeshed in and around that grieving. But one thing I'm clear about is that I'm going to keep observing myself and keep myself moving on through this process. Even in the worst of these situations, I notice that I'm still walking two and a half miles every day with my neighbor and having my silent prayer times. Something strong is there, even in the middle of all these complications.

RECOGNITION OF WAYS THE LOST PERSON CONTINUES TO BE PRESENT

A granddaughter recounts a realization:

The morning after my grandmother died, my husband wrote a little epitaph for her and put it by my coffee cup at breakfast. It read: "For Grandmother, I'd wear jogging shorts and a New York Mets cap." I knew why he said this. My grandmother at seventy-nine was active beyond most people's imagination. She had just recently finished painting the outside of her house herself, even managing to fall— with no repercussions—into the kitchen through the back window one day when the concrete blocks slipped out from under her. She was also an avid Mets fan who would take her portable radio to bed with her when they were playing on the West Coast so she could follow the game, even though it was two o'clock in the morning.

I missed Grandmother after she died; she had been a spirited presence in our family. Then one day I noticed something: I had started buying stationery and cards that had beautiful flowers on them. "Ah," I said to myself, "that's Grandmother!" Grandmother always had flowers in her yard, and these flowers were always a topic of conversation when you were with her. I would say that she and flowers were so connected in our family that you couldn't say one without thinking of the other. I had also begun to write to my family, who live in different parts of the country, every week instead of my usual once or twice a month. Grandmother wrote all the children in the family every week, no matter what, and chided the rest of us when we were with her for not "keeping up the family tradition," as she put it. "Family is important," she would say. "You must write your family."

So without even realizing it, I had started doing what Grandmother said—"keeping up the family tradition." This was comforting to me, because I knew this was a way that Grandmother was still present in my life. She will never go away as long as there is flowered stationery and family letters!

THE FOCUS DURING OBSERVATION

What ways of thinking and behaving are the most useful during this phase of the mourning process? What are the issues that predominate? In some ways the experiences of Observation result in confrontation: we face facts and situations that are painful. Yet in other ways the experiences result in calm: we begin to focus on something over which we *do* have control—our own thoughts and reactions. Here are some of the opportunities of Observation:

Distinguishing Between Loneliness and Solitude

There is no question that after the loss of persons important in our lives we are lonely. Their absence is part of our constant awareness; we miss them every day. In our loneliness, we feel an incompletion, a lack, a deficit. Our need to bond, to connect, to love, has been tampered with; our desire for communion and companionship with this lost person has been denied.

Solitude, however, is different. While we are still *alone* when we allow ourselves time in solitude, we are not lonely. The companionship we have is with ourselves, our own thoughts and dreams, our relation to life around us. We explore our internal world, making discoveries that enlarge us, having insights that feel like openings. We find ourselves more creative. Perhaps we experience unexplainable feelings of union and connectedness or oneness with all living things. Solitude brings growth and stillness, nurturing those parts of us so hurt by our loss.

In her spirited and inspirational book *Getting Better All the Time*, Liz Carpenter, that vivacious woman who became so beloved by the public when she worked with Lyndon and Lady Bird Johnson in the White House, tells the story of making the critical distinction between loneliness and solitude after her husband died suddenly of a heart attack and she moved from Washington back to Texas:

No gradual transitions for me—I wanted it all to happen immediately. I confessed this to my doctor, John Tyler, confessed it with tears that I couldn't stop.

"Stop racing and look around. Let your environment enrich

your life," he said. "You have a place you love, so stay put long enough to love it."

One morning as I sipped a cup of coffee while I was on the phone talking with an editor in New York, I looked out the picture window and saw a baby deer walk gingerly by, sniffing at the pink geraniums. It paused, framed against the pink granite dome of the capitol of Texas in the distance. Here it was, God's world and my new world laid out before my eyes.

"I'll have to call you back," I hastily told the editor. "I've got to take this in."

And I sat there for a full five minutes gazing at the wonder of it all, reflecting that I had just learned how to move from loneliness to solitude. There is a vast difference.

That's what I had prayed for. That's what I had made the move for, and I had found it at last. God had really given me a chance at a second life, and gradually, in a different way, it became as full as the old life, the Washington life.

Reminiscing

Sadly, I have heard people advise others who were grieving, "Quit thinking about the past. The future is what you can do something about, so that's where you now need to be looking." But this advice is wrong. For reminiscing—recalling events, conversations, occurrences from the past—is one of the important ways we mourn. (In fact, the word *mourning* in Sanskrit means "to remember.") And, paradoxically enough, reminiscing is a way of thinking that can result in our getting free from our depression and sadness.

"How so?" someone might ask. "How can thinking about the past help break the darkness of the present?" Pietro Castelnuovo-Tedesco, who has studied reminiscence, points out that this form of thinking is "one of the principal means by which a person continues to have a relationship with old parts of the self." Through reminiscing we are able to maintain an "inventory" of the key images of ourselves from the past and are therefore able to keep "a thread of continuity among them."

Reminiscence also allows us to discover that the past "has not vanished but is still available and serviceable." "Serviceable?" someone might ask. "How can a past we can never return to be serviceable?"

Because reminiscence "comes close in substance to thinking as a form of trial action." Through reviewing both our past accomplishments and our failures, we can better set goals for the future. Reminiscing, too, "offers guidance and direction" because we are reminded of those ideals and precepts that we have believed in.

Reminiscence is a type of thinking that may occur with others but mainly "occurs silently, when the individual is alone, and is a most private form of mental activity." It allows us to be "simultaneously observer and participant," which is why reminiscing is such an important part of the Observation phase of our grieving process. For now, during this time of solitude and reflection, it is necessary for us to begin to reflect on how we are reacting to the loss and to make judgments, decisions, and changes in relation to those reactions.

Castelnuovo-Tedesco reports that reminiscence "may even be positively related to freedom from depression and to personal survival." When we reminisce about the past, this way of thinking can actually provide consolation because it can serve "as buffer against loss and depression." Reminiscences confirm "that *something* actually took place," and that what remains "has enough substance to comfort and reassure." Through this way of thinking we find that our minds are 'peopled.' The figures of the past are not just 'memories' or mere abstractions but are still present and available to us in certain ways: as sources of awareness, learning, and wisdom; as reminders of goals and ideals; as part of the context we have for making decisions in the present.

Acknowledging Both the Bad and the Good in Our Relationship with the Lost Person

In the beginning, we are prone to go to extremes. We are tempted either to idealize the person who is gone—turning the individual into a saint—or to find fault—painting the one who is gone as the blackest of villains. We may also remember our role in the relationship from a skewed standpoint or attempt to gloss over unresolved issues.

At this point in the grieving process, however, we have an opportunity to begin to find a balance. This is no small point, for Beverley Raphael warns: "Critical to the issue of resolving the loss is the way in which the average of the good and bad of human relationships is accepted and balanced." In fact, one of the benchmarks we have for measuring our progress in mourning is that we begin to remember our relationship with this person as a combination of the plus and the minus. "When the bereaved remembers the dead person as the 'real' person he was to her," Dr. Raphael says, "then mourning is progressing successfully."

I remember talking to a mother whose daughter had died in an automobile accident. The two of them had constantly fought because the daughter had dropped out of college just six hours shy of graduation, an act that infuriated her mother. After the young woman died, her mother would not admit that there had ever been an argument between them. And everybody else in the family skirted the issue also, being careful never to allude to the animosity and anger between the mother and daughter. The cost of this unwillingness to see the bad as well as the good in a past relationship? The mother was caught in her mourning, unable to reach any resolution.

Taking Responsibility for Our Guilt

One of the inevitable outcomes of looking at the past from a balanced point of view is a feeling of guilt. Human relationships are complex. We cannot live and relate to others without doing *something* that, in retrospect, we feel or know was wrong or harmful or insufficient or thoughtless. Therefore, no one who tells the truth is free of at least some degree of guilt after the person is gone. The question to ask, then, is not "Did I do anything over which to feel guilty?" but rather "What responsibility am I taking for dealing with my guilt?"

Ambivalent feelings. There are several reasons we have difficulty resolving the issues related to our guilt. A chief one is the presence of ambivalent feelings toward the person who is gone and our wish not to admit these ambivalent feelings. Perhaps we lived in a love/hate relationship with the person, not only experiencing alternating happiness and unhappiness but also actually having "contradictory and interdependent feelings of love and hate for the same person." Perhaps there were unresolved angry issues between us. Perhaps we even harbored fantasy death wishes about the lost person. Perhaps even now we have mixed feelings about the person's absence—in some ways we are glad, and in other ways we are sorry.

Not to admit these ambivalent feelings—which, by the way, are common to everyone—is to determine that we will never complete our mourning. Says Lily Pincus, "The greatest obstacles in the way of making new relationships after bereavement and being able to live meaningfully again are ambivalent feelings about the deceased and the denial of one's own hating self. By denying his hate," the family therapist goes on to say, "the mourner impairs his love, and with it the capacity to be in loving contact with other people."

Desire to deny our helplessness. A statement once made by Alfred Camus, the French essayist and novelist, suggests another reason we do not take responsibility for our guilt. He wrote: "A world that can be explained, even with bad reasons, is a familiar world." Thus the guilt we feel after a loss may be an attempt to keep our world familiar even if we must use "bad reasons."

Colin Murray Parkes helps us understand this. "A major bereavement," he tells us, "shakes confidence in [our] sense of security. The tendency to go over the events leading up to the loss and to find someone to blame even if it means accepting blame oneself is a less disturbing alternative than accepting that life is uncertain. If we can find someone to blame or some explanation that will enable death to be evaded, then we have a chance of controlling things. It is easier to believe that fate is indifferent, or rather positively malevolent, than to acknowledge our helplessness in the face of events."

We don't want to feel impotent, of course. Therefore we continue to search for causes and to assign blame and guilt. When my husband died, for instance, I felt responsible for his death because I had been the one who wanted us to take up jogging—even though the coroner told me that Greg's death had nothing to do with the fact that he was running. I had to give up that guilt when I realized how much it belittled Greg for me to act as if he did not have full choice in the matter of whether he jogged or not.

But I also had paranoid fears. Hadn't I caused his death by wishing at times, after we had had a fight, that I wasn't married to him, even fantasizing that he was dead? The turnaround in this situation came for me one day when I was telling a friend how guilty I felt, and he said, "Well, if you had the power to cause his death by wishing you weren't married to him or by fantasizing his death, why don't you bring him back by wishing or fantasizing something now?" That ended my preoccupation with grandiose imaginings that my thoughts had controlled my husband's life and, therefore, I was guilty somehow of causing his death.

Accepting responsibility. On the other hand, we may have actually played a part in the event(s) that brought about the loss we have experienced. It is important in that case to examine our behavior. "Wrongs committed," Glen Davidson says, "cannot be addressed unless it is possible to identify what they are.... Rather than trying to suppress the feelings, mourners should express them in order to be able to discern what the limits of their responsibility are.... Only in clarifying what they should feel guilty about—either through omission or commission—can they know what they need feel no guilt over."

It is our potential development that is at stake when we engage in authentic questions about our responsibility for what has happened. What we stand to discover are those things that will allow us to know ourselves, to rectify our behavior, to make appropriate commitments that bring feelings of restitution and completion.

Finally, the bottom line of any engagement with the subject of guilt it is this: We must forgive, ourselves and others. There is no alternative if we are ever going to live freely and fully. If we are ever going to finish our grieving. So it isn't just a moral issue—it's a personal issue of our own well-being as well.

Realizing That Earlier Losses Have Been Reactivated

As if the loss we are currently mourning weren't enough, we must often deal simultaneously with upset and pain from earlier losses for which we were not able to finish grieving. It's as if one loss reminds us of all losses. We think we are grieving for this thing, and we are actually grieving for that. It's hard to discriminate.

To sort out these losses is one of the tasks of the time of Observation. To recognize that to the mourning we are doing now we may sometimes have to add mourning for something in the past. I remember talking to a young woman who was angrily denouncing her husband who had just left her. Suddenly she began to cry almost uncontrollably. "It's the same way it was when I was fifteen, and my daddy died," she said. "I've got to make changes now just the way I did then."

"What kind of changes?" I asked her.

"Since I was a little girl," she said, "it had been set in our family that when I went to college I would go to my mother's alma mater in the East. That was where I wanted to go more than any other place in the world. Then when my father died, all that changed. There wasn't enough money for me to go away to school when I graduated from high school, so I had to attend the local public junior college. Everything about my future life was determined by that decision."

As she talked, the young woman realized that although she had mourned her father's death, she had never mourned the "inconsequential" loss related to her choice of college. Yet the anger and the sadness had been there for fifteen years. The similarity between her situation now—things she would have to give up, changes she would have to make as a result of her husband's leaving—stirred a deep memory. She was grieving now for a seventeen-year-old teenager as well as for a thirty-year-old woman.

Releasing Resentment and Anger

This is an issue that particularly plagues those whose loss comes as a result of divorce or separation. Of course, almost everyone experiences anger when there is a significant loss of any kind—anger at the person who is gone, anger at people whom we think could have prevented what happened, anger at ourselves, anger at "the system." But during the experiences of Observation, if they have not done so before, many people begin to see the importance of expressing their resentment and anger and thereby becoming free of it. They see the damage they are doing to themselves, as well as to others, by continuing to harbor these negative feelings and they try to find a way to release them.

But this resolution does not happen for some—particularly those who feel they have been rejected by their partners, done wrong, treated unfairly, used and taken advantage of, lied about, abandoned. The other day a social worker told me that the people she works with who seem never to get over their losses are those who will not give up their anger and their bitterness. These individuals, she told me— many of them divorced women—determine everything about their lives in relation to its value as retaliation. And even if they choose to express their anger passively, the anger hampers their self-expression and sets the parameters of their lives. The cost, of course, is enormous: constant conflict, fear of living, withered existence, early aging, and disease and ill health.

Another kind of resentment and anger that is extremely difficult to overcome is that which comes when individuals are hurt by acts of prejudice, ignorance, and callousness. Many people who have lost a loved one to AIDS know too well the damage such unconscionable behavior can inflict. Unfortunately, there are those in our society who arrogantly evaluate and blame the life choices of the deceased and the survivors. Those who disallow the survivors the right to mourn. Those who refuse to recognize the devastating impact of multiple deaths— and the constant continuing fact of death—on the psyche of individuals, as well as on a community as a whole. Those who overlook the dislocation and disequilibrium men and women feel when the entire social structure of their lives crumbles around them.

Yet somehow, as hard as it may be, the anger and resentment resulting from such responses must be worked through and released. During Observation we have an opportunity to reflect on the cost to ourselves of harboring these self-devouring emotions and to grapple with ways to expend them. For some, the answer is to work within the community to better the circumstances of those experiencing the ravages of AIDS. For others, it is to become involved in educational programs designed to alter attitudes in society. For still others, it is to raise money to be used to search for a cure to the disease. Through these and other activities, the energies of resentment and anger are transformed into work and action that not only bring a healthy release to the survivors, but also contribute to the good of those for whom they care so much.

Shifting Our Focus From What Happened to How We Are Reacting to What Happened

Victor Frankl, the Viennese psychotherapist and a survivor of the Holocaust, once said, "Each man is questioned by life; and he can only answer life by *answering for* his own life...." During the experiences of Observation, we have the opportunity to begin to "answer for" our own life. We begin, during this time, to direct our gaze to ourselves, to our reactions, to our role in determining how our mourning is progressing.

This is a time of hard appraisal. How am I behaving in the face of this loss? Am I in any way taking advantage of the situation to get sympathy or to avoid responsibility? Are there things I could do to make the situation better? Why am I not doing them? Do I really want things to be different? Or do I want to grieve forever? During Observation we check ourselves in order to give a true account of the responses we are making to what has happened. Excuses are detected; fears pinpointed; strengths called forth and acknowledged.

Much of this analyzing is done when we are alone. When we are by ourselves we can think, reflect, reminisce, plan. We can be quiet so that we can assess where we are today and what is possible for tomorrow. In solitude, we can take stock of what has happened and is happening in our lives. We can see things that in the hustle and bustle of daily life we are unable to see.

Authorities tell us that even babies need solitude in order to "discover [their] personal life." If infants are capable of being alone, says Dr. Donald Winnicott, first "in the presence of someone" and then without the "actual presence of a mother or mother-figure," the children will learn how to "have an experience which feels real." And, Dr. Winnicott points out, "A large number of such experiences form the basis for a life that has reality in it instead of futility." Anthony Storr, commenting on Winnicott's study, says that "the capacity to be alone thus becomes linked with self-discovery and self-realization; with becoming aware of one's deepest needs, feelings, and impulses."

One of the primary opportunities, then, of the time of Observation is to be alone in order to become aware of our "deepest needs, feelings, and impulses." The discoveries we make as a result of this introspection, in turn, can result in changes in our thoughts and behavior and move us forward toward a constructive outcome to our grieving process.

There are practical benefits, too, that accrue from our time of solitude. Psychiatrist Paul Horton suggests that "the ability to give solace to oneself is the basis of such major positive feelings as joy, awe, forgiveness, and generosity." Work he has done shows that spending time alone talking to oneself, reading, listening to music, praying, going for a walk, and recalling pleasant memories bring solace. He emphasizes the importance of this "private behavior" in our being able to comfort ourselves and "lift the weight of a depression."

Richard Sackett, clinical director of the Cognitive Therapy Center of New York, likewise points out the value of certain activities that one does when alone. "It often helps," says Dr. Sackett, "to write down one's thoughts." This writing can take the form of a list, "with a column listing one's thoughts and feelings about the matter, and another column enumerating a rational response to each thought." Such writing makes it "easier to see when you are distorting things—imagining the worst thing that could happen, or being too harsh on yourself."

Bernie Siegel, formerly a physician at Yale University School of Medicine, also points out the value of spending time alone writing: studies show that those who keep journals about their feelings and dreams have "more active immune systems and fewer colds" than those who didn't keep journals, even up to six months after they stop keeping a journal.

I think of a friend who told me of experiencing a powerful shift in her life as a result of choosing to spend three days totally alone. Lucia was bruised and angry after a divorce she had not wanted.

The young woman reported:

For a long time I would just escape. With the radio in the car, with TV, with friends. But one day a customer gave me the key to her cabin on Camp Creek and said, "Go; stay as long as you like." So I arranged to be gone for three days. It was the first time in my life I had been alone like that. It was the first time I could hear silence, could listen to myself talk. I had no distractions; so I began to sit and ask myself: What do I want to do? Is this what I want to do—just sit here wallowing in self-pity—or do I want to get on with my life, good or bad, take risks, continue?

I wrote down every thought that came into my mind; it was desperate soul-searching. What do I want and why do I want it? Why am I doing this and not that? When I wasn't writing, I read A *Woman of Independent Means,* a wonderful book that shows you how easy it is to spend your life doing things you think will benefit others; and, as a result, you give up your independent thoughts. As a result of reading and thinking and writing, it all came together. I saw how easy it was to get trapped into doing things for others and how important it was to do things for yourself. As I wrote, I realized what an angry, destructive situation I had created. It was something inside that said, "You don't want this. This is not good. This is not how you want to be. Get out of this, and go on."

I realized during that weekend that when I died I did not want people to be able only to say, "She was a good mother; she was a good friend; she was fun." I wanted to know that I did something that helped more than my immediate community. Or at least I wanted to know that I had tried. It became clear to me that weekend that I wanted to go to my native country in Central America to see what I could see and then return to America to set up some kind of project that could help.

I must admit that when Lucia told me her story, I recognized the authenticity of the experience she had had in solitude, but I suppose I thought that, as time went on, the realities of life as a divorced mother and businesswoman would alter the form and scope of her dream. But imagine my surprise—and pleasure—when I saw this lead to an article in our local newspaper: "Lucia Adams is on a mission to provide Central American refugee children with the necessities of life." The article went on to state that Adams had formed Friends of Central American Children, a nonprofit organization established to collect clothing, food, and toys for refugee children. And accompanying the article was a photograph. There, among eight small Nicaraguan children in a refugee camp, stood my friend Lucia.

THE CHOICE

There is only one choice of value during this period of Observation:

We must choose to look honestly.

This is a choice that requires enormous courage. It requires us to be alone with our thoughts; to focus on our responses rather than on the event of the loss itself; to remember in a balanced way rather than to remember only the good or the bad; to admit the cost of guilt and anger and be willing to forgive; to recognize that there are ways in which the lost person can always be present.

The choice of Observation requires us to call a moratorium on what we may have been doing to "cope" with the loss we have experienced— things like losing ourselves in our work, involving ourselves excessively in the care of others (usually weak others), running constantly, focusing only on the past, depending on sleep, drugs, alcohol, television, or partying to ease our pain. Instead of these, we choose now to grapple with the only questions that can lead to wisdom: What meaning does this loss have in my life? How am I choosing to respond to what has happened? How do I intend to act in the future? These are questions of import, questions of power.

WHAT WE NEED FROM FAMILY AND FRIENDS DURING OBSERVATION

I remember a young widow telling me about her dilemma during Observation. A neighbor came rushing to her back door one afternoon in a panic: "I've been calling and calling," she said to the young widow. "Are you all right? I saw your car in the driveway, but when you didn't answer the phone I just knew you were sick or depressed or something."

The young woman had to speak to her neighbor firmly. "You know, Alicia, that I told you I wanted time alone. And that I was not going to answer the telephone every time it rang. I've realized I need to be by myself more now. I'm finding this time alone very valuable."

"You just don't need me anymore," the neighbor said with a catch in her voice, "and it's terrible not to be needed."

Unfortunately, the behavior of this neighbor was well intentioned but uninformed. She did not know that the need to withdraw, to be alone, was a sign that her friend was progressing in a healthy way through her grieving. In similar situations, we must do as this widow did and take the initiative to ask for time alone if others do not understand, explaining that this is an important and necessary part of the process of our grieving.

But often we are ambivalent about the matter ourselves. What if people forget about us while we are engaged in matters solitary? What if those with whom we like to do things get accustomed to our absence and stop thinking of including us? What if there is no one to listen when we do want to communicate, perhaps to talk with someone about an important insight we had while we were being private?

Again, it's a matter of balance. For although we need time by ourselves during Observation to begin to make sense of our reaction to what has happened, to think toward the future, to commune with ourselves, we also continue to need our friends and family. For we do still get lonely, and we are often sad. A requirement of Observation is not that we cut ourselves off from our family and friends, but that we engage with them in ways appropriate to the grieving we are doing now. Perhaps they can be a sounding board for the ideas that come to us when we're alone. Or they can offer suggestions that can help us implement changes we now want to make. Or perhaps they can share our happiness over the new possibilities we have seen. Family and friends may also be able to provide guidance and advice in areas about which, in our silence, we have discovered particular pain.

The solitude of Observation, I think, is as much an attitude as it is an action. We can be alone in a crowd, if we choose to be introspective and contemplative. This doesn't take the place of the time we need alone, of course, but an attitude of solitude can serve us anywhere and anytime. Because this is so, I think another role our family and friends play in our lives during Observation is to be a source of things to read, do, and think about. What we couldn't hear months ago because we were experiencing the pain of separation or were engulfed in the bleakness of depression, we can now respond to: a book someone recommends; a place to go for inspiration; an activity that others found beneficial. Often during Observation a casual comment by another will open up whole vistas for us. A conversation will lead us to entirely new areas of inquiry. A movie or television program will spark ideas for our future. A discussion, a sermon, or an event will lead to a powerful reevaluation of our beliefs, our values, and our faith. So with the *attitude* of solitude—in addition to the actions—we can be both with our family and friends and separate from them.

I saw Armand DiMele, the grief therapist in New York, a few months after he had given me the "only number you dial is your own" poem. This time I told him, "I have a poem for you." It was Richard's Brautigan's short poem called *"Karma Repair Kit: Items 1-4."* After listing silence, sleep, and food, the poet gives his final instructions:

4.

Seeing Armand smile at this wordless instruction for how to repair one's life by being quiet, I said "This is to let you know that I got the message."

Such is the wisdom of Observation.

4

The Turn

Life can only be understood backwards.

It must be lived forwards.

SØREN KIERKEGAARD

At Easter I went to Greece. A friend I worked with invited me to go home with her to visit her family. The flight was "cheaper than flying from Houston to Los Angeles," she had promised—and we would be staying with her mother and father. After having been so financially irresponsible, I was worried about making ends meet. This, however, looked like something that I could do without wrecking my budget.

Chrysoula's parents live on the island of Crete on the outskirts of the town of Kania, where Mr. Bouyotopoulos runs a small woodworking business. The rest of the family—uncles, aunts, cousins, grandfather—live in Vlatos, the ancestral village, high in the mountains at the end of the island. "A very simple life," Chrysoula told me, "raising goats and tending olive trees. Nobody has much, but when I go there I find it hard to leave."

Being in Greece at Easter was a mixture of pleasure and pain. The pleasure was everywhere. Walking in the strong sunlight on the baked dirt outside the Bouyotopoulos house. Picking bright orange kumquats off the trees and pressing their warm flesh through my teeth. Bicycling with Chrysoula and her mother to visit a monastery back in the hills, where brown-robed monks served us schnapps in a stone-floored room as cool as a cellar. Hiking to the ruins of another monastery—this one built by the Venetians centuries ago, many of its arches and bridges still standing—scrambling down steep rocky slopes to find caves with secret altars. Eating fish fried whole, chicory salad, and homemade "flower cheese" that tasted like cake. Drinking Greek coffee and pouring the dregs on the plants growing in pots outside the door. Playing with new kittens. Watching the way the light came through the lace curtains that had been part of Mrs. Bouyotopoulos's dowry. So much pleasure.

Yet equal amounts of pain. I was full, almost to bursting. Only someone who knew me the way Greg did, who cared about what

touched me, who loved to know what I thought and to tell me what
he thought in return—only Greg could make the experiences complete. Without someone to share them with, the place was almost too
beautiful, the experiences too poignant.

There was Good Friday when we went to the neighboring
village of Gavalachori....

In the village everyone gathers in the churchyard for the ritual of
ringing the bell commemorating the start of Easter weekend. One
after the other, mothers, fathers, and children walk solemnly up to
the bell rope and pull it. When the last person is finished, Mr.
Bouyotopoulos turns to me and says, "I will teach you to ring the
bell. You must learn to ring the bell sorrowfully." There was something in the incongruity of ringing a bell sorrowfully that made some
statement about life, but I couldn't quite put my finger on it. I
needed to talk to Greg.

There was the religious procession through the streets of Kania
the night before Easter...

Everyone rushes to get from one good vantage point to the next
in order to catch a glimpse of the holy statues. Chrysoula's family
and I run through the streets trying to catch up with the procession, a
human chain, each of us holding the hand of the next. As we turned
corners and were pulled along by the momentum, I thought of the
whip games I played when I was a child. When we finally caught up
with the procession, we fell against each other in breathless pleasure. It was like the day Greg and I jogged up a ski lift and finally
made it, leaning on each other when we got to the top because we
were so tired but laughing because we were so happy. But who here
would understand, even if I told them how this event reminded me
of that earlier one?

There was midnight mass...

We sat in a small village church built in the 1200s—dark, quiet,
solemn. Sitting in the shadows, we watched the service as if it were
a tableau being performed in the center of an illuminated circle. At
home, following the mass, we ate the traditional Easter supper,
which we did not finish until almost daybreak.

In bed later I could not sleep. The service had been so simple and
so beautiful; when I closed my eyes the images swam in front of me.
And at the supper table I had felt that I was living the meaning of

family and *tradition*. Without Greg there was no one to talk to who would understand that every cell in my body was alive from the impact of these experiences.

Chrysoula's family spent every Easter with Mr. Bouyotopoulos's father in the ancestral village. Papa Bouyotopoulos, seventy-seven and a widower for many years, prided himself on his self-sufficiency. It was he who always prepared dinner every Easter. This event was a family tradition.

During the three-hour car ride to Vlatos, on treacherous roads that seemed to hang between the mountains and the sea, I sank into moroseness. Perhaps it was because the stay was almost over. Perhaps it was because the previous day had been so exuberant. Perhaps it was because it was the morning of the Resurrection, and in my life I felt no resurrection. Who can say what was the source of my depression? All I knew was that I felt so alone and empty, as if I were being slowly but inexorably sucked into an immense black hole of nothingness.

Mr. Bouyotopoulos parked the car in the sandy square of the small village. "Papa lives a few miles farther up the mountain," Chrysoula told me. "We have to walk from here."

We twisted back and forth on the trail for almost an hour, walking silently, single file. Then, suddenly, the path ended. We were there. In front of us was a small yard surrounded by orange and lemon trees. A kitchen table, set with bowls ready for soup, occupied the center of the open area. "We can never all get into Papa's kitchen," Chrysoula said, laughing, "so we always eat out under the trees."

Papa must have heard us coming, for when we stepped into the yard, he was standing at the table breaking eggs. "When you make lamb and rice soup," Mrs. Bouyotopoulos explained, "the egg yolks always have to be whipped at the very last minute."

"Oh, and when you taste it . . ." Chrysoula added, turning her eyes toward the heavens.

Two widowed aunts, who also must have heard our footsteps on the rocky path, came into the yard simultaneously. They were dressed all in black, even to the babushkas that covered their heads. The aunts rushed to the orange trees and picked a piece of fruit for each of us. "Sit . . . sit down and eat . . . this will refresh you. Jacob's soup will soon be ready."

We ate the soup, while the aunts worried about us. Papa was busy removing the young goat from the spit where it had been roasting at the edge of the yard. He brought it to the table and began the carving. When we finished the soup, we ate the succulent meat with its crisp, almost-burnt edges pressed between pieces of thick, coarse bread and washed it down with pungent homemade retsina.

As I sat there—simple, satisfying food in front of me, hospitable, generous people around me—I felt my depression lifting. I looked across at Papa and his two sisters, each bereft of a partner but clearly relishing being alive. I looked down at the sun-baked earth beneath my feet and then up toward the blue patches of sky that were showing through the orange and lemon trees. Suddenly I felt a shift occur in my body; there was an actual physical alteration. Something released inside me. This shift was immediately followed by an inexplicable sense of well-being, of calmness and serenity. The vague foreboding— the sense that "something is not right; something bad is about to happen," which had been a constant presence in my life since Greg's death—had left me. Instead, sitting there as if in a round of sky and trees and light and earth, I felt in touch with something elemental, strong, ineffable. In touch with what seemed at that moment all one would ever need to know, with something deeply healing.

After dinner, it became clear that Papa had plans. "He wants us to go with him up the mountain; he has something he wants to show us," Chrysoula told me. We followed the spry old man, who was carrying two wooden buckets filled with water, as he led us to a path that seemed to go straight up the mountain. We climbed for many minutes.

Then we turned a final curve in the path. Ahead was what Papa had brought us to see. Planted in the large clearing were hundreds of tiny oak seedlings. Row after row of little trees lined the steep hillside, narrow furrows plowed between them. It was Papa's forest. He proceeded carefully to water every tiny tree.

I stood there in amazement, looking first at Papa and then at the hillside of seedlings. I could imagine the amount of work this project required: how the old man's back must hurt from all the bending and how his arms must ache from hauling water up the mountain.

"Why would he do this?" I asked myself. "This is a man seventy seven years old. He cannot possibly live long enough to see these seedlings become a forest." Chrysoula's mother seemed to read my mind, for she turned and said, "Papa has planted these trees as part of a reclamation program sponsored by an environmentalist organization active here on the island. 'For the land,' he says. 'So the family will always have trees on the land.' "

I thought about this all the way down the path as we walked back to our car at the end of the afternoon's visit. Seeing Papa Bouyotopoulos's forest had deeply stirred me. I didn't quite know what it was that had touched me so, but it had something to do with caring about something bigger than you are, something to do with making a contribution that will live on after you, something about *looking out at life* instead of always obsessively staring inward. I knew the experience had made an opening in my thinking. Because for the first time since Greg's death, I found myself considering the idea that there might be some projects worth doing in life, some commitments worth making. I looked forward to getting home from Greece. I was enthusiastic. It was going to be the start of a new era.

But that wasn't how it happened.

When I returned, instead of energy I experienced a new depth of depression. It was just like the weeks right after Greg's death. I was afraid to be in the house by myself. I lost my appetite and couldn't sleep. I cried constantly and could not make myself go to work. The worst part about it was that I had no way to understand the backset. I *knew* I had made progress in grieving; why, then, was this happening?

Confused and distraught, I called Armand DiMele in New York. "Now, just exactly when was it that Greg died?" Armand asked me. "I know it was last summer, but what was the date?"

"July 2," I replied, just a little aggravated. I could not see what the date of Greg's death had to do with how I was feeling now.

"I'm looking at the calendar," Armand went on to say. "That's been nine months . . ." pausing as if I would find that useful information. Then he continued, "For some uncanny reason, people often

have a severe relapse nine months after the loss. It happens often
enough that researchers even write about it.

"So," he continued, "if you consider that you may be experiencing the nine-months-since-death syndrome, and if you add to that
the fact that you spent the Easter season in Greece where you participated over and over in activities associated with death and
resurrection . . ."

"And with a family who has lived in the same place as a unit for
hundreds of generations," I added, beginning to see the picture.

"Then you came back," he went on to point out, "with the idea
that you would start life newly . . ."

"But what I found," I interpolated, "was the same old empty
house and a pattern of life that was no different."

"Enough to make one depressed, isn't it?" he asked me.

"It feels just like that day," I said—and as I spoke I began to
experience the undefinable but almost suffocating fear—"when I
realized that I'd have to make new patterns for my life like new
veins for blood to run in. But what I did then was fall to pieces and
spend months living in desperation. I don't want to do that again."

"You won't have to," he responded. "You're much stronger; now
you'll be able to look at what you need to do more quickly and more
directly."

Still depressed, I returned to work. The nights were especially
difficult—I kept dreaming I was driving on what I thought were
open, spacious highways, only to find, at the end of every road I
took, the impenetrable wall of a heavy concrete underground bun-
ker. When I was with people, I felt separate from them, as if I were
encased in a shield of plastic. I was present, but I was not present.

One evening my neighbor asked me over for dinner. While she
was making the picante sauce and her husband was putting the
fajitas on the grill, I went into the dining room to set the table. "Add
a couple of extra plates," Ann called from the kitchen. "Beth and Joe
are joining us; in fact, they should be here any minute." I went to the
hutch to get the silverware and the dishes.

I put five brown ceramic plates down on the white linen table-
cloth. Suddenly, the place where the sixth plate should have been
laid stood out so prominently that it actually startled me. As I stood

there, looking at the blank spot on the table, anger welled up in waves from my stomach to my throat. I felt hot tears in my eyes, and my nose was stinging. "I must get out of here," I said to myself, "before somebody comes in and sees me." I could hear Beth and Joe arriving as I ran from the dining room to the empty den to take refuge.

I grabbed a pencil and began writing furiously. It was as if I were possessed; the words seemed just to appear on the page in front of me. In rapid-fire progression, I wrote these stanzas:

Tonight

The 6th place at the table.
Empty.
Like a socket with no eye.
I hate it.

Wipe It in Your Face

The 6th place at the table.
Shouting, "You're by yourself."
"Ha, ha, ha, ha, ha, ha
Ha, ha, ha, ha, ha, ha
You can't come and get me."

Golgotha

The 6th place at the table.
White mark of the cross.
No way to ignore it.
Even a bowl of salad doesn't help, really.

Empty Alone

The 6th place at the table.
The white marking the spot.
Leading all eyes to notice.
You couldn't help but see it.

Say What?

The 6th place at the table.
What kind of plate can a ghost eat from?

In Your Honor

There really should have
Also been
Flowers
    And butterflies
        And stars
            And rainbows
At that 6th place at the table.

Delphi

A praise offering.
That's what should have been
At that 6th place at the table.

Celebration

To commemorate your release
To the cosmic playground
Airy ferris wheels
Ethereal merry-go-rounds
And plenty of room for washing your car.
Who needs that limiting, earthly, binding 6th place at the table?

When the last word was written on the page, I felt light, unburdened. I sat there for several seconds wondering what had happened to me, and then I understood. As I wrote those lines, I had stopped thinking only about myself and my loss and had begun to think about Greg: what was good for him? what did he deserve? what would honor him? I had changed from being Greg's angry critic and enemy to being his champion and friend. And I had finally located him somewhere that I wasn't. In a place where he had some other form and was happy.

Yes, it was quite an alteration. No wonder I felt light and unburdened. I went across the hall and joined my friends in the kitchen. No one had even had time to miss me.

Over the next weeks, I turned my attention to several things that, up until this time, I had been avoiding. I wrote the remarks to be delivered at a regional conference where the first Gregory Cowan Memorial Teaching Award would be given: "Tonight, with Karen Davis presenting this award, there is evidence of the best kind of immortality. Greg's dedication to students and to teaching is recreated in Karen, one of his dearest friends and students. He would not want a better legacy." I decided how to spend the money colleagues and friends had contributed to a memorial fund at the university. I would invite the poet William Stafford, who had been Greg's friend, to come from Oregon to present a special evening of poetry and to honor ten of Greg's graduate students by giving them gold Cartier writing pens. As I worked on these activities, I could see that there were many ways Greg would continue to be a part of the lives of the people who knew him even though he was not present. It was a different way of thinking.

The first anniversary of Greg's death was approaching. I had read many books warning that birthdays, anniversaries, holidays, and the anniversary of the event were dangerous times; you could almost count on having a painful relapse in your grieving. I thought at first that I'd do whatever I could to avoid paying attention to the anniversary . . . perhaps my sister and I would go on a trip, or I would go stay with my parents.

But finally I decided not to do any of these things. "I know I am capable of facing whatever I need to face," I said to myself. "I will go to work as usual and perhaps have some friends over for dinner. But I'm not going to run from Texas to Tennessee to try to escape this anniversary."

I continued to talk to myself. "Yes, you'll be able to do it," I said confidently. "You know by now that you don't die from pain even if you don't like it. As bad as it is, you do live through it...."

So I went to work as usual on the day Greg had died one year earlier. With a group of other professors, I spent most of the morning discussing a possible exchange program with a dignitary from the Middle East.

It must have been two o'clock when I arrived home. The light was flashing on the answering machine; I pushed the button.

"Hey, Sis, are you ready to be an aunt?"

I could hear the excitement in my brother's voice.

"Your niece, Sarah, was born a couple of hours ago. She weighs four pounds seven ounces, and is seventeen inches long. She'll have to stay in the hospital for a little while, but basically she's okay. She has all her essential parts."

I sat down on the couch, dumbfounded. My brother's first baby was here! And she had arrived six weeks early! Then came the realization: the baby had been born on the very afternoon Greg had died twelve months earlier! A birth and a death—both unexpected—had occurred in our family on the same afternoon. Greg dying one year; baby Sarah being born the next. This was amazing! On a day that our family had expected to be sad and lonely, we would now also be cheerful and happy. Every year this particular afternoon would always be a reminder: there is exit from life, and there is *also* entrance.

I suppose I needed something to deflect me from the intensity of the moment. So I picked up the magazine the gentleman from the Middle East had given me a few hours earlier and began to flip through it while my mind tried to accommodate what had happened.

As I turned the pages, several poems caught my eye, and I began to read. When I came to the second poem, I could hardly believe what was before me. It was as if the poem had been written for *today* for *my family;* it was as if the gentleman had given me the magazine *just for this occasion....*

A Song

I sing a sad song—
sadder than the sunset's walk
in the city streets;
I feel grief in my blood
flowering from some hidden spring;

my friends, we die—
we sail into the end
without pausing to say good-bye;
our dreams, hopes, loves
come to an end
like footprints in the sand
chewed by the desert.
I sing a happy song—
happier than the sunrise
on another shore;
happier than the smile
a birthday-child smiles;
happier than a new kiss;
I feel a stubborn joy
conquering my blood;
my friends, we live—
we live each instant
to its deepest cores, collect
its treasures, trifle with its secrets,
lave ourselves within its ecstasy.

Of death and life I shall
a happy/sad sad/happy song
    sing . . .

        SHAIKH GHAZI AL-QUSABI

When I finished reading, I thought to myself, *"The cycle of life. You hear that phrase all your life; you understand with your mind the truth of it. But then comes the day when you know what the words mean. You know with your whole being."*

There are some things you never understand, however—things that defy all logical explanation. The note from my mother, written on the morning of the anniversary day of Greg's death, arrived a few days later. I stood at the kitchen counter, reading.

Dear Sister,
    We're thinking of you this morning and pray that everything works out well.... An almost unbelievable instance happened

*yesterday! As we were going to church last night, about 6:30—
way before dark— when we got to the exact spot where Greg
fell, there came a young man jogging, facing us on the exact
side of the road. As we passed him, we noticed that he had a
dark beard, close-cut like Greg's. Was such a feeling, seeing him
right at that spot, resembling Greg so much. Neither of us said a
word and haven't mentioned it since. Seems almost sacred-like.
Don't mean to make you sad, just wanted to mention what a
coincidence it was! Especially right at this time.*

*Daddy is in the garden seeing if it is too wet to pick beans.
We had a little rain yesterday.*

*Lots of love,
Mother*

I was packing a box to put in storage. As I reached for a piece of
the newspaper I was crushing to protect the breakables, an article
caught my eye. THE WORDS OF JEAN-PAUL SARTRE, the headline read. Melvin Maddocks of the *Christian Science Monitor* had
written a perspective on the philosophy of Sartre, who had died a
few days before the article was written.

The piece intrigued me, and I began to read. It is hard to anticipate that sitting in your den packing boxes can be the occasion for a
life-changing epiphany, but it happened. As I read through the
article, one sentence jumped out at me. A character in one of the
philosopher's plays had said:

"Freedom crashed down on me and swept me off my feet."

When I read this, I finally understood why the aftermath of
Greg's death had been so devastating: freedom *had* crashed down
on me. Until Greg died, my life had purpose and it had a structure.
After he died, I was free—within the bounds of my abilities and my
resources—to do anything, live anywhere, act any way. But this was
freedom that I despised; freedom I did not want; freedom that
frightened me. For the freedom was a form of emptiness, of nothingness. The freedom provided only openness; it offered no structure.

And without structure, without some specific shape to my life, I was dangling out in nowhere. I could only flail and flounder.

I don't know why, but just *understanding* what I had experienced, just *understanding* what I had been running from, why I had been so crazy, so erratic, so scared, so tentative, and so uncertain, made me feel stronger. I think I realized, perhaps for the first time, that I had reacted in a normal way to a frightening condition of human existence. Greg's death had destroyed everything that mattered to me; and the freedom that resulted—"the absence of necessity or constraint in choice or action"—had almost undone me. Somehow it made a difference to me that day to realize that words like "crashed down on me" and "swept me off my feet" had been used by others who felt condemned when they experienced that kind of freedom.

The article also summarized the credo of the philosopher:

"Let us say that one can improve one's biography.... There is always a possibility for the coward to stop being cowardly.... [There is always the] possibility of being a hero.... The self is a choice; we are what we do."

When I read this, I knew—as in really *knew*—that I was responsible for my life and that it would be the choices I made—not the circumstances in which I found myself—that would determine the kind of life I had in the future. There are hardly words to describe the exuberance, the opening, of that moment. I felt enormous energy. There was something I could do! I did not have to be a victim of what had happened. I did not just have to resign myself to some sublevel existence . . . to the defeatist philosophy I had heard from so many people.... *There's nothing you can do about it, so you might as well accept it and just get on with living.*

No, I did not have to have as my highest goal "accepting and living with" what had happened to me. My doom was not sealed. My fate was not set. It was true that I could do nothing about what had happened, but I could do everything about how I continued to react to what had happened. I could act on the realization that I had the power to make choices about my future, and then I could make choices that served me. *One can always improve one's biography. There is always a possibility for the coward to stop being cowardly. There is the possibility of being a hero!*

I did not just suddenly stop grieving as a result of this experience, but from that point on I did hold my grief in a larger context. The best I could describe it to myself that morning as I sat in the den was that I now felt a sense of *possibility*.

I didn't know the context for this philosopher's credo; perhaps the way I interpreted those few quotations in the newspaper was completely in error. But it didn't matter. In reading them, I had seen a new future for myself, and that was the interpretation that mattered.

I don't know whatever possessed me. I was walking across the campus when I got the idea. I would go over to the university president's office and ask if I could come to work for him!

No matter that I didn't know him and had seen him only once in the three and a half years I'd been on the faculty. We could get to know each other! No matter that no professors worked in the office of the president. I could be the first! No matter that I wasn't exactly sure what I would offer to do for him. I'd make a list! The more I thought about it, the more excited I became. This job would be perfect. It would give me something new and challenging to do at the same time that I maintained some familiar structure, teaching a reduced load in the English department, staying in my home, being with my friends.

That afternoon I called and made an appointment. As soon as I got off the phone, I began to make my list and to decide what to wear that would look "administrative."

"President Tyler," I said when we had completed the introductory amenities, "I'd like to come to work for you. Here's a list of ten things I can do." Balancing the cup of coffee the secretary had brought me in one hand, I reached awkwardly across the president's desk with the other.

In the few minutes it took the president to read that short list, I lived a dozen scenarios. He would laugh and find the whole thing ridiculous.... He would feel sorry for me and be as nice as possible while he summoned the secretary to see me out the door.... He would be embarrassed and awkward at finding a way to refuse me.

... I wouldn't like to work over here anyway.... What would a hare-brained idea like this do to my schedule?

Then he looked up. "Professor," he began, "there are four or five things on this list that I have been losing sleep over. I can see how you might be a help in these areas. Give me a couple of weeks to see what I can do; I believe we'll be able to work something out."

And that's how I came to be assistant to the president in charge of liaison and communication between the president's office and the faculty. That's how I started taking action and being responsible for the direction my life took. That's how I launched my new future.

This is the set of experiences called the Turn—a series of realizations, understandings, actions, and commitments that allow us to establish a new framework for our grieving. We shift our focus. We experience a change in perspective.

Up to now it was important to concentrate on acknowledging and experiencing all the ways the loss had hurt us. By necessity, we spent most of our time looking inward. Now, however, because we have let ourselves experience our grief, because we suffered the depths of aloneness, because we took time to reflect on our experiences, we have arrived at a new place. We are no longer forced on a daily basis to deal only with our emotions; we are not required to struggle only with feelings of helplessness and hopelessness. We can now imagine our lives extending out into the future, something that did not seem possible, or even likely, earlier in our grieving.

Psychiatrist John Bowlby explains the change this way:

Because it is necessary to discard old patterns of thinking, feeling and acting before new ones can be fashioned, it is almost inevitable that a bereaved person should at times despair that anything can be salvaged and, as a result, fall into depression and apathy. Nevertheless, if all goes well this phase may soon begin to alternate with a phase during which he starts to examine the new situation in which he finds himself and to consider ways of meeting it. This entails a redefinition of himself as well as of his situation.... Until redefinition is achieved no plans for the future can be made.... Once this corner is turned a bereaved person recognizes that an attempt must be made to fill unaccustomed roles and to acquire new skills.

The Turn does not happen automatically. It does not just "naturally follow." Bowlby reminds us that it is not with our emotions and feelings that we make this commitment to redefine ourselves and our place in the world around us. This is a *cognitive act,* he says, something that happens in our thinking and speaking. It is because we *decide*— not because of a change in our circumstances—that we commit to making the longer-term adjustments that are so essential to the completion of our mourning.

I remember an ad sponsored by Shearson Lehman/American Express that ran in the *New York Times* and the *Wall Street Journal.* "Commitment," read the bold headline. Then these words followed: "Commitment is what transforms a promise into reality. It is the words that speak boldly of your intentions. And the actions which speak louder than the words.... Commitment is the stuff character is made of; the power to change the face of things. It is the daily triumph of integrity over skepticism."

This message, it seems to me, reflects the kind of thinking and behavior we do at this point in the mourning process. It is the "words that speak boldly of [our] intentions," it is with "the daily triumph of integrity over skepticism" that we make the Turn.

We change our attitude during the Turn because we realize that our past thinking and behavior have served their purpose and, if continued, can only deceive and defeat us. (During this period of the grieving process we come to understand Anthony Storr's assertion that "mourning is . . . a long drawn out mental process leading to an eventual change of attitude.") We question our assumptions, correct misconceptions, see our situation in a larger context. We begin to   dismantle old ways of thinking and behaving that are no longer appropriate—that could only keep us caught in some kind of permanent "grieving limbo"—so that we can create new ways of thinking and behaving that are useful—that will allow us to create a satisfying life for the future.

Over and over as I have talked with people in the process of writing this book, I have been awed by their heroism. They have not been stopped in their grieving by the traumas of Impact or the depression and disorganization of the Second Crisis. They have taken the opportunity of Observation to begin to make sense of their responses to their losses. And in the Turn they have had the conversations with themselves and have taken the actions that move them forward so that they can finish their grieving.

When I asked these men and women to describe the insights and actions that characterize the Turn, they reported that this phase of the grieving process includes....

RECOGNIZING THAT YOU HAVE SURVIVED
A young widow speaks:

I feel that I am finally beginning to make sense out of my experience of the loss of my husband. You know, there's really no making sense out of the loss itself. To keep on attempting to figure out why *him* on that particular day or why the valves weren't capped on the machine or why he didn't have his hard hat on . . . that's useless. There's just no sense to be made of it.

But I see that there is sense to be made out of my *experience* of the loss. I am beginning to make sense out of who I am and how I am about that. I feel that I'm beginning to sort out what's worth keeping out of the experience, what's worth recognizing about myself and about life and what's not.

For instance, one thing that has come to me in the last few days is the realization that I survived. I survived, and I really actually am turning out well in the face of such a traumatic event. I see today that I didn't die from it; I didn't go permanently crazy; I didn't kill myself. I did things, of course, that hurt me; but that's relatively minor compared to the part of me that was strong enough to endure a process like that.

Now what I have to do is make a stronger identification with that important part of myself. I don't think you get that kind of training when you grow up. You have to decide on your own to cultivate the part of yourself that is strong.

BEING ABLE TO MAKE AN ASSESSMENT
A divorced father relates:

I'm not sure that this loss is anywhere near complete, but I do feel that I have definition. I am Mark Allen, a stockbroker, a friend to a lot of people, and I'm the father of a couple of children. I'm also the ex-husband of a lady who appears to be very unhappy. I'm a person who can now maintain a nice household, who fixes some very good meals, who is beginning to write again, who is getting some national recognition in my field, who is being called on to be a consultant. I'm a person who can now sleep well at night and get started early in the morning. My life has started forming again, from a liquid to a solid, so to speak. And, incidentally, the solid turns to liquid every once in a while. So I'm not without my troubles and everything is not settled in my life, but I am beginning to see where I am and where I have come from. I feel good about myself. That's a wonderful thing to be able to say again, and I am so glad I can say it.

MAKING DISTINCTIONS
A widow states:

It is very educational to be left behind. You realize that there are some things you can do something about and some things you cannot. You can control your own destiny up to a certain point. You can decide what kind of clothes you want to wear; you can pick a house to live in; you can decide what kind of career you're going to have; you can decide where to pursue it. Your everyday life you are in charge of.

But there's a higher level of existence, and I think when you've experienced loss you come to realize that you don't have control of that higher level. You're not one hundred percent in control. Something else is involved. You realize that at that level you have to be prepared to roll with the punches. If something happens and you didn't plan it, it's still a part of life. If you are a survivor. And you have to decide whether you'll be a survivor or not. You have to choose to continue making choices on the everyday level, no matter how enticing it might be to throw your hands up and quit because you don't control the higher level.

I recognized this so clearly a few months after Ash's death. I told my son: "Look, we are not killed; we didn't die; we're not dead.

We're alive, and we've got to stay alive. We can't just go into a cocoon and shut ourselves up, because we won't be able to exist like that. We have to decide to be a part of life. We have to make decisions in all the parts of life that we have any control over."

EXPERIENCING EVENTS THAT ARE UNEXPLAINABLE YET ENLARGING

A woman remembers the loss of a close friend:

For many years I attended a parish church as an active and involved member. When a new mission church was established, I made the extremely difficult choice to leave the old parish. My relationship with the priest at the church that I left was a bumpy one. We had struggled together for more than twenty years—both with our faith and with the ups and downs that come with a close friendship.

One place where Tom and I consistently experienced a warm bond over the years was Camp Afton, a beautifully wooded church camp. Here he led children on nature walks in the woods, and I often went along. It was at Camp Afton that we saw each other again. The occasion was the dedication of a massive wooden cross that had been erected at a new campsite on the lake. After the service Tom and I walked toward each other, and he surprised me with a big hug. There was a positive, healing spirit between us. Some time later, Tom died unexpectedly of cancer.

One day I drove to Camp Afton. I felt such sorrow about Tom's dying. About halfway through the fifty-mile drive, I began to cry, and I cried all the way to Camp Afton. When I got there I parked at the new campsite, and still crying, I walked to the cross on the lake.

There were two large white birds, Moscovy ducks, perched on the arm of the cross. The ducks just sat there, on the arm of that cross, for a long time. Finally, they flew off in unison, completely circled the lake, clockwise, and landed back under the cross, in the water, directly in front of where I was standing. I was transformed in those moments, my sadness replaced with a feeling of peacefulness. It was as if Tom's spirit, and perhaps mine, too, made that flight with the ducks and settled gently at the base of the cross. The experience was, for me, the beginning of a unique and very special healing of a deep loss.

RECOGNIZING THAT THERE IS CONTINUITY
A widow recalls:

It was when we took Akio's ashes back to Japan that I got a sense that life itself has continuity—in spite of the death of individuals. We went to central Japan to the place where Akio's parents are buried. Actually, it's the family graveyard, and there's a temple that has been the family temple for centuries.

We had a burial service at this family temple, and then we walked to the graveyard and the Buddhist priest put the ashes in the stone. The gravestones there are hollow inside with a place to put the ashes.

I felt a deep calm after that ceremony. For me, Akio was now part of that temple that had been there for centuries and, as far as I know, will be there for centuries long after I'm gone. I got a real sense there that life started before we were born and will go on afterward. For me this was very peaceful.

When I got home, I found myself building on that sense of continuity. I became very clear that I wanted to keep up the Japanese side of my life. I am an American, but Akio and I were married for over twenty-five years; and I have been greatly enriched by the Japanese people and culture.

So I said to myself when I got back from Japan, "I'm not going to lose all that." So I read about Japanese things. I keep myself abreast of the culture. This is providing me continuity.

MAKING AN INTERNAL DECISION TO TURN FROM LOSS TO LIVING
A senior citizen whose sister had died asserts:

It has taken me a while, but I've decided life is worth doing anyway. Because you have to live until you die, so you might as well perk up. Attitude is everything. The hardest thing to do after a loss is to know when to say, "I've grieved enough." It's hard to time. But you do get to the place where you know you have a choice. I mean, if you're a living, breathing, semiconscious person, you realize finally that you have to make the choice to have enough nerve to do something.

DECIDING NOT TO BE A VICTIM

A divorced woman told this story:

One day I said to myself, "Sally, you've pined long enough. Get up from this couch and make yourself some clothes. You've got to go out and get a job." So I began to sew. As soon as I had a couple of outfits made, I decided it was time to start looking for work. By this time I had contacted my friends and said, "If you hear of anything, let me know." Something came open rather suddenly, and so it was take myself down there and get the job because no one else is going to do it for you.

I also had to relearn all kinds of things—like how to reconcile a bank statement and balance the checkbook. And establish a whole new network. You know, like find someone you can trust to tell you really what's wrong with your car and not charge you an arm and a leg for fixing it. Who you can get to fix the lawn mower when it breaks. Who puts up part of a fence when it blows down in a storm and who comes right out when you have a plumbing emergency. Where the safety lane sticker place is and when do you need to go there. All those things. You have to establish a whole new network of people in the community, and you have to just move out there and do it. I've seen women carry on about this forever. But the way I see it, you can complain or you can do it. And your life is a heck of a lot happier if you just do it.

ACKNOWLEDGING THAT YOU ARE RESPONSIBLE
FOR YOUR OWN HAPPINESS

A mother says:

You can't drag around a ghost and be happy. That's a choice we all make. And the way I had been operating was a dead-end street. I had been dragging the past around and feeling sorry for myself and waiting for someone else to do something that would make me feel happy. But I know now nobody else is responsible for your happiness. Nobody! Not your husband, not your parents, not your children, not your best friend—*you*. Every tub must sit on its own bottom.

And that goes double for anybody who wants to be happy after losing. Your state of mind is literally your choice, no matter what happens to you. And I'm not saying that I won't remember something tomorrow that will put me back into this business of saying one more time, "Here I am, little Janinne, saying 'Poor me.'" But I can assure you that I may go ahead and feel sorry for myself for a little while, but then I'll do something to get myself out of it. I choose not to stay miserable, and I know I'm the only one who can do anything about it.

Recently, I was lonesome and blue, missing Meredith terribly. So I got out my knitting needles and started knitting a sweater for her boyfriend. I knitted and cried into my knitting. I put all my love for Meredith into that sweater for a few hours, and I got myself out of feeling sorry for myself.

My husband said to me when he saw me crying: "Go ahead and feel sorry for yourself for a little while. That's okay. Because I know you well enough to know that you're going to get tired of this before twenty-four hours have gone by, and you're going to do something about it." Isn't that a wonderful attitude for a husband to have?

UNDERSTANDING THERE HAS TO BE A NEW FORM FOR THE RELATIONSHIP

A widow recalls:

One day I realized that it had been almost three years since Martin had died, and I still had so much of his "stuff" everywhere. I had gathered a lot of his things and put them in one place upstairs, and there they were staring at me every time I went in that direction: his briefcase just the way he had left it. The notes he took at our Lamaze class before Jimmy was born. All the notebooks from the classes he took years ago when he was in college. And downstairs it wasn't much better. The cabinet was full of his albums, most of them left over from college days. The bookshelves had so many of his books on them that I had no room to store new ones. The desk in the family room had something of his in every drawer: old receipts from the gas station, figurings he had done for building a deck on his brother's house, notecards for presentations at work.

Suddenly, I had the urge to get rid of all this stuff. The urge shocked me, but that was what I really felt like doing. I asked myself, "What are you trying to do—forget Martin? Pretend he never existed?" But that wasn't it. All those things belonged to a Martin I had loved who had lived in this house. And the Martin I loved now was different; he was not present; he didn't need old college notes and service station records. I knew I would always be close to Martin —he would always be with me—but that closeness was not related to hanging on to his things.

So I went into the living room and made a fire in the fireplace. Then I started burning everything that would burn. It was a chilly day, but can you imagine how hot a fire gets when you are burning years of accumulation? I finally had to turn on the air conditioner. I took all the albums and books down to the half-price bookstore, and they bought them. My sister-in-law happened to come in when I was gathering together the things I was going to get rid of. "You mean, you're going to throw away these notes he took at your Lamaze class?" she said. "How can you throw away anything that has his handwriting on it?" I realized then that if you're going to do something like this, you should probably do it in private. Because it is only *you* who knows why you are doing this. It is only *you* who knows that the relationship you have now with the dead person doesn't rely on objects or things for its reality.

FINDING SATISFACTION THROUGH OTHER WAY OF RELATING

A son tells this story:

I keep my dad with me symbolically through this old truck. One of the things Dad and I always worked on together was old trucks. That was a big part of our lives. He'd cruise the countryside and find trucks sitting in people's backyards—old clunkers, it didn't matter— and he'd make them an offer: "Hey, I'll give you fifty dollars to haul that old thing off." And they'd say, "Sure, get rid of it." He'd bring the old thing home; and he and I would tinker with it, get it running, and then sell it. Once in a while we painted them. We painted one bright orange with green bumpers and called it the Pumpkin.

I always wanted one of those trucks, but we were never in the position for me to have one. Now when this truck came along—Dad bought it from a rancher up around Sacramento; I don't know why the man sold it, he came back the next day and tried to buy it back— Dad and I agreed it was the best truck we had ever run into. Everything on it was original. So we kept it. When I got ready to leave home, I said to Dad, "If you ever get in a position where you need to sell this truck, you tell me because I'll find the money somewhere to buy it so we can keep it." It never got to that place, though; and when he died the truck was about the only thing he had left, and I got it. It's a family heirloom, and it's my obligation to keep this truck as long as it exists.

So now when I go to teach my classes at the university, I drive this truck every day. When the transmission jumps out of gear, which it invariably does at about forty miles per hour, I laugh and think, "Oh, that's Dad saying, 'You're going too fast for this old truck; slow down.'" This old truck keeps me in touch with him. I get in here and talk to him. It's not "talk" to him, really, but I feel close to him when I'm in the truck. It's a kind of connection.

STARTING TO REBUILD YOUR BELIEF SYSTEM
A widow says:

I don't know what I believe in since Jim died. Everything I thought was true in the past now seems suspect. But the other day I did have an insight. I was asking a friend of mine what she thought was in the hereafter, and she said she didn't know, that she had her ideas and these ideas gave her life meaning but that certainly didn't mean they were accurate. She said, "Whatever the hereafter is like, it is going to be completely different from this world. So I relish every day I live on the planet because I want to know as much as possible about life in this form. I want to do everything there is to do here and learn everything there is to learn." As soon as she said this, I felt an intense desire to do the same. I realized this life I had now was something to be explored, to be known. My attitude really changed as a result of that conversation. I don't want to be sick even one day now! I don't want to miss anything.

RECOGNIZING WHAT IS GOOD FOR YOU
A divorced woman tells this story:

In getting myself pointed toward a new life, I've had to get rid of some old friends. I know this may sound negative, or maybe even tacky, but there are some people who are happy only when things are bad. They enjoy the drama of hard times. I have a few friends who fall into this category. If I'm feeling low and terrible, they want to be right there; but if I'm feeling up and happy, they keep saying things like "I know you really miss David," or "I'm sure glad to see you having a good day; I know it's rough for you," etc., etc.

Well, by now, this far along after the divorce, I want to move on, and I think they subconsciously don't want me to. The other day I ran into a friend at the grocery store, and she said, "Oh, I never see you anymore; you don't ever call." I just stopped my cart right there and said to her, "You know, Karen, you're really a sweet person. I'm fond of you. I'd like always to be your friend. But I haven't called you because all you want to do is talk about the past. Every time I see you, your conversation is all about how is my ex-husband, have I seen him, how are the children adjusting, how am I doing. And while I care—" Then she interrupted me. "Oh," she said, "I know, it's just too painful." And I interrupted her and said, "No, Karen, it's not painful now at all. It's just boring."

RECOGNIZING THAT YOU MAY NEED PSYCHIATRIC HELP TO MAKE THE TRANSITION

A young widow with two children reports:

One morning I realized that I was not able to love my children. I was just getting through the day with them the same way I was just getting through the day at work—fifteen minutes at a time. The only thing that occupied me fully was thinking about Darrell's death. On this particular morning I realized that this was how I was coping—I had just shut off all feelings, including feelings for my children. I was now aware of how much I missed the feeling of love and companionship with them. I knew we needed each other, but I was not available.

So I made the choice to take my life insurance money—which I was guarding with my life—and go see a psychiatrist. For me, this was one of the scariest things I had ever done. First of all, people I know just don't go to psychiatrists. It was like an admission that you're crazy, and you just don't go. And second, it seemed like so much money!

But I was determined to do whatever it took to get back in touch with my love for my children. I said, "I'll go Monday, Tuesday, Wednesday, Thursday, and Friday if it's necessary. I'll tell that psychiatrist everything that's happened since kindergarten!" That's how willing I was to do anything to return to the land of the living.

What I've discovered by going to the psychiatrist is that I already had many of these problems and they just came to light as a result of Darrell's dying. I'm working on the problems now, and already I can tell a difference. I've made the choice to change and not live the way I did in the past. Just going and asking for help was the first step.

DECIDING TO DO SOMETHING THAT IMPLIES YOU WILL BE RESPONSIBLE FOR YOURSELF AND YOUR FUTURE

A widower recalls:

One day I decided, "Hey, I'm sick and tired of eating in restaurants. I'm not willing to keep on running away from myself and from learning how to do things on my own. Tonight I'm going to fix round steak and cream gravy!"

So I stopped at Kroger's and picked up a beautiful piece of round steak—a little expensive and far too much for one person. But I'd just eat the leftovers, I said to myself. "I'll have parsley boiled potatoes that you can put gravy over, a fresh loaf of bread, and a little salad—lettuce, tomato, some mayonnaise on it."

So, I started preparing all of this as soon as I got home. I was really anxious. I cooked the steak, cut up the salad, got the potatoes to boiling. Then I thought, "Oh, my God, I don't know how to make gravy." I'd tried when Laura was alive, and it always came out in one piece instead of liquid. "Well," I thought, "it's time for you to learn. If you're going to have gravy, that's what you got to do. What you gonna do, otherwise—invite Mama down from Oklahoma to cook it for you?"

I began. "Settle down and think about it: if you do this first and this second, it's probably going to turn out all right. Do it carefully, do it slowly, take your time, learn how to do it." I ended up making the most beautiful pot of cream gravy you've ever seen. The only thing was that I made too much; but I saved it and put it on my toast the next morning.

You know, I found myself to some extent—I found this independence, this ability to live on my own—through cooking that cream gravy. After I made the gravy, I took on an even bigger project—doing my own washing. I had always divided everything into man's work/woman's work before Laura died. Now it all was my work.

Riding the crest of the wave of the gravy success, I said, "I'm going to do some hot-water washing with some bleach. I'm going to get my things really white."

So I read the instructions on the washing machine and the instructions on the bleach bottle. I put all that information together, and I did a wash and then I did a dry. I remember that when I took those things out of the dryer, it was dark. I reached in and bundled them all up and took them to the living room where I had been listening to music and put them on the sofa to fold them up.

I was so pleased that I almost wanted to say, "What do I need a wife for?" This was another mark of success. Success at taking the responsibility for putting yourself together again. You know, all the king's horses and all the king's men couldn't do it, so how can you? You don't think that finding out how to put yourself together again consists of things like washing clothes and making cream gravy.

THE FOCUS DURING THE TURN

When we hear these stories, the Turn seems like such a logical— and positive—development in the grieving process that we wonder, "Why do people find it hard to make the Turn? What makes it so difficult? Why do some actually choose not to make it?" The answers to these questions lie in the changes in our thinking and behavior that have to occur to make the Turn possible.

New Form for the Relationship

The first thing that stands in our way of making the Turn is a fear that if we look to the future, we will have to turn our backs on the past. I remember a widow's outrage at a suggestion in a book she was reading on grieving that she put a chair in front of her, mentally place her husband there, and say good-bye to him. "I didn't want to say good-bye to him; I wanted him in my life forever," she said vehemently. "So I threw the book down and never finished reading it."

I understand this reaction. The widow was equating saying good-bye to her husband with forgetting him. I am sure this was not the intent of the author's suggestion, but it is easy to see how there could be a blurring of distinctions. I remember I kept asking after Greg died, "But how do you love a dead person?" The feelings I had for this man were as strong and deep as they had ever been, and the fact that he was not present to receive my affection only increased my attachment.

In his book *Loss and Change,* Peter Marris talks about this dilemma. If the very purposes and meaning of our lives are integrally connected with this lost person, how can we put our past behind us? Would that not denigrate the central role played in our lives by that person? And if we were able to let the person go, wouldn't that devalue what he or she meant to us and, by association, devalue all our relationships? And would we not be callous persons if relationships could be changed so easily?

Of course, one way that we attempt to solve the dilemma is to keep the person in our minds—and as much as possible in our lives—the way they were in the past. This is the only way we know how to express the fact that we still love them. We see this behavior in the extreme in Queen Victoria's legendary order that her late husband's shaving articles be laid out every morning as if he were still alive. We see it in less extreme fashion in the lives of those people who two or three years after a person's death or departure have made few if any significant changes that indicate the person is no longer present.

The fact that we can understand the motive for behavior such as this does not make the behavior any less debilitating. No matter how hard we attempt to keep the lost persons present in our lives through such means as talking about them as if they were still alive, avoiding disposing of their ashes or getting a headstone, and keeping their possessions around us, we are not successful. In reality they are absent, no matter how much we want the situation to be otherwise. So we remain stuck, not able to make even those changes we want to make and know would be good for us. We are stretched taut, wanting to remain close to the person who is gone but going about it in a way that can only bring failure. As time goes on we have more and more upsets, with ourselves and with others, upsets associated with the way we are trying to continue to relate to the lost person. Life is made all the more miserable.

As a part of the experiences of the Turn, we must learn how to alter our relationship with the lost person so that she or he remains a part of our lives but in ways that are appropriate. Dr. Sidney Zisook and his colleagues put it this way: "It is as if the survivor ultimately finds a comfortable place for the deceased, a place where memories, thoughts, and images exist but no longer overwhelm or predominate...." It is a mistake, they say, to expect that the death of someone means that the relationship is over, for a healthy adaptation "includes the evolution of a new form of this relationship and its integration into the changing life and personality of the bereaved."

At this point in the grieving process we must make a clear distinction between those "patterns of thought, feeling and behaviour that are clearly no longer appropriate . . . which only make sense if the lost person is physically present" and those that allow us to remain linked to the person in a positive way through maintaining values and pursuing goals that we shared with the lost person. We are able, as John Bowlby points out, to "retain a strong sense of the continuing presence of [the lost person] without the turmoils of hope and disappointment, search and frustration, anger and blame, that are present earlier."

I recently saw a beautiful example of a mother and father working to establish this kind of altered relationship. The son, who had been killed in an automobile accident, and his father were alumni of the same university; both had participated in the same military program, a program that for more than a hundred years had created strong bonds among its members. To perpetuate a record of this shared history, the university had established a collection of class rings worn by the cadets in this program, a collection that went back to the 1800s. The parents of the young man who had been killed decided to give their son's senior class ring to this collection and did so in a lovely ceremony, conducted with strength and dignity.

Through this ceremony the parents were acting on the reality that their son was no longer present to wear his ring, yet they were showing their love for him through honoring a commitment they had shared together, a commitment to the principles and practices that had been so important in both the father's and the son's training. Every time the story of these rings is told in the future to new cadets and their parents, the values and ideals of this young man's life will also be present. How he had chosen to live his life will, therefore, continue to make a contribution. Although finding ways to establish a "new form" for their relationship with their son will, of course, be an ongoing process, these parents have made a positive beginning.

New Ways of Thinking

To make the Turn we must also identify and change old ways of thinking that would keep us from going forward in our grieving. Observers have pointed out that people who are destined to remain stuck in their mourning think repeatedly: "I am incapable of changing the situation for the better; I am intrinsically unlovable and thus permanently incapable of making or maintaining any affectional bonds." These individuals focus constantly on their own suffering and become "morbidly introspective." They also often become hypochondriacs.

Persons engaged in healthy mourning, on the other hand, work during the Turn to recognize self-defeating thoughts and substitute for them more accurate assessments. Aaron Beck, M.D., describes the process this way, using the analogy of learning a new language:

> When an adult . . . attempts to learn a new language, then he has to concentrate on the formation of words and sentences. Similarly, when he has a problem in interpreting certain aspects of reality, it may be useful for him to focus on the rules he applies in making judgments. In examining a problem area, he finds that the rule is incorrect or that he has been applying it incorrectly.
>
> Since making the incorrect judgments has probably become a deeply ingrained habit, which he may not be conscious of, several steps are required to correct it. First, he has to become aware of what he is thinking. Second, he needs to recognize what thoughts are awry. Then he has to substitute accurate for inaccurate judgments. Finally, he needs feedback to inform him whether his changes are correct. The same kind of sequence is necessary for making behavioral changes....

At the Turn we must examine what Dr. Beck calls our "automatic thoughts" to see if they are keeping us from changing. We are able to do this by recognizing that "it is possible to perceive a thought, focus on it, and evaluate it" just as it is possible to identify and reflect on a sensation such as a backache or an external stimulus such as a request that we turn down the radio. Then we must challenge and replace the thoughts we have that are "maladaptive" with the kind of thoughts that will empower us to move on to complete our mourning.

Reassessing Our Worldview

Look at these two quotations, both from the same scientific study ("A Multidimensional Model of Spousal Bereavement"):

> One of the mainstays of the bereaved is the operation of their faith. This is a powerful and effective means of coping with death and seems to operate in a number of ways: it can facilitate acceptance, provide meaning, offer help and support through God, combat loneliness, and offer the bereaved a chance to reunite with their spouse in heaven.

> The bereaved . . . go through a significant and at times radical alteration of their world view—the set of beliefs by which they operate. Following their loss, the bereaved are frequently floundering for direction, often well into the second year. This loss of direction and meaning is precipitated by the disruption of the plans and hopes they shared with their spouses, or by shattering of belief systems which governed many of their actions: beliefs in being able to control one's destiny, maintain invincibility, belief in a just and merciful God.... All such beliefs are challenged, fall short, and leave a vacuum that only gradually becomes filled again....

These seemingly contradictory statements illustrate the complexity of the role of faith and belief in the mourning process. We can only reconcile the seeming contradiction when we focus on the words in the second quotation: "a vacuum that only gradually becomes filled again." Our belief systems are like the phoenix that burns, only to rise to life again from the ashes. At first we question everything. Then, as we grapple with what has happened, we begin to discover those things we can say we believe in, those ideas, convictions, and experiences that we return to again and again as the context for our thinking and our action.

By the time we reach the Turn, we are becoming clearer about what we can and do believe in. For some, it is a reconfirming of a traditional faith. These individuals come to see that "biblical faith does not shield us from the facts of life," as Glen Davidson points out. But, he continues, "God does not disappear in the presence of imperfection—death, loss, or suffering...." The "human sufferer can live the seeming contradiction of growing through losing."

For others, the vacuum is being filled not with reconfirmed beliefs, but instead by "modified" reassertions of these old beliefs and even "at times with totally new ones, reflecting the finiteness and fragility of life and the limits of control." I know that in my own case, the quite dogmatic belief system I had before Greg died—a system that had *me* and *my actions* at the center—was being replaced by the time I had reached the Turn by a faith that contained a much greater sense of reverence, awe, and mystery. Sidney Zisook and Stephen Shuchter point out that these reconfirmed, modified or new belief systems play a very important part in the lives of the bereaved, showing up in many ways: the bereaved become "more appreciative of daily living, more patient and accepting, and more giving. They may develop new careers or change them, enjoy themselves with more gusto, or find new outlets for creativity." Such insight and understanding is one of the marks of the Turn. We begin to see what we do believe in and to use that belief system to support our commitments and our actions.

THE CHOICE

What is the only choice of value during the Turn?

We must choose to make an assertion.

Assert, declare, and *affirm*. These words have a shared meaning: *to state or put forward positively, usually in anticipation of or in the face of denial or objection.* That is exactly what we have to do during the Turn. To proclaim, either in words or in actions, that we *will* go forward, even though our pain is still present, our future unknown. With conviction, we declare that we will incorporate this loss into our life in a way that will enable us to move forward. We make an internal decision to replan our lives to include this change.

In a study of widows carried out at Harvard University, an important finding revealed the relationship between making an assertion and the Turn. John Bowlby, remarking on this study, points out that for those women whose grieving was moving toward a creative outcome, "at a particular moment during the year they had asserted themselves in some way and had thereafter found themselves on a path to recovery." In the study itself, the authors speak of "the first determined movement of a widow" and write, "Often this is a painful task.... But when it was completed it became a statement that one era of a widow's life had ended and another was beginning." For some this assertion took the form of sorting through the husband's clothes. For some there are other commitments and actions. But each one of these women in some fashion—in the terms of the definition of assertion: "to put oneself forward positively"—had made a statement that she would not remain stuck in her grieving.

The assertion we must make during the Turn exists first as an internal commitment, a private decision: *I will live through this loss. I will contribute to my own rehabilitation. I will incorporate this loss into my life and move into the future. I will make the necessary changes.* This commitment, then, after it is made internally, shows up in external action.

What makes such an assertion difficult?

There is a danger in giving up the role of helpless griever. We are required to be responsible for ourselves. We may not always know what to do in certain situations. We may be awkward and even fail. It is a risk, then, to make an assertion. For some, this fact is a serious deterrent.

Perhaps making the assertion will cost us the support of some of our friends or decrease the amount of attention that is paid to us. If people don't have to look after us and help us, how do we know they will still call and come over? And aren't some people comfortable only with those who are weak and needy? If we make an assertion that reveals strength and forward movement, we don't know what will be the repercussions among those around us.

Perhaps the most difficult hurdle of all in choosing to make an assertion relates to the basic issue of loyalty to the lost person. If we love this person, how can we go on without her? If we were deeply connected, wouldn't we naturally exhibit ongoing dejection? Many people believe that remaining inconsolable is the only way to show how much the lost person meant to them. This is a powerful myth. And it takes courage not to be persuaded by it. To make an assertion toward the future carries with it the task of making a distinction between forgetting about the person and what he or she meant in our lives and finding appropriate and comfortable ways to include the lost person in what is nevertheless going to be a new future.

I don't think it is too dramatic to say that the choice of the Turn—*to make an assertion*—is a life-or-death issue. We will either make an assertion that shows we are committing to the second half of the mourning process—which centers on the longer-term adjustments related to roles and identity, to relationship patterns, to resolution of past/present conflicts and issues—or we will stagnate and wither. Instead of experiencing the grieving process, many people choose to make permanent a life-style based on those coping defenses that they hope will protect them from pain and awareness. Speaking of the attitude of such individuals, the editors of the Institute of Medicine's report on bereavement point out: "Not only is there no movement, but there also is a sense that the person will not permit any movement." The loss has become the explanation for why life has to be the way it is; the loss has become an excuse.

Those who choose not to make the Turn but choose instead to have their grief become a way of life live different fates. Some become chronic mourners or compulsive caregivers; some avoid mourning, continuing behavior begun soon after the loss occurred: losing themselves in work, alcohol and other drugs, frantic activity, delinquent behavior, destructive living patterns. Some become or continue to be ill, and some die. Some become clinically and/or chronically depressed. Some become recklessly euphoric, perhaps even manic.

But many who do not make the Turn are not so easily identified. In fact, they may look as if they are unaffected by their unfinished grieving. Perhaps they will be "self-sufficient . . . proud of their independence and self-control, scornful of sentiment." They may act as if nothing has happened, yet a closer examination of their behavior reveals that they have become tense and short-tempered. They may have "headaches, palpitations, aches and pains. Insomnia is common, dreams unpleasant." In some, "cheerfulness seems a little forced; others appear wooden and too formal. Some are more sociable than formerly, others withdrawn; in either case there may be excessive drinking. Bouts of tears or depression may come from what appears a clear sky. Certain topics are carefully avoided." These who have not grieved may also become compulsive caretakers, always finding someone to look after who is weaker than they are.

A third group who choose not to finish their grieving may show neither aberrant behavior nor take on a persona of self-sufficiency. In fact, these people seem to suffer no breakdown or change of any kind. Yet research shows that, as a result of not finishing their grieving, they "feel none the less deeply dissatisfied with their lives." Their personal relations are empty. They feel depersonalized and have a "sense of unreality." They exist as what Donald Winnicott calls a "false self." Many are brittle and hard; "difficult to live and work with," having "little understanding either of others or of themselves," often "responsible for the breakdown of others; readily aroused to smoldering jealousy and resentment"; feeling isolated, unloved, and sad in the extreme but not revealing these feelings.

WHAT WE NEED FROM FAMILY AND FRIENDS DURING THE TURN

I remember the way a friend of mine put it when I was living the experiences of the Turn. "Elizabeth," he said, "what you need now is tough love and ruthless compassion." And that was how he interacted with me, a fact for which today I am very grateful. He—and others—acted as if they expected me to establish my own autonomy, gave support as I started the work of establishing a new identity, even helped initiate certain turning points such as planning the first vacation I would take alone, and applauded me because I had exhibited a change in attitude and begun to take important steps toward a new future.

One of the things we may have to do during the Turn is to winnow out those companions and acquaintances who want to dwell only on the past, who continue to make sympathetic gestures of rallying around us and relieving us of our roles and obligations, who perhaps are themselves incomplete with their own grieving. We may also have to ask for the kind of support we now need. Those around us may be in a habit of responding to us in certain ways out of respect for the difficulties they know we are experiencing. "You have to retrain your environment," is the way one widow put it. "At this point the most important thing you can do," she added, "is to let people around you know that you are committed to starting a second life and that you would appreciate their help and their support."

Once when I was in Santa Fe I bought a book about D. H. Lawrence's experience in New Mexico. In one of these essays Lawrence writes about the thoughts and practices of Native Americans, whose stories he had heard and whose ceremonies he had witnessed. Native Americans, he states, so long as they are pure, have "only two great negative commandments.

Thou shalt not lie.
Thou shalt not be a coward.
Positively, [their] one commandment is:
Thou shalt acknowledge the wonder."

For this phase of the grieving process, The Turn, I don't think we could find any better guidance.

5

Reconstruction

If you're doing nothing, you're doing wrong.

LORD MOUNTBATTEN

The surf was so strong that I had to turn up the volume on the cassette player under my lounge chair. Taking advantage of the lull between the summer and fall semesters at the university, I had invited my parents to join me at this isolated spot on the coast of North Carolina. It was early in the week, but the three of us had already settled into a comfortable routine. After breakfast my father fished, my mother crocheted, and I came out to the sand dune in front of our rental cottage to read, write, and listen to music.

The first task of the morning was to set up my "work area"— make sure the rickety side table was close enough to the lounge chair so I could reach my coffee, stack up the cassette boxes on the sand in a certain order, put out my books, pen, and writing tablet. As I got organized, I kept thinking of a line from *Moby Dick*—something about "When it's November in my soul, I get myself down to the sea." Today, perhaps more than ever before, I could understand Ishmael's motivation and appreciate his wisdom. For even though we had been here only two days, already the rhythm of life by the ocean had begun to enlarge my spirit and wear away my sharp edges.

Haydn's 100th Symphony was playing, and I was reading Anne Morrow Lindbergh's *Gift from the Sea*. This was not a book I had brought with me but one I had found in the bookcase in the cottage. Greg had been reading *Gift from the Sea* on the afternoon he died; the book was lying on his work table, with a passage marked that he intended to insert into the manuscript on which he was working. It had made me happy to find the book because Greg, never far from my thoughts in the entire fifteen months since his death, had been on my mind a lot since we had arrived here.

I recognized the passage he had planned to use when I came to it. "But I want first of all. . .to be at peace with myself. . . .an inner harmony, essentially spiritual, which can be translated into outer harmony." This passage struck me again, as it had when I first read it, as the perfect epitaph. If Greg had known he was going to die, I thought to myself, he couldn't have picked a more appropriate final testimony.

But today there was something else about these words . . . I couldn't put my finger on why, but reading the paragraph today bothered—even provoked—me.

I put the book down in my lap and looked out at the ocean. A fleet of shrimp boats was passing in the far distance. The scene was mesmerizing: the flat plane of the ocean, the center poles of the boats rising against that horizon, the high booms turning first left and then right as the nets were moved in the water. As I watched, I realized . . . what was it? Ah, the clue was in the geometry. In looking at those lines and angles, I was seeing not only ocean and boats, booms and center poles; I was seeing *harmony*.

Harmony that in my own life was not present.

I looked back at the paragraph. *I want a central core to my life . . . purity of intention, singleness of eye. . . I want to be at peace with myself. . . inner . . . outer harmony . . . at one.* Those words stung me. I realized that even though I had turned toward the future, even though I had found a new job that brought me into contact with different people and gave me some diversion, those things were not the same as the "purity of intention" that Anne Morrow Lindbergh was writing about. In spite of these changes, my daily life still had no central core, no true purpose. Where everything meaningful had been when Greg was alive was still only a vacuum.

"Great," I said, slapping the book down on the table. "I'll put it in my schedule: *Get meaning in daily life at ten o'clock next Thursday.*" I was sick and tired of always having to work on something related to Greg's death. When would life feel just like normal living? When would I be through with all this adjusting? I reached down to change the music, putting the Bob Seger tape into the Sony. As I began to gather up my things to go inside, "Against the Wind" was the song that was playing.

The sun was just starting to go down as I headed out to the beach for my daily run. Off and on all day, thoughts about the passage in *Gift from the Sea* had aggravated me; but as I jogged along, seeing the reflection of the strong afternoon light on the wet

sand, I began to feel less irritable. A line from Proust came to my
mind—"If I were dying," he had said, "and the sun made a patch of
light on the floor, my spirit would rise in happiness." It made me
happy to remember the quotation.

I thought about the fascination light had had for me since earliest
childhood. I could remember many days before I started to school
sitting alone, perfectly content to do nothing but watch the light
move across the wide boards of our front porch all morning. As an
adult, I had finally understood this drawing I felt to light when I
read Camus's observation that in all of our lives there are two or
three important images in whose presence our hearts were first
opened. I knew that light was one of my images.

As I jogged along, I thought, too, of the day Greg and I first met.
It had always been the light of that afternoon that had stood out in
my memory. But I realized, almost with a start, that since Greg had
died light had not been very important to me. In fact, light was now
something that I very seldom noticed.

It was then that the idea occurred to me. One way I could start
building harmony in my daily life would be to change my home environment. I could move furniture, paint the walls another color . . .
why, I could even put in a skylight! The thought made me feel
almost giddy. Even as I ran, I could see the light streaming into my
den, making moving patterns on the ceramic tile floor. By the time
I got back to the beach cottage, the skylight was already installed
and I was sitting under it.

The next day I woke up excited. The idea of rearranging my
house and installing a skylight had released a whole ream of other
possibilities. About midmorning I got to my "work place" on the
beach and took out my pen and tablet. "Decide how you want your
life," I tutored myself, "and then start working to make those things
happen."

The first thing I did was write at the top of the page: "A Credo
for My Life." Then these were the points I listed:

1. Be good to yourself.
2. Have fun.
3. Love others.
4. Make a contribution.

I began to make a list of things I wanted: To create a new beautiful and nourishing home environment.... To have a wonderful man to share my life with.... To spend and invest money wisely.... To eat well and continue to exercise faithfully.... To learn to dance and swim.... To enlarge my circle of friends.... To feel safe and secure alone.... To get satisfaction every day from how things are.... Making this list, I felt almost euphoric. What many people had told me before, I was now beginning to realize for myself: I *did* have my whole life ahead of me. I *could* rebuild the central core of my life. I *was* strong and able.

Later that day I was looking through one of those sophisticated women's magazines. ELEVEN RECORDS TO MAKE LOVE BY, the headline read: Ravel's *Bolero,* Debussy's *Prelude Afternoon of a Faun,* Santana's *Abraxos, Rainstorm,* Gato Barbieri's *Caliente!,* Bolling's Suite for Flute & Jazz Piano, Mozart's Piano Concerto No. 21, Faure's *Requiem,* Marvin Gaye's "I Want You," Stephane Grappelli's "Uptown Dance," and *Ella Fitzgerald Sings Cole Porter Songbook.* I knew something very important had shifted in my outlook when I found myself copying this list into my journal.

But the euphoria didn't last.

I discovered when I got back home that it is no small task to turn goals set on a beach in North Carolina into reality back in Texas. Putting in the skylight was just one example.

When the carpenter came to give me an estimate, he found there was only enough space to put a very small skylight in the den roof. But, he pointed out, if we removed one wall of Greg's office and incorporated that space into the den, we could put in a much bigger skylight. This was much more of an undertaking than I had counted on, of course, but to have a minuscule skylight would defeat the whole purpose. I decided to do the remodeling.

One of my first tasks was clearing out Greg's office. I wrote an advertisement for the typewriter, desk and desk chair, and bookcases and also decided at the last minute to include his motorcycle, which was doing nobody any good stored out in the utility room. When the ad came out on Saturday, several people came to see the items. It pleased me to lower the price of the typewriter so that a young mother who was a new graduate student could buy it. The woman who bought the desk and chair was getting them as a surprise for her husband's birthday, and that made me happy. When I saw that Greg's helmet would fit the young boy whose parents were buying him his first motorcycle, I threw that in for good measure.

But after the last buyer left late in the afternoon, all my composure disappeared and I went to pieces. It felt as if I had sold every piece of furniture I owned and that the whole house was empty. I walked back and forth in the house crying, doing my best to avoid looking at Greg's vacant office. I turned on the television, but every program was boring. I tried to eat but immediately became sick to my stomach. I poured a glass of wine, but all I managed to do was turn the glass over on a beautiful area rug from Norway and ruin it. I finally went to bed, hoping that when I woke up I'd feel better.

But I wasn't so lucky. The next day was Sunday. When the clock radio came on, Kris Kristofferson was singing. It couldn't have been a worse selection: "There's something on a Sunday makes a body feel alone...." I missed Greg so much. The pain in my lower back was so severe that I couldn't turn or bend. "Those are tears in my back," I thought. "The tissues and muscles are knotted up with all my aloneness." It hurt so to move that it took me several minutes to get out of bed and down to the kitchen.

I fixed a cup of coffee and turned on the radio in the kitchen. Again; luck was with me. The song that was playing was "For the Good Times." "How favored can a person be?" I asked sarcastically. "The disc jockey has picked all these songs just for me."

I could not ever remember being so lonely. I tried to call my girlfriend Felicia in Tennessee, and when she wasn't home I picked up the pad and pencil by the telephone and began to write her a letter:

> *It's chilly this morning here in Texas. Right now I'm listening to Emmylou Harris and thinking of cold rainy winter days when Greg and I were so content and satisfied and dwelled in the sky called love.*

*The stew in the pot, his bringing the wood in from the yard,
his bare legs sticking out from under his green trench coat—
oh, I miss him so much today. I miss the softness, the lack of
trying, the not being constantly under the demand called
resolving and adjusting. I am so tired of being brave and
getting on with it and learning from my experience and beginning a new life—all those positive things that you're supposed
to do after losing. Instead, I'd like to roll in the rug called
"the world's good," the rug called "I love you. "*

As I wrote, the tears splotched the paper in front of me. I had to
wait a few minutes before I could finish the letter.

*It's hard for my arms to reach all the way round to the back;
my fingers won't meet to give me a hug. And try as I might, I
can't manage to rest my head in that comforting, warm, secure,
hollow place in my shoulder.*

Over the next weeks the tension was almost unbearable. But I
knew I could not run from it. I had to resolve this painful conflict.
"Otherwise," I asked myself, "what is your alternative?" Already I
knew the answer: regression and stagnation. Living life in a coma,
as a colleague put it.

But it was a constant battle. Nothing pulled me. I was almost
overcome with lethargy; I was bored, listless. When the carpenter
began the skylight renovation, I wasn't interested. I had to force
myself to call someone to help me pick out new colors for the
interior. It took enormous effort to do something as simple as invite
a new faculty member in our department over to have lunch on
Saturday. In fact, I had to *make* myself do everything; nothing
came easy or naturally. All I really *wanted* to do was curl up in a
ball and hide under a blanket.

Then my friend Felicia wrote back from Tennessee. "I know
this time is hard. I know everything feels like chaos and devasta-
tion. But be patient. Remember, you are a project under reconstruction."

A project under reconstruction. That statement gave me perspective. How things were now wasn't how they would always be.

Everything wasn't final. My life was in process, and this uncomfortable feeling of betwixt and between, this phase of confusion and unsettledness, was just something I had to live through.

When I answered Felicia's letter, I sent her a copy of a Jack Kerouac quip I had found and also taped up on my bathroom mirror: "Look, walking on water wasn't built in a day." I wanted Felicia to know that I had gotten the message.

But the loneliness persisted. Even in a group, even with my friends, even with my family, I was lonely. It was the loneliness of being separate, of being without an intimate connection, of having no one I could plan my life with. Everything felt so incomplete, so tentative.

What I wanted more than anything in the world was a relationship like the one I had had with Greg. I wanted to matter and be important to a special man, to have him be central in my life and me in his. I wanted someone to drink hot buttered rum with when we finished decorating the tree on Christmas Eve, someone to help me dye the eggs that went on the circle of cinnamon buns I made every Easter, someone whose legs curved around me when we were asleep. I wanted sex that was an expression of love, not conquest and need. More than anything else in the world, I wanted to be married.

I had thought early on that I had found the right person. "How could I be so lucky," I marveled, "that the first man I go out with after Greg's death would be just perfect?" Even now I still remembered his genuineness, his tenderness, the way I felt strong and light when he left after that first date. In fact, that was the day I had taken the towel down from the uncurtained kitchen window; somehow the outside had not seemed so threatening.

For a few weeks I had thought our relationship was heaven. I loved to go to the house with big windows he had built himself in the middle of the woods. I loved the meals he cooked—biscuits, chicken fried quail, gravy. I loved his curiosity. "How would you like to see the underside of a house?" he asked one day when we were stalled behind an old structure being transported on a trailer.

He pulled over to the side of the road; we got out and crawled under the house to see its construction. I loved his teaching me to shoot a pistol. I loved finding books by Nietzsche on his night table.

But I tried too hard to be wanted. I was too needy. I made everything too serious. Things became strained between us. When I pressed for more togetherness than he was willing to give, he left. Even though I could now see that it had been for the best—that it was the potential for friendship and not romantic love that he had offered—then it had been a very hard lesson.

Since that time—not counting the one or two other good men who also came and went in my life very briefly—I had met no one I could picture spending my life with. In those months after I returned from Chicago, when I was so off-center and depressed, I had had my fill of dating men I didn't admire and didn't like just to have somebody to go out with. So for a long time now I just hadn't dated.

And in a few months I would be forty. All I could picture was a dismal future. When I saw an older woman who looked as if life had not been good to her, I would think, almost in a panic, "I'll look like that soon; then for sure nobody will ever want me."

Then the miracle happened. On the plane flying home from a meeting I had attended in Boston, I met the man I wanted as my future husband. Taller than Greg but with features very much like him, Chandler was everything a woman could dream of—handsome, wealthy (he owned a successful software company in Dallas), kind, and generous. We were the same age, and the irony of it all was that our spouses had died within a few months of each other. Even though his wife's death from diabetes had been preceded by several years of lingering illness and Greg had died suddenly, we were still experiencing the same twists and turns on the road back to equilibrium. And his daughters . . . I loved them the minute I saw them. I wanted immediately to mother the little girls.

As time passed, I could not believe my good fortune. I took Chandler to ball games where we sat in the president's box with all the other couples, and once again I felt normal. He had me meet his family and took me to dinner with the neighbors with whom he and his wife had been a constant foursome. We shared books with each other, wrote long letters. He gave me a beautiful antique copper kettle for Thanksgiving, and I placed an early order with L. L. Bean

for a chamois shirt for him for Christmas. Life again was wonderful. I knew we were always going to be happy.

"I have just found out I have to be in New York this Friday on
business," Chandler called to say, "so why don't you go with me?
We'll fly up on Thursday, stay at the Plaza, and have the whole
weekend free after I finish my meetings." I loved the city and I
loved the Plaza (although I hadn't been back since Greg and I
had stayed there to celebrate one of our anniversaries); so, of
course, I would go. But then I remembered. I had to give a
speech at Western Illinois University on Friday morning. But a
solution was quickly forthcoming. I could fly straight from
Illinois to New York and be at the Plaza by the time Chandler
finished his meetings.

I was sitting in the Houston airport gate number 31 when it
dawned on me that on the way to Western Illinois University I
was going through St. Louis. I knew the St. Louis airport almost
as well as my own living room; it would be hard to count the
times I had flown in and out of there when Greg and I were
dating. This would be the first time I had been in that airport
since Greg moved to New York when we got married.

I decided to call Greg's best friend, Dick Friederich, before I
left Houston to see if he could come to the airport for a short
visit during the layover. As soon as I dialed the area code—
314—I remembered every call I had ever made to Greg when he
lived there. I began to cry. Waves of memories, sights, images,
and smells rushed over me. I almost missed the plane. Just went
unconscious after they called the flight. They slammed the door
right behind me. I was the last person on.

———————

I suppose I will never know what really happened that weekend in New York. Was it me or was it Chandler? Or perhaps
both? Here I was with a man with whom I had felt a fit from the
beginning. There had been none of the awkwardness that I had
experienced with other men. But now I was uncomfortable,
upset, edgy—as if Greg had just died last month instead of more
than two years ago. I was haunted by questions that were as

irrational as they were deeply disturbing: Wasn't I dishonoring
Greg by being at the Plaza in the company of another man? How
could I forget him so easily?

The weekend passed in haze, and even now I can remember only
scattered events....

Realizing while we were eating lunch that I had left my diamond
earrings on the nightstand in my room at the Plaza, the diamond
earrings Greg had bought me at Tiffany's on *his* fortieth birthday.
Rushing back to the room and being so relieved to find the earrings
still lying where I had left them.

Not being able to sleep, lying there listening to low night music
and watching light snow fall outside the window, feeling only
distance and deadness. Then suddenly hearing the disc jockey
sometime in the wee morning hours abruptly break into the music to
announce that John Lennon had been murdered. Getting caught in a
traffic jam later that day in front of the Dakota, the apartment house
where John Lennon had lived, and watching a young girl jogging in
the snow in Central Park across the street from the Dakota, making
no attempt to hide her tears as she ran.

Don't I also remember Chandler getting several telephone
messages? Perhaps from one of his neighbors, the woman he
later married?

No, I really can't say what happened. I just know that I did
not tell Chandler that weekend about the fortieth birthday party
I had just learned my friends were planning for me. And I know
that after the weekend in New York, Chandler did not call me.

In one way, the fortieth birthday party was wonderful. I loved
what I was wearing: high-necked Victorian-looking blouse
trimmed in lace, jeans, boots, and a new cinnamon-colored
cowboy hat. The old barn my friends had rented was perfect for
making chili, which we did right on the premises, and for
country-and-western dancing. Three friends who, like me, had
Christmas birthdays were also honorees at the party, so there
were many wonderful people who came to shower all of us with
love and well wishes.

On the other hand, the party was terrible. The next morning
all I could think about was the attractive bachelor's remark.
"You scare me," he had said while we were dancing, and then I

didn't see him for the rest of the evening. I remembered something similar an acquaintance had said to me some months before: "You act so strong and independent," he'd said, "that I don't know why you ever got married." Thinking back over the party, I wrote in my journal, "I'm so afraid of the next ten years, of being unattractive, aging. No one will want me. I'm discouraged and scared. Feel the emptiness of it all after the party last night. My aloneness. The facade. The faking that hides the loneliness."

I knew I had to go forward, but what do you do when you can't get free of whatever it is that keeps pulling you back? I knew I wanted to stop being a *widow* and just be a plain human being; but what do you do when, in spite of the commitments you have made and the actions you have taken, it's just not happening?

One afternoon I saw a Lawrence Durrell novel I hadn't read on the shelf in the library. When I opened it later that night at home, it seemed as if the book had been written to me as a personal message. Lines like these were so applicable that they startled me: *"Such a lack of theme.... Everyone who dies takes a whole epoch with them.... It's always now or never—since we are human and enjoy the fatality of choice. Indeed the moment of choice is always now.* "Darn it," I thought, "I can't even check out a library book without being forced to see evidence of my predicament."

As coincidence would have it, I saw the graffiti and got the letter inviting me to apply for the job on the same day a few weeks later. I walked into the bathroom in one of the buildings where I taught my classes and saw written over the sink:

"What do I want?"
This is the world's most disturbing question.

Seeing the graffiti filled me with rage. "Hoodlum," I said, "defacing public property."

"Come on," another voice said, "people have been writing on walls since cave days. Something else is making you angry."

The second voice was right. It was the message that I found so confronting. What did I want? I had no idea, and that was my whole problem. It was as if all the world were out there and I could make my life up now that Greg was dead in any new configuration I wanted, but what was that going to be? I just kept floundering.

The state of mind I was in when I got back to my office made the letter in my mail tray all the more enticing. "The University of South Florida in Tampa will be hiring a new Dean of Liberal Arts this semester. The search committee has been given your name as a possible candidate, and we invite you to apply for this position." I was excited; this could be the answer. I liked Tampa, and the university had a good reputation. I would have new work, make new friends, perhaps meet a man with whom things would go better than they had with Chandler. Yes, it would be a good move. I decided to send in my application.

Every two or three weeks I got another notification. My application was under consideration . . . the screening committee had made the first cut and my application was still being considered . . . a group of finalists were being asked to send in additional information, and I was one of those included.

Then came the really good news: the committee had winnowed the applicants, and my name appeared on the final short list. Would I come to be interviewed on the campus? I bought a new lilac-colored linen suit and off-white silk blouse for the occasion, and a bunch of dark purple silk violets to pin on my lapel just because they looked jaunty. My spirits were high. This could be the new beginning that I needed so desperately.

The interview schedule was grueling. Dinner with the president and his wife, breakfast with the search committee, meetings with the Council of Deans, with students, with this department chair and that one, each one seeming to be housed as far as possible from the other. By the end of the day I was physically and mentally exhausted. But I had liked what I had seen—a thriving university, energetic administrators with expansive ideas for the future, a liberal arts college poised for change and growth, a mix of interesting students.

On the plane coming home, I tried to assess the situation. I knew they had selected five individuals for the final round of interviewing, so the selection process was almost over. Surely I'd hear something in one to two weeks.

Liberal arts dean—I liked the sound of the title. I began to imagine a high-rise apartment looking out over Tampa Bay, dinners of pompano baked in parchment, maybe even a little place on the beach that could be a getaway cottage. Already I could see myself swinging my briefcase as I walked along under the palm trees going to my office at the university.

"You have a telegram," the secretary said almost before I had time to step through the door when I got back to work on Monday. It was clear that the arrival of the telegram had made a stir in the office. The president, with whom I had developed a close working relationship, had gotten up and come to his doorway when I arrived, where he stood now drinking a cup of coffee.

"A telegram?" I said in surprise as the secretary handed me the windowed envelope. I had no idea what this could mean or who it could be from, but my heart was pounding. I always associated telegrams with bad news; even at this moment I was remembering the day when I was a preschooler that Mother got a telegram saying her brother had been shot down in action in France and his status was undetermined.

I opened the envelope where I was standing. No, they couldn't have already decided. I had only been there on Friday. But here it was in black and white. "The search committee is happy to inform you that you have been selected for the position of Dean of Liberal Arts at the University of South Florida. Letter to follow." I looked over at the president, who, it turns out, had already received a courtesy call informing him of my selection, and he was smiling. The secretary came around the desk to hug me. I was stunned with the news; but, oh, I was so happy!

In the letter that arrived a few days later, the committee asked me to indicate in writing within a week my acceptance of the position. I surprised myself when I did not sit down that very night and type out my affirmative response; but then it had been a long day, and I knew I could do it tomorrow. But the next day and then the next came and went, and I still had not written the acceptance letter. "Why?" I chastised myself again and again. "Why haven't you already sent the letter saying you will be thrilled to take this position? It is everything you could ask for." But for some reason the closer the deadline came, the more some other part of me was reneging.

I could not understand my behavior. I had spent days working on the application to get this job. I had read up on the university and the community diligently before I went on campus. I had done everything I could to be at my best during the interviews. And now, after all that work, now that the job was mine, I was hesitating to take it. It was very embarrassing. To be undecided *after* I was named to the position made me look so foolish and uncertain.

"The best I can describe it," I said in frustration to my friend Emma, "is that it just doesn't feel like the right direction for me to go in. I just can't make myself say yes to starting a new career as a fulltime university administrator. Now that the actual opportunity is present, I realize how many other options this decision cuts out and how firmly it turns me toward a specific future."

"Well, what do you want to do instead?" she asked kindly.

"I don't know," I answered. "That's what makes me so angry at myself. That's the whole problem. If there were something else I was choosing, it would make more sense that I was turning down this job. But I don't have anything. I don't know what I want to do. I can't think of a good alternative. I just know that I can't make myself do this. And that leaves me with nothing again that represents a new future."

It was one of the hardest things I had ever done to send the letter saying I would not be accepting the position. Not only was I turning down a chance to start a new life for myself, but I was sure I was forever cutting out the option of being a university administrator. When word got out that I had been offered and had declined this position, no one else would put me on any list to be considered for comparable positions. If I knew for sure that I was making the right decision, that would be one thing, but I didn't have that certainty. So I didn't know what I was doing to myself. I just knew I wasn't going.

There was only one counterpoint to the misery I felt after I made the decision. I still didn't know if I had done the right thing. I still didn't have an alternative. But I did have a brochure Armand DiMele had given me once, on the back of which had been printed a quotation. Carlos Castaneda's mentor, Don Juan, was instructing him:

> Anything is one of a million paths. Therefore you must always keep in mind that a path is only a path; if you feel you should not follow it, you must not stay with it under any conditions.... Look at every path closely and deliberately. Try it as many times as you think necessary.... [Then ask one question.] I will tell you what it is: Does this path have a heart? . . . If it does, the path is good; if it doesn't, it is of no use.
>
> Both paths lead nowhere; but one has a heart, the other doesn't. One makes for a joyful journey; as long as you follow it, you are one with it. The other will make you curse your life. One makes you strong; the other weakens you.... A path without a heart is never enjoyable. You have to work hard even to take it. On the other hand, a path with heart is easy; it does not make you work at liking it.... For me there is only the traveling on the paths that have a heart, on any path that may have a heart. There I travel, and the only worthwhile challenge is to traverse its full length. And there I travel—looking, looking, breathlessly.

I read this quotation often in the weeks after my decision. For I knew that even though I had not taken this particular job, I was going to make a change. I knew I was in the process of making a new life for myself, even when it looked as if things weren't going so well; and part of that life had to be work that gave me a sense of renewed meaning and purpose. Somehow, somewhere, I would find a path with a heart. About that I felt an unshakable commitment.

This is the set of experiences known as Reconstruction. It is during Reconstruction that our grieving moves out into life. We start imagining possible new directions; we set goals and begin to work toward them; we take steps to establish a new identity. During Reconstruction we begin to do the work that is necessary to resolve the conflict between the pull of the past and our desire to be happy.

This is a time of paradox. On the one hand, we begin to feel alive again, to feel enthusiastic. We no longer live every moment of the day in the slough of despondency. At the same time, we are confronted by the blank canvas of our future. We do not know what to recommit to. We do not know how we are going to reestablish our life purposes. We are unclear about our direction.

This is a difficult time. We feel like an emigrant who must carve out a new life in an unfamiliar land. We feel like a mountain climber who can find no sure footing. The past looks like our only place of safety, our only place of refuge. All the while, then, when we are trying to move forward, we must accommodate our memory of the past and at the same time reckon with our desire and need for a new future.

Peter Marris, the British social scientist, helps us understand this dilemma. We need our past, he tells us. In fact, the only way we can understand the present is by referencing it to the past. It is from previous experience that we discern the principles by which we operate our world. Although these principles may be different from those of our neighbor, they nevertheless provide a framework that tells us the meaning of events—whether they will be "good, bad, or indifferent." Each discovery we made in the past, for instance—if I touch a hot stove, that stove will burn me; if I have a companion with me to watch the sunset, I am happier—leads to the next until finally we have, in Professor Marris's words, "a series of interpretations which gradually consolidate, with more or less assurance and consistency, into an understanding of life." We cannot therefore just decide to jettison our past, no matter how much we want to get on to the future. Our past is the basis of everything we have learned about what does and does not make our life happy.

Furthermore, it is extremely difficult to separate what we learned in the past from the person(s) with whom we learned it. (This is why it is often as difficult for individuals who disliked or even hated the lost person to reconstruct their lives as it is for those who loved the one who is missing: so much of the structure and shape of the past is tied up with the person who is no longer present that it requires a herculean effort to separate principles for living from the people with whom we have lived.)

What we are trying to do during Reconstruction is to find the activities, the people, the kind of work, the experiences, that will give us a sense of continuity with our past and yet allow us to move beyond it. And this is enormously difficult. We feel a lot of pain as we work to find a way to extract the purpose and meaning from the past and experience it in some new, appropriate form in the present, for so much of that purpose and meaning was associated with the lost person.

Yet I've seen again and again as I've worked on this book that, no matter the difficulty, people step out and begin the tasks of long-term change that are required during Reconstruction. I've been moved by their courage to muddle around, to take action with no security about the outcome (writer Sheldon Kopp said once that he had finally accepted that all of his important decisions had to be made on the basis of insufficient data), to grapple with a scary, open future even while they are still trying to figure out their relationship to the past. The conflict is excruciating (which is why every serious researcher writing about loss asserts that learning how to make these longer-term adjustments is as much a part of mourning as the earlier, more easily recognized forms of acute grieving). But brave individuals take on the tasks of Reconstruction for the same reason immigrants work so hard to make a life for themselves in a new country: it is these experiences that allow us finally to create a life that both honors the past and has new shape and meaning.

Individuals with whom I have talked during their period of Reconstruction report that we can expect experiences such as these....

A RECOGNITION THAT IT IS TIME TO MAKE CHANGES
A young widow says:

I've made a list of all the things I've been doing out of habit but that I really don't like to do. For instance, I've been in a study group for over five years, and it dawned on me the other day that I don't enjoy being there. I've also been in a tennis league for a long time. I realized lately that I was in that activity because some of my friends participated but that I didn't enjoy tennis, either. So I've canceled both of those activities and signed up to take a genealogy class at the community college. That's something I've been wanting to do for a long time. I think I've hesitated to make changes like this, thinking that a widow needs to keep doing things with her friends as much as possible. But I realized the other day that a widow can also decide what she likes to do on her own account and do that. I've felt better ever since.

THE NEED TO BEGIN TO ESTABLISH A NEW IDENTITY

A senior citizen who was recently widowed recalls:

There's the shock of being regarded a widow. It's . . . the word has a very unhappy connotation. And it's brought home to you on all the forms you have to fill out. Married, divorced, widowed. You never get used to this thing you now are.

You just don't know who you are anymore. Most women my age in my situation have had forty or fifty—I had almost fifty—years of discussing everything. Everything was a joint decision, whether it had to do with business or personal affairs. Now that he is gone, I feel so strongly that my identity has been removed.

You know, they invited Marge and David. And suddenly, now, I walk into a room as an alone person when before we always walked in as a couple.... That's an excruciating thing. And, you know, you're asking yourself all the time, "Do people like me? Do they accept me because I was David's wife or because I'm me? And if it's because I'm me, what do I have to offer?"

I caught myself the other night relying on my relationship with David to insert my own opinion in the conversation. At dinner we were talking about something David always had very strong ideas about. And I said, "Well, since David isn't here to say this, I'll say it for him; because this is the way he felt, and I agree with him." I haven't decided how to handle all this yet, but one friend of mine, also widowed, found an answer for herself—she moved to another environment, away from all her couple friends. And she is loving her life in the new location. She's made new friends who never knew her husband.

A RECOGNITION THAT SOME OF THE DIFFICULTIES WERE NOT CAUSED BY THE LOSS

A grandmother recently widowed tells this story:

It has been a shock for me to realize that I have other problems besides the death of a husband. I thought for a long time that that

was it. I realize that I am faced with an issue of self-development.
And I can tell you, that's a lot more confronting even than the death.
I've now got to pick up where I left off as a person when I married
Clayton— and develop myself from there. And that's scary.

Up till now, my life has been my husband and my children.
Marrying so young, you know, I didn't have a full youth. We got
married when I was sixteen, and Clayton was already the dominant
one. He was the one who received the education, with my help to be
sure that everything went just fine. But I never became a whole
person.

I really need to go back and learn a lot of things. I was a good
mother; I was a good wife; and I was a good friend to my neighbors.
But I—this is hard for anyone to believe—I cannot swim. I cannot
dance. I can't type.

I have realized since Clayton died that my life has been full of
excuses, and I had such good ones. I couldn't drive, so I couldn't get
there. Or I was doing something for someone else. You know, I
would really love to learn to dance. Or to swim. I know that's not
talking about things that would help others, but they're just some of
the things that would give me a full life.

My first hurdle is to learn to drive. Because until I do that, I am
still so limited. I still must call everyone to get me places.

Someone I was talking to the other day just came out and asked
me bluntly, "Well, do you think you will do any of these things?" At
first I said, "I hope I will," and then I said, "I must." I can't keep on
like I am. I could, but what would it be? Since my children all live
in the same town as I do, I would just be a little old lady, baby-
sitting her grandchildren. I enjoy doing that, of course; but that's not
a very full life. So I just must develop myself. That is the answer.

But, you know, I asked myself the other day, "Are you just
talking, or are you going to get out there and do it?" I keep wanting
someone else to make it happen, and I realize they can't. It has to be
me. It digs at me, something I read in *A Road Less Traveled*—that
laziness is evil. I believe that! I know I'm not lazy in things like
mowing an acre lot or going over and cleaning my daughter's house.
But there's a particular kind of lazy—not doing the kinds of things
that I have said I want to do, like learn to drive or swim or take
classes. That kind of laziness is my own fault. So the big question

I'm asking myself now about the way I want to develop my life as a whole person is, "Well, will I do it?"

A FEELING OF CONTINUING LONELINESS
A senior citizen confides:

It's the loneliness that discourages me as I try to make a new life. I've been lonely, of course, ever since George died. But I thought when I moved into this new apartment and made new friends, things would be different. But even here I feel as if all I have ahead of me is being a lonely old woman, just waiting to die.

I can get through the days very well without brooding. I've joined a few other people in the building in starting a Friendly Hour. First we have refreshments and then a program. We've had a wonderful performance of Dorothy Parker's *So Here We Are,* done by three retired drama teachers. The former head of the English department at our local university came and talked about the pleasures of reading. The third program was a talk by a nutrition expert. We have five retired doctors living in the building, so our next program is going to be a symposium in which each doctor will talk about his or her most interesting or unusual case. And I've also started a personal project: putting together a cookbook.

But my activities are restricted because I can't see to drive at night. And at night is when it hits you. When there's nobody to nudge. When something comes on TV that's either funny or particularly perceptive or a drama that's well done, and there's nobody you can talk it over with. Or if it's poorly done, you want somebody to help you analyze and decide why was it done poorly, and that's when the loneliness gets you.

RECOGNIZING IT IS TIME TO LOOK AT THE FUTURE
A widower says:

I've come to think of my life in much the same way as I do my work. I work as a historian at a research center where we write many grant proposals; and, when one proposal isn't funded, we sit down and write another one. I've started thinking about my life as a widower as something I have to write a new proposal for. But, in a case like this, I don't know yet what kind of proposal to write. I have to do a lot of searching, and I've begun to do some of that.

Among the things I think about are selling the house and taking off. I used to do a lot of consulting internationally. Maybe I'll go back to South America and work with the Rockefeller Foundation there. Or go to the Soviet Union.

Doris and I had a plan that when we retired we would go back to Rockbridge County in Virginia, and either take one of the old family farms up there and restore the house or buy land and build a house on it. We thought we'd have a couple of horses and a dog and a place to go fishing. Every now and then I'd go into Washington to do some consulting. I might still do that; but to tell you the truth, I don't really have a burning desire to go back to Rockbridge County now that Doris is dead. So I'm considering other alternatives. I wish I knew. It's the most uncomfortable place in the world to be in, not to know what direction your life is going to go in; but from all I can see, that just comes with the territory.

THE RECOGNITION THAT THE PAST PULLS
WHEN THERE IS FEAR ABOUT THE FUTURE

A young widow told this story:

I decided to go back to school to take a few courses, and philosophy was one of the subjects I decided to study. I went in to see my philosophy professor one day to discuss my research topic, and near the end of the conversation Dr. Fernando asked me a very ordinary question. "What is next for you? What is in your future?"

The minute he asked me that question I was overwhelmed with sadness about the death of my husband. At that moment all I could think about was how much I longed to see Terry. I mean, it was like a knee-jerk reaction: the professor asks me about my future, and I get upset about the past. Instead of responding to his question, I began to cry and tell him about the accident two years ago and what had happened and how much I missed Terry. It was as if there was something so frightening in thinking about me being out in the world, in thinking about my identity, my self—as if somehow I was going to have to be exposed. I had never seen the mechanism so clearly before: in the face of fear about the future, I turned immediately to the past.

After the conversation was over, I went up on the hill above the philosophy building and sat in a little park thinking about what had happened. I thought about things we had talked about in class—how a clearing or an opening produces anxiety; how you feel, when faced with existential choice, that you are going to fall into an abyss. After what had happened in the professor's office, these were no longer theoretical concepts for me. I knew firsthand the feeling of that anxiety. And I recognized that in the face of that anxiety I had wanted to take refuge in the past.

But a funny thing happened as I walked back down the hill to go to my next class. In one of the rooming houses across the street, an upstairs window was open. Someone had put one of those big music boxes in the window, and the loudest piece of reggae music I have ever heard in my life was playing. It was such a juxtaposition: thoughts about a heavy subject like existential anxiety and the sounds of happy, boisterous reggae music. I can't really put it into words, but I learned something in that moment. Something about how to live life in the face of fear and anxiety.

THE REALIZATION OF CERTAIN PRIORITIES
A divorced man says:

One of my main aspirations is to have a wife. That's what I miss. To come home to an empty house is a difficult thing. The kids did something thoughtful after their mother left—they got me one of those timers that turn the lights on. At least then I didn't have to walk into a dark house when I got home from work.

There's a book called *Creation Is a Patient Search.* It's about architecture, but I've borrowed the author's idea and applied it to my situation. Searching for a wife is a creative search and requires patience.

I've got the whole world to search through. So, I'll just conduct a creative search, with patience, and I'll find a new wife. I'm sure of it.

THE RECOGNITION THAT EMOTIONS ARE SEDUCTIVE
Listen to a mother whose son committed suicide:

It's very difficult when you're involved emotionally to be able to pull yourself out of it. That's one reason I'm very careful not to let myself fall into that emotional trap. It would be so easy to do. But I know that there's almost a delight in wallowing in your emotions, if you allow yourself to continue to do it. There's a certain pleasure you get out of feeling melancholy . . . "Oh, poor me." A certain pleasure in telling people, "Oh, I've gone through so much." Then you go through the stories of "My trauma is worse than your trauma," and it can go on forever.

I've learned that if you get in the emotional trap, there is nothing that is going automatically to trigger your getting out of it. One of the things I do when that happens is remind myself of a poem I learned once. I think it was Rossetti who wrote it:

> Go, you may call it madness, folly.
> I would not, if I could be, be glad.
> I love this melancholy.

So when I'm tempted to give in to my emotions, I remember that poem and say to myself, "Eee gads, there must be something more to life than this." I've even gotten to the place now where I can laugh at myself when I succumb to the emotional trap. I think that's very important.

MAKING THE COMMITMENT TO TAKE ON NEW PROJECTS
A divorced woman recalls:

I felt new energy the minute I decided to take on the project. I finally had something to focus my time and attention and my work on. I joined with a team of people who were putting together a special for public television about business leaders, educators, and professionals in the medical field who were offering new solutions to age-old problems. With this project I had something bigger than myself and my own grief and sorrow and pain to focus on. I couldn't talk about my kids or my husband anymore—I'd worn that subject out—and since this television special was of great interest to a number of people, I had something to talk about that made me feel worthwhile. I felt as if I were doing something. I felt that through this project I was in some way contributing to the lives of other people.

While I was working, I wasn't home crying in my beer about my busted relationship. It was real simple. I couldn't be two places at the same time, and I couldn't think two thoughts at the same time. As long as I was working on this project and working with other people, I wasn't dwelling on my miserable little existence.

I've discovered that every new thing I do is like a little grain of sand. I add one grain of sand to another. It's beginning to feel as if at some point they will form one big block of granite that I can stand on.

AN EXPERIENCE OF CONFUSION ABOUT THE FUTURE
A widow says:

It's a shame to have to say at age thirty-three, "What am I going to be when I grow up?" but the truth is I don't know what to do with the rest of my life. I just sold the equipment business that Jack had; it wasn't something I wanted to run or felt I had any talent for running. But I do want to do something. I majored in Russian history in college, planning to go on to graduate school. But then Jack and I decided to get married. Now I've got to think about what to do. Should I resume studying history, or should I do graduate work in business since I've got three girls to raise and could benefit from learning as much about finance and accounting as possible? Can you imagine? Three girls in college at the same time! So, it's all confusing. I don't know what I'm going to do. Everything looks like a possibility, and that's the problem. How do I choose? What if I make a mistake? You can't make many mistakes at my age and in my circumstances and have it not seriously affect your future and the futures of lots of other people. It just seems so important to make the right decision, but what is that right thing to do?

A DESIRE NOT TO REPEAT MISTAKES
A divorcee tells this story:

It was wonderful when Trey and I met and got married. "I am making a total commitment to this relationship," I said to myself. And it was interesting how the first test of that commitment came about.

We were trying to mesh our two households. What do you do with two toaster ovens, two hand-held mixers, four sets of spatulas? I pulled a treasure from the box I was unpacking. "Here is the best spaghetti pot in the world," I told Trey proudly. "Well, that can certainly go in the discard pile," he responded. "We have a lot better cookware than that to use to cook our spaghetti."

I was stunned. Of course, he didn't know that for almost twenty-seven years every strand of spaghetti I had cooked had been in that pot—ever since Michael was a baby. He didn't know about all those times over the years when the boys came running in and seeing this pot on the stove yelled, "Oh, boy, spaghetti and garlic bread for supper!" He didn't know that every time I had moved, this old pot had gotten a favored place in the packing. I could have told him, but I didn't. I wanted so much for everything in our relationship to go smoothly. So the spaghetti pot got discarded.

After our relationship went sour and Trey moved out, I thought about that spaghetti pot incident. I realized that what happened that day, if I could have seen it, was a foreshadowing of what was going to go wrong later. I wanted the relationship so much that I was untrue to myself in an effort to try to keep it. And that didn't work. I honestly think now that I smothered the relationship to death with my "commitment." I have to put commitment in quotation marks when I say it because it wasn't really a commitment. It was an obsession, a fear that I would lose this man, too. And, of course, with that attitude, with that little belief in myself, I did lose him. It is so important to me now, as I start dating again, not to make the same mistakes.

THE FOCUS DURING RECONSTRUCTION

We have all had times in our lives when the task at hand and our ability to meet that task were a marvelous fit: we were able to accomplish what had to be done with velocity and ease and a sense of deep satisfaction. Not so during the experiences of Reconstruction. As these stories show us, Reconstruction is a time of groping and stumbling, of not knowing, of making changes without having any certainty of the outcome. A time when we are beginning to have goals and dreams for the future but very little clarity about how those goals and dreams will be accomplished. It is the phase of the grieving process when we have to "try out" new roles and new activities, with all the awkwardness and chance that such speculative efforts entail.

I think it was writer Thomas Szasz who once said that you have to be humble to learn. During Reconstruction we have little choice but to be humble because we are finding out, often painfully, that although the past pulls powerfully, everything about how to create a new life for ourselves is ahead of us to be learned. This requires us to examine our ways of thinking and behaving to determine what can be useful in helping us construct this new future and what will be destructive and detrimental.

New Identity/New Roles

Naturally, the mutual roles we shared with the lost person, the things we did with that person that gave our life structure and meaning, the ways we related, are still very present. This behavior is familiar, comfortable, and, most of the time, automatic. Even this far into the grieving process, we still find ourselves often thinking and acting as if the past were still present (or certainly wishing that it were still present), only to have to acknowledge once again, in still another painfully abrupt "test of reality," that the person is not here and will not be here, and that our thoughts and behavior are useless and inappropriate. (I've always used as a touchstone for this kind of behavior the experience I had of saving a letter from my editor in New York because I wanted to show Greg the last paragraph—and the paragraph was about Greg and his death!)

During the experiences of Reconstruction we are required actually to begin to relinquish these old roles and identities and reinvent ourselves appropriate to our present circumstances. We have to remake ourselves, to start to establish new roles and new identities. This would be painful enough within itself (we all remember what it was like to face such tasks during adolescence); but added to the grief we feel for the loss of the past, the situation is often overwhelming. That is why we go down so many blind alleys, often look and act so indecisively, and walk around in such a quandary. We don't know who we are yet in this new situation, and it seems that we are always practicing.

One of the things we have to acknowledge in order to negotiate this period of Reconstruction is that there is no way around this confusion and trial and error. It is no small task we are undertaking— forging a new identity, finding new ways of relating and new sources of satisfaction—so we should not disparage ourselves when we don't always go in a straight line toward a new destination. "Such disorganization," John Bowlby writes encouragingly, "though painful and perhaps bewildering, is none the less potentially adaptive."

But it is often more than just establishing new roles and identities. We may also find ourselves in a delayed developmental crisis. We see that we do not have certain skills and behaviors that we must have if we are going to be able to perform our new roles successfully. I think about the widow who married young and lived a sheltered life throughout her marriage having to take on the financial management of her personal accounts, starting with learning to photocopy papers and checking books out of the library to do research. That was as challenging for this woman as traveling alone in the Antarctica would be for another person (and probably took about as much courage). She had to redefine who she was in order to take over these accounts, and she had to develop latent skills and abilities to learn how to handle them. (A few months later she even tackled the computer!)

So it isn't just a matter of swapping this identity for that one (although even such a simple exchange as that is painful when the swap is involuntary), but the fact that we often have to change ourselves fundamentally, take on things we have never done and don't know how to do, come to see certain ways we are behaving that hold us back and alter that behavior. And while "this may be an immensely painful and difficult process for some," Dr. Beverley Raphael reminds us, "when it is satisfactorily worked through, the new identity may be more stable and secure and linked to the core aspects of the self." This is, of course, the result we want to achieve. And when we do so, we will have made of the work of Reconstruction a transforming process.

Understanding Self-Perpetuating Emotions

Reconstruction is a time of strong emotions. We may even feel that we are regressing because images from the past are so vivid and haunting. In touching the past, we are swept by emotion.

If this emotion runs its course, all is well. We empty out our sadness, our regret, our longing. We are released and can move forward. But this may not be what happens. For our emotions are also capable of acting as an autonomous system. This means that the emotion can trigger itself—again and again—with no new stimulus. We then become the puppet of the emotion; our feelings are at its mercy. During

Reconstruction, then, one of our greatest challenges is to understand how our emotions operate so that we can distinguish between the healthy expression of emotion and the unhealthy feeding upon themselves of which our emotions are also capable.

An emotion is a whole system. It is "penetrated throughout by an impulse that organizes it, which accepts certain thoughts and rejects others, and directs them to its predetermined end." This system is made up of three distinguishable parts: the emotion itself (for instance, sadness); the memory, both conscious and unconscious, of that emotion that includes all past experiences of the emotion; and the bodily reactions to the emotion (our hand trembling when we are afraid, our face getting red when we are angry, and so on). Any one of these three parts can trigger off the system: this means that without ever having a new stimulus, the emotion can keep itself going. A memory triggers the emotion itself; the emotion triggers the bodily reaction; the bodily reaction triggers a memory; the memory triggers another bodily reaction; that bodily reaction triggers the emotion; and on and on, ad infinitum, like one of those perpetual motion sculptures you sometimes see in airport lobbies.

This emotion system is a force that performs certain valuable functions, but the system can also exceed its function and take on this self referential operation. That's why we hear someone say something like "I want to get over my upset with her, but I can't. It's as if my anger has me by the throat." If we are able to discern when the emotion is feeding off itself, resulting in our thinking and behaving in a self-defeating manner, and when the emotion is serving as a valuable release mechanism, we can take appropriate action.

Fortunately we have available to us systems of organization higher than our more primitive emotional system—systems Alexander Shand, a pioneer thinker in this area, referred to as the "better self," sentiments of friendship, self-love and self-respect, respect for others, love, "respect for conscience." Our emotions can be controlled by these systems of higher organization, and this is how we are able to intervene and break the vicious cycle when we are experiencing self-referential and self-perpetuating emotions.

In practical terms, the interventions can take such simple forms as thoughts like "If I keep on crying like this, I will be so exhausted I will not be able to make dinner for the children" or "I have a project to complete which means a lot to me, so I am going to get to work on it and stop nursing my anger at the hospital administrator." Or intervention can take the form of an approach like Dr. Aaron Beck's cognitive model: thoughts and feelings are reported on, the relation of thought to feeling is determined, and then generalizations are made about what kinds of thoughts lead to which emotions. Thus, as a result of changing our thoughts, we are able to do something about controlling emotions that up until now ran rampant. Through the use of this cognitive model, Dr. Beck asserts, the "whole matter of arousal of emotion [has been brought] back within the range of common-sense observation."

Dr. Beck's protege, David Burns, M.D., suggests an activity he calls: "Hot Thoughts/Cool Thoughts" as a way to work with destructive emotions. First you write down the thoughts associated with the emotion: *I will never be happy again; I miss those Sunday nights so much—when we put our supper on TV trays and watched* 60 Minutes; *I do not want to go to this party alone....* These are the "hot thoughts," the thoughts that keep the emotional system turning on itself. Then write down a "cool thought" for each "hot thought" you have written—an answer or an observation. *I may not ever be happy again, but it's too soon to know; I will invite Stan and Marty over to watch* 60 Minutes *next Sunday; I will weigh the advantages and disadvantages of going to the party alone.*

Dr. Burns also suggests making a chart that he calls "Daily Record of Dysfunctional Thoughts," which can help a person caught in a self-defeating emotional cycle. The chart has five columns: first the "provocative situation" is described; then the emotion that has been triggered is named; then in the third column "hot thoughts" are recorded and in the fourth column "cool thoughts"; then the outcome of the situation is written in the final column. Even though this and the "Hot Thoughts/Cool Thoughts" approach are simple, the research of Dr. Burns and others has shown them to be highly effective in giving individuals control over their emotions.

How can we make the distinction between the times we need to *release* our emotions and the times we need to *discipline* our emotions? People tell me that they soon learn to tell the difference based on how they feel afterward. When individuals "bump" into a pocket of emotion that needs to be expressed and choose to vent their feelings, they report that they feel cleansed, washed out, released, free when the experience is over. On the other hand, when the emotion is part of a seductive, repetitive cycle, individuals say they feel worse when the experience is over. (If it ever is over. Some people remain stuck in these defeating cycles.) They say that no matter how long the thoughts and feelings persist, they never feel "finished" with the experience and find instead that feelings of resentment, anger, fear, and depression increase as a result of the presence of the emotion. To learn to recognize the difference between authentic emotional release and self-destructive emotional cycles is one of the tasks of Reconstruction.

Recognizing Different Kinds of Loneliness

Of course, from the very beginning loneliness has been part of our response to the loss we have sustained. But during the experiences of Reconstruction we often feel even more isolated, separate, without companionship and comradeship, unnurtured. We are now required to be "out in the world" more as we begin to build a new life for ourselves, and that activity seems to accentuate our aloneness. We are making decisions by ourselves that in the past we shared with another; this, too, increases our sense of being by ourselves and vulnerable. As we begin to make plans for the future, we realize that the lost person will not be there, and we have intensely poignant feelings of aloneness.

In his study of relationships, Robert Weiss of Harvard points out two kinds of loneliness: the loneliness of *emotional* isolation and the loneliness of *social* isolation. The loneliness of emotional isolation is experienced when we lose a person whose presence provided us with a sense of place, of belonging, of meaning, attachment, and security. The loneliness of social isolation is experienced when we do not have relationships that provide us with the opportunity to discuss mutual interests, exchange ideas and information, engage in social events, and feel a sense of companionship. During Reconstruction we experience both types of loneliness. We feel socially isolated as we work to establish a new identity; perhaps we are not invited to places where we used to go as a couple, do not feel comfortable with groups we used to enjoy, have less interest in things we used to do. This kind of loneliness can be at least partially assuaged by deciding to participate in new activities, make new friends, take the initiative to invite people over, and volunteer in civic, church, and community activities.

But the loneliness of emotional isolation is another matter. This is the loneliness we feel because we have no mutually committed relationship, no one with whom we are "affiliated" in a one-to-one partnership. In most cases, relationships with our family, friends, and children do not diminish this kind of emotional loneliness. Part of emotional loneliness may be the need and desire for sexual intimacy and almost certainly includes a longing for closeness.

This feeling of emotional loneliness is usually not alleviated until we have established another potential long-term relationship. This may be, Dr. Weiss suggests, through marriage or some other form of committed partnership. With some women it can happen through a special relationship with a close friend, sister, or mother; and, among some men, it may be achieved through a relationship with "buddies." There are those, too, whose relationship with God, with themselves, with nature, or even with pets assuages their feelings of emotional loneliness. But for others the tasks of Reconstruction must be carried out under the heavy weight of both emotional and social loneliness.

A danger we face is that in order to avoid this intensely painful experience of emotional (and social) loneliness, we will pursue and establish unhealthy relationships. We are especially vulnerable to this danger as time passes and our loneliness continues unabated. Dr. Beverley Raphael outlines the negative types of relationships we may be tempted to establish:

A fantasy relationship with the lost idealized partner. The partner is "ever-loving, perfect, unable to desert or die," and the bereaved finds fault with all other relationships and becomes hostile and negative.

A replacement relationship. The bereaved becomes attached to "someone who is seen symbolically, unconsciously, or actively as a replacement for the lost person." Perhaps another spouse or partner who "is valued only in terms of his [or her] similarity to the dead spouse" and, hence, with whom the relationship is usually doomed. Perhaps a child who is expected to take over the role filled by the lost person, causing psychological damage to the young person that can last a lifetime. Perhaps a person involved in the care of the bereaved, such as a clergy person, counselor, friend, family member, or neighbor who is expected ongoingly to "fill the gap" left by the dead person.

A *self-destructive relationship*. The bereaved attempts to punish herself or himself by establishing a relationship that will bring pain, punishment, and feelings of low self-worth.

An *avoidance relationship*. The bereaved, deciding never again to risk becoming close to another person, chooses someone who is incapable of giving and receiving intimacy.

A *compulsive care-giving relationship*. The bereaved must always have someone weak, helpless, bothered, or needy to do and care for, counting on the fact that this person will require support so much and for so long that separation will be impossible.

I don't think we can leave the subject of emotional and social loneliness without talking briefly about the awkwardness adults often feel as they attempt to establish new primary relationships. When our loss has been a spouse or a companion, we often don't know what to do when we finally venture to go out with others. We feel so awkward worrying about whether or not he or she will want to kiss us—but we worry nevertheless; about what the new rules are— does he always pay or should we both contribute; about what we will do if the person (or we) want(s) to be intimate. (A person, of course, doesn't have to be middle-aged to have concerns such as these; anyone who is having to shift from the coupled to the single life has similar experiences.) And there are so many other questions: What about wearing one's ring or keeping pictures on display? How to approach the subject of dating with the children? We wonder if these new interactions will ever feel natural, or if we are always going to feel guilty, scared, like a kid, so awkward. During the loneliness of Reconstruction we face these thorny issues which each of us must solve appropriate to our own situation.

It is certainly true that the loneliness we experience until we are again part of a satisfying social structure, and until we have reaffiliated with another with whom we have emotional intimacy, does not make the tasks of Reconstruction any easier. But neither do relationships that deny our value. Loneliness, at least, is open-ended, existing in a space of possibility. The fact that at some unexpected point or moment the loneliness might end is somewhat comforting; I know that in my own passage through grieving this was often a fact that I clung to.

But there is one kind of loneliness that cannot be assuaged either by finding a place for ourselves in a new social structure or reaffiliating with another. This is the loneliness an adult feels after the loss of a parent. Some who have not experienced the loss of a parent might pooh-pooh the impact of such a loss—after all, the parent had lived a long life; the sick person is finally out of her or his misery; the surviving adult children have their own lives to return to, lives that often include their own offspring. The justifications and explanations are logical and reasonable. But they are also often irrelevant. For the relationship of child to parent is special and long-lasting. Recently, I called a friend whose mother died last year to congratulate her on being nominated for an award of national recognition. My friend said, "It is a wonderful honor, but I've been sad ever since I got the notification because I can't call and tell my mother." It may also be the case that there is no relationship more fraught with the possibility of estrangement and awkwardness, and we mourn our incompletion with the deceased or wrestle with our unresolved conflicts.

The bond we have with our parents is unique, and one mourns the sundering of this bond, no matter the age or situation of the lost one. The only kind of "reaffiliating" we can do, in the words of one friend of mine who has lost both of his parents, is to "become our own father; become our own mother." Perhaps this is what many adult children mean when they report that they grow up in some special way after the loss of a parent. "I've realized since my father died," one young woman told me, "how much I still depended on him. Since he is gone, I have become much more responsible for myself and feel much more capable."

THE CHOICE

What is the choice of value during Reconstruction?

We must choose to take action.

The way John Bowlby talks about this is that we must have "active interchange between ourselves and the external world." When we are involved in this active interchange, he reminds us, we are in the process of organizing our lives toward some new object or goal. This activity will likely result, as the accounts in this chapter have shown us, in a mix of subjective experiences—"hope, fear, anger, satisfaction, frustration, or any combination of these...." But no matter how much we go back and forth, up and down, during the interim, so long as we stay in "active interchange" with the external world, we are still moving forward. By taking action—which inevitably involves risking changes, some of which work out and some of which don't—we are finding out what it will take for our lives to be satisfying, for us to feel happy. We are "trying out" alternatives to see what will be the appropriate shape for our new future.

What makes this choice to take action so difficult is that we are not yet complete with the past. As George Pollock puts it, "Little episodes that are suddenly recalled may serve as poignant reminders of the past. They may rekindle the dying fire of grief and tears for a short time.... Slips in conversation may indicate that the [loss] is still partially unaccepted...." Yet, Dr. Pollock points out, at the same time as we are experiencing this painful pull of the past, we are finding in our daily lives "various manifestations of adaptive mechanisms attempting to integrate the experience of the loss with reality so that life activities can go on." We have begun the work of "more lasting adaptation" even if it is not yet finished.

The noted family therapist Lily Pincus discusses the seemingly contradictory experiences such as those we have during Reconstruction: "People who believe strongly in self-discipline and control may be puzzled by regressive behavior in themselves and others," she says. "Identification and restitution, anger, hostility, and guilt may all be interwoven during the mourning process. There are no distinct boundaries or timetables." But this longing for the lost person, this seemingly regressive move back toward the past, "is a filling up, a replenishment of the self, in order to become a stronger, better integrated, more separate person."

Melanie Klein, who has done significant work on grief and loss, gives us further insight into why the choice to take action is difficult:

> The pain experienced in the slow process of testing reality in the work of mourning seems to be partly due to the necessity, not only to renew the links to the external world and thus continuously to re-experience the loss, but at the same time and by means of this to rebuild with anguish the inner world, which is felt to be in danger of deteriorating and collapsing.

The choice to take action during Reconstruction will result in "contradicting drives toward maturity and regression." This is unavoidable, because we are in a new situation. "All the usual responses are completely out of tune and inadequate to meet it." Therefore, our behavior "becomes unpredictable." As Lily Pincus says pointedly, "It is not just losing a state in which one had found one's balance, but rather as if one has lost one's balanced self. In attempting to regain it, one may try out some new ways of coping, giving up certain wishes, defining a new task."

This is what happens during Reconstruction. We begin the work necessary to replan our lives. To regain our balanced self. We try out new ways of living. We initiate an "active interchange" with the external world.

WHAT WE NEED FROM FAMILY AND FRIENDS DURING RECONSTRUCTION

Dr. Beverley Raphael reminds us that during Reconstruction we are still grieving. This time of longer-term adjustments, she says, is still "a period of ongoing mourning." The problem is that many of our family members and friends will not recognize that this set of experiences is part of the grieving process and will assume that because we are now "out and about in the world" everything is back in balance. And we may hesitate to tell them what we are experiencing—the ambivalence, the sadness, the fears, the loneliness—because we too think we should no longer be grieving. We are often ashamed because we find ourselves slipping back into the past when we thought we were moving into the future.

It is important, however, that we let those to whom we are close know what we are experiencing. We should not attempt to wear a facade that hides the continuing pain or to act as if the changes we are making are easy when, in truth, they are hard. If we are honest and let our family and friends know, in a responsible way, the difficulties we are experiencing, they will realize that their support and help are still needed.

Reconstruction is the time that we often find self-help groups the most useful to our grieving process. If we seek out the kinds of groups that concentrate on the necessity for change and that provide training and practice in how to accomplish this change, we are certain to meet some people in such groups who can be role models, people who have already done the work of Reconstruction. We can ask advice from these individuals, talk over specific problems with them, and include them as part of our network of support. Both these new friends and our old friends and family can help us in practical matters we must now engage in—learning how to manage finances or to write a good resume or to cook a wholesome meal or to locate excellent child-care facilities, for instance. It is important, both to us and to our friends and family, that we ask for this kind of help.

Edna St. Vincent Millay once wrote about the human being's amazing ability in the very midst of terrible pain to do amazing things: write music, play tennis, even plan. Since my bathroom mirror was already covered with poems and sayings taped there to encourage and inspire me, I put Millay's lines in a small picture frame and placed the frame on my bedside table. I played these lines in my head like an anthem, an anthem celebrating resiliency and courage. *In the very midst of terrible pain I can plan.* A theme song for Reconstruction. When, in spite of everything, we start to plan and build a new life for ourselves. We begin to take action.

6

Working Through

For a long time it had seemed to me that life was about to begin—real life. But there was always some obstacle in the way, something to be got through first, some unfinished business, time still to be served, a debt to be paid. Then life would begin. At last it dawned on me that these obstacles were my life.

ALFRED D'SOUZA

Sometimes the way a solution shows up is just amazing.

For months I had continued to stew about the future. What kind of work did I want to do? Continue teaching? Choose some other type of employment altogether? Perhaps work in the area of communications for a large corporation? I debated, too, about moving. Didn't I need a new location? Wouldn't I be happier in a new environment? At least twenty times a day, if not two hundred, these questions nagged me.

Then one morning, in that hazy time between sleep and waking, I knew the answer.

"Mother, can I go to the library after we eat? Judy Blake said she'd go with me."

I was eight years old again, and it was the middle of the summer. My mother and I were in the kitchen of the house that stood at the foot of Lookout Mountain. She was mashing margarine back and forth in one of those thick plastic bags, the kind we used to put the little pill of color in to make the margarine yellow.

"You can't walk to that library in this hot broiling sun. You'll get heat stroke."

"But, Mother, I've got to go. All my books are due today. I'll walk in the shade . . . let me go . . . please let me."

"Well . . . if you promise to wear a hat . . . and you'd better not take those shoes off! If you come back from that library barefooted with tar all over you, I'll give you a whipping. Last time, I think you just tried to find melted tar to step in."

I loved to go to the library in the summer. You could talk to Mrs. Miller then without having to elbow a hundred kids who were standing around her desk waiting to check out books or to ask her something.

"How many books this week?" Mrs. Miller asked. She was reaching into the little tray where she kept the stars for our reading records that were displayed on bulletin boards all around the library.

"Ten," I answered proudly.

"Ten!" Mrs. Miller responded, with just the right amount of appreciation. "It's a good thing we keep getting new books. At this rate, you're going to have read all the books in the library!"

Then came the blessed moment. Mrs. Miller reached into that wonderful, magic second drawer on the left that almost always held some books she had been saving. "How about this Caddie Woodlawn?" she asked me. "Or these two biographies, one about Jane Addams and the other about George Washington Carver?

"You know, Elizabeth," Mrs. Miller said as she handed me the latest treasures, "anybody who loves books the way you do is bound to become a writer. Why, you know what? I bet someday we'll have books you've written in this very library!"

For several seconds I could not figure out what was happening. For I knew the event was occurring at this moment, and I also knew I was reliving it decades later. How could I be both a little girl eight years old and a woman just turned forty? Then I realized I had been dreaming. No, not dreaming, for everything I had seen had really happened. What I had been doing was recalling something I hadn't thought about in over thirty years. I had been remembering.

And when I got up, the memory would not leave me. Something about it had stirred me very deeply. All during breakfast, I thought about Mrs. Miller and her prediction. Had I been moving toward becoming a writer ever since that day, and just hadn't known it? Was that why I had majored in the eighteenth-century novel in graduate school? Was that why I had become a teacher of literature and writing? Had the college textbook Greg and I were working on when he died been just one more link in the chain of events that would finally lead to my becoming a full-time writer?

As I sat there at the breakfast table, I began to formulate the answers to the questions that for months had been hounding me. What I really wanted to do with my life was to be a writer. And I wanted to write something besides the academic articles, monographs, and textbooks I had been doing. I wanted to write about life, not just about teaching and writing. I wanted to write all kinds of books on all kinds of subjects, books that, if she were still librarian, Mrs. Miller would want in the Rossville library.

But how could I do that? How could I make my living? Everyone knew the precariousness of book publishing, how writers never know if a book will be accepted and then, even if it is accepted, whether it will be bought and read by the public. I had no one to support me, no cash in reserve to fund such an excursion. How could I even think about giving up a secure job for such unpredictability?

It must have been my day for remembering, for at that point my mind went back again to my childhood. Grandma Harper and I were sitting in rocking chairs on her front porch in middle Georgia. I could hear myself asking: "Tell me the Civil War story again, Grandma, please . . . will you tell me?"

All the men were fighting in the army. Your great-great-grandpa got captured and died in a Union prison in Rockford, Illinois. They said he died of typhoid fever, but we always thought he starved to death. Then when the troops got pinned down in Franklin, Tennessee, that's when your great grandpa knew he had to join the war.

That left only the womenfolk on the farm. Your great-great grandma and her daughter took the silver and china they prized so highly, and they buried it before the Yankees came through, below the house in the little swamphead. During Sherman's march, soldiers came through our section and stole all the horses that were left, leaving one old broken-down, sway-backed mare.

One day a stray soldier came into the yard. In a few minutes he came around the side of the house with three or four chickens tied together in his hand. Then he went into the kitchen and cut down the only piece of meat the womenfolk had left, the remains of a cured ham. When the soldier came out, he said, "Thank you, ma'am. I'll just take these chickens and this ham."

Your great-great-grandma said, "That's the only piece of meat we have in the house. Those are our last chickens. Over my dead body you'll take them."

In the meantime, the soldier had crawled up on the swaybacked mare. Not only was he taking the last food the women had, but he was also stealing the only animal they had left to farm with.

From under her long apron, your great-great-grandma pulled an old double-barreled, muzzle-loading shotgun. The gun was loaded only with dried peas and sand, but the soldier didn't know that. He didn't know the women had no ammunition.

"You won't use that gun," the soldier said.

"You believe that?" she replied. "Sometimes it pays the difference to have the difference," she said as she pulled back both hammers on the gun. And with that she pelted him right in the backside.

When she did, he fell off the other side of the horse, turned the chickens loose, and dropped the ham. But your great-great grandma got more than she bargained for. That soldier was so cut up from the sand and dried peas that she had to take care of his wounds before he could go on to join his regiment.

Grandma and I always laughed hard at the end of the story, thinking of the predicament our ancestor's bravery got her into. Then we'd sit there a while longer, rocking. I always knew there would be more if I kept still and waited.

"After Appomattox," Grandma would continue, "one of their men came back—but he was never to be well again—and the other one didn't. The women salvaged what they could, moved to a smaller piece of land, and started over."

And then Grandma would look at me and say, "Now, that's what it means to be a Harper woman." That, I knew, was the point of the whole story.

"Well, perhaps it is time for me to carry on the tradition," I thought as I sat at the table. "Surely some of the blood of those brave women runs in my veins. Surely I have inherited at least some of their grit and determination. When, then, am I going to start acting like a Harper woman?"

I don't know the exact moment when I made the final decision. I just know when I took the action. When I got my next semester's schedule in the mail, I sat down and wrote the department head a letter. "The work that Greg and I started together in the department and that I have been continuing has been gratifying. But it is time now for me to make a change. I am resigning as a commitment to becoming a full-time writer."

I had worked out a plan for supporting myself: with a long-term consulting assignment I had recently gotten from a nonprofit charitable organization publishing a book on world hunger, with one or two prospective coaching jobs working with executives who wanted to learn to do their own writing, with the royalties I was hoping to get from the textbook Greg and I had written that was finally about to be published, and by paring my living expenses to the bone, I thought I could make it. But I was to find out almost before I got started how precarious these plans were and how quickly a source of income could disappear. I was to discover how unpredictable the life of a self-employed person could be and how much I would have to be responsible.

The editor of the textbook had called from New York. "By having the book shipped directly from the printers, we're going to be able to introduce it in San Francisco at the convention of the Modern Language Association," he told me. "We've made reservations for you and hope you'll be there."

Of course I would be there. I was counting on this book to be a major source of income, but it was also important to me for many other reasons. The book was the culmination of more than a decade of research and teaching; it presented an approach to writing that Greg and I had developed and believed in. It was the last project we had worked on together; in fact, we had been working on it up to the minute he left for his jog. And there had been such uncertainty after Greg's death—should I go ahead and finish the book? How much longer would the project now take than had been planned? How would the market respond?

It was past midnight when I arrived in San Francisco. I was very tired when I finally reached the hotel and planned to fall into bed immediately. These plans changed, however, when I walked into my room. For the first thing I saw, lying on the desk, was the new book! The editor had been there before me.

The book was beautiful. There was a Kandinsky painting on the cover, and on the first few pages were four-color photographs of a young couple building a cabin. I had used the metaphor of building a house to talk about writing, and that section of the book, I thought, was especially eye-catching. I was proud of it.

I continued to leaf through the book. It was so exciting to see what had once been scribbled on yellow legal paper now appearing as printed words on the page. I felt like a kid at Christmas. The fatigue had all left me.

Then a piece of folded paper fell out of the book. "Call me no matter what time you get in," the note read. "All I can say is, 'I'm sorry.' " It was signed by my editor.

I was dumbfounded. Why was he sorry? Had something happened that he thought I knew about but didn't? I stared at the words on the note as I called the room number he had listed.

"Have you seen the book?" was Robert's first question.

"Yes," I answered. "I love it. It's so beautiful."

There was a long pause before he continued the conversation. "Well, have you noticed the second color? . . ."

"The second color?" I echoed. "No, I didn't pay any attention to the second color. Is something wrong with it?" I was turning as fast as I could to find a page with a second color.

"Yes, something is wrong," Robert answered. "The second color isn't the brown we specced. It's purple!"

Now I saw. All the headings in the book, all the explanations under the drawings, everywhere color had been used for emphasis . . . all of these were *bright* purple.

"Well," I said quickly, trying to toss the mistake off lightly "I bet English teachers will love purple for a change. The color will get the book a lot of attention.

"There was a long pause, and then Robert said, "Elizabeth, this is really serious. Our marketing department spent several thousand dollars doing a survey to determine the best second color for this book . . . you know that many of the ideas in the book are innovative, so it was critical that the design and color be traditional. This bright purple trivializes the book, makes it look trendy. We'll never be able to sell it in the conservative English market."

I *did* see the gravity of the situation. And I was getting angry. "Well, what happened?" I asked, realizing that my voice was several decibels louder. "How, after all that research and planning, did we end up with a book with purple as the second color?"

"It was a clerical error," Robert answered. "Someone confused two orders as the book was going to press."

I just stood there holding the phone for a few seconds, trying to think of something to say. But there was nothing. Robert's voice was low as he closed the conversation. "I really am sorry, Elizabeth," he said. "Everyone in the company is sick about the mistake. But the book is dead. All we can do now is try to cut our losses." I knew what that meant. No special sales thrust. No special advertising. Everybody trying to forget the book instead of trying to sell it.

I hung up the phone and fell across the bed, crying. So many years' work . . . for nothing. An approach to writing that Greg and I believed in and knew was effective . . . to be discounted. All thoughts of the sale of the book being a source of income . . . a pipe-dream fantasy. I was sick. Discouraged. Devastated.

I cried for hours. I had never felt so defeated. When I finally got up and went to the bathroom to wash my face, I could see that it was almost daylight. The sky was beginning to show pale pink and yellow on the horizon. Since it was useless to think of sleeping, I pulled a chair out onto the small balcony and just sat, looking.

At some point while I was sitting there, something snapped in me. "I will not have it be this way," I said defiantly. "I will not have it. Too much work and effort have gone into this project for such a miserable ending. I just will not have it." Was it my grandma's voice I was hearing in the background? . . . *Then after Appomattox the women salvaged what they could, moved to a smaller piece of land, and started over.* Was finding a way to salvage this book what it meant in the twentieth century to be a Harper woman?

I had never been more resolved in my life. The situation had to be remedied. Whatever it would take, I was going to do it. As the sun came up and the city in front of me took on definition, I made plans. Plans that I was going to put into effect as soon as the stores were opened.

Ten o'clock found me on Union Square waiting for the doors to be unlocked at I. Magnin's. I headed straight for the men's department. "I want to buy some purple shirts," I said to the salesman. "Solid purple."

If he had said there were no men's shirts in solid purple, I was already prepared with an alternate plan. But plan B turned out not to be necessary, for the gentleman said, "Let's go over to the sportswear department. Pierre Cardin has designed some solid-colored shirts this year in bright colors, and one of them is purple."

It was probably the most purple shirt I will ever see. I could not imagine anyone in normal circumstances buying it. "It's a little bright," the salesman said tentatively, "but it's the only thing we have in purple."

"I'll take two," I said without hesitating, "one large and one medium. I'd like them gift-wrapped," I added, "and may I now see the ties you have in paisley?"

I asked the gentleman to pull out every paisley tie that contained the color purple. We spread these out on the glass countertop, and I began choosing. "How many do you need?" the salesman asked me. It was clear that he was no longer making ordinary assumptions. If this lady bought two Pierre Cardin solid purple sport shirts, who knows how many purple paisley ties she needed?

"Ten," I answered.

Expanding our definition of purple to allow for lilac, violet, and blue purple, we found ten paisley ties that filled the bill. "Please giftwrap those, too." I said.

Everyone was at the booth when I walked into the exhibit area The national sales manager was there, as well as my editor. "I have something for you," I said, handing each of them a box containing the shirt. Then I gave each of the sales reps one of the gift-wrapped ties.

"Do you want us to open these now?" the men all asked me. They seemed a little pleased but mostly awkward.

"Yes," I responded. "Now is the time to open them."

It was one of those situations where the gift is so bad that it's wonderful. These were not men who wore loud purple shirts and purple paisley ties. These were men who wore wing-tipped shoes and conservative button-down collars. That, of course, made these shirts and ties all the more ridiculous.

At first the men did not know how to react. Were they supposed to like these? Were they supposed to show their appreciation? But then, first one and then the next began to laugh. Soon all of us standing around this serious college textbook publisher's booth were laughing. Bending-over-double laughing. Holding-the-shirts-up-in-front-of-themselves laughing. Matching-paisley-tie-to-pinstripe-suit laughing. Suddenly the color purple had lost its heaviness, its significance. One could even imagine, standing there, that these men might be able to sell a new college textbook to a conservative market, even if it did have a second color that was purple.

The next few days proved that supposition to be accurate. The reps had good reports: teachers liked the books; many had said they would be ordering. I knew that by the time the news of this success at the national convention reached the entire sales force, the book would stand a good chance of being heavily promoted. Naturally, this made me happy. But I was also mentally and physically exhausted. I had no idea that a person had to work this hard to be courageous.

Even though the textbook sales were going well and I had been able to get consulting jobs that paid the bills while I worked on a new book proposal, I was still a basket case about money. Even if I could see making ends meet for a particular thirty-day period, I was already worrying about the next one.

I was not used to generating income by the month or by the project. Since I was twenty-one, when I got my first teaching job, I had received a regular paycheck. Now I always had to keep an eye on how much I needed, how much had already come in, how much was expected. And I was always afraid that the next month nobody would need or want my services and I would not be able to make it. I knew millions of individuals chose to be self-employed and thrived on the challenge, but in my case it just about made me crazy.

Yet, on the other hand, I had never been more content with the nature of my work. My schedule was flexible; I could set it any way

I needed to in order to have time to write. The consulting jobs were with interesting, creative people who brought to my life a whole new perspective. The proposal I was working on was going well. I knew I wanted to be doing what I was doing.

The conflict, however, was taking its toll. It was wintertime, the days were gray, and my spirits were grayer. I had now been self-employed long enough to realize that the cycle was never-ending: see how much money you have to have, find a way to earn it, finish those projects, see how much money you still have to have, find a way to earn it.... "I've just swapped one disadvantage for another," I told myself, "a teaching job which paid well but left little if any time to write, for a life with plenty of time to write but nothing sure to count on."

It had gotten so bad that I was having nightmares. One morning about four-thirty, I spoke to myself very honestly. I had been tossing and turning for much of the night, having woken up with a start, dreaming that I was shriveled and old and dying in poverty. "You have got to do something to break the hold this thing has on you," I told myself. "It's beginning to color everything, including your enthusiasm for writing."

As I lay there, I realized the root of the difficulty: it wasn't the type of work I had chosen that was the problem, but the fact that I did not have self-confidence. I claimed that I didn't like always having to think about budgets and income, but the truth was that underneath that complaint was a constant fear that no one would hire me, that my books would not be good, that I would not be capable of getting work when I needed it. What I had to do something about was the level of my self-confidence, not the way I had chosen to work.

I was surprised at how much difference it made just to identify the problem correctly. Now I had something I could grab hold of, something I could work on. I was so sick of the way this unspoken, unacknowledged fear had been sucking energy away from things I deeply cared about and spilling its ugly spew over the new life I was building. "What you need to do," I instructed myself, "is to take some action so drastic that in the future you will feel courageous just by remembering that you did this." But what could I do that would be that drastic?

"Give some money away," came the answer from somewhere inside.

"Give money away! Are you crazy!" I felt fear making accordion pleats in my stomach as the internal dialogue continued.

"What was it that Emerson said—if you are afraid to do something, that is the thing you should do, if you want to build character?"

"But I don't have any money to give away; I'm barely making enough as it is."

"Yes, you do. You have your teacher retirement."

"My teacher retirement! But I can't give part of my teacher retirement away; that's absolutely my only security."

"You don't have to give it all, but you might give five thousand dollars to that organization you consult with that's working to help end world hunger."

"But I don't have a lot in my teacher retirement, and five thousand dollars is a big chunk of money."

"I know, but you did say you needed to do something drastic to break the back of this fear that is constantly gnawing away at you."

"Yes, but I didn't mean that drastic!"

But the more I thought about it, the more I could see that making that donation would be making a statement about my belief in myself: that I could take five thousand dollars out of my teacher retirement because I had confidence that I could build another retirement fund out of my self-employment; that I saw myself as the kind of person who could make a contribution of that magnitude; that I was a strong enough person to do something that I was scared to death of doing.

So I gave the five thousand dollars. And although it wasn't the last thing I was ever going to have to do to build my self-confidence, it made a big difference.

_____

As the months passed, I felt more and more centered in my work; I felt that I had reconnected with what gave me meaning and purpose. I had picked up the thread again, a thread that, in effect,

had been present all of my life in some form or another. The plays
and stories I had written as a child. All those poems I had taken so
much care to print in that little brown spiral notebook. The social
studies assignments that I would always ask if I could turn into a
story—*Miss McKensie, do you care if I write about the everyday
life of a set of twins living in colonial America? I'll be sure to get in
all the information about the war with the English.* Then the academic study in literature and writing. All those books and articles I
had edited or written. Marrying and working with Greg, who was a
writer. I felt that what I was doing now had always been there at the
beginning and I had just come back to it.

But I couldn't feel that way about other areas, particularly about
my personal life. What I had shared with Greg had been like a
destination, the place I had dreamed about all my life, the place I
most wanted to get to. So what was there to reconnect with there?
Nothing. So even when my work was going well, I still had to fight
off depressing feelings of "What's the use?" Everything was still so
empty; I was so lonely. What was I to do with the memories of a
man I loved who no longer existed?

Then came the dream and the student's letter.

The dream was very simple. There was a large green plant that
had been thrown aside on the lawn. But when I picked the plant up I
made a wonderful discovery. The plant had roots! I knew in the
dream that the plant could be repotted and would stay alive. The
discovery in the dream made me deliriously happy.

A few days later I received a long letter from one of Greg's
former graduate students with whom I had not had contact since
shortly after Greg died. Chuck wrote:

> *Greg was the first person close to me who ever died. He was my
> mentor, the teacher I wanted to be. And he just passed right out of
> my life. He went out so quickly, so irretrievably, so irrevocably. I
> couldn't go to the funeral, so I didn't get a chance to say good-bye.
> I did say good-bye one night out in the backyard of my house, but
> things still always seemed unfinished.*
>
> *But something happened recently that allowed me to see the
> place Greg has and will always have in my life. It happened as I
> was completing a writing seminar prior to taking my doctoral orals.*

Then the student told the story. Dr. Graves, the professor in the writing seminar, had instructed the graduate students: "Read Scott Momaday's tribute to his grandmother—'Now that I can have her only in memory, I see my grandmother . . . standing at the wood stove on a winter morning and turning meat in a great iron skillet; sitting at the south window, bent above her beadwork....' Then write a model of Momaday's paragraph, using someone as the subject whom you can have now only in memory."

The student told me he had chosen Greg, and that this was what he had written:

> *Now that I can only have Greg in memory, I recall the sense of continuity that was shattered when he fell off a road in East Tennessee and out of all our lives forever. I think of Greg and I see Kris Kristofferson, grizzled beard, deep voice, sparkling, deep-set eyes. He was my teacher, my colleague, my friend, who showed me how to step across a boundary and leave all the tangled messes behind. It was the crossing that mattered.*
>
> *Once we were going into a Japanese restaurant. You had to cross a little bridge to get to it. Greg was bothered by something that had happened at the university . . . I didn't know what it was, but something had disturbed him. As we started to go into the restaurant, Greg said, "When I go across this bridge, I'm leaving the problem here and I'm going over there. It's not going to be with me anymore, and we're going to go ahead and have our time together."*
>
> *We did have a wonderful time, and it was one of my greatest lessons in life, watching Greg do that. What he taught me was to let go of things and move on. I think that's why I had such a hard time letting go of him —because he taught me how to let go and I couldn't imagine letting that go. Continuity. The smooth movement from here to there, from then to now, and on into tomorrow without getting caught in any one place too long. That's what he taught me, and it's always with me.*

The student ended his letter: *I'm convinced the reason we are here is to remember, if we understand memory to be that uniquely human ability to create from the past a sense of meaning in the present and a trembling anticipation of possibility in the future.*

When I finished Chuck's letter, I knew I had gained wisdom: a person who is gone can live on in memory as an *active* agent in one's life, not just as someone you love and miss, not just as a nostalgic sadness. Greg had been remembered by his student; and that remembering had altered the quality of the student's life in the present and informed his life for the future: . . . *if we understand memory to be that uniquely human ability to create from the past a sense of meaning in the present and a trembling anticipation of possibility in the future.*

That, I realized, was how a person we love and have lost can remain in our lives forever. In a way that is neither morbid nor regressive. And in a way that honors the lost person at the same time that it makes room for others. We *make meaning* of the memories. From the memories we extract values, ideals, insight, pleasures, awareness.

This, then, was how Greg would fit into my life. I knew, for instance, that I would always care for my family in a different way because Greg had enabled me to see them in a new light. I would always feel more connected to the out-of-doors because with him I had learned new ways to see the woods, the mountains, the sea. I would always be more awake to the sensuous pleasures of life— colors, smells, sounds, tastes—because I had been able to experience life with him. And I would always know what love was because he had loved me.

I would always enjoy the opera and ballet, which I first discovered with him. I would always read books about the Lewis and Clark expedition because I had followed the trail with him one summer and caught a glimpse of how that trek symbolizes a journey that is possible for all of us. I would always like red geraniums by the front door and eggs scrambled with brie. I would always want to drive a clean car, and I would always ask if the saltwater taffy were made on the premises.

It was just a pleasant interlude, but the experience I had that evening gave me insight into how to be happy.

It was New Year's Eve, and my girlfriend and I were in Mexico

City. Felicia's boyfriend had recently been transferred here, and she had invited me to join her when she came for this holiday visit. We were now seated in an elegant hotel dining room, regaling the two men across the table from us with stories about what had happened to us during our sight-seeing activities.... Did they want to hear about the woman who had enticed the parrot she was carrying on a stick to bite me on the elbow when she wanted to pass us on the sidewalk? Or perhaps they would rather hear about the taxi driver who could not understand our Spanish and delivered us to an open-air market way out in the suburbs instead of to the downtown cathedral where we were going. Or perhaps they'd like to see all the tiny glass turtles and frogs and prisms we had bought at the park from the street vendor....

The colleague Brad had brought as my date for the evening was taking all this hilarity in stride, and I liked him for it. The men soon matched us story for story with their own tales of adventure that accompanied being transferred from the United States to a foreign city. We were a light-hearted foursome.

It was almost midnight. "Let's have our champagne downstairs in the discotheque," Brad suggested. "Then we can dance till morning if we want to." I was stunned when we entered the room. I had never seen a club as beautiful as this one. Dark blue velvet banquettes curving around tables covered with white linen, silver, and crystal. A domed ceiling of lights that looked so much like stars and planets that, if you had not known better, you would have sworn you were looking up into the heavens. Beautiful people everywhere. Long gowns, jewels, tuxedos. "This certainly doesn't look like any discotheque I've ever been to," I whispered to Felicia as we were being seated. "Can you believe we're in such an elegant place?"

I realized as we sat down how much I was enjoying this evening. I couldn't remember when I had last felt so at ease, so natural. "What is the difference?" I wondered. Then I answered my own question. I looked at the person sitting next to me and realized that here was a man I had not once all evening thought about marrying! I had not once imagined us in an ongoing relationship. I had not once worried about how I could get him to like me! What a shift. Finally, I was able to be with a man just for the pleasure of his company. Just to have fun. With no hidden agenda. It was a wonderful feeling.

We began to dance. I felt exuberant. The beat of the song was strong, and I was moving in rhythm to it. I could feel the sound reverberating in my fingers, in my feet. As I continued to dance, it was as if the definitions of my body began to melt and I became one with everything around me, the music, the people, the lights above me. It was a moment of pure ecstasy. Total happiness. Complete freedom. In that experience there was no yesterday, and there was no tomorrow. There was only this moment. There was only *now. I* was just dancing.

I knew my friend would never understand if I tried to tell her on the plane ride back home that I had learned how to live my life while I was out on that dance floor. But the truth was I had. *Hold nothing back. Engage fully with what you are doing at this very moment. Focus only on the thing right in front of you. Live in the present, not the past or the future.* The extent to which a person chose to do this in all areas of life, I now realized, was the extent to which a person experienced being free and happy.

These are the experiences of Working Through. A time of learning new solutions, forming new assumptions, reworking old issues. We begin to redefine our place in life around us, to reinforce our competence, to assume new roles alongside those old ones that are necessary or appropriate for us to continue. We find new ways to predict and guide what happens in our lives; we reassess our talents and capabilities.

During Working Through we experience life as a double thread: we must solve problems and deal with issues related to the new life we are building, and we must do the same for problems and issues continuing from the past. At first glance, it may look as if each of these arenas is an additional demand put on top of the one before. But often we are surprised to find them working in tandem. The confidence we gain as a result of solving a new problem, for instance, will often enable us to face and solve a knotty problem of the past. As we find ourselves able to act in the present, we discover new ways to experience continuity with the past.

But there is a gap. All of this Working Through is not done in a day. It takes time for the plans and assumptions that were changed for us *externally* by the loss to change *internally* also. There is much trial and error, much scratchy unsettledness as we engage with the conflicts. We "proceed by tentative approximations"; we "grow by delays." But we can take satisfaction from the fact that we are not only solving problems and working out issues during this period, but are also altering ourselves. We are being changed by the experiences: to become more independent, more competent, more knowing. To become more our true self.

A number of men and women who have lived in this gap we call Working Through say that this period of the mourning process includes these experiences....

EMERGENCE OF NEW ASPIRATIONS
A man reports:

Probably the hardest thing for me to tolerate after Leslie died was the lethargy. I lost all ambition. Up until that time I had been gung ho about everything; I had a game plan that excited me. I worked out regularly at the gym. My brother and I were turning a small electrical company into a good business. I had high goals in life and total confidence that I would reach them. But with Leslie gone, I just didn't care about anything. I tried to fight it, but it's a contradiction in terms, I guess, to think you can fight lethargy.

Lately, though, something has started to change. It's like I'm waking up. The thing that has excited me is the idea of simplifying my life. I'm looking to see how many things I can get rid of around the house that's just clutter. I've got my brother interested in simplifying at the office. I'm getting him turned on to the idea of building a smaller but a more quality business. It's a game now for me to find as many ways as possible to make things more simple.

But I also have to admit that sometimes it's upsetting. Many of the changes involve things related to my life with Leslie. For instance, we were into buying old—I mean really run-down—houses and fixing them up to rent. We fixed them up together, and then

Leslie managed them. Now every time I sell one of those houses, I feel like another part of Leslie has been taken away from me. But the rewards of simplifying are strong. So I just keep moving on with the project.

REACTIVATION OF FEARS

A young mother relates this story:

Only someone who has ever had a firstborn die a crib death can know what it takes to decide to have another baby. Right before Kimberly was born, I dreamed again and again about Tommy's death. That made me afraid something was wrong with the baby I was carrying. We didn't even talk about the possibility of crib death, just whether or not she would have all her fingers and toes—would she have anything wrong with her.

Even though it's highly unlikely that a second baby in a family will die of crib death, we still keep Kimberly hooked up to a monitor. The fear is residue left over from Tommy's death, I know. One day when Kimberly was about three months old, the monitor's beeper went off. It's customary for babies to breathe irregularly at times and if the monitor beeps, you're supposed to stand there and count to ten to see if the baby corrects herself, which is what is normal. My first thought, of course, was that she was dead; and it was the hardest thing in the world to stand there and count to ten to see if she started breathing again. I knew I had to, though; I had to face that fear. In just a few seconds everything was back to normal. That experience has given me courage to take her off the monitor more often.

OPPORTUNITY FOR RISK TAKING

A divorced mother of two tells this story:

One day the thought came to me, "I'd like to start dating." The divorce had seared me, as I guess they most always do; and I hadn't been interested in men for a long time. I had concentrated all my time and attention on Ben and Stacy, doing everything I could to make their adjustment easy. But as time passed I realized I was lonely. I really missed male companionship.

I had never thought of John as a potential date. I saw him often at the boys' school where he was the principal, and I knew he had been divorced many years, but beyond that I knew little about him. Then, one night I dreamed about him. The next day I asked another volunteer at the school who had known him for many years what he was like, and she said he never dated. "He reminds me of an ascetic monk," she said. "His life is devoted to the students."

I debated for several weeks, and then I got up the nerve to call him. "I'd like to have an appointment," I said to him, and we set a time when I could come in. "I'll get right down to the purpose for my visit," I said to him as soon as I sat down in his office. I was nervous; I had no idea what would be the outcome of this venture. Would things now be so awkward between us that it would be impossible for me to continue to volunteer? Would he laugh? Would we both be totally embarrassed? But I went ahead. I told him about the dream I had of him. And then I said, "I would like to get to know you better. Is that a possibility?"

Of course, I shocked him to death. The first thing he did was sit back in his chair. He was speechless. When he finally managed to speak, his words were, "I admire your courage." Then he started two or three other sentences and couldn't finish them.

I interrupted. "I've made you uncomfortable, haven't I?"

"Yes," he answered.

And I replied, "I'm sorry."

"No," he said, "you shouldn't be sorry. It's not you. It's me."

So then we talked a little more, and he said, "Do you know how long it's been since I dated? I don't even know how to date."

"Well, I don't either," I answered, "but I can ask my sister. She knows all about those kinds of things."

That was where we left it. The next time we saw each other, he waited for me outside the meeting room and said, "Well, how would you like to go out next Friday night?"

"I think it would be great," I answered.

We made the arrangements; then he said, as he was leaving, "I'm looking forward to it," and I said, "Me, too."

We dated and went through all the ups and downs of that process, but my hunch all along was that we'd finally get married! Which we are doing this coming May. And the whole school is invited to the wedding.

NECESSITY TO TAKE RISKS

A young widow recalls:

Of all the things Ed had been involved in, the only piece of the business that I could see being able to make a living at was running the two doughnut shops. They were potentially income-producing, and the kids and I had to have an income. I knew it was a big gamble. I had never even run anything before, much less a doughnut shop. And I knew I would be excused if I said, "I just can't do this." Everybody would have understood and said, "Oh, that poor widow."

But I saw the possibility in the doughnut shops. "The risk of making them better," I said to myself, "has got to be worth what you're going to lose if it doesn't work out." So I made a choice. I knew this was for the long haul, not just something I could flit in and out of in a few days. I decided I would get into those doughnut shops and work to change things over time and not be stopped by my fear of economic failure. I knew things were going to be changed anyway, and I decided I would be the one in those shops doing it. If time for the next payment came around and I couldn't meet it, I'd just say, "Hey, I can't do this. I don't know how to run a doughnut shop." But if I succeeded, the kids and I would be in much better shape financially.

It's now been two years, and I'm happy to report that I'm making it. A big equipment loan just came due at the bank last week, and it made me feel so good to know that every penny of the money used to pay off that loan had been earned since I had been managing.

NECESSITY TO COME BACK FROM FAILURE

A divorced mother of three tells this story:

After the divorce, I had to get a better job. The boys and I couldn't live on what I'd been making, even with the child support their daddy was giving. I'm a bookkeeper, and you can make only so much working for others. So I decided to go into business for myself. It was a risk, but it was also the only way I could see being able to make it.

At first I did great. The business grew; I rented larger office space and hired someone to help me. Unfortunately, I hired someone who was also a friend who I thought knew a lot about bookkeeping, but it turned out she couldn't do anything. So I had a lot of losses related to her work. Then several people who had been clients from the first month I was in business died. The economy in our area took a nose-dive, and I must have written off $10,000 in bad debts. I could not keep everything going, so I had to declare bankruptcy.

I filed Chapter 13 because I wasn't willing to run out on it, so for the next five years I'll be paying off everything. This was hard on my sense of self-worth; it took a long time for me to put it all in perspective. I was embarrassed and felt like a failure. But as time went on, I saw the truth: Just because I went bankrupt didn't mean I was any worse a bookkeeper. I let people know I was still in business, and I started getting a lot of referrals. The irony is that in the long run the bankruptcy seems to have helped my business. It has made me very knowledgeable about bankruptcy law and has allowed me to help my clients avoid similar situations.

NECESSITY TO REINVENT ONESELF
A young man recounts:

The whole structure of my life was smattered to smithereens by the death of my mother. I was eight and didn't understand what had happened—that my mother had become addicted to barbiturates three years earlier and finally was dying from this addiction. Within those three years, then, we went from a very midwestern, middle-class, very typical early-fifties St. Louis kind of family to a disintegrated, poor, Deep South kind of family. It was just incomprehensible. Very bewildering. Confusion and more confusion. I changed from being very outgoing to never going out. Just staying home and reading and having no friends. Our family just withdrew as a group.

So as an adult I've had to reinvent myself. Come up with a personality and a person to be. When someone asks me how you do that, I say, "You pick what you like. You learn." For a long time I was a very unfocused, undirected person.

But life placed me in contact with people who taught me that I could pick and choose from the menu of what I had seen and say, "Well, I like that and I like that and I don't like that. That's a good way to be, and that's not a good way to be."

I made choices. I just became aware of reality and that I had to make choices and those choices were my life. Everybody, of course, has to do that; but loss forces you into an absolute realization of that.

And I'm still doing it. Making choices isn't something that you do once and then no more. Making choices is for the rest of your life.

CHALLENGE OF ESTABLISHING A NEW IDENTITY
A divorced woman recalls:

It had always been through this other person that I had fulfilled myself in life—take care of a man, help him in his work, raise his children, keep his life in order and on track, and make him look good. That was my life's purpose and had been for twenty-six years. Suddenly, when he fell in love with another woman, all that was not there any longer, so I had to relook at all of my values, all the things I believed in, and start over. Or just start, I guess. Just start.

It was terribly frightening. My career went with the divorce since I worked with my husband in our own company. My children were almost grown. I was even located physically in unfamiliar territory. I had no idea what to do with the rest of my life. It was like, "My God, what am I going to do?" I was not prepared at all to live my own life. I had no idea what it was like to be my own person, be responsible for my own time, my own emotions, my own circle of people.

Now, however, I'm beginning to get something of a new iden- tity. I looked at some of the things I did most successfully when I worked with my husband's company and realized that over the years I had developed a lot of skill in strategic planning. So I've zeroed in on that and am offering my services to small businesses that need help with their planning.

I've also taken up ballroom dancing, something I always wanted to do but that my husband wasn't interested in. It's opened up a whole new world to me. The people in that arena are very different from those in the business world. These new friends are very inter- esting people. New doors are opening in my personal life, my emotions, my self-expression. I've discovered I've had to unlearn just about everything I knew about dancing. And the stamina re- quired—it's amazing. There's no end to the challenge. It's exciting and so open-ended. I have won first place already in several compe- titions and am going to Hawaii to compete again in January.

I still have my ups and downs. It's not easy to become a new person. But one day when I was moaning and groaning to a friend about all the decisions I have to make now, she looked at me and said, "Don't you ever get tired of whittling on your own finger?" Boy, that was a breakthrough. Now every time I start thinking negative thoughts, I say to myself, "Brenda, you're whittling on your own finger."

NECESSITY TO REEXAMINE ASSUMPTIONS

A young man whose father died and who himself just recovered from a life-threatening disease says:

The way I see it, everybody has a kind of contract with the world. According to the terms of that contract, the world acts in a certain way and you act in a certain way and the world responds in a certain way. It's a contract that builds up over time.

And I think one of the most fundamental clauses in that contract is the immortality clause. The immortality clause says the world doesn't go on without you and those you love in it. We wouldn't admit to believing the immortality clause if we were pinned down to it, but we act as if it is true nevertheless. We believe that the world will stay the way it is while our lives unfold as they are supposed to.

Then something comes along to contest that clause. With no warning, with no signs pointing to it, with no pain beforehand. Like my father dying. Like my going in three years later for a regular check up and finding out that at age twenty-nine I had cancer. All of a sudden everything is shattered. It's a horrible thing.

So I have realized that the clause has gotten canceled, and I have to rewrite the contract completely. The whole contract with life has to be renegotiated because none of it any longer makes sense. I'm now in the process of doing that renegotiation.

THE RECOGNITION THAT CERTAIN PROBLEMS WERE NOT CAUSED BY THE LOSS BUT MERELY REVEALED BY IT

A widow reports:

At first I was prone to say that I had certain problems because I had been hurt so by Jim's dying. But I know now that these problems already existed. For instance, since his death, I have realized it is very difficult for me to show affection to the children; and I said for a while that this was related to being in mourning. But the truth is that I have always had trouble showing affection. When Jim was alive I wasn't the only parent to love and nurture the kids, so any deficiency on my part was not so apparent. Now, I've had to work hard to learn how to show them my affection.

My relationship with my in-laws is another area that I had been able to handle by hiding behind Jim when he was alive. For instance, if I got upset with them, I'd tell Jim and he'd say he'd talk to them or he'd do some kind of mediating. Now if I don't want to go some place they want to go or if I don't want to do something or don't want the kids to do something, I have to come right out and say it. I now have to deal with them as an adult, on a one-to-one basis. Now I have to be right on the front lines ready to take any shots that come at me. I'd like to say all this is because of Jim's death, but I know it isn't. I know the problems were always there, and now there's just no convenient way to hide them.

THE NECESSITY FOR SELF-MANAGEMENT
A divorced father says:

Really, you almost have to build yourself over, decide again who you really are. There are a lot of alternatives. And you're pushed to the emotional limit and perhaps the physical limit as well. You have to see where the boundaries are so you can build on your strengths.

I've discovered that to do this I have to discipline my mind. Most of us will discipline our bodies pretty well, but not our minds. If I don't discipline my mind, I fall back to where I was right after Nancy left me. For instance, I'll be lying in bed at night, not able to go to sleep, and my mind will go to town. "Oh, woe is me. Why did she leave me? What could I have done that I didn't do?" And so on. I've come to see that I have the choice to keep on thinking those thoughts—which I've learned produce only negative experiences— or I can discipline my mind to stop thinking them. This isn't easy; it takes a lot of work. It's really a behavioral change I'm talking about. Bringing about a behavioral change in oneself. But I've found out that this idea of self talk and disciplining your mind is very helpful and necessary.

ACCOMMODATING RECURRENT GRIEF
A woman whose grandson died at age eighteen months recounts:

I think the loss of a child may be one of the hardest things to get

over. When Jason died, I became very bitter, very angry with God.
How could an innocent baby die when there were so many mean,
evil people walking around alive in the world? How could a bright
child's potential be denied?

But I am able now to deal with my grief constructively. One
thing I've worked through is my desire to know *why*. Why did Jason
die? For so long I was dominated by that question. I tried to find the
answer through reading books, talking to wise people. But I see now
that I will never find a satisfactory answer. I now know the question
"Why?" is not a good question. So I have ceased to ask it. And I am
at peace even though I don't know the answer.

I also realize how important it is to continue to speak of Jason
when I am sad or on special occasions when I miss him. Talking was
the best therapy I found after his death. Many of my friends were
uncomfortable hearing me speak of Jason—they would want to take
me out to lunch or shopping to help me forget it—but I had one
friend who encouraged me to talk. And, you know, one friend can do
it; you don't have to have a whole support system. By this time,
however, I don't feel a need to talk about the death all the time. But
there are times when it is necessary: maybe it will be Christmas and
I will think of the child and say, "I'm sorry Jason is not here to get
and give presents." The rest of my family never respond when I
speak about Jason. They won't talk about him or the death at all.
At first this bothered me a lot, but now I just remind myself that
I've got to do what keeps me healthy, no matter what others do or
don't do.

NEED TO FIND NEW SOLUTIONS

A divorced father recounts:

Carrie and I have been divorced three years now, and all this
time I've said to myself, "You can't date because you don't have
enough money." Before the divorce I had taken the money we made
for granted. We weren't rich by any means, not even close, but we
had some cash flow we could live with. We could go skiing and
things like that. And all of a sudden now I can't go skiing or do
anything extra. And I have a lot of pride. It was just one more insult
to the injury—to go from being solid middle class to being a
pauper.

So it's taken me a while to stop being the victim of the situation and do something about it. I kept thinking, "Just to go out to eat on a basic date anymore costs you fifty or sixty bucks." And I was living on fifty bucks a week! (Of course, I set that up myself; it was my own generosity and because I love my kids that I give Carrie so much of my paycheck.) But lately I've gotten real creative about what to do, real cheap. I'll go running down at the Hike and Bike Trail, and I've met some neat women that way. Women who like to do things outdoors and don't demand that a lot of money be spent on them. I've started perusing the paper to see what's going on around town, like free symphonies, and that's where I'll take a woman.

Sometimes I think you develop a real good sense of humor to keep from going crazy. The decision is yours: to be miserable or to be happy. To make light of it or let it depress you. And lately I've decided to choose to make light of it as much as I can.

OPPORTUNITY TO ABSTRACT FROM THE PAST
WHAT GAVE LIFE MEANING

A fifty-nine-year-old widow told this story:

Family was always so important to my husband and me. His four brothers and their wives would come to see us, all at the same time, and we would have such a good time together. I enjoyed cooking for them—"the old-fashioned way," they called it. I enjoyed every minute of it—making biscuits for every meal, bowls of cream gravy, fried pork chops. (Makes me shudder now to think of all that cholesterol! But we didn't know any better then.)

After my husband died, we didn't have family events like that anymore. We were all still close, but we just didn't visit the way we did before. I really missed the experience of "family." Then I discovered one day that writing about the past put me back in touch with all those good feelings. I wrote a little vignette about my childhood— about the day my papa's drugstore burned down—and although it was simple and might not be to others great writing, I really enjoyed it. So I began putting together a collection of stories from the past, which I gave to all the family one Christmas.

The funny thing was that to write all those stories I ended up visiting every one of the four brothers to get facts and details. It was a new way to enjoy the family.

THE DISCOVERY THAT YOU HAVE FOUND A COMFORTABLE PLACE IN YOUR THOUGHTS FOR THE LOST PERSON

A woman whose mother died tells this story:

The day after my mother died, I drove to the funeral home to take some clothes for her to be buried in, and my thirteen-year-old son was with me. We got to the parking lot outside the funeral home, and I started to cry. I said to William, "You know, all that we have left of Nanny is in the funeral home." And he looked at me like I was crazy.

"Why, Mama," he said, "you know we'll always have Nanny with us. We'll always think about her and what we did and what a nice time we had together. She's not going anywhere; she'll always be with us." And then I thought, "What an idiot I am." Here is a thirteen-year-old boy who has it all figured out.

And as time has gone on, I've realized even more that he was right. That we would always have good memories of Nanny. And I think you should think about those things—you can't stop yourself from thinking about them anyway; things are always reminding you. So we still talk about her, and now it's not hard to talk. We can even make jokes about things that happened. I think we have the tendency to make a martyr out of the person who died, and they become perfect in our minds. For a while. And then all of a sudden you realize they were just a human being like everyone else. They didn't always do the right thing, and sometimes you even got disgusted with them.

I still talk to my mother, too. She was a very wise woman. When she was alive, I would talk things over with her. She would always let me make my own decisions; but she had some very helpful things to say always. So now if I have something I'm trying to figure out, I have a conversation with her. The only difference is that I both ask and answer all the questions! She also had a wonderful sense of humor. The day before she died the doctor was using some instrument to look into her eyes and she thought he looked so funny twisted around trying to see what he needed to see that she burst out laughing. To this day, the doctor still mentions that when I see him. I find myself now seeing more humor in situations than I used to, and I always think of her when I am laughing.

THE FOCUS DURING WORKING THROUGH

Needless to say, the tasks that make up this part of the grieving process—tasks that include problem-solving, grappling with old issues that have resurfaced, working to establish a new identity, and numerous other challenges—tax and strain us. This is clearly a *working things out* period in our lives, and most of the time we feel that there is little, if any, respite from this labor. How do we keep ourselves moving forward under these circumstances? What can we do to keep ourselves committed to sticking with these thorny issues until we achieve a resolution?

Positive Self-Management

There is no question that this is a time when we are required to manage ourselves in order to move on through the process. I remember a poet writing that instead of feeling as if he were just one person, he felt as if he were a whole boarding house full of people who would never come all at the same time when he called them to dinner. That's often how we feel during this Working Through period. We know what we must do, but some renegade pieces of us won't join the confederation.

I have seen individuals who have lost do many courageous things to manage themselves during this period. I think of my neighbor, a man in his fifties whose wife had died unexpectedly, walking several miles every morning about four A.M. It was his way of saying, I will not become a vegetable; I will move forward. I think of another friend—a woman who has remarried after a painful divorce and is working diligently to merge two households—who schedules into her busy life at least an hour every day to listen to tapes that inspire and instruct her. "I know I've got to work on myself," I've heard her say again and again. "I've got to work on my own thinking. That's the only thing that will make any difference." This woman looks at least ten years younger than her years, and I have to believe the regimen of private study and quiet reflection that she does each day with her tapes contributes to and enhances her beauty.

I think also of the numerous individuals with whom I've talked who have developed for themselves what amounts to a creed that they use again and again to keep themselves going: pieces of poetry, verses from sacred scriptures, aphorisms and quotations, remembered and often even verbally repeated to encourage themselves when it is time for more courageous action. What all of these people have in common is a sense that their thoughts and behavior affect their lives and that they are not, therefore, helpless in the face of adversity.

Current research supports this conclusion. Not long ago, the *New York Times* reported that it has now been proven that "optimism—at least reasonable optimism—can pay dividends as wide-ranging as health, longevity, job success, and higher scores on achievement tests" (and, I would add, success in completing the mourning process). "Our expectancies," says Dr. Edward Jones from Princeton University, "not only affect how we see reality but also affect the reality itself."

Dr. Michael Scheier from Carnegie-Mellon University reported that people who think positively handle stress better than those who think negatively: optimists, for instance, respond to being turned down for a job by formulating a plan of action and asking other people for help and advice; pessimists try to "forget the whole thing" and assume "there is nothing they can do to change things."

And Dr. Martin Seligman from the University of Pennsylvania has pointed out that it is the way people explain their failures to themselves that determines the degree of their future successes (and also their health; an attitude of helplessness, for instance, is associated with weakened immune systems). Those who think negatively "construe bad events . . . as resulting from a personal deficit that will plague them forever in everything they do." They punish themselves for their setbacks. Those who think positively see "the same setbacks more optimistically, as being due to mistakes that can be remedied. They feel they can make the necessary changes." Those who take the stance that there is nothing they can do are much more prone to depression.

The important thing for us to note about this in relation to the Working Through phase of the grieving process is that we must engage in some form of self-management based on the belief that we play a significant role in how our lives turn out and whether or not we are happy. Whether that self-management takes the form of self-talk, books, tapes, prayer, assertions of faith, words of wisdom, exercise, planning, conversations with others, or some other method depends on the particular bent of each individual. But, given the complexity of the tasks, we have no alternative except to commit ourselves to some form of self-management as we move through this Working Through period.

A specific self-management action that some individuals find useful is a tool we called project management. When a person determines to make a particular change, accomplish a certain goal, or do a specific activity that is not part of her or his ordinary repertoire of actions or that is especially hard, the individual decides if the goal or proposed activity is serious enough to turn into a project. "Turning an idea into a project" means that the idea is put in writing and a structure is created that supports the accomplishment of the project. For instance, questions such as these are answered: What is the purpose of this project? What makes this project worth doing? What is likely to go wrong and what will you do when this happens? What tools, equipment, supplies, information, and so on do you need to do this project? Who will coach you in this project? What is the timeline? What will be your next project? What outcome do you want? Want can cause this project to fail?

Men and women during Working Through have used the tool of project management to do everything from putting a fifty-year collection of photographs into albums to learning to drive at the age of seventy to setting up a budget to manage personal finances to finding a solution for how to discipline the children. People are amazed to discover that a tool as simple as project management could give them such a sense of control and personal power. (But didn't Einstein say that the most elegant things were the most simple?) Again and again, I've seen the structure that this self-management approach provides give people dealing with the experiences of Working Through just the lift off, order, and purpose they needed.

Detaching and Reattaching Purpose

One of the most crucial and most difficult of all tasks during the mourning process is to retrieve the thread of purpose that ran through the life we had with the lost person and find a way to reattach that thread in our present circumstances in order again to have a sense that life has meaning. There is no quick fix that allows this to happen. I've seen men and women attempt to find immediate purpose and meaning through "practical busy-ness"—through taking classes, going on trips, joining groups. But such a flurry of activity does not give these people what they want. It is not possible just to tack on activities and expect these to matter deeply to us. It has been over a lifetime that the purposes that give our lives meaning have been learned and brought together. Any new purposes we establish, therefore, "remain meaningless, until they can be referred to those which have gone before." And such helter-skelter activities can actually be dangerous; they can result in a fragmentation—a disintegration—of our identity that is "more lastingly damaging" than having to retrieve a purpose from the "wreck of dead hopes."

As Peter Marris tells us:

> A sense of continuity can, then, only be restored by detaching the familiar meanings of life from the relationship in which they were embodied, and reestablishing them independently of it.... Thus grief is mastered, not by ceasing to care for the dead, but by abstracting what was fundamentally important in the relationship and rehabilitating it. A widow has to give up her husband without giving up all that he meant to her.... [This is a] task of extricating the essential meaning of the past and reinterpreting it to fit a very different future.... This is what happens in the working through of grief....

Professor James Carse has another way of talking about the outcome of our attempts to reestablish meaning and purpose in our lives. When we do find a way to pick up the threads of the past and connect those threads with something in the present, we discover that, as hostile a force as it is, death has not taken away all of our freedom. We recognize that we still have one very important freedom: the freedom to "reconstitute the continuities" that the loss has destroyed. When we experience this, we realize that we do have "the power to sustain continuity in the face of death." And this, the professor says, is the highest form of freedom.

Internalizing the Lost Person

I have a close friend, a writer, who told me recently about his experience of "internalizing the lost person." Adam's best friend, Paul, also a writer, died three years ago. "This has been hard," Adam said. "You know, you expect your parents or someone older than you to die, but a friend isn't supposed to die. That's why you have friends your own age—to go through life *with you,* not to die *before you. So* I had strong anger and resentment. I felt as if he were a victim, and I felt as if I were a victim.

"But," Adam went on to tell me, "I find that now I am assuming for myself many of the things he did. I have found myself experimenting with his way of writing and really getting into it. It's as if he's not here to do it, so I'll do it for him. And it's also as if that way of writing is a part of Paul that is left with me. I also find myself writing much more autobiographically, which Paul did a lot, but which, until after his death, I had never done. When I run into old friends who knew Paul, I find myself, as Paul's best friend, being an authority on his work. I know things about his craft, his assumed attitudes, that others don't. I also notice that at times I take on Paul's way of behaving: 'Let's get drunk and not talk about it,' I might say, or, 'Let's have a good time and forget it.' But the way I have internalized Paul the most," Adam concluded, "is by having much more confidence in my own work. It's as if Paul, who always believed in my writing, is still reassuring me, except that it is *I* who am now doing the reassuring."

I have heard many people tell similar stories: a wife who learns to make wise business decisions in ways similar to her ex-husband; the father who is able to tell funny stories to his teenage daughters of his courtship days with their late mother; the widow who learns to make the same dishes her husband did; the husband who begins to sing in the choir because his late wife had done so and realizes how much he enjoys it; the ex-wife of a writer who has become an editor, incorporating his love of words into her own work; the mother who relishes flying kites every spring because she flew them with her deceased children; the son who uses memories of the self-destructive actions of a deceased parent to enable himself to make wiser decisions in his own adulthood; the daughter who finds herself incorporating into her own life her deceased mother's values—eating well, taking walks, mixing with people of many ages; the elderly widow who holds imaginary conversations with her late husband. (I. O. Glick and his colleagues at Harvard point out: "Often the widow's progress toward recovery was facilitated by inner conversations with her husband's presence . . . this continued sense of attachment was not incompatible with increasing capacity for independent action." John Bowlby adds, "That for many bereaved people this [talking to the lost person] is the preferred solution to their dilemma has for too long gone unrecognized.") All of these are ways we internalize lost persons so that they remain a valuable part of our lives.

Lily Pincus talks about internalization this way:

> This process of internalizing the dead, taking the deceased into oneself and containing him so that he becomes a part of one's inner self, is the most important task in mourning. It does not happen immediately; for a varying span of time the bereaved is still in touch with the external presence of the lost person. Once the task of internalizing has been achieved, the dependence on the external presence diminishes and the bereaved becomes able to draw on memories, happy or unhappy, and to share these with others, making it possible to talk, think, or feel about the dead person.

When the task of internalization has been accomplished, it is as if the lost persons "can be summoned to life and made to appear three-dimensional, in the mind as on a stage where, like veteran actors, they play once more their classic role."

THE CHOICE

If there is any one thing that has become clear as we have explored the various sets of experiences that make up our mourning, it is that movement through this process is not automatic. We determine whether we make movement or not, and the way we do this is by our choices. What is the choice, then, that we must make during the Working Through phase of the grieving process?

We must choose to engage in the conflicts.

Conflict, we are told, "is a very powerful organizing principle of behaviour, simplifying and clarifying immediate purposes." As we weigh pros and cons, look for solutions, grapple with issues, we are, in effect, determining our values, setting our priorities, deciding on what is and is not acceptable to us. We are drawing the contours of our future.

Choosing to engage in the conflicts of this phase of mourning, in perhaps an unexpected way, makes our internal grief more manageable. By engaging with the difficulties and problems that have resulted from the loss and from our commitment to reconstruct our lives after that loss, we have an arena, a kind of external field, where by trial and error we can work through our grieving.

The choice to engage with the conflicts, however, is not easy, for it means acknowledging situations we might rather pretend not to be aware of, sticking with problems until we find satisfactory solutions, doing those things that are necessary to change ourselves to be consistent with our new life environment. This *working through,* however, is "the central, most urgent task" because we "cannot repair the ability to learn new meaningful ways of coping" until we have engaged in the conflicts. But when we have accomplished this working through, we "will find vitality and confidence for other purposes."

The Working Through phase of the grieving process has several areas of special difficulty: the challenge this period represents to the family unit, and the extra strain and stress for those whose loss is the result of divorce or the loss of a homosexual partner, family member, or friend.

As Dr. Beverley Raphael alerts us, "The family unit as it was before dies, and a new family system must be constituted. The death," she says, "will be a crisis for the family unit as well as for each individual member...." What is the nature of this crisis?

Perhaps before the loss, the family's well-being was nurtured by a mother who had chosen the career of a homemaker. When she is gone, there is no one for the family to constellate themselves around, so the family unit disintegrates. Or perhaps the adult children of a family maintained a modicum of congeniality and chose to cover up seething resentments to avoid open conflict while their father was alive, only to reveal their real feelings of anger, distrust, and jealousy after his death. These families now must reconstitute themselves, and this reconstitution can be very painful.

After the loss, family members must also find appropriate new roles for themselves. Who will take over the lost person's duties and responsibilities? How will the other family members react to this replacement? What dynamics will come into play as family members attempt to cohere themselves into a reorganized unit? What will be other family members' responses to the changes that occur in the life of the primary mourner? These are difficult questions. Often the *working through* of each individual family member's personal mourning process is exacerbated and, if one is not careful, even hindered by the dynamics involved as the family unit is reconstituted.

Another kind of working through often required at the family level is the recognition of and response to young children's delayed or prolonged grieving. A young mother whose husband died accidentally two years ago told me about her ten-year-old son, who until recently she had thought was moving through the grieving process in a timely and normal fashion. Yet, suddenly, he became a frantic student at school—afraid at every turn that there was some part of his homework he hadn't done because he didn't remember the complete assignment; afraid that he wouldn't get to soccer practice on time; afraid that he wouldn't be able to do the tasks required for his next Boy Scout badge. Fortunately, the young mother was cognizant of the phases of the mourning process and recognized that the change in her son's behavior might be related to aspects of the loss that he had not yet worked through. The child is now seeing a psychologist once a week—"my other teacher," the child calls him—and positive changes are already apparent in his behavior. Paramount among them is a noticeable increase in the child's spontaneous mentioning of his father—when the family is eating supper, when they ride by buildings his father's company constructed, when the child is about to go to sleep. There has also been a noticeable decrease in the child's franticness.

Another group for whom the Working Through phase of the grieving process is awkward and often extremely difficult are partners, kin, or friends of homosexuals. Professionals who have worked with recovery groups in the gay community point out ways this segment of grieving individuals differs from others; they live a life-style often condemned by others, and they are often shunned themselves because people think they may carry the AIDS virus; they sometimes are plagued by low self-esteem and guilt; they may feel abandoned and isolated because the deceased was their only real "family," their own family being perhaps emotionally and geographically distant from them; there is no tradition for gay mourning and no societal approval; the survivors usually do not get financial benefits and often lose jointly acquired property; they are often not given a role in the making of funeral plans; reentry and resocialization are difficult and often complicated by the AIDS crisis; there are few outside resources or sources of support for gays who are grieving. Care givers often must deal with their own feelings about loss and about homosexuality in order to offer genuine help. There is an extreme need during the Working Through phase of mourning for individuals to recognize and respond to the special needs of the gay community who may not only be grieving for "their dead and dying friends, but also for a way of life that is gone and may never come back."

Finally, let me say a word about divorce and the Working Through phase of mourning. Having been both divorced and widowed, I can attest to the fact that it is a delicate matter to find a point of balance in a situation where you must continue to interact with the former partner. In death there is a finality; new memories will not be created nor new conflicts ignited. But even if one's relationship with a divorced spouse is congenial, there are always decisions to be made and questions to be answered: What is the right thing to do when your ex-father-in-law dies? Do you call when you return to your ex-husband's hometown? And these are slight concerns compared with questions of child rearing, support payments, visitation rights, and so on, which are an ongoing part of life when there are children.

But, as hard as it may be, the Working Through must be done by those who are divorced. Some kind of balance must be established. Peter Marris has pointed out that with divorce it is not the meaning of the lost relationship that must be retrieved, but "the hopes and purposes it betrayed." The *working through* of grief, then, for the divorced person is a matter of a "restoration of faith that such hopes are not futile; that one is not, after all, incapable of giving or receiving love." And for this the divorced person needs the same support we might have expected to give only to a person who had experienced a death.

Issues such as these make the choice to engage with the conflicts even more difficult, but as we have learned at each juncture in the grieving process, the only alternative we have is to make the affirmative choice, no matter how hard it is. For that is the only way we will be able to reach a constructive outcome in our grieving.

WHAT WE NEED FROM FAMILY AND FRIENDS
DURING WORKING THROUGH

The kind of people we need around us during Working Thorough are those who indicate that they know we have conflicts to work through to reestablish ourselves in life—all part of our grieving—and that they also know we are capable of meeting and resolving these conflicts. Colin Murray Parkes points out how important such individuals can be: "In a situation in which well-established norms are absent, the expectations of those around are potent determinants of behaviour." Choosing to be around people who *expect* us to grow and change, who *expect* us to face and handle the challenges of this period of our grieving, can be a powerful incentive for resolving the conflicts that are always part of change. The kind of people we do not need to be around during Working Through are those whose "caretaking" and "sympathy" would keep us weak, dependent, and afraid.

If we have not already been working with a professional, this period during which we must find a way to solve many difficult problems is an excellent time to seek professional advice and support—perhaps a child psychologist to help us understand a youngster's delayed grieving; perhaps a therapist or counselor who can assist us in understanding our fear of change or in learning how to assume new roles that are awkward and unfamiliar; perhaps a coach who can direct us in the work we have to do in areas that are new to us; perhaps a minister, rabbi, or priest who can help us reconstitute our faith. I remember one divorced father telling me that the work he did with a professional counselor in learning how to change long-standing negative patterns of thinking was the single most important thing that allowed him to move on through his grieving. "I learned," he said, "that I could alter my thinking, could actually intervene in and *manage* my thinking, so that old habits of thought did not continue to make me feel insecure and unworthy. Without the assistance of someone trained to help me spot my negative and defeatist thinking," he said, "my mind would have gone on forever, I suppose, running in its worn-out, habitual grooves."

The bottom line is that during this time of problem solving, we should seek out and ask the assistance of those individuals around us who are solution-oriented, who understand the necessity for change and even some risk taking, who expect that our progress will not occur in a smooth, straight line, and who acknowledge and support us for having the courage to engage with the conflicts that are an unavoidable part of Working Through.

I happened to be going through the Denver airport at one extremely hard time during my own Working Through process. As I was waiting for my flight, I picked up a paperback at the newsstand, a little book called *Markings* by Dag Hammarskjold, a private journal he had kept for many years. Only after he was killed in an airplane crash in Africa while serving as secretary general of the United Nations was the journal made available to the public.

There were many entries in *Markings* that spoke to me. But one sentence in particular stood out. "I am committed to a life of no return," Mr. Hammarskjold had said. That, I decided, was worth remembering and repeating often. *I am committed to a life of no return.* The life of balance and promise that I so desperately wanted lay nowhere except ahead; and going forward was, I knew, the only way I was going to reach it.

7

Integration

The tales we care for lastingly are the ones that
touch on the redemptive...the singular idea that is the
opposite of the Greek belief in fate: the idea that
insists on the freedom to change one's life.

CYNTHIA OZICK

Looking out the window, I could see dark clouds ahead. Streaks of lightning were flashing every few seconds. The pilot, the only crew aboard the small commuter plane, announced: "A thunderstorm has moved in faster than expected. Looks like we're going to be going through the worst of it. Be sure your seat belts are fastened."

The wind began to toss the small plane around as if it were made of paper. We turned from side to side. Sheets of rain hit the windows. The plane bucked again and again as we hit air pockets. The metal began popping and cracking. It was only four o'clock in the afternoon, but there was now nothing but black outside, punctuated by the bursts of lightning. I could see the pilot in the cockpit, his hands gripping the wheel in front of him. The muscle in his right jaw was twitching violently.

I began to cry. I knew the plane was breaking up and we were going to crash. I knew death was imminent.

Suddenly the motion of the plane threw me violently to the right, the seat belt cutting into my abdomen. The gentleman across the narrow aisle reached out to steady me, and I grasped his hand. Immediately I was strangely affected. An actual feeling of heat traveled through my entire body. I continued to hold on to the stranger's hand as I wedged myself back into my seat. The plane rocked as uncontrollably as before, but something amazing had happened. All fear had left me; I was completely at peace.

When we finally passed through the storm, I released the gentleman's hand and looked over to thank him. He must have been in his mid- to late sixties, a tall, thin man with big hands and a wind-whipped face. I could see nothing in his appearance or demeanor that would explain the warmth and the strange calming effect his touch had had on me.

"I'm Ernest Naudon," the gentleman said, "a well digger from British Columbia, on my way to the Turks and Caicos islands. I'm just stopping off at Texas A & M to pick up some equipment."

"What will you do in the Turks and Caicos?" I asked him, searching for a clue that would help me understand what I had just experienced.

"Help build some houses for the poor and a place of worship. I'm of the Baha'i faith, and each year I do three months' work at some pioneer mission. This year it's the Turks and Caicos."

I sat a few seconds trying to think how to broach the subject. I finally asked straight out:

"You weren't afraid at all when we were going through that storm, were you?"

"No," he answered. "I was not afraid."

"But you knew we might crash, didn't you?"

"Yes," he answered, "I knew we were in great danger."

"Do you mean, then," I asked incredulously, "that you knew we were in great danger, and you still were not afraid of dying?"

"No," he said, "I am not afraid of dying." The man looked me straight in the eye when he answered.

"But how can you not be afraid of dying?" I asked him. "Death is so terrible."

Without answering, the gentleman opened the book he had been reading, tore a blank end sheet from the back, and printed in large block letters:

> Know, you are where you are
> Not by accident but by the design
> of your Creator for your own
> development or for the development
> of those around you.
>   ABDUL BAHA

Below this verse he wrote a second one:

> Is there any remover of difficulties, save God? . . .
> All are his servants and all abide by his bidding.
>   THE BAB

"That," he said, "is why I am not afraid of dying. I know there is a design, and I know I participate in that design by God's bidding. What, then, is there to fear—whether one is dead or living?"

I knew Mr. Naudon believed what he spoke; I had seen the evidence a few minutes ago. I envied this man his peace about dying. I envied him his freedom.

When the plane landed, I walked with him to the terminal. As we shook hands and said good-bye, I tried in an awkward attempt to thank him. "I certainly hope there is someone like you on the next plane I'm flying."

"Oh, there will be," Mr. Naudon answered with a smile that was as enigmatic as his answer.

The aftermath of the scare in the airplane left me with two recurring memories: the frightening sounds of popping and cracking, which I had been sure meant the plane was breaking, and the inexplicable warmth and sense of calm that had come when I clasped the gentleman's hand. I would lie awake at night, playing these two experiences against each other: the one reminding me of how afraid I was of dying; the other reminding me that, for some, there was another alternative.

The truth was this was the first time I had considered my own dying. And it was very upsetting. A whole raft of memories flooded my mind every time I let myself think about it: A filmstrip we saw when I was in the eleventh grade—wasn't it one of Chaucer's tales, where the Grim Reaper came, at his pleasure, through the window with his hourglass and his sickle? The experience of stepping across the threshold of a room in a southern plantation I was once touring, feeling the air suddenly and inexplicably change from pleasant to cold and finding out only after the tour guide entered the room and told the story that this was the place the master of the house had died after putting up a terrible struggle. The shock of being touched personally by the force of death, unveiled and unmitigated, when I saw for the first time a dead body not already in a mortuary—and that dead body was the body of my husband! No, thinking about my own death was not a subject I found pleasant.

But I was not able now to forget it. I thought of the truths I had long believed in, truths reflected in St. Paul's "O death, where is thy sting? O grave, where is thy victory?"; in the Buddha's "Death is a temporary end of a temporary phenomenon"; in the Sufis' "Death is the tax the soul pays for having had a form and a name." Until I had faced my own imminent death, these truths had been sufficient. But now I realized that a gulf existed between what I *believed* about death and how I had responded when I thought I would soon be dying. As a result of that experience on the commuter plane, the shield had been removed that up until that moment had protected me from seeing into the abyss called my own dying.

But now the shock of the glimpse had registered. "How much does this unacknowledged, unexamined fear of my own death determine the parameters of my life?" I wondered. "Is it possible," I quizzed myself further, "to express in daily life an attitude and behavior that include death in the whole picture rather than doing everything possible to exclude it?"

As synchronicity would have it, a friend whom I had told about the airplane incident brought me a book a few weeks later. "I found this," he said. "Thought it might be interesting, in light of your recent experience." The book was called *Death and the Creative Life: Conversations with Prominent Artists and Scientists* by Lisl Goodman. Who would have thought that it would be from the words of a physicist and a scientist that I would get the first glimmer of how to bring my faith and my behavior together, my first insight into how to build a frame for thinking that included death and life as a whole?

Goodman had interviewed the physicist John Wheeler, famous for his study of "black holes" and his work in gravitational physics, asking him if he thought he had come to terms with death. Professor Wheeler answered by affirming how much he loved life:

> If my airplane tomorrow night had to ditch in the ocean, I would struggle with all my might to survive. Life is just too precious to give up.... Each remaining year seems more precious than ever; but even more, the contact with every friend enhances the preciousness of life.

The writer then pressed the physicist, "But suppose you had finished everything you possibly could? . . ."

"In my office," Professor Wheeler answered, "I keep a two-inch white box for every project that I plan to do someday.... The number of new projects that I add each year exceeds the number that I accomplish. So now there are about 150 such two-inch boxes in my office—misery for my poor secretary. To me each is a precious tie to the world. So it is hard for me to think of myself ever being tired of the world."

But, then, would he banish death, if he could?

The scientist answered: "Taking a responsibility for the trees at my children's summer place makes me aware of how a great old spreading tree kills the future for promising new young trees which are too close to it. Death is essential for renewal. We know that the earth is renewed from underneath."

And furthermore . . .

Life without death would be a picture without a frame. To have the body go is proof before one's eyes that the survival of mankind, its essence, is of the spirit—the flame handed on from one runner to another. How else are we to realize that life is more important than the ones who do the living?

It was clear to me as I read this interview that John Wheeler saw death as a paradox. On the one hand, he was a man with a hundred and fifty projects waiting, a man who loved his friends and family, a man who didn't want to give up a single precious day of living. On the other hand, he was a man who, tending his children's trees, knew that death was necessary. A man who recognized that death proved that the very essence of life was spirit.

I read further. Howard Gruber, a scientist noted for his work on creativity, spoke about a paper he had written called "And the Bush Was Not Consumed." In it, the scientist said, "I don't speak of death, but about the 'unquenchable flame.' "

A creative moment is part of a longer creative process, which in its turn is part of a creative life. How are such lives lived? How can I express this particular idea that such an individual must be a self regenerating system? Not a system that comes to rest when it has done good work, but one that urges itself onward. And yet, not a runaway system that accelerates its activity to the point where it burns itself out in one great flash. The system regulates the activity and the creative acts regenerate the system.

Then Dr. Gruber added:

If you ask me how I am planning my life. . . I am planning it around the idea that I am going to die. I know I am going to die and I want certain things to be accomplished, so I'm working within certain probabilities about getting old, losing my resources, my energy....

It came to me as I read: instead of focusing on the fear of death, I could focus on not dying incomplete. This would mean that I would strive at all times to be a "self-generating system," to concentrate on living my life to its fullest potential. That way, *whenever* I died—whether suddenly or at a ripe old age—at that moment of going I would feel that I had died alive, active, working to be who I had the capability to be.

As I put the book away, it seemed ironic to me that it would be the conversations of a physicist and a scientist that suggested to me a way to think about dying. It also seemed ironic that the frightening experience on that commuter plane had turned out to be such a gift, enabling me to confront the idea of my own dying. And while the context I had begun to frame for myself was perhaps not as explicit a statement of faith as had been those lovely words the gentleman had written that day on the plane, there did seem to be something about the insights I had just realized that was sacred.

———————

It happened in the wilds of the Mojave Desert in southern California on a late afternoon in mid-November four years after Greg had died. The moment—the symbolic moment—when I knew my grieving process had reached equilibrium.

The setting was an Outward Bound wilderness survival course, which I had first thought of taking three years earlier but until now had not been able to muster the courage to tackle. And I still wasn't sure about the whole thing. In fact, since being here I had questioned the decision to come at least ten times a day, if not a hundred. What was a klutz like me doing rappeling five hundred feet down a mountain, climbing fifty-foot boulders, hiking ten hours at a stretch, hoisting a fifty-pound backpack, and learning to assemble camp stoves and to read compasses? It was only with great difficulty that I could remember the litany I had repeated to get myself here . . . *new experience, a physical challenge, something you have never done before, it will keep you young, an opportunity to expand your limits.*

And now I had even graver doubts about the wisdom of such an adventure. We had reached that dreaded point in the schedule: it was time for the experience known as the solo. Each of us was going to be left alone to fend for ourselves in the desert. "Naturally," our course leader said, "you'll learn from the physical challenge of having to survive...." We all laughed nervously. The course leader smiled and continued, "But perhaps the greatest benefit you will gain from doing the solo is the time you spend in conversation with yourself. Take this opportunity to ask important questions: What do I want in life? What gives my life meaning? You know, those universal questions that people in all cultures have asked as far back as there is record."

"Consider writing in a journal," the leader suggested. "Drawing pictures. Making a piece of art from found objects. Building something from the dirt around you. Or just sitting doing nothing."

I had cleared the site where I had been dropped off, unrolled my sleeping bag on the ground, gotten out my food and water. It was late afternoon—I guessed there were two or three hours of daylight left—when I sat down with my journal. A "copybook," I called it because I put everything in it—not only my own jottings, but quotes I found meaningful, poems, clippings from magazines and newspapers, addresses given out on National Public Radio for ordering tapes and transcripts of their programs. The pages were a hodgepodge of many things that over the past couple of years had interested or inspired me.

"I wonder what I will find here?" I asked as I adjusted myself next to a Joshua tree. Even though I picked up the journal often at home to add an entry, I had never just sat down and read it. "Will I find out something about myself that I do not know? Will there be some pattern behind what looks just like a bunch of random entries?"

The first entry I turned to was the paragraphs I had copied from Woody Guthrie's posthumous autobiography, word pictures of a family gathering to eat. "Chow is now on! Red bean a green bean a white bean a flitter, corn bread dry bread a wheat bread fritter! Come get it before I throw it to th' hogs in th' pen!" I laughed. Discover myself in these extravagant lines? Find a pattern that said something about the eternal questions of existence? In words like these?

Then I asked myself, "Now, why in the world *had* I copied that?"

"Because you're southern and love to eat, especially black-eyed peas and cornbread," was my first answer. And although that was all true, I knew there was more. As I sat there reflecting, the words on the page now just a blur in front of me, I knew the answer to my question. I had put this excerpt in my journal because I had an empty place in my heart. These words were a celebration of life, a celebration of family. Woody Guthrie had written about the kind of easy, light, fun togetherness I had with Greg and that I hoped I would someday create with another man I would marry.

But I also realized as I read this entry that at some point during this long grieving process I had come to recognize that a new husband was not the answer. That I had to complete my grieving. Then if a man did come along in my life, I would be able to relate to him not out of need, but out of genuine connectedness. And, I wondered, if I don't meet a man . . . is there some other way I can celebrate family . . . perhaps by special times spent with my little nieces or by inviting the family to my house for Thanksgiving instead of going to one of theirs or by broadening the meaning of family?

I brought my mind back from its reverie to what I was supposed to be doing. I noticed the bushy purple cactuses all around me and out of the corner of my eye caught a glimpse of a jackrabbit moving across the desert in the distance. Now, what was our assignment?

"Hold a conversation with yourself. Think about your life. Reconsider the eternal questions," the leader had said. I turned on in my journal.

Why, I had even saved an obituary. For Buckminster Fuller. What had made this important enough for me to put it in my journal? I could not remember. But as I read, I knew. In the obituary, some of Bucky's own words had been quoted:

> I live on earth at present, and I don't know what I am
> I know that I am not a category. I am not a thing—a noun.
> I seem to be a verb, an evolutionary process—an integral function
> of the universe.

These lines reminded me of the scientists' conversations: *We are a self-regenerating system.... Life is a bush that will not be consumed.... Life is more important than those who do the living....*
Below the obituary I had taped another quote by Bucky:

> My brother collected stones.
> I collected papers with my name on them
> As written or printed by someone else
> Letters, postcards ... school reports....
> As a consequence of surprises
> Emanating from my collection's
> Progressive patterning
> In 1917, at the age of 22,
> I made a grand strategy decision.
> I determined to make myself the guinea pig
> In a lifelong research project....

I leaned back against the Joshua tree and gazed up at the sky. That was an interesting way to think about the evolution of one's life . . . as a lifelong research project. In that context, I wondered, "By the end of a woman's life, what kind of investigation would the death of a husband have turned out to be? How would such a life-changing event as this fit into the lifelong research project?"

The end of a woman's life . . . My eye lighted next on an excerpt from an interview with Marguerite Yourcenar, the French novelist.

When she was in her late eighties, an interviewer had asked Mme. Yourcenar to speak about what she thought was the purpose for living. I had copied:

I believe that perfecting oneself is life's principal purpose.... We may not reform the world, but at least we can reform ourselves, and we are, after all, a small part of the world.

Yourcenar went on to quote the eighteenth century philosopher, Saint-Martin, who had said about his friends, "They are the beings through whom God loved me." This seemed to me as I sat that afternoon in the desert a worthy purpose for a person to have for her life: to be someone through whom God loved others.

A few pages over in the journal I saw an entry that made me laugh out loud. Somewhere I had come across the phonetic transcription by a French composer of a nightingale's song:

Tiou, tiou, tiou, tiou—Spe, tiou, squa—tio, tio, tio, tio, tio, tio, tio, tix—Coutio, coutio, coutio, coutio—Squo, squo, squo, squo—Tzu, tzu, tzu, tzu, tzu, tzu, tzu, tzu, tzi—Corror, tiou, squa, pipiquiZozozozozozozozozozozozozo, zirrhading—Tsissisi, tsissisisisisisisis— Dzoree, dzoree, dzoree, tzatu, dzi—Dlo, dlo, dlo, dlo, dlo, dlo, dlo, dlo, dlo—Quio, trrrrrrrr—Lu, lu, lu, lu, ly, ly, ly, ly, lie, lie, lie, lie, lie—Quio didl li lulylie—Hagurr, gurr, quipio—Coui, coui, coui, couri, qui, qui, qui, gai, gui, gui, gui—Goll, goll, goll, goll guia hadadoi—Conigui, horr, ha diadia dill si—Hezezezezezezezezezezezezezeze couar ho dze hoi—Quia, quia, quia, quia, quia, quia, quia, quia, ti Ki, ki, ki, io, io, io, ioioioio ki—Lu ly li le lai la leu lo, didl io, quia—Kigaigaigaigaigaigai guiagaigaigai couior dzio dzio pi.

I decided that I must have put this piece in the journal to help me keep my perspective, because right underneath it I had written two other quotes. One was from a sacred Indian scripture:

There are three things which are real:
God, human folly, and laughter.

The first two are beyond our comprehension
So we must do what we can with the third.

And then came what someone had told me were Socrates' last words: *Please the gods, may the laughter keep breaking through.*

It was at this moment that I knew the work of grieving for Greg was over. Not, of course, that I believed I would never feel sadness again or longing or pain. Not that the experience of his death would not be with me forever. Not that issues, particularly about myself, that had been revealed, though not caused, by his death were not present for me to continue to grapple with. But what I now realized was that I *had* found a new balance for my life. I did again take joy in living. My life was no longer dominated by the presence of grief. I had done the work that was necessary to be able to say, "I have grieved."

After I prepared my noodles and vegetables, ate my bickie crackers and peanut butter, cleaned the boiler so it would be ready for making coffee the next morning, it was time for bed.

I would be lying if I said I wasn't scared as I climbed into my sleeping bag and zipped it up around me. But I wasn't nearly as afraid as I had thought I would be. Even when I woke in the wee hours of the morning and saw a coyote standing at the end of my bedroll, I only yelled five times to make him run instead of ten or twenty. And I think I was even able to go back to sleep, maybe sometime shortly before daybreak.

This is Integration. The set of experiences that culminates in our recognizing that we feel released. No longer do we feel dominated by the loss; every day we are not forced to do combat with debilitating memories. Our life no longer is one gaping hole of emptiness and pain. We are stronger. We find that we are able now to grapple with those existential questions of our own death and living. We experience release from the weight of the burden of grief; we enjoy an increased sense of play and freedom. We have a renewed interest in living; and, once again, when we look up, we can see a horizon.

All of this is possible because we have chosen to *experience fully* the complete grieving process. Dr. George Pollock calls this a transformational "mourning-liberation" process that he asserts is normal, found in all people and throughout history, and a universal means for adapting to unwanted change. This mourning process has been our private ritual.

During rituals—which anthropologists also call rites of passage—an individual always passes through three states: the state of separation (imagine an ancient initiation rite: the state of separation would occur when the young man or woman being initiated is isolated from regular societal life and taken perhaps to a forest or to a tepee to begin the tasks of the ritual); the state of transition, or "limen" (the time during which the tasks are faced, either successfully or unsuccessfully); and the state of aggregation, or reincorporation (when the young person is brought back from the place of initiation to take her or his new place in society).

In our own private ritual, the event of the loss was our point of separation. The mourning process up to this point has been our period of transition, or our "limen." Now, during the experiences of Integration, we are entering the final ritual state, reincorporation. We are emerging from the experiences of mourning and returning to a life that again has balance and structure. We are finding that we have integrated the loss into our lives and can now integrate ourselves back into the world.

What has made this possible, of course, is our willingness to have passed through the ritual. As anthropologists Victor and Edith Turner point out, individuals are "inwardly transformed and outwardly changed" when they take on the difficult and challenging tasks of a ritual. A rite of passage, they remind us, is a time of "betwixt and between," a time when our experience is that we are traveling through a "realm or dimension" that has few or none of the qualities of our lives in the past and few or none of the qualities our lives will have in the future, a time they compare "to death, to being in the womb, to invisibility . . . and the wilderness," like falling into the dark and living in floating worlds.

But the Turners also point out that the ritual, which, to be sure, is marked by this terrible ambiguity and confusion, is also marked by enormous potentiality. It is a time of "major reformulation," a time of open-endedness and of possibility, a time not only of *what is,* but a time of *what may be.* Any time that our "previous orderings of thought and behavior are subject to revision"—as they certainly are during mourning—there is a strong chance that we will come up with "hitherto unprecedented modes of ordering relations between ideas and people." We experience a "freedom of thought" that helps us reformulate our lives and come up with "new experimental models" for living

It is at Integration that we can finally recognize this potentiality that resided in our painful private ritual of mourning. Dr. George Pollock calls the gains we recognize during Integration "creative outcomes." Our creative outcomes may include gains like these:

- the ability to feel joy, satisfaction, and a sense of accomplishment
- a return to a steady state of balance
- the experience of an increased capacity to appreciate people and things
- a realization that we are more tolerant and wise
- a desire to express ourselves creatively
- the ability to invest in new relationships
- the experience of a sense of play and freedom
- a deepening of our faith

We do not experience these creative outcomes because we have been able to re-create how things were before the loss. No, we have achieved much more than that. What we experience now, because the mourning process is an adaptive-transformational process, is a "new creation." A new creation that derives "its energy and perhaps inspiration and direction from the past," to be sure, but is nevertheless a "successor" creation, not a replacement. We have been changed by the grieving process, and as a result, we have changed things around us.

The women and men with whom I have talked speak of the release and new life that come during the experiences of Integration.

FINDING DEEPER RESOURCES

A divorced mother of two comments:

Oh, I admit it was awful. I had been living in a real comfort zone. I had everything made. My husband made good money; he was loving and caring. I had two beautiful children I adored. My whole purpose in life was to be a good wife and a good mother. And I was great at both of those things. Then he fell in love with somebody else, and I lost almost everything. I went from a Jaguar to a Toyota. I went from going in limos to eat out in fancy restaurants to driving my car to the store to buy groceries.

But today I no longer dwell on what I lost but look instead to see that I've made it in the past and I'll make it now. This is not just wishful thinking or sheer determination talking. I have looked around and seen evidence that I've survived. I have the love of my children in spite of what has happened. I am now able to be civil and adult with my ex-husband. I see that I've been forced to take a new path and to see that a world that I thought was perfect and working so well can be interrupted and then destroyed. I've had to call on my resources; I've had to dig deeper. I've had to call on something I had forgotten was there, things I hadn't ever given myself credit for. And, you know, to tell you the truth, it's kind of exciting.

ACHIEVING CLARITY OF THINKING

A mother says:

When our son committed suicide, I was so angry at him. "He didn't have to do this," I said again and again. "He had many other alternatives." But now I see that, yes, he did have other alternatives, but he also had the alternative of suicide. That was an alternative. Certainly not the alternative I would have chosen, but it was his choice. For him, he thought that he could be out of whatever trauma he was living in his life, and so therefore I have to respect that even if I don't agree with it.

And I don't hold our family or God responsible. For a long time I kept going back over our lives. What did my husband and I do wrong? Perhaps we didn't provide him what he needed. And how could God allow this? Where was God's love?

I no longer ask these questions. My husband and I did make

some mistakes, but that is part of being human. And any mistakes we might have made did not cause our son to choose to kill himself. Even if we hurt him inadvertently or overlooked some way we could have helped him, we still did not have the power to determine how he responded to what happened to him. Every human being chooses how he or she responds to what happens. Over that nobody but the single individual has any control.

RECLAIMING LOST VALUES
A friend tells this story:

I used to be an avid deer hunter. Nothing could keep me away from the lease during the fall of the year. Now, I'm no longer interested in killing deer—I don't know how much of it is related to Whitney's death—but for a long time there was only a void in my life where deer hunting used to be.

I've discovered lately, however, that the interest is still there, but it's just taken a different form. I've found something new to involve myself in—duck hunting. Well, actually, it's more duck observing, I suppose, because what I'm interested in is figuring out the world of ducks, not shooting at them. I'm reading about duck hunting. I've got a great old book, *Travel and Traditions of Water Fowl,* that I'm reading. A classic in the field. So I'm looking into ducks now. And once I figure out ducks, maybe I'll go for wild boar or something. I'm really enjoying it.

One thing I see out of this is that you never really lose a real interest. That interest just recurs in another form. I enjoyed deer hunting before and now I enjoy ducks. It's the same interest, just showing up in an affiliated field; between the past and the present there is a fit.

UNDERSTANDING ABOUT SELF-MANAGEMENT
A divorced woman talks:

It's now been five years since my divorce, and when I feel what I would generally call pain, I can usually transform that into something else by looking for the explanation: I'm learning something new or doing something that is uncomfortable or letting go of another piece of the past. I'm getting to the place where I can have a sense of humor about it. I know now that everything in life is temporary, everything, and that even what we call pain is just growing through an experience we didn't expect.

But, you know, because my ex-husband is alive and well, there is still the daily reminder that the relationship with him didn't work out. In my case, I made the decision about the man I was going to spend my life with when I was sixteen years old. So the commitment goes really deep; it's so ingrained.

This creates a contradiction. I have my life here, and over there is still a life unfulfilled. When I say that, I get a mental picture of a railroad track, with me on one of those little one-wheeled scooters railroad workers ride to check on the track. One side of the track is the unfulfilled commitment to a life with a former husband. The other side is the joy, fulfillment, and wonderful things in my life now. On any given day, I can travel on my one-wheeled scooter along either of those tracks. If I want joy, peace, and harmony, I can go down one track. If I want to think about what I lost and will never have again, I can hop over there and be miserable for a little while. It's really kind of nice. It's like—get over there and be sloppy sad; and then it feels so much better when you do go back to the fun part. Maybe that's why we don't totally let the past go, because we always want to have this sad part available to us.

DECIDING TO ENGAGE WITH LIFE FULLY
A son recalls:

Before my father was killed, I would say that I was very much with the program of life. I excelled in sports; I had reams of trophies; I had medals for singing; I made straight A's in school; I was honor society and class president. I did all the achievement-oriented things that regular everyday life is about—winning and succeeding.

Then for a long time after my father's death, I wasn't interested in succeeding or participating. But now I think differently. I am going to take what I have learned since my father's death and bring that back with me into the mainstream of life where most people live—which is to be successful and have a nice house and great cars and win awards in your industry and be all you can be. Everything that the great American dream and the American way—go for the gusto, tonight's Miller time, living it up, taking a vacation to Hawaii, and all that.

And I know all that is absolutely meaningless. It just has no meaning in and of itself. It can't, when you put your face up to the fact that you're going to die and all that is going to be left here. You get real clear when somebody dies that none of that stuff means anything. I mean, I threw all my trophies away after my father's death because they didn't mean anything to me anymore. And the truth was, they meant a lot to me.

So, when I say that I'm integrating back in with life, I mean I'm going to hold the reality that those things have no meaning in and of themselves, *and* I'm still going out there and get them. That's the game to play. That's how life is set up; that's how you grow; that's what there is to do. So if you're going to get with the program, you've got to get back out there and participate. I think what grows when you do that, when you change and master something you hadn't mastered before, is your soul. And the soul is just something you might take with you. If I don't do that, all that learning I've done since my father's death would be of no use if I didn't bring it to bear somewhere. It would have been for naught.

The important thing to do is to put the arbitrary occurrence in a larger context. There isn't anything I can do in terms of how the cards fall. Sometimes I can control them, and sometimes I can't. So I've begun to get the picture that there's something bigger that's running the show, and I have to learn to get along with whatever it is that's running the bigger program. So I guess that's what I mean when I say that I'm beginning to find my place. And it's taken a lot of trial and error. Trust is important. Trust in yourself and trust in the overall process. You just have to do it and see what works. That's how you learn to get along with the bigger program. I think I have to say that when you finally come back and integrate with life, if you're aware of what really happened to you and of what the overall program is in life, then your integration is going to be intertwined with a spiritual approach to life. It's surprising to hear myself say that, but I truly believe that it's so.

RECOGNIZING LOSS WILL ALWAYS BE PRESENT
A mother says:

I don't think you ever get over the loss in your heart. We were down at the beach when we got the news that our son had died. The phone rang, Dean answered, and a neighbor told him that Cliff was dead. I was standing near the glass doors, and every time I pass that spot now—and it's been ten years—I think, "I'll never be able to pass this spot without thinking of that phone call." I think you have to acknowledge the fact that when you love someone and that person is gone, you're going to miss him or her. And that has nothing to do with your spiritual strength or trust or even with how you've dealt with the loss. It's a perfectly human thing to continue to miss someone. I can know my son is just fine wherever he is and that I am fine; yet when Christmas time comes, Christmas Eve, and there's no Cliff who's going to walk in the door with a big stack of presents and say, "Hi, Mom!" I have a hard time.

We don't agonize over Cliff now, Dean and I, and go over it and over it. If something beautiful happens or we're somewhere Cliff would have been, we'll say, "Hi, Cliff, how's it going, ole boy?" something like that, but it's not heavy. I do wonder, though, if I'll ever be willing to sell that house at the beach where I first heard the news. I doubt it. I really doubt it.

ACKNOWLEDGING THAT THE PAST CONTINUES
A divorced father of three children says:

You know, the divorce will never be over. You've got a relationship whether you want it or not. Regardless of who you're in love with, regardless of where else you choose to live, regardless of how much money you're going to make. Hey, you've got a history. It's there, and about the best you can do is try to keep some sort of amicability about it, or I think it can make your life miserable. But the little murders still occur time after time, the squabbles about the kids, about money, about life-styles. You realize that you'll always be connected. Andrea is eight now, but when she's twenty-five and getting married, both Teresa and I are still going to be invited to the wedding and I'm sure we're going to have disagreements over how much I should pay on the wedding dress.

The only thing I know to do is to try to make a damn good income, try for the best possible relationship, stay in the same locale if it is at all possible. What holds me is love for the kids. I realized this one day when I was feeling desperate, even thinking about running away from it all, disappearing and never seeing any of them again. A lot of people do that, I know, and I can understand it. But when the kids left one weekend to go back to their mother's, I sat down and wrote a poem that helped me put things in perspective:

Three Children

yeah, I've got an old lady
who still haunts some rooms in my
subconscious
because, see, we still share some things . . .
    three children
who revolve between us like a
bank door,
their love keeping us linked
even when we're over.
    three children
always reminding me
that love extracts a price,
people change,
good things do go bad when effort
goes to ambivalence.
this gray morning I contemplate
the frosty roofs . . .
I don't want to leave this house,
this woman who loves me,
return to the discomfort of the past
but I feel invisible strings pulling
my heart like a reluctant kite
so that although I hate leaving
I want to see
    three children.

FINDING CONTENTMENT

A widow recounts her situation:

We were married fifty-four years. He lived to be seventy-eight. I'm eighty-three now and have been widowed for four years. Of course, he still lives on for me. I have tapes of his speeches, and I listen to them sometimes. There's one tape he made with the grandchildren when they were small, and he's so natural. He laughs, and I just love to play that tape. I keep it turned to the point where he's laughing because that's what I miss most about him—his sense of humor.

Of course, I don't associate him with my new apartment, but when I turn on programs that we used to look at together, that's when I think of him. And I surprise myself by crying a lot when I'm watching sad movies. I just weep and wail, use up ten handkerchiefs, and cry and cry.

If I die tomorrow, it's all right; but if I live ten more years, I'd like it. But I don't have the least fear of dying. I trust in the goodness of the universe. If I die, I think God knows what's best for me. If there's something to preserve, He will. If not, He won't. The Great Intelligence knows the best.

I'm perfectly content. I stay busy. Keep house, get the groceries, fix my meals, vacuum the rug. And, of course, I do my reading and play my records: Beethoven's C-sharp Minor Quartet, the meditation from Massanet's *Thais,* the "Song to the Evening Star" from Wagner's *Tannhäuser,* Liszt's *Liebesträume.* I agree with Beethoven that "music is in very truth the mediator between the life of the senses and the life of the spirit."

And I stay out in the yard as much as I can. I couldn't live without my swing. My swing is not only a tranquilizer when I swing gently, but an energizer when I swing vigorously as high as I can. I'm instantly in a state of joyful, exultant, childlike wonder which keeps me young at heart. And I walk every day to the park to see the squirrels and get in some exercise.

GAINING PERSPECTIVE
A widower says:

You've got to be able to see that this is some sort of learning process and that you don't always know everything that is happening. It's like the old Chinese story of the farmer whose champion stallion ran away and all the neighbors gathered to say, "That's bad." And the old farmer said, "Maybe." The next day the stallion came back with a whole herd of wild horses, and the neighbors all said, "That's good," and the farmer said, "Maybe." Then the farmer's son broke his leg trying to tame one of the wild horses and the neighbors said, "That's bad," and the old farmer said, "Maybe." Right after the son broke his leg, the army came through and drafted all the young men and took them off to war, but they left the farmer's son because his leg was broken. All the neighbors said, "That's good," to which the old farmer only said, "Maybe." And, of course, the story never ends.

That illustrates to me that whatever is happening now, you don't really know what is going on. And I've seen during these years of grieving for Dianne that this is true. It's a real irony, isn't it, that I would have ended up coming out of this thing an optimist!

CLARITY ABOUT WHAT ONE BELIEVES IN
A father says:

I'm very clear that loss is just the other side of gain. It's going to happen to you. If you live long enough, you're going to lose it all. And sometimes you lose it all before you live long enough, like our son dying before he even started to school. When I was a kid, a young man, I was terribly concerned about getting my philosophy together. But since David's death, I've given up on that and settled on a pretty simple deal: the object of life is to gain wisdom. And that's what I'm trying to do. I've come up with some guiding principles: the world's full of creeps, so try not to be one. Remember that what saves us is style and grace. Have tolerance, reserve judgment, and be easy on people because we're all weak. Just try to conduct yourself with a little dignity. Be quiet. Don't pop off.

I read a book one time . . . I think it was called *Master Game.* The author divided the book into Object Games and Metagames. The purpose of a metagame is to endure, to keep on playing, to share enlightenment. Whereas in an Object Game the purpose is the worship of money or prestige or recognition or winning. My aim is to play the metagame.

Even though I'm faithless, I'm not pessimistic. I think the world is indifferent, not that it's ganged up on us. I relish life. I get up earlier in the morning now more than ever. I bounce out of bed. I guess it's curiosity. I like to get up and watch the sun come up. I like to feel the sun on my back. I enjoy a pretty day. I enjoy a cold rainy day. It's life. And it beats the alternative all to hell. And what gives life meaning, I've come to see, is love and affection and knowledge.

EVALUATING THE CHANGE

A widow says:

I know it is a terrible thing to say, but it's the truth: I'm happier now than when my husband was living. He was one of those overbearing men who gave a woman no opportunity to have any self-confidence. He was tough and hard and wanted me to be just the way he thought I should be. I could never cry; he forbade it. He just told me what to do and I was supposed to do it. Even with all the pain that came with his death, I'm better off now. I have a chance to find out who I am. I am thinking about going to school. I went on my first vacation this past summer. I bought a blousy top the other day that I knew he would have hated, and I even asked myself when I saw myself in the mirror, "Is this me?" But I knew it was; I just wasn't used to asserting my own self-expression. But I'm learning. And life continues to get better.

COMING TO TERMS WITH ONE'S OWN DEATH

A brother says:

I spent every possible minute at the hospital with Frederick, and the closer he came to dying, the more I stared my own death in the face. This was my kid brother! If he could die in his early thirties, I could, too. It really shocked and unnerved me. One day I carried *Little Big Man,* which has been one of my favorite novels since high school, with me to the hospital. I remembered that great scene at the end of the book where Old Lodge Skins says:

There is no permanent winning or losing when things move, as they should, in a circle. For is not life continuous? And though I shall die, shall I not also continue to live in everything that is? The buffalo eats grass, I eat him, and when I die, the earth eats me and sprouts more grass. Therefore nothing is ever lost, and each thing is everything forever, though all things move.

When I finished reading that, something inside me had shifted. Late that afternoon I climbed up on Frederick's bed with my guitar and I sang one of our favorite beer-drinking ballads, even though he was in a coma. And then I said, "You know, buddy, we'd love to have you stick around; but it looks like you're on your way out. So, if you I are, I want you to know that it's okay with me. I love you, but I'll dismiss you." I left the hospital, and Frederick died, they said, in the next thirty minutes.

That whole experience really affected me. I'm different now about my own death and everybody's. I've decided that the timing of death may be sad, but death itself is not sad. I mean, we are here; then we're not here; but we live on in some form or another. I am now not bothered.

ASKING THE PERENNIAL QUESTIONS
A widow says:

Being a scientist, I'm not particularly religious, certainly not religious from an organized religion point of view. But since Carl's death, I have thought a lot about the kinds of questions that religion raises. Why are we here? What is the purpose of life?

You know, if you're a scientist, you have to think that there must be something higher than what we can study. How can you explain a cell? All that marvelous organization? I mean, how can you explain that 100 percent on a scientific basis? I'm not sure that you can. And I've thought a lot about it. So, I guess that lately I have become more religious in a sense—even though it's not what a lot of people think of as being religious.

I've decided that the purpose of life is to try to live as good a life as you can, and it should be happy. You should try to enjoy yourself. You should try to do something for other people. You should try to —I suppose it's the old Puritan ethic coming out in me—but you should try to make a difference in the world. That's why we're here —to make a difference. It doesn't have to be a huge difference, but everyone should contribute something to change the world to make it just a little bit better. You should not be a liability to society, but you should try to leave something positive behind you. That's how you live your life until it's time to die.

And about dying, I've got a new perspective about that, too. Not long after Carl died, I met a man at a friend's house, a philosopher visiting from Greece, and he asked me if I had ever considered that we may just have everything backward. That what we call living may be death, and what we call death may be living. Ever since then, I've been intrigued with the idea that that just might be possible.

FINDING A PURPOSE FOR BEING

A son whose mother had died comments:

One of the things that happens when the whole structure of your life falls apart is that you start wondering what you're supposed to be doing here. When it becomes clear to you that the purpose of life isn't for you to be perpetually happy, then you have to ask, "If not that, what?"

I've given a lot of thought to this, and I think our purpose here on earth is to get organized. To organize ourselves to do something. Everything, if you look at everything, if you look at the universe, and especially astronomically, all of the processes that are going on are organizing themselves toward some end, and then that isn't the end. Like a star. It is formed out of moving clouds that swirl into a center, and it becomes a star. Then it explodes and becomes a black hole and then absorbs everything. But then it turns into something else. Things constantly organize themselves toward an end, but it's not the end; it's the start of something. And to whatever end our process is—and I don't know that it makes a difference what that end is—our purpose on earth is to be a part of that. I think it's either irrelevant or presumptuous to overanalyze what *that* is. Because if you look at the way everything else is except us, everything else is busy being here, busy being itself. I think when we finally get down to it, what we are supposed to be doing is just being here, being who we are.

ESTABLISHING A NEW RELATIONSHIP

A divorced father says:

They billed themselves the "Non-Desperate Singles." I had tried out the singles scene off and on during the first couple of years I was divorced and felt so silly and uneasy. But a friend at the office told me this group was different, so I decided to go. And it was there that I met Linda. We both grew up in small towns not far from each other in northern Ohio, and I had dated one of her friends in high school. But Linda and I didn't remember each other, even though we're in the same senior prom picture in her high school annual. We left the party and went out to get a bite to eat. And I guess the thing that still amazes me is the intimacy in conversation that you can share with a woman. That was missing from my marriage. After that night, Linda and I never dated anyone else. It's been two years now, and we're planning to get married at the end of the summer. We've worked through many problems—our relationship comes first, but we have had to consider lots of things about the kids. We each have a freshman in college, and Linda still has a child at home. Just the logistics—do you buy a house with enough bedrooms for each child, even though some will soon be leaving? Things like that. We've set some goals now and we're working toward them. She's quite a lady, a bright, fun lady.

SEEING THE GLASS AS HALF-FULL
A mother says:

I noticed people thought that since I had lost a young child who suffered seven years before she died that I would be very heavy and significant about life. But, the truth is, through the pain I learned that you can be miserable anywhere you want to be and you can be happy anywhere you want to be. It's what you make of yourself.

Once when I lived in Okinawa, it wasn't the best living conditions, and there were wives there who were just miserable. They sat around all day being miserable. Well, hell, anybody can be miserable. It doesn't take much of a person to be sad and miserable. It takes a heck of a person to make the best out of what's the worst. When you go to the commissary and you want butter and they say, "Well, there's no butter; there's not going to be any butter for two weeks." What do you do? You ask, "Well, do you have any whipping cream?" "Yes, we've got whipping cream." So you buy whipping cream and make butter out of whipping cream. Add a little salt and a little yellow food coloring, and you got butter. That's how you should take life. That's what life is. Whipping cream.

BEING WILLING TO TAKE RISKS
A widow tells this story:

I find that since I've lived through a traumatic experience of loss I prefer lively people. People who are doing things. It's as if surviving and returning to life brings with it a new kind of lightness and freedom. In fact, I don't even mind if people are outrageous. I enjoy being outrageous myself at times. In fact, I like people who are willing to take a risk, and being outrageous is taking a risk, isn't it?

About three years after Tom died, I was in England. The fad in London that summer was spraying your hair all kinds of fanciful colors—green, pink, blue, purple. You could wash the paint out, so if you didn't like blue hair, the next day you could try red or yellow or green.

Well, that fall I had a huge class—225 students in biochemistry— and one day before I went to class I sprayed my hair electric blue with some of that hair paint I had bought in England. I just went into the room— me, this sixty-year-old scientist—and started my lecture. In a few minutes this serious kid sitting in the front row raised his hand and said, "Dr. Williams, why is your hair blue?" I looked him right in the eye and said, "Because I just felt like being outrageous." He continued to look puzzled all during class, but I went right on with my lecture. On the teaching evaluations at the end of the term, several students commented: "That blue hair was marvelous!" Now, can I prove that my ability to have fun like that and my having experienced Tom's death are related? I can't, of course, but I *know* there is a connection.

EXPERIENCING DEEPER COMPASSION
A young man says:

Loss is the *disease* of human life. It's what happens to you, and you cannot stop it. And the damage to the spirit is the *illness* that you suffer after that loss. You can't stop the disease, but you can address the illness. You can actually work at getting over the illness.

I had to learn how to address the illness of the spirit when within a three-year period my mentor died, my father died, and I almost died of cancer. I had to let go of the disease itself—the loss—and concentrate on handling the illness—the damage to my spirit. The way I found to do that was to reach out to community. To create a lot of horizontality in my life. To reduce hierarchies.

I grew in compassion. I was no longer above people. I realized I didn't exercise power over them. I was no longer the toughest guy around. I became a person among people, recognizing that there really is a human family. I gave up isolation and became willing to be a part of the human community.

If you choose to work on the illness of loss—the damage to the spirit—you grow to understand the term *compassion,* which is a fellow feeling. Community actually becomes communion. Communion is the act of love, which is the giving up of one's self. Not in a namby-pamby way, which means "I'm going to do all for my fellow man." Communion is just giving up that sense of isolation and becoming willing to share deeply in the human condition.

I've come to see that love and loss are exactly the same four-letter word. The degree to which we can feel loss, I think, is just the degree to which we can feel love. And the degree to which we recover from the illness of loss is just exactly the degree to which we can recover the capacity to love.

THE FOCUS DURING INTEGRATION

It seems to me that one of the saddest things we could ever say after a loss is that, like the speaker in Eliot's poem, "We had the experience but missed the meaning." When I listen to these women and men talk about their experience of the grieving process, however, I know that they will never have to speak this lament. For these are courageous individuals on whom nothing has been lost. They have observed themselves, taken note of what helped and what hindered, and changed accordingly. And because of the choices they have made, they are able now to say during Integration, "We have finished our work of grieving." What ways of thinking and behaving brought them this sense of completion?

Facing Our Own Mortality

Dr. Beverley Raphael tells us that the "death of a loved one means not only the loss, but also the nearness of personal death, the threat to self.... All the personal and internalized meanings of death will be evoked by the death.... All the personal vulnerabilities associated with death will be aroused by its closeness to the self." Through the loss we have been put in touch with our own dying.

And family therapist Lily Pincus tells us bluntly: "The bereaved who has never been able to face his own death cannot successfully make [the necessary] adjustment." Being willing, then, to think about, to ponder, our own mortality allows us to finish our grieving. We have been in touch with death, and we must come to terms with that profound experience.

In an article entitled "Facing Your Own Mortality," Jane Brody, personal health columnist and science writer for the *New York Times*, writes: "If any good came from my mother's death at age 49, it was my recognition, at age 17, of *my* mortality and my decision . . . to live each day as though it might be my last." She goes on to say, "Taken to the extreme, fear of death can rob people of life, keeping them from taking the kinds of risks that can yield rich rewards...." My experience in talking with people who have been willing to think about their own death confirms Jane Brody's assertion. The freer one is to consider one's own dying, the freer one is to experience full living.

Yet it is not easy. Ernest Becker, citing the work of Frederick Perls, tells us that we have four layers of tactics that we use to avoid such painful subjects: the first two are our "glib, empty talk, 'cliche,' and role-playing layers." Many people, he says, never go beneath these. The third layer is the "impasse" we use to cover our feelings of "being empty and lost," and that is a tough one to penetrate. Finally, there's the fourth—the "fear-of-death layer"—which is the "terror that we carry around in our secret heart." It is only when we penetrate all the way to that fourth layer, Mr. Becker says, that we are able to find our "authentic self." And, I would add, to be able to come to terms with one's dying.

Acknowledging that death is inevitable and seeing death as an important part of life are the most important things we can do to prepare for bereavement. Lily Pincus writes:

> Thinking and talking about death need not be morbid; they may be quite the opposite. Ignorance and fear of death overshadow life, while knowing about and accepting death erases this shadow and makes life freer of fears and anxieties. The fuller and richer people's experience of life, the less death seems to matter to them—as if love of life casts out fear of death. A

child therapist once said to me "Children of parents who are not afraid of death are not afraid of life." In that sense, education for death is education for life....

"Education for death is education for life...." Do we need more incentive for being willing to think about our own dying?

Recognizing How We Have Been Altered

Almost everyone who has grieved, at some time or another, has heard words like these spoken by well-meaning persons: "You will come out of this catastrophe stronger"; "Someday you will be able to see how much this loss has taught you"; "Having gone through this tragedy, you are going to be able to contribute so much more to others." Such bromides, of course, ring hollow to our ears, for we are grieving the loss of a person important to us, not trying to fulfill the requirements for a curriculum of self-development we never signed up for.

But when we begin to assess our situation during Integration, we find that we truly *have* been changed by the event. And that change *does* have some positive repercussions. Therefore, when we take note of such "pluses," we are not trying to persuade ourselves or others. We are just reporting.

Heinz Kohut, M.D., talks about the kind of "attainments of the ego" and the "attitudes and achievements of the personality" that we recognize during Integration as part of the legacy of the completed grieving process: an enlarged capacity for empathy, the ability to think beyond the bounds of the individual, a heightened sense of humor, and a recognition that there has been an increase in one's wisdom.

We say someone is empathetic who is able to look at other people, notice how they are behaving and what they are saying, and then, using this data, accurately imagine what they are experiencing inside even though we cannot directly observe these inner experiences. To express empathy, we have to curb intentionally our usual ways of thinking—analyzing, critiquing, scrutinizing, and so forth—and recognize instead the humaneness of all individuals—that others hurt just the way we do; others are as confused or off-center or frightened as we know that we have been. Many of us, during Integration, recognize that the experiences of the grieving process have resulted in our being much less judgmental and much more humbly empathetic.

Another transformation I've observed in the lives of people who have reached Integration is one Dr. Kohut also mentions: a new outlook on life, a kind of "quiet pride" in knowing and being able to acknowledge that human existence is finite. This new outlook results in an increased ability to hold life's ups and downs in perspective and to put attention on what really matters. It's as if individuals who have mourned have an elevated place from which to view life that enables them to see events as if they were being played out on a stage. When I am talking with individuals whose way of thinking and seeing has been altered this way, I remember that vivid scene in *Troilus and Cressida* where Troilus, already killed in battle, is now in heaven looking down at the war that is still fiercely being waged. But Troilus now can only laugh as he watches. For he knows such skirmishes mean nothing in the overall scheme of things. He now has life and death in perspective.

But humor? Is Dr. Kohut right when he asserts that a transformation of the self—which is what happens during the grieving process—reveals itself in an "increased capacity for humor"? My observation tells me this is so. People who have grieved a significant loss and faced their own death in the process are not as easily ruffled by day-to-day problems as are those people who have not gone through a similar experience. They display a kind of detached cosmic humor that allows them to put the vagaries, the caprices, of life in perspective. Kohut describes this trait not as a "picture of grandiosity and elation, but [as] . . . a quiet inner triumph with an admixture of undenied melancholy."

Expressing empathy, acknowledging the transitory nature of our existence, experiencing an enlarged capacity for humor—these three shifts in our personality constellate, and we form new attitudes. People around us take note of our new attitudes and say that we have increased in wisdom. Often I have heard individuals speak of family members or friends who have passed through the grieving process: "She has become so wise," one will say. "He is a much deeper person now," another will say. Or "Have you noticed how much her faith has deepened?" This achievement of wisdom—which Dr. Kohut refers to as a victorious outcome—occurs when we accept our limitations and discover how to be comfortable with the way life itself operates.

What contributes to our being able to attain this wisdom? Attention to forming, reestablishing, and maintaining a set of cherished values. Individuals have told me again and again that they have finished their grieving clearer than they have ever been in their lives about what they believe in, about what they think matters in life, about their relationship with God, and about what they are willing to give their commitment and time to. A sense of proportion, too, is the mark of this hard-won wisdom and "a touch of irony toward the achievements of individual existence, including even [our] own wisdom."

When we talk, then, in Integration, of how loss has altered us, it is not just an attempt to persuade ourselves that some good has come of our experience. We have been genuinely changed; our characters, our personalities, our thought structures and value systems have been affected. It is a hard-won shift, to be sure, but a change through which our very self has been altered.

Understanding the Time Frame of the Grieving Process

Some of the questions I hear most frequently when people have finally finished their work of grieving are, "But did it have to take so long? And did it have to be so painful? Did I have to make so many mistakes and see things so slowly?" It's as if we wish the wisdom and insight we have gained could be retroactive. We forget so easily that what we see clearly now has come only because we allowed ourselves to experience fully the grieving process. Therefore, we have to remind ourselves during Integration that we don't reach end results without making all those necessary intermediate choices.

Someone once pointed out to me the difference between time *Chronos* and time *Kairos*. Time *Chronos* describes a continuum of past, present, and future; it is the experience of time measured by clocks and calendars; time measured *chronologically*. Time *Kairos*, on the other hand, refers to "the time within which personal life moves forward." Time *Kairos* is not measured by temporal means but is movement we experience as a result of moments of awakening or realization. Time *Kairos* refers to a deepening process that results from our paying attention to the present moment, a process through which we are "drawn *inside* the movement of [our] own story."

As we experience the full grieving process, time *Chronos* is valuable only in that it gives us a span within which to experience time *Kairos*.

The passing of days and weeks and months does not, as we have seen so clearly, within itself bring resolution to our conflict. We each have, to use a word favored by the anthropologists, our own "entelechy," our own "immanent force controlling and directing development." Therefore, the calendar time it takes us to finish the work of our grieving depends completely on time *Kairos* (which can only move forward through our choices) and on our own "entelechy."

Nevertheless, people still wonder: "How long will this take? What can I expect? Am I progressing in a normal fashion?" The best I can offer are the average statistics, and we know how mythical are all things "average." Reminding them of the caveats, I discuss with individuals the research findings that have been based on studies of persons mourning significant losses:

- Psychiatrist John Bowlby, remarking on those people who successfully follow through the process of mourning, says: "A majority of those who do recover their former state of health and well-being are more likely to take two or three years to do so than a mere one."
- Dr. Beverley Raphael, in *The Anatomy of Bereavement,* suggests that even though survival may be clear by the end of the first year, "There is no fixed end point of mourning during the first or even second year.... There are many end points...."
- The Institute of Medicine, in its comprehensive report on bereavement published in 1984, reports, "Despite the popular belief that the bereavement process is normally completed in a year, data from systematic studies and from clinical reports confirm that the process may be considerably more attenuated for many people and still fall well within normal boundaries.... Thus a precise endpoint in time cannot be specified."
- Glen Davidson of Southern Illinois College of Medicine, citing his study of 1,200 adult mourners carried out over a two-year period, reports that near the end of the second year the bereaved person begins to feel a "sense of release, renewed energy, makes judgments better, [and regains] stable eating and sleeping habits...." Research into bereavement, Dr. Davidson asserts, "has made it clear that the mourning process is complex and the period of mourning lasts far longer than most people expect." In Dr.

Davidson's study, the phase of shock and numbness dominated the first two weeks of mourning; searching and yearning dominated the first four months; disorganization dominated the fifth through ninth months; and characteristics of reorientation dominated near the end of the second year after the death.

- Based on data from his study of three hundred widows, Dr. Sidney Zisook and his colleagues report in an American Psychiatric Press volume in 1987: "One of the most important findings of this study . . . was that for many widowed persons the time course of grief was much more prolonged than generally expected.... In general, we can say that the widows and widowers in our study appear to be relatively well adjusted by the end of four years."

The most common response people give after hearing this information is a sigh of relief. So many had been thinking they should already "be over the loss" and were embarrassed that they weren't. Once individuals have the context of the full grieving process, however, they recognize the complexity of what they are doing and award themselves a considerably larger amount of patience and understanding.

There are so many variables that play a part in each individual's time *Chronos* and time *Kairos:* the griever's personality and style of responding to unpleasant events in life; the degree to which the lost person was a part of or involved in what gave the grieving person's life order, structure, and meaning; the nature of the loss; the kind of support given by family and friends; past losses and the degree to which they have been mourned fully; the amount of ambivalent feelings a person has toward the lost one; the social, economic, and personal circumstances in which individuals must do their grieving; the number of other crises that must be dealt with simultaneously; the grieving person's health; his or her sex-role conditioning.

A brief look at these variables will help us understand why the length of time it takes each of us to grieve is different:

The griever's personality and style of responding to unpleasant events. Since moving through the mourning process depends upon persons being willing to make hard choices, those individuals who establish "dependent, clinging, ambivalent" relationships and who pull back from making decisions on their own will find their mourning extended, fixated, arrested, or perhaps stopped altogether until they are willing to change their behavior.

Also, if an individual's habit is to avoid painful situations and realizations, to draw back from working through difficult problems, then the length of the mourning will depend on how soon these persons become willing to change this habitual behavior and begin to engage with their grieving.

The degree to which the lost person was a part of or involved in what gave the grieving person's life order, structure, and meaning. If the lost person were central to the organization of the grieving person's life and/or to the sense of self, the mourning process is likely to take longer than if the person were part of the grieving person's life but not central to it. This means that it is not possible to make blanket judgments about what an individual's death will mean to another. It is possible, for instance, for the death of a brother whom one seldom saw and did not know well to have less impact than the death of a next-door neighbor who was central in those things that gave life meaning. And a husband who was violent and despicable may have to be mourned as extensively as if he had been loving and generous, simply because he was central in the organization and structure of the life of the family.

The nature of the loss. The nature of the loss is a central factor in the length of mourning. Sudden deaths or losses, the death of a child or a young person, violent or traumatic deaths, and suicides present special problems in grieving. There are often more shock, a greater sense of injustice, more guilt and blame, and a greater sense of helplessness; and these greatly complicate mourning. (Suicides and the deaths of children present some of the greatest complications.)

With some losses, several of the phases of the grieving process might telescope into each other, creating a quick mourning period, i.e., the loss one often feels at graduation or after getting a promotion. Other losses—like a divorce when we feel deserted and rejected or a death which seems untimely or especially unfair—seem to attach themselves at a particular bend in our psychological makeup and we stick at one phase of the grieving process for what seems like an inordinately long amount of time.

What about the opportunity to anticipate the loss? What effect does this have on length of grieving? Although knowing in advance does give individuals a chance to prepare, this advance preparation may not, in the long run, shorten their mourning period. Researchers find, for instance, that at the end of one year there is no difference between widows and widowers who had experienced anticipated grieving and those who did not (although those who have a chance to prepare do show less likelihood that their mourning will become pathological). The fact that a loss can be anticipated and planned for may be offset by the emotional drain that occurs as a result of a long illness, the ambivalent feelings of both relief and sadness that occur when the death finally happens, or by the emotional bonding and attachment that developed during the period before the death.

The kind of support given by family and friends. If those grieving have people around them who understand the mourning process and assist them appropriately in each of its phases, they will move through their grieving with more velocity. If those grieving feel loved, supported, and aided, and if the family and friends act as if they know that they are capable and expect them to move through the mourning process, then the outcome of grief will reflect these favorable situations. If, on the other hand, those around are uncomfortable with mourning, if they act as if the grieving person should already be finished mourning, or—heaven forbid, but it does occur—if they actually encourage the grieving person to dwell in her or his mourning, then grieving time may be extended.

Past losses and the degree to which they have been mourned fully. Imagine that when she was a child of seven or eight, a woman's mother died. And imagine that, as a child, the woman had no guidance in how to mourn and, subsequently, buried the loss as best she could, developing a way of life that always managed to skirt that delicate, painful, and incomplete issue. Then the woman's husband dies. His death, reaching deep into her psyche, activates the earlier ungrieved loss of her mother (and possibly even many more losses).

In such a circumstance, the length of the grieving process may reflect the fact that multiple losses have to be mourned.

The amount of ambivalent feelings a person has toward the lost person. The more ambivalent the grieving person feels toward the lost person, the longer and more difficult the mourning period. Perhaps there is unexpressed or unacknowledged resentment and anger. Perhaps there is guilt over disagreements and arguments that were never worked out. Perhaps there is relief that the person is gone at the same time that there is sorrow; and the grieving person does not forgive himself or herself for this seeming contradiction. In order to deny negative aspects of life with the lost person, individuals may idealize the past and thereby make their mourning harder. Any or all of these feelings of ambivalence may trigger most negative images of one's own worthlessness, which must then be worked through, thus often adding additional time and complication to the mourning.

The social, economic, and personal circumstances in which the individuals must do their grieving. Those people who have financial difficulties concurrent with the loss, are emotionally upset about other issues, do not have good health from the beginning or become ill during the mourning process, or are constrained as a result of previous sex-role conditioning (e.g., men don't cry; women are helpless in the face of decisions) will find that these factors complicate their mourning.

Men and women often respond to a loss differently. A woman may be more inclined to display her grief to others, to reach out to one or more persons around her, to talk more openly about the loss. Men, on the other hand, often tend to keep their grief to themselves, work hard to avoid losing control in front of others, and refrain from asking for help or assistance. For many women, feeling related or connected is of paramount importance, while for many men feeling independent and autonomous is critical to their having a positive view of themselves. These varying orientations to others, naturally, can affect the way an individual mourns.

Phyllis Silverman, codirector of the Child Bereavement Study at Massachusetts General Hospital in Boston, points out that there is a "male model" of loss, in which one speaks of "learning to break away from the past." Persons who follow this "male model" prefer to " 'get

on with life' and quickly involve themselves in work or other activities." A female model of grief, however, emphasizes connection rather
than disengagement and separation. Those who identify with this female model, the researcher says, are more comfortable behaving in
ways that indicate "you don't break your ties with the past, you change
your ties." Those who act on the male model often need assistance in
learning how to reconnect and relate after a loss, and those who act on
the female model often need help in learning how to be independent and active in taking care of themselves.

These variables affect not only the length of time of our grieving
process, but also the "smoothness" with which we move through it. I
don't think I have ever talked to anyone who had finished the work
of her or his grieving who did not say at some point in the conversation, "I wish I had done certain things differently when I was going
through the process; I wish I hadn't hurt that person; I wish I hadn't
been so destructive to myself; I wish I hadn't made that decision; I
wish I hadn't spent that money; I wish I had made the right choices
sooner; I wish . . . I wish." I always remind the individual that these
kinds of regrets are unavoidable. Given the complexity of what we
must experience during the grieving process—we *are,* after all, doing
the work of rebuilding our very self—we will not proceed in a straight
line. Our route will be convoluted. It must, then, be part of our experience of Integration to remind ourselves of this truth and to forgive
ourselves for the mistakes and the regressions.

One final point about time and smooth, linear progress: We have
no statistics to be able to determine what difference education about
the grieving process can make in both the length of time of the process
and smoothness of progression. Nevertheless, there is a strong con-
sensus of opinion among those in the medical and health communities
that education can make an enormous difference in the success with
which individuals conduct their mourning. I agree with this observation. My contact with individuals who are grieving tells me that it is
education—not courage, not heroism, not willingness, not desire—
that is lacking.

THE CHOICE

Since Integration represents a time when we recognize that we have finished the work of our grieving, what choice could there possibly be left to make? It would seem that none was necessary. In fact, have we not arrived where we are because we have already made choices? But it is part of the recognition of Integration to understand this inevitable truth:

We must choose to continue to make choices.

I think it was Madame de Stael, the eighteenth-century French novelist, who said, "The human mind always makes progress, but it is a progress of spirals." That is the way of life, too. And the way of loss. The loss we have just mourned represents just one of the innumerable losses we will need to grieve for during our lifetime. (No one has pointed out this fact of life more persuasively and poignantly than Judith Viorst in her book *Necessary Losses.*) In fact, at times, in order to move through the grieving process, we have had to create other losses. When we make changes in order to start to build a new identity, for instance, we often have to leave behind certain activities, habitual ways, even people, and each of these losses starts a mini process of grieving inside our larger ongoing process. Spirals within a spiral.

Losses, too, reactivate earlier losses. Lily Pincus says, "The loss through death of an important person strikes at the deepest roots of human existence, recalls the experience of previous attachments and losses, and reactivates the pain of earlier bereavements, physical as well as psychological in nature." (The process of writing this book, for instance, activated for me some long-forgotten losses of childhood, which I have mourned, phase by phase, as I moved through this writing project.) Therefore, the choice of value during Integration is to be willing to continue to make the choices that will allow us to experience the mourning-liberation process for all of our resurrected and our future losses.

Recognizing that life does present us with both a repetition and a succession of losses is part of the wisdom we gain as a result of engaging in the mourning process. We also have a larger context for holding our losses that, while giving them their due, makes them only part of the whole mosaic of our lives, not the total picture.

One way of speaking of this context is to see our lives as an ongoing adventure. (It's telling, isn't it, that the dictionary definition of the word *adventure* is "an undertaking involving danger and unknown risks" and that the word's root means "that which arrives.") Paul Tournier, in a book called *The Adventure of Living,* which he wrote when he was a practicing physician in Geneva, Switzerland, says that the adventure each of us lives is a manifestation of ourselves, a form of self-expression. "Each individual," he writes, "plays the cards he holds, and that is his adventure." And we want to play this adventure, Dr. Tournier asserts, because "the instinct of adventure is closely linked [with what prompts us] to make some personal mark which will survive [us]"—some creative work, some contribution to our family and others, some commitment to new paths, some original invention.

Given that adventure always includes the possibility of risk, the adventure that life is goes from "resurgence to resurgence, because of obstacles it meets and the problems to which it gives rise...." And that is where loss comes in. Obstacles and problems include losses, and the grieving process is our way of responding. Even this response, Dr. Tournier would say, is a sort of adventure, for he asserts, "The greatest of adventures is not action, it is our own development."

The renowned British educator James Britton tells us that it is *language* that we use as a way of *working upon* our representation of events. It is with language that we regulate our lives. Through the words we use, we set our direction. Because we have the use of language, we have "a power of coordinating, stabilizing, and facilitating other forms of behaviour." Including our mourning. Which brings us back full circle, then, to making choices. We make choices only through language—spoken language, internal language, body language. These choices are what allow us to direct our grieving.

To be willing to continue to make choices allows us to participate, as Ernest Becker speaks of it, in the "mysterious way in which life is given to us in evolution on this planet...." "Who knows," he says, "what form the forward momentum of life will take in the time ahead or what use it will make of our anguished searching. The most that any one of us can seem to do is to fashion something—an object or ourselves—and drop it into the confusion, make an offering of it, so to speak, to the life force." This is reason enough to commit to doing the work that is necessary to move through our losses.

WHAT WE NEED FROM FAMILY AND FRIENDS DURING INTEGRATION

Now, at this point in our grieving process, it is not so much a matter of what we need from our family and friends as what we can contribute to them. One of the things we recognize after we have experienced and worked through a traumatic loss is how pervasive grief and sadness are in the world. We are more aware of the pain and confusion around us; we can often intuit or recognize what a grieving person needs simply because we have had a similar experience. We have become—without ever desiring it, of course—one of the "wise ones," as Armand DiMele used to say to me. And on this wisdom we can now draw, not only for understanding our own losses that will continue to occur, but also for helping others understand theirs.

I remember a grandmother whose grandson had died before he was two years old. "I needed to talk about the baby's death so much in those first few months," she told me, "but my friends tried to direct my mind to other things—playing bridge, going to fashion shows, anything to keep my mind off the child. They thought they were helping, but they did not know that they were withholding the one thing I needed—permission to talk about what had happened. I would get so desperate for someone to talk to," she concluded, "that I would go shopping just so I could tell the salespersons that my grandson had died." Now that this grandmother has reached Integration, she makes it a point to spend time with family members and friends who experience a loss, allowing them to talk about the event as much as they want to. "I realize now," she said, "that so many people are uncomfortable hearing grieving persons talk about the loss. I make a special effort, therefore, to give them an opportunity to talk." This grandmother's actions are just one example of the kind of contribution we are able to make to our family and friends after we have moved through the mourning process.

Even though in Integration we are now released from the suffocating weight of our grieving and find our lives in a new balance, the love and companionship we have with our friends and family continues, of course, to be important. Not only for those times of surprise in the future when we will experience a recurrence of our sadness and grief or suffer a new loss and for the times when our family and friends will, in turn, need our support in a loss, but also for the times of quiet togetherness, of joy, of celebration and play. For we recognize now, probably to a much greater degree than we ever did in the past, how integral friends and family are to our well-being and how nurturing are the bonds of love in our life.

When I was mourning, William Stafford once sent me a poem he had written called "Rescue," which goes like this:

> A fire was burning. In another room
> somebody was talking. Sunlight slanted
> across the foot of my bed, and a glass of water
> gleamed where it waited on a chair near my hand.
> I was alive and the pain in my head
> was gone. Carefully I tried thinking
> of those I had known. I let them walk
> and then run, and then open their mouths the way
> it used to cause the throbbing. It didn't hurt
> anymore. Clearer and clearer I stared
> far into the glass. I was cured.
>
> From now on in my life there would be a place
> like a scene in a paperweight. One figure in the storm
> would be reaching out with my hand for those
> who had died. It would always be still in that scene,
> no matter what happened. I could come back to it,
> carefully, any time, to be saved, and go on.

It has now been ten years since that July afternoon when, driving along the road to find my husband, I instead found myself a widow. And today I think I can say that I understand the poem that Bill sent me.

For there *is* something redemptive about the mourning process, something that resides in the power and opportunity we have to make choices. These choices, of course, allow us to make for ourselves a new life in the external. For instance, I now write books and no longer teach school; I am now married to a wonderful man with whom I deeply enjoy the adventure of living; and today I can, most of the time, remember the value of living in the moment. I also know the value of recuperative silence. My daily life is full, rich, and deeply textured. But the real impact of the choices, I think, resides in their power to alter our very way of being. As Emily Dickinson once wrote, "Heavenly Hurt, it gives us—/ We can find no scar, / But internal difference, / Where the Meanings, are." This "internal difference" is what we create by our choices.

Somehow it seems fitting that as I write the last lines of this book a soft rain is falling on the skylight that, with so much love *and* pain, I installed such a long time ago. As I listen to the sound, I remember the cabin in Tennessee; I remember the day Greg and I sat on the front porch eating buttered toast and watching the rain run down the screen in rivulets. It is like that glass paperweight in Bill Stafford's poem. I can visit the still scene, so quiet and so beautiful, and then return peacefully to the present.

The rain also makes me think of the Northwest, and that brings to my mind Greg's sons and his mother. It isn't quite so easy to visit that memory and then return to the present, for I often long for Greg to know how well his family is doing. His mother, when she moved to a smaller apartment after she reached her eighties, calling to say, "I am sure I will like it here, for I can see the Blue Mountains." Or his son David writing to tell me about the Philippine mahogany and cherrywood bookcase he is building: "The overall look as observed from afar shall be one of a subtle two tone of dark orange and an ash/charcoal gray/tan; and if my sense of color and design doesn't fail me now, it should look good." I cry because in that action he is so much the son of his father. Or when Fred sends pictures of his two sons who are preschoolers or lets me know he has been named the number-one motorcycle safety education instructor in all of North America, I want his father to know these grandchildren and to be able to congratulate his son. But that's the part of the loss that is never over. All the rain can say to those memories is, "I'm sorry."

But then I remember the rain falling on another cabin, one the Trappist monk Thomas Merton wrote about in one of his essays, and I am returned to myself:

> The rain . . . fills the woods with an immense and confused sound. It covers the flat roof of the cabin and its porch with insistent and controlled rhythms. And I listen, because it reminds me again and again that the whole world runs by rhythms I have not yet learned to recognize....
>
> I came up here from the monastery last night, sloshing through the cornfield, said Vespers, and put some oatmeal on the Coleman stove for supper. It boiled over while I was listening to the rain and toasting a piece of bread at the log fire. The night became very dark. The rain surrounded the whole cabin with its enormous virginal myth, a whole world of meaning, of secrecy, of silence, of rumor. Think of it: all that speech pouring down, selling nothing, judging nobody, drenching the thick mulch of dead leaves, soaking the trees, filling the gullies and crannies of the wood with water.... What a thing it is to sit absolutely alone, in the forest, at night, cherished by this wonderful, unintelligible, perfectly innocent speech, the most comforting speech in the world, the talk that rain makes by itself all over the ridges, and the talk of the watercourses everywhere in the hollows!
>
> Nobody started it, nobody is going to stop it. It will talk as long as it wants, this rain. As long as it talks I am going to listen.

And now, as the rain continues to make a soft sound on the skylight, I sit back in my chair, and I listen.

EPILOGUE

It has now been eight years since I completed writing *Seven Choices*. What has happened in this almost a decade? Especially what has happened that I can trace back to the painful, terrible event of having a young husband drop dead?

That last question in particular is one that cannot be answered. For when a loss is integrated into who we are, everything that has happened since is in some way related to what we have experienced.

I see today the externals of my life:

I continue to be privileged to live the life of a writer. I have been remarried for almost thirteen years. My husband and I reside in a big city alive with the comings and goings of human activity and with the performing arts that enliven the human spirit. I have two dogs, Dusty and Lacey, who think my writing studio is their dog house. I have three nieces instead of two. My parents have died. I consult with Fortune 500 companies in the United States and with executives and managers of multinational firms from many countries in the world, bringing ideas on how the leaders in these organizations can respond productively to the complex changes that are occurring in global business. I also lead women's spiritual retreats.

But who am I and how am I different from the woman who finished writing *Seven Choices*? That to me is a much more important question.

If I had to say it in one word, it would be quieter.

What do I mean?

I'm quieter in my spirit. Wisdom did come, as researchers predict it can, from living the full grieving cycle. I'm on the go less. I don't try to do everything that comes along that I could do. What is even more amazing is that I don't even set goals any more. I

make commitments and keep them. I get things done that are there
to be done. But I have no goals I'm striving for, no gold ring I want
to reach.

To be sure, I have desires. I have dreams. I have wants. I have
a picture of things I want to have happen. But something has shifted
profoundly in the last eight years. I no longer drive toward these
dreams. I no longer turn the world upside down to get them. Much
more, I let life take its course. I follow—as one philosopher put it
once—the movement of the showing. I work and work hard. I take
action when action is needed. But I don't push for my idea of what
ought to be happening. I don't set my eye on one thing and do
whatever it takes to get that.

It is a paradox, isn't it. I'm not lackadaisical. I'm not drifting.
I'm not waiting for things out there to just happen. I am an active
participant in the enterprise. But somewhere along the way I've
realized that any goal I set, any direction I lay out precisely, might
be too small or too limited or too one-dimensional. This I do not
want.

I now have time to do things that I did not even want to do in the
past—like water flowers, cut bouquets, visit antique stores, hunt for
bargains in thrift shops. My home is much more a home and less a
place to stay when I wasn't working, volunteering, going, doing, as
in the past.

I know the process of grieving now and have had on many
occasions in the past eight years to yield to that process. Just this
spring my mother and father died eight days apart, and I am still
doing the work of grieving the loss of the two dear people who gave
me life. What is different is that I can now recognize where I am—
though when it's Second Crisis or Working Through it's no easier
even if I do know where I am—and, most important of all, I know
there can be Integration!

I express my creativity more now than I used to. Not long ago I
took a two-hour course on collaging at an art supply store nearby—
and my husband had the piece I made framed "That's art," he said,
when I brought it home. (For one whose art making ended in the
third grade—when her cotton-ball-box-horse with pipe stem cleaner
legs was the only one that wouldn't stand up in the entire class—
making the collage was a breakthrough.)

What began during the grieving process I wrote about in Seven Choices as silent prayer taught to me by the history professor at the university has now become the focus of my life, my core, and my center. Connection with and communication with the Divine— listening as well as talking—is now, in the words of theologian Paul Tillich, my ultimate concern. Being in relationship with God is now always my first commitment. Learning how to love more and more graciously and totally is my highest intention. Giving gratitude to the Holy Other brings me now the greatest sense of purpose and fulfillment.

All this could, I suppose, sound platitudinous. Pompous. Even pious. Funny, though. It's none of that. It's my life. That is truly how I have changed. I experienced through Greg's death another kind of death—death of the view of life as I had it then. The view I have now of life allows me to be much more at peace. Much more confidence. Much more able to wait.

And even more in awe of Mystery.

Last year when I got a new plant for the garden—a native Texas Star red hibiscus—I took a picture of the first bloom and sent it to my mother in Tennessee. All summer, after she got the picture in the mail, she would ask about the plant when we talked on the telephone: how many blooms now; are they still big as a dinner plate, like the one in the picture? This year the Texas Star red hibiscus froze during the winter. So when growing season came there was nothing there except the cut-off-to-the-ground stalk from last year. Imagine my joy—some days after Mother died—when the hibiscus began to grow. And imagine my—and neighbors' and friends'— amazement to see that the plant has grown to be more than twelve feet high in this one growing season—and has multiple new blooms as big as a dinner plate on it every day.

Yes, I stand today in awe and gratitude of the unfathomable, glorious, loving Mystery. I live to honor God.

NOTES

Prologue

Complex process: Terms used in talking about this process vary. The Institute of Medicine, in its study *Bereavement: Reactions, Consequences, and Care,* edited by Marian Osterweis, Fredric Solomon, and Morris Green, uses these definitions: *"bereavement:* the fact of loss through death; *bereavement reactions:* any psychological, physiologic, or behavioral response to bereavement. The term 'reaction' is not meant to suggest automatic, reflex responses nor to imply that any particular reaction is universal, *bereavement process:* an umbrella term that refers to the emergence of bereavement reactions over time; *grief:* the feeling (affect) and certain associated behaviors, such as crying; *grieving process:* the changing affective state over time; *mourning:* in the social science sense, the social expressions of grief, including mourning rituals and associated behaviors. This definition of mourning is a departure from Freud's usage, where the term refers to an internal psychologic state and process" (pp. 9-10).

Beverley Raphael, M.D., professor of psychiatry at the University of Newcastle in New South Wales, Australia, in her definitive book *The Anatomy of Bereavement* uses these terms: "Bereavement is the reaction to the loss of a close relationship. Sometimes grief is also used to describe this reaction, but in this work grief will be used to refer to the emotional response to loss: the complex amalgam of painful affects including sadness, anger, helplessness, guilt, despair. Mourning will be used here to refer to the psychological mourning processes that occur in bereavement: the processes whereby the bereaved gradually undoes the psychological bonds that bound him to the deceased" (p. 33).

George Pollock, M.D., Ph.D., whose work based on his research as professor, Department of Psychiatry, Northwestern University Medical School, director of the Chicago Institute for Psychoanalysis, and president of the Center for Psychosocial Studies in Chicago, has for more than twenty-five years provided a definitive perspective on loss and grieving, uses the term *mourning process to* cover both *acute grieving* and *chronic grieving. Chronic grieving* includes the adaptive mechanisms that allow an individual to integrate the experience of the loss with reality. In his seminal article "Mourning and Adaptation," published in *The International Journal of Psycho-analysis*, vol. XLII, parts 4-5, Dr. Pollock says, "The acute stage of the mourning process refers to the immediate phases following the loss of the object. These phases consist of the shock, grief, pain, reaction to separation, and the beginning internal object decathexis with the recognition of the loss.... As the acute stage of the mourning process progresses, the chronic stage gradually takes over. Here we find various manifestations of adaptive mechanisms attempting to integrate the experience of the loss with reality so that life activities can go on" (p. 352). Dr. Pollock considers *bereavement (loss* of a meaningful person by death) to be a subclass of *mourning* and refers to bereavement, as well as to other kinds of losses, in his discussion of the mourning process. (See Pollock, "Process and Affect: Mourning and Grief," *The International Journal of Psycho-analysis, vol. 59*, parts 2-3, p. 273.)

For purposes of simplicity and familiarity, in this book I use the terms *grief, mourning, grief process,* and *mourning process* interchangeably to refer to the full range of experiences that allow individuals to find their way from the shock and numbness of a loss to reorientation and balance in life. These experiences include the emotional and psychological responses to loss as well as the longer-term adjustments that help persons develop new identities, establish new purposes, and build new assumptive worlds. I use *acute grieving to* refer to the initial intense emotional responses that occur following a loss.

I am deeply indebted to the writings of the individuals cited above, and others whose works are cited in later notes, for my theoretical understanding of the mourning process, as well as for the illumination I have gained about my own mourning process.

Page 2
"Creative outcome": See George Pollock, "Mourning and Adaptation," *The International Journal of Psycho-analysis,* vol. XLII, parts 4-5, pp. 354-355; "The Mourning Process and Creative Organizational Change," Journal *of the American Psychoanalytic Association,* vol. 25, no. 1, pp. 1328; "Process and Affect: Mourning and Grief," *The International Journal of Psycho-analysis,* vol. 59, parts 23, pp. 267-273.

"Intense distress or depression": See "New Studies Find Many Myths About Mourning," Daniel Goleman, the *New York Times,* August 8, 1989, p. Cl.

On the otherhand: Beverley Raphael writes in *The Anatomy of Bereavement,* "The levels of morbid outcome or pathological patterns of grief are known in only a few instances, but they may represent at least one in three bereavements" (p. 64).

Page 3
East African man: I am indebted to Lily Pincus's excellent book, *Death and the Family: The Importance of Mourning,* pp. 255—256, for knowledge of this ritual.

Page 4
Alaskan Tlingit Indian: For a description of this ritual, see Fried and Fried, *Transitions: Four Rituals in Eight Cultures,* pp. 156—158.

Page 5
"Interior terrain": Nor Hall, *The Moon and the Virgin,* p. 167.

Mental process: Anthony Storr, *Solitude: A Return to the Self,* p. 32.

Sets or clusters of experience: The editors of The Institute of Medicine's *Bereavement: Reactions, Consequences, and Care* state, "Despite the nonlinearity of the grieving process, most observers of it speak of clusters of reactions or 'phases' of bereavement that change over time. Although observers divide the process into various numbers of phases and use different terminology to label them, there is general agreement about the nature of reactions over time. Clinicians also agree that there is substantial individual variation in terms of specific manifestations of grief and in the speed with which people move through the process" (p. 48).

Impact: These Impact reactions are universal, and they are automatic. The responses are elemental, ancient, connected to human beings' need for balance and order in our lives and to our desire for remaining bonded to those around us. For millenia, such bonds have been synonymous with survival. Many of the responses we make during Impact are instinctual; we share them in common with other animals—such as greylag geese and the primates—who search for their lost partners and are sad when they cannot find them. Elephants mourn their dead. They will stop at a carcass of one of their own, become quiet and tense, and then slowly and cautiously begin to touch the bones as if they are trying to recognize the individual. See Colin Murray Parkes, M.D., *Bereavement: Studies of Grief in Adult Life,* p. 40, as well as Pollock, "Mourning and Adaptation," *The International Journal of Psychoanalysis,* vol. XLII, parts 4-5, pp. 359-360. Also see Cynthia Moss's beautiful book, *Elephant Memories: Thirteen Years in the Life of an Elephant Family.* Chapter 3 of this book, called "Migration," contains a moving account of an elephant family's response to the death of one of their members from a gunshot wound (pp. 72-75). Chapter 10, "Life Cycle and Death," details additional information about elephants' reactions to death (pp. 270, 271).

Observation: Anne Morrow Lindbergh once said that if suffering alone made one wise, everybody in the world would be wise. The difference between those who suffer and become wise and those who suffer and do not is the experience of Observation. During the set of experiences that constitute this phase of the grieving process, the kind of rejection and discernment and assimilation that can lead to wisdom is begun.

Observation is not synonymous with acceptance. In fact, acceptance can be the booby prize in the grieving process, because most people, when asked their definition of *acceptance,* will indicate that the word means something like *resignation.* Observation, instead, is a time of "living in the question," of forgiving oneself, others, and life; of noticing how the loss has changed us, altered our environment, scattered our past. It is a period of keeping open the mourning process in order to have time to think, to experience. It is a time of ambiguity as well as a time of clarity; a time of not knowing and a time of wonderment.

Page 6

The Turn: John Bowlby, in *Loss,* speaks of the importance of this phase of the mourning process: "If all goes well . . . [the griever] starts to examine the new situation in which he finds himself and to consider ways of meeting it. This entails a redefinition of himself as well as of his situation.... Until redefinition is achieved no plans for the future can be made.... Once this corner is turned a bereaved person recognizes that an attempt must be made to fill unaccustomed roles and to acquire new skills" (p. 94).

Reconstruction: Beverley Raphael, in speaking of these longer-term adjustments and adaptations, asserts in *The Anatomy of Bereavement,* "The time taken for the longer term adaptations will vary enormously.... The period of readjustment may be seen as a period of ongoing mourning" (p. 57). George Pollock also states, "This mourning reaction is an ego-adaptive process which includes the reaction to the loss of the object, as well as the readjustment to an external environment herein this object no longer exists in reality" ("Mourning and Adaptation," *The International Journal of Psychoanalysis,* vol. Xl.ll, parts 4-5, p. 343).

In *Bereavement: Reactions, Consequences, and Care,* the editors cite the Widow-to-Widow Program conducted by Phyllis Silverman from 1964 to 1974 at Harvard University. The goals of that program did not center around "recovery"; instead, the work with the widows centered around change. Recognizing that it is never possible to return "to all prebereavement baselines," the program taught that reaching a constructive outcome to the mourning process depended on the mourners' "ability to adapt and alter their images and roles to fit their new status." Commenting on this program and its emphasis, the editors observed, "Although emotional support from a person who has also been through the experience was considered important, the women's most fundamental need was to learn how to change" (pp. 242-244).

In *Loss,* John Bowlby says that a mourner will do one of two things: he will either "progress toward a recognition of his changed circumstances, a revision of his representational models, and a redefinition of his goals in life, or else [he will stay in] a state of suspended growth in which he is held prisoner by a dilemma he cannot solve" (p. 139).

Working Through: George Pollock points out that "the need to give up a house, a social group, or the like as a result of the separation may serve to institute new mourning processes and increase the integrative task of the ego, but these also are gradually worked through." He also says, "New mourning experiences can serve to revive past mourning reactions that may still have bits of unresolved work present" ("Mourning and Adaptation," *The International Journal of Psycho-analysis,* vol. XLII, parts 4—5, p. 354).

Peter Marris, the British social scientist who has studied the complexities of change in a variety of settings—bereavement, slum clearings, entrepreneurial enterprises in Africa, and others—writes in his highly regarded book *Loss and Change:* "A sense of continuity can, then, only be restored by detaching the familiar meanings of life from the relationship in which they were embodied, and re-establishing them independently of it. This is what happens during the working through of grief" (p. 34). Marris also states, "The working out of a severe bereavement represents, as a personal crisis, a general principle of adaptation to change. Life becomes unmanageable, because it has become meaningless. The context of purposes and attachments, to which events are referred for their interpretation, has been so badly disrupted by the loss that it at first seems irreparable" (p. 38). He adds, "The meaning of life must be retrieved and reformulated, so that it can continuously survive the relationship which may no longer contain it" (p. 40).

Integration: Dr. George Pollock asserts that mourning is a "normal transformational adaptive process [that has] an outcome of gain and freedom once the process has been completed." A "change creative-gain sequence," says Dr. Pollock. The mourning process, available to all of humankind as "one of the more universal forms of adaptation and growth," is what allows us to deal with the trauma of our loss; and through this process we find a way to achieve "continuity, integration, cohesiveness, preservation, survival, and further additional development." Because we choose to experience the full mourning process, we achieve what Dr. Pollock calls a "creative outcome" when we finish our grieving, defined by him as the ability to feel joy, satisfaction, and a sense of accomplishment; a return to a steady state of balance; the experience of an increased capacity to appreciate people and things; a realization that one has become more tolerant and wise; a desire to express oneself creatively; the ability to invest in new relationships; the experience of a sense of freedom and revitalization. See Pollock, "Process and Affect: Mourning and Grief," *The International Journal of Psycho-analysis, vol.* LIX, parts 2-3, pp. 267-273; "Mourning and Adaptation," *The International Journal of Psycho-analysis,* vol. XLII, parts 4-5, pp. 345, 354-355; and "The Mourning Process and Creative Organizational Change," *Journal of the American Psychoanalytic Association,* vol. XXV, no. 1, pp. 11-28. Dr. Pollock also says, "It is my belief that the mourning process, a universal adaptive process to change and loss with an outcome of gain and freedom once the process has been completed, is a means of reestablishing balance intrapsychically, interpersonally, socially, and culturally" (Ibid., p. 18).

Particular choices: George Pollock writes, "As the ego passes judgment on the truth and permanence of the loss, action and thought processes are utilized to facilitate appropriate alterations of reality with subsequent adaptation" ("Mourning and Adaptation," *International Journal of Psycho-analysis,* vol. XLII, parts 4-5, p. 348). This action and these thought processes inform our choices.

Remain stuck: George Pollock writes, "The mourning process can have four outcomes: *normal resolution* which results in creative activity, creative reinvested living, creative products. Memory traces become the end product intrapsychically of the resolved and completed mourning process; *arrestation of the mourning process* at various stages; *fixations at various earlier stages* which become reactivated when a mourning process is initiated; and finally, *pathological or deviated mourning processes* that are variously diagnosed as depression, depressive states, apathy. These may result in anniversary suicides, anniversary homicides, serious delinquent behavior, psychotic decompensations, etc." ("Process and Affect: Mourning and Grief, *The International Journal of Psycho-analysis* vol. LIX, parts 2-3, p. 273). Citing John Bowlby, Pollock defines *pathological mourning* as "(1) anxiety and depression where a persistent and unconscious yearning to recover and reunite with the lost object is present; (2) intense anger and reproach, frequently unconscious, directed towards various objects including the self; (3) absorption in caring for others who have been bereaved; and (4) denial that the object is permanently lost" (Ibid., p. 266).

Page 7
Map of the complete grieving process: First some caveats . . .

1. The clusters of experiences that make up the grieving process are not like a series of tightly
    defined steps that an individual moves through in a linear, lockstep arrangement. (Because this
    is true, the word *stages* is too rigid to describe the parts of the process; the more fluid words
    phases or *clusters* or *sets of experiences* are more appropriate.) The process is experienced in a
    recursive manner characterized by movement that is back and forth and overlapping. At the
    same time, the clusters or sets of grieving experiences do occur in a sequence. That sequence,
    although not an uninterrupted chain of happenings occurring one right after the other, does
    gradually move in a forward direction: toward reorganization, reorientation, and a return to
    equilibrium.

    The editors of the Institute of Medicine's *Bereavement: Reactions, Consequences, and
    Care* state: "The committee cautions against the use of the word 'stages' to describe the be-
    reavement process, as it may connote concrete boundaries between what are actually overlap-
    ping, fluid phases. The notion of stages might lead people to expect the bereaved to proceed
    from one clearly identifiable reaction to another in a more orderly fashion than usually occurs.
    It might also result in inappropriate behavior toward the bereaved, including hasty assessments
    of where individuals are or ought to be in the grieving process" (Institute of Medicine's *Be-
    reavement: Reactions, Consequences, and Care*, p. 48).

    About movement that is back and forth, Beverley Raphael writes in *The Anatomy of Be-
    reavement:* "The bereavement reaction may be described as comprising a series of phases,
    representing some of the processes of adaptation to loss. It must be acknowledged, however,
    that any such phases are not clear-cut or fixed, and that the bereaved may pass backward and
    forward among them or may indeed become locked in one or another, partially or completely"
    (pp. 33, 134). George Pollock says of the phases that "though somewhat unidirectional, [they]
    do on occasion oscillate and revert back temporarily . . . as part of the back and forth transfor-
    mational process" ("Process and Affect: Mourning and Grief," *The International Journal of
    Psycho-analysis,* vol. LIX, parts 2-3, p. 262.)
2. No two people experience the mourning process at the same pace or in the same manner. Each
    individual has her or his own timing and way of grieving. Also, the various phases of the
    process assume different proportions for different kinds of losses. Yet we can speak of grieving
    as a universal phenomenon experienced throughout history by all people.

    George Pollock says, "The mourning process . . . is a universal adaptation, goes on
    throughout the life cycle of the individual, is found in all cultures, and, when ritualized, can be
    found throughout man's existence in his religious, social, and cultural practices ("The Mourn-
    ing Process and Creative Organizational Change," *Journal of the American Psychoanalytic
    Association,* vol. XXV, no. 1, p. 16). He also writes: "Mourning is a normal transformational
    adaptive process, found in all people and throughout history" ("Process and Affect: Mourning
    and Grief," *The International Journal of Psycho-analysis,* vol. LIX, parts 2—3, p. 273).
3. Some individuals report that they experience no intense distress during their grieving. They are
    able to find a way to think about their loss that allows them to bypass many of the phases of the
    grieving process. Such people, in the word of one psychologist, bear their grief "lightly." For
    such individuals, perhaps, the phases of the grieving process would not hold. For more infor-

mation, see "New Studies Find Many Myths About Mourning," Daniel Goleman, the *New York Times*, August 8, 1989, p. Cl.

4. The grieving process is not to be confused with the process through which people may move when they find out they are dying. The valuable research of Dr. Elisabeth Kübler-Ross, in which she identified five stages—denial, anger, bargaining, depression, and acceptance—experienced by individuals prior to the occurrence of death, has been mistakenly identified by many as a description of a full grieving process. And although the situations—responding to the news of one's anticipated death and finding one's way back to life after a traumatic loss—share some aspects in common, the two processes associated with these events are very different. See Elisabeth Kübler-Ross's *On Death and Dying: What the Dying Have to Teach Doctors, Nurses, Clergy and Their Own Families,* pp. 38-137.

The map included here, while based on my own experiences and research, also includes, amplifies, builds on, and adds to phases delineated by other researchers.

John Bowlby, whose pioneer work was conducted with the World Health Organization and at the Tavistock Clinic and Tavistock Institute of Human Relations in London, lists in *Loss: Sadness and Depression,* the third volume of his definitive three-volume study *Attachment and Loss,* these four phases of mourning. "1. Phase of numbing that usually lasts from a few hours to a week and may be interrupted by outbursts of extremely intense distress and/or anger. 2. Phase of yearning and searching for the lost figure lasting some months and sometimes for years. 3. Phase of disorganization and despair. 4. Phase of greater or less degree of reorganization" (p. 85).

Glen W. Davidson, Ph.D., professor and chairman of the Department of Medical Humanities, Southern Illinois University School of Medicine, and a leader in the field of bereavement education and counseling, lists in *Understanding Mourning: A Guide for Those Who Grieve* these phases: *"Shock and numbness:* resistance to stimuli, judgment making difficult, functioning impeded, emotional outbursts, stunned feelings; *Searching and yearning:* very sensitive to stimuli, anger/guilt, restless/impatient, ambiguous, testing what is real; *Disorientation:* disorganized, depressed, guilt, weight gain/loss, awareness of reality; *Reorganization:* sense of release, renewed energy, makes judgments better, stable eating and sleeping habits" (pp. 50, 59, 68, 78).

Sidney Zisook, M.D., associate professor, University of California, San Diego, UCSD-Gifford Mental Health Center, San Diego, lists these phases in *Biopsychosocial Aspects of Bereavement:* I. Shock—denial and disbelief. II. Acute mourning. A. Intense feeling states: crying spells, guilt, shame, depression, anorexia, insomnia, irritability, emptiness, and fatigue. B. Social withdrawal: preoccupation with health, inability to sustain usual work, family, and personal relationships. C. Identification with the deceased: transient adoption of habits, mannerisms, and somatic symptoms of the deceased. III. Resolution—acceptance of loss, awareness of having grieved, return to well-being, and ability to recall the deceased without subjective pain" (p. 25).

Beverley Raphael, M.D., in *The Anatomy of Bereavement* refers to: *Shock, numbness, disbelief; Emotional experience of separation pain:* "intense yearning, pining, and longing . . . restlessness, agitation, and a high level of psychological arousal . . . preoccupation with the absent person . . . pain and emptiness . . . anxiety and helplessness . . . anger and aggression"; *Psychological mourning:* "intense reexperiencing of much of the past development of relationship . . . undoing the bonds that built the relationship"; crying, sadness, regret, resentment, guilt, despair, disorganization; *Longer term adjustments:* engaging in adjustive tasks, defining identity, relinquishing old roles, establishing "new patterns of interaction and sources of gratification," evolving "new and satisfying roles, interactions, and sources of gratification" (pp. 34-58).

Page 8

"The grieving of widowhood": Marris, *Loss and Change,* p. 22. Further, Marris states, "Bereavement presents unambiguously one aspect of social changes—the irretrievable loss of the familiar. And since it is a common experience in every society, the reaction to bereavement is perhaps the most general and best described of all examples of how we assimilate disruptive change. If we can understand grief and mourning, we may be able to see more clearly the process of adjustment in other situations of change, where the discontinuity is less clear-cut" (p. 23). He also states, "I have been writing of death. But these suggestions can, I think, be adapted to any severe personal loss" (p. 154). George Pollock states: "I have studied the loss through death as it is simpler to date the loss and subsequent mourning. I believe the general principles are applicable to other loss situations, e.g. divorce, serious illness with prolonged separation, etc." ("Process and Affect: Mourning and Grief," *The International Journal of Psycho-analysis,* vol. LIX, parts 2-3, p. 271). Also, see Beverley Raphael, *The Anatomy of Bereavement,* pp. 227-228, for a discussion of divorce and dissolution of partnerships in the context of the death of a spouse.

There are, of course, differences in the intensity, duration, and the like of the grieving process when we mourn different kinds of losses and when different people mourn the same losses. For a detailed discussion of this subject, please see section 7 of this book.

Age, too, makes a difference. In discussing the mourning process, George Pollock points out that "the earliest phases of the process [are] the ones that can be seen in young children, whereas later phases appear in older children. Adults are capable of participating in the entire process, whose resolution and outcome can be freedom, revitalization, and, in gifted individuals, creative products" ("The Mourning Process and Creative Organizational Change," *Journal of the American Psychoanalytic Association* vol. 25, no. 1, p. 18).

1. Impact

Page 9

Epigraph: For notice of this Shakespeare reference and the Thomas Paine epigraph introducing Section 3, I am indebted to John Schneider's *Stress, Loss, and Grief* pp. 79, 9.

Page 21

"Bring in the axe": From poem "After Work" by Gary Snyder, published in *The Back Country,* p. 22.

Page 27

Brains secrete: Institute of Medicine, *Bereavement: Reactions, Consequences, and Care,* p. 162.

"Virtually closes its boundaries and defenses": Raphael, *The Anatomy of Bereavement,* p. 34.

Deep evolutionary roots: See Raphael, *The Anatomy of Bereavement,* p. 3, and Parkes, *Bereavement: Studies of Grief in Adult Life,* pp. 40-42.

Page 28

"Searching and Sounding": Cited by Parkes, *Bereavement,* p. 40.

Page 35

Flight-or-fight: See Wayne Barrett, et. al., *The Brain: Mystery of Matter and Mind,* pp. 9899.

Medical studies: For comprehensive information about the relationship of grief and health, see the Institute of Medicine's *Bereavement: Reactions, Consequences, and Care,* chapters 2, 3, and 6.

Page 36
"Standard of care": Glen Davidson, in *Understanding Mourning,* reports on physicians' tendency to interpret the prescribing of barbiturates or tranquilizers as a "standard of care," citing statistics that showed that 87 percent of physicians in Illinois indicated they held such a position (p. 22).

The majority of the general public: "As many as 89 percent of the general public polled in 1980 understood mourning basically to be an illness, whose characteristics must be suppressed.... Most of those polled thought it appropriate for physicians to prescribe drugs as a means for suppressing the symptoms" (Davidson, *Understanding Mourning,* pp. 22, 23).

Page 37
Alternatives: Davidson, *Understanding Mourning,* p. 70.

Page 39
Giving attention to ritual: In the excellent book *Dealing Creatively with Death: A Manual of Death Education and Simple Burial,* written by Ernest Morgan and edited by Jenifer Morgan, one can find sample death ceremonies, including (1) a service with a flower communion, (2) a service using writings of the deceased, (3) a service with organ music, (4) a service held for a teenaged girl, (5) a memorial walk, (6) an unstructured service held in a farmyard, (7) a Quaker service, (8) a love memorial for a son, (9) a service based on recognition of death, (10) committal services, and (11) a good-bye ceremony for children. This book also contains general selected readings, as well as readings for a child, the aged, a parent, burial committal services, and cremation committal services (pp. 125-145). *Dealing Creatively with Death,* with its simple and loving approach to matters of grieving, is well worth reading in its entirety. The book can be ordered from Celo Press, 1901 Hannah Branch Road, Burnsville, N.C. 28714.

Page 41
Earliest phases: Pollock, "The Mourning Process and Creative Organizational Change," *Journal of the American Psychoanalytic Association, vol.* 25, no. 1, p. 18.

Different phases: Claudia L. Jewett, *Helping Children Cope with Separation and Loss,* pp. 22-49.

"What happens when the body": Lawrence Kutner, "Death Is No Friend, So Take Care When Introducing Him," the *New York Times,* March 10, 1988, p. 19.

Page 41
"Almost everyone": see Jane E. Brody, "The Facts of Death for Children," the *New York Times,* August 12, 1987, p. 18.

"In a special place": Ibid.

"Feels no pain"; "all agree"; "Going to the funeral": Ibid.

Page 42
"It is critical": Jewett, *Helping Children Cope with Separation and Loss,* pp. 41, 42. Books that may be useful in helping children deal with loss include *How to Teach Children About Death,* Audrey K. Cordon and Dennis Klass, Prentice-Hall, 1979; *Caring About Kids: Tallying to Children About Death,* National Institute of Mental Health (free from Public Inquiries, NIMH, 5600 Fishers Lane, Rockville, Md. 20857); *Talking About Divorce,* Earl A. Crollman, Beacon Press, Boston, 1975; *Divorce Book for Parents: Helping Your Children Cope with Divorce and Its Aftermath,* Vicki Lansky, New American Library, 1989; *How Do We Tell the Children! Helping*

Children Understand and Cope When Someone Dies, Dan Schaefer and Christine Lyons, Medic Publishing Co., Redmund, Wash., 1987.

Page 43
Many theories: For a review of such theories, see Allan L. Combs, "Synchronicity: A Synthesis of Western Theories and Eastern Perspectives," *ReVision,* vol. 5, no. 1, pp. 20-27.

Page 44
"Mourning is treated": See Geoffrey Gorer, *Death, Grief, and Mourning,* p. IS 1.

Page 45
Objective studies: Storr, *Solitude: A Return to the Self,* p. 30.

"There is an optimal 'level of grieving' ": Parkes, *Bereavement,* p. 162.

Page 46
Need from family and friends: Beverley Raphael summarizes the chief goals of care in the early phase of grieving: "to facilitate the emotional release; to assist the bereaved in recognizing and expressing their yearning for the lost person; to facilitate reality testing by a review of the death and its meaning; to promote other social support; and to initiate the basis for an ongoing caring relationship" *(Anatomy of Bereavement,* p. 358).

Page 47
"Not the only one"; "By contrast": Bowlby, *Loss,* p. *193.*

Page 48
"Pluck at the heartstrings"; "connive"; "in endless attempts"; "Both probing"; "a painful and difficult task": Parkes, Bereavement, p. 161.

Page 49
Move forward by trial and error: In her personal story, *The Grieving Time: A Year's Account of Recovery from Loss,* Anne M. Brooks recounts the phases of acute grieving with poignancy and clarity.

2. The Second Crisis

Page 51
Epigraph: From "Years Vanish Like the Morning Dew," in *In the Midst of Winter: Selections from the Literature of Mourning,* Mary Jane Moffat, ed.

Pages 66
"Keystone"; "whole structure of meaning"; "important anxieties"; "resentments": Peter Marris, *Loss and Change,* p. 33.

Page 67
"In the course": John Bowlby, *Loss,* p. 91.

"Restore the bond": Ibid.

Page 71

Sympathetic illness: Beverley Raphael says in *The Anatomy of Bereavement:* "Many bereaved widows and widowers experience transiently body symptoms reflecting the dead partner's terminal illness" (p. 215).

Page 73

Increase in accidents: Lily Pincus, in *Death and the Family,* comments on the occurrence of accidents following loss. Speaking of her own accident after the death of her husband, she writes: "I managed to fracture my ankle within ten days of my arrival in Israel.... When I asked the orthopedic surgeon who treated me whether people often fracture bones after bereavement, he said, without even looking up from my injured foot, 'Naturally, people lose their sense of balance,' and perhaps some have to fracture limbs or hurt some other part of themselves before they can acknowledge what has happened to them. Is it possible to enable them to do so in less self-destructive way, by encouraging and supporting them in their mourning process?" (p. 13).

Page 76

"Assumptive world": See Colin Murray Parkes, *Bereavement,* chapter 7. Also see James Britton's essays, chapters 8- 10, in *Prospect and Retrospect,* edited by Gordon Pradl.

"I have been surprised": Albert F. Knight, "The Death of a Son," the *New York Times Magazine,* June 22, 1986, p. 34.

Page 77

Don't burn our widows: Parkes, *Bereavement,* p. 9.

"No allowance for grieving": Julie Rose, in "Mourning a Miscarriage," *Newsweek,* August 3, 1987, p. 7, gives a poignant account of society's reaction to the loss of an unborn child.

Page 78

Probably no age: Bowlby, *Loss,* p. 72.

"Bereavement may also be fatal": Raphael, *The Anatomy of Bereavement,* p. 62.

Increase of almost 40 percent: Parkes, *Bereavement,* p. 16.

Page 79

4.8 percent died within the first year: Ibid.

"The mortality rate"; 10 times higher; 34.3 percent over five years: Institute of Medicine, *Bereavement: Reactions, Consequences, and Care,* pp. 21 -22.

Suicide rate: Institute of Medicine, *Bereavement: Reactions, Consequences, and Care,* p. 26. *For an* excellent discussion of suicide *and grieving, see Silent Grief: Living in the Wake of Suicide,* Christopher Lukas and Henry M. Seiden, 1987, Charles Scribner's Sons, New *York. This* book contains a comprehensive eighteen-page appendix entitled "Where to Find Self-Help Groups."

Partial list: For a discussion of illness and grief, see *the* Institute of Medicine's *Bereavement: Reactions, Consequences, and Care,* chapters 2-3.

Seven illnesses; "chronic depression": Glen W. Davidson, in *Understanding Mourning,* discusses *Lindemann's list and his own,* pp. 21 -22.

Page 80
Second and third years: Institute of Medicine, *Bereavement: Reactions, Consequences, and Care,* p. 35.

"Sick role": See Glen W. Davidson's *Understanding Mourning,* pp. 71, 72.

"Derelict role": Ibid., p. 70.

"All studies": Institute of Medicine, *Bereavement: Reactions, Consequences, and Care,* p. 40.

"Antisocial, delinquent": Raphael, *The Anatomy of Bereavement,* p. 61.

Page 81
Personal relationships: Ibid., pp. 219-221.

Pathological mourners: See Beverley Raphael, *The Anatomy of Bereavement,* pp. 59, 60; pp. 205-209; also Bowlby, *Loss,* chapter 9.

New and special role: Raphael, *The Anatomy of Bereavement,* p. 60.

As though nothing: Ibid., p. 205.

"Toned down": Ibid. p. 206.

Intense pervasive anger: Ibid., p. 208.

Page 82
"The best that can be determined": Davidson, *Understanding Mourning,* p. 23.

"The levels of morbid outcome": Raphael, *The Anatomy of Bereavement,* p. 64.

Deep bouts of depression: The Institute of Medicine reports in *Bereavement: Reactions, Consequences, and Care:* "Grief may . . . give way to depression; approximately 10 to 20 percent of the widowed are still sufficiently symptomatic a year or more after their loss to suggest real clinical depression. Although this proportion *is* relatively small, out of the approximately 800,000 people who are widowed each year, this means that 80,000 *to* 160,000 people suffer serious depression in any given year. The number of depressed individuals following other types of bereavement—death of a child, sibling, or parent—is not known" (p. 284).

British anthropologist Geoffrey Gorer in *Death, Grief, and Mourning,* speaking of people suffering depression, says: "None of these people in despair were very recently bereaved; at least twelve months had passed since the death of the person they mourned so insistently; their unhappiness was of a quite different nature to the intense grief which so many of the time-limited mourners reported in the first three months of bereavement.... The number of people in despair ... was a surprise to me. I am inclined to see a connection between this inability to get over grief and the absence of any ritual either individual or social, lay or religious, to guide them and the people they came in contact with" (pp. 90-91).

There is conflicting opinion, however. A recent report in the *New York Times* ("New Studies Find Many Myths About Mourning," Daniel Goleman, August 8, 1989, p. Cl) asserts that "elements of the prevailing wisdom that now seem more myth than fact include the idea that 'healthy' grieving includes a period of intense distress or depression shortly after the loss." Citing psychologist Camille

Wortman's research at the University of Michigan, the article pointed out that five different studies of widows and widowers have shown that "between a quarter and two-thirds of those who are grieving are not greatly distressed." Previous estimates of the number of people who become depressed have been based, psychologist Wortman says, on studies of people who sought therapy for their problems. "It is not inevitable that severe distress or depression must follow a loss. Nor is the absence of such a response necessarily 'pathological,' says psychologist Wortman.

In this book I report on my own personal experience and the experiences of other individuals, most of whom had not visited a therapist, who report that they did experience, in greater and lesser degrees, distress, depression, and disorientation.

Common symptoms of depression: "Depression," *Newsweek,* May 4, 1987, p. 49.

Page 83
Four of these symptoms: Ibid.

"Know, and name, and express": Raphael, *The Anatomy of Bereavement,* p. 358.

"It is characteristic": Ibid.

Alexander Shand: John Bowlby, in his book *Loss,* says: "Shand, drawing for his data on the works of English poets and French prose-writers, not only delineates most of the main features of grief as we now know them but discusses in a systematic way its relation to fear and anger. As a sensitive and perspicacious study his book ranks high and deserves to be better known (pp. 2425).

"While we think of Despair": Shand, *The Foundations of Character,* p. 491.

"Despair tends to elicit": Ibid., p. 492.

"Despair tends to evoke": Ibid., p. 495.

Page 84
"Sadness as 'depression' "; "actually be experiencing": Raphael, *The Anatomy of Bereavement,* p. 45. Dr. Raphael also points out on page 216: "There is often a semantic confusion: the bereaved widow states her feeling as depression when she really means sadness, for the word sadness has become little used, particularly when speaking of personal feelings which are more frequently labeled depression." See also David Burns's chapter, "Sadness Is Not Depression," *Feeling Good,* p. 207.

Page 85
"If a mourner is developing an illness": Davidson, *Understanding Mourning,* p. 70.

Mental dysfunction: See Morton Hunt's "Sick Thinking," the *New York Times Magazine,* January 3, 1988, p. 22.

"Acute grief frequently creates": Zisook and Shuchter, "A Multidimensional Model of Spousal Bereavement," in *Biospsychosocial Aspects of Bereavement,* p. 43.

Page 86
"I think a stranger": Marris, *Loss and Change,* p. 153.

Page 87
We either choose to fight: Parkes, *Bereavement,* p. 35.

"An approach", "of problem-solving": Ibid., p. 36.

"Peculiar attribute", "this age-old": Ibid., p. 37.

Page 88
"Continuity": Ibid., p. 152.

3. Observation

Page 94
Poem by Natasha Lynne Vogdes: In Fredric Leer, "Running As an Adjunct to Psycgho-therapy," *Social Work,* January 1980, pp. 20-25.

Page 100
"I want": Gina Cerminara, *Many Mansions,* p. 284.

Page 101
Realize first: Ibid., p. 286.

Page 105
"Mourning requires", "at the nub", "allows an update": Quoted in Daniel Coleman's "Mourning: New Studies Affirm Its Benefits," the *New York Times,* February 5, 1985, p. 23.

"A very intense": Beverley Raphael, *The Anatomy of Bereavement,* p. 44.

"Not growing": Ibid., p. 47.

"Piece by piece": Ibid., p. 187.

"Many powerful": Ibid., pp. 186, 187.

"Studying and investigating": Webster's *New Collegiate Dictionary.*

Page 106
"The work of mourning": Anthony Slorr, *Solitude,* pp. 31, 32.

"To confirm": John Bowlby, *Loss,* p. 232.

Page 119
"No gradual transitions": From Liz Carpenter's *Getting Better All the Time,* p. 42.

Pages 120-121
"One of the principal means"; "inventory"; "a thread of continuity"; "has not vanished"; "comes close"; "offers guidance": Pietro Castelnuovo-Tedesco, " 'The Mind As a Stage.' Some Comments on Reminiscence and Internal Objects," *The International Journal of Psycho-analysis,* vol. LIX, part 1, p. 22.

Page 121
"Occurs silently": Ibid., p. 20.

"Simultaneously observer": Ibid., p. 21.

"May even be positively": Ibid., p. 20.

"As buffer"; *"that* something"; *"has enough substance":* Ibid., p. 23.

"Peopled": Ibid., p. 24.

"Critical to the issue": Beverley Raphael, *The Anatomy of Bereavement,* p. 187.

"When the bereaved ": Ibid., pp. 187, 188.

Page 122
"Contradictory and interdependent": Lily Pincus, *Death and the Family,* p. 118.

Page 123
"The greatest obstacles": Ibid., p. 268.

"A major bereavement": Colin Murray Parkes, *Bereavement,* p. 85.

Page 124
"Wrongs committed": Glen W. Davidson, *Understanding Mourning,* pp. 58-59.

Page 125
Releasing resentment and anger: In *The Grief Recovery Handbook: A Step-by-Step Program for Moving Beyond Loss,* John W. James and Frank Cherry provide exercises and activities designed to enable a grieving person to come to terms with guilt, blame, and anger. Anyone stuck at this phase of the process would benefit from working through this book.

Page 127
"Discover [their]": Anthony Storr, *Solitude,* p. 20.

"In the presence of someone"; "actual *presence";* *"have an experience";* *"A large number":* D. W. Winnicott, "The Capacity to Be Alone," in *The Maturational Processes and the Facilitating Environment,* pp. 34, 35.

"The capacity": Storr, *Solitude,* p. 21.

"The ability"; *"private behavior";* *"lift the weight":* Quoted in Daniel Coleman's "Talking to Oneself Is Good Therapy, Doctors Say," the *New York Times,* February 4, 1988, p. B12.

Page 128
"It often helps"; *"with a column":* Ibid.

"Easier to see": Ibid.

Those who keep journals: Bernie Siegel, "How to Improve Your Immune System," *Bottom Line* vol. 9, no. 18, September 30, 1988, p. 1.

Page 129
"Lucia Adams is on a mission": The Bryan/College Station Eagle, November 19, 1988, p. 2A.

Page 131
Matter of balance: Beverley Raphael points out in *The Anatomy of Bereavement* that this time of review is "both private and public" (p. 44).

4. The Turn

Page 137
Physical alteration: This is a common occurrence reported by bereaved individuals. There is a point in their grieving when they experience an actual visceral change. This physical alteration, which is both spontaneous and unexplainable, is followed by a sense of peace, release, ease, and confidence.

Page 139
Relapse nine months after: Beverley Raphael writes in *The Anatomy of Bereavement:* "*It is* interesting to note that there is sometimes an upsurge of distress, or even a peak of morbidity, about nine months after the death. This may, perhaps, be linked to deep inner fantasies that something led behind, some bit of the dead person, will be reborn again then. And when it is not, and his 'death' continues, then fresh pain is once more experienced. Other peaks of renewed mourning . . . are often related to a special occasion: festivals without the deceased . . . anniversaries of the relationship or death which reiterate that the dead person is of the past" (page 58).

Page 141
To commemorate your release: John Bowlby in *Loss* references a study that showed a grieving mother's emotions "changed in parallel with the direction of her concern." When she began to think of her son and his fate instead of concentrating all her attention on her own suffering, she began to care for her son tenderly and became calm (p. 144). Bowlby also states: "In healthy mourning a bereaved person is much occupied thinking about the person who has died and perhaps of the pain he may have suffered and the frustration of his hopes" (p. 248).

Page 142
The first anniversary: For a full discussion of behavior associated with the anniversary of the event of loss, see George Pollock's "Anniversary Reactions, Trauma, and Mourning," the *Psychoanalytic Quarterly* vol. 39, no. 3, pp. 347—371.

Page 143
"A Song": From *Embassy News* vol. 4, no. 1, p. 20. Unfortunately, despite weeks of research and efforts, I was unable to locate the author of this poignant and significant poem.

Page 144
The cycle of life: Lily Pincus, in *Death and the Family* speaks of "the ever-recurring theme of 'one life for another' which I have frequently noted." She points out that, while this idea can create fear and anxiety, nevertheless, such an experience can also "suggest the joyful experience of rebirth, the completion of the life cycle, and the continuation of the dead" (p. 274).

Page 145
"The Words of Jean-Paul Sartre": Melvin Maddocks, "The Words of Jean-Paul Sartre," *The Christian Science Monitor,* April 21, 1980, p. 22.

"Freedom crashed down": Ibid.

Page 146
"Let us say": Ibid.

Page 148
"Because it is necessary": John Bowlby, *Loss,* p. 94.

Page 149
Cognitive act: Ibid.

"Mourning is": Anthony Storr, *Solitude,* p. 32.

Pages 155-156
New form for the relationship: Some choose not to find a new form for the relationship, equating such a change with loving the lost person less. Geoffrey Gorer writes, "Although these people's grief was genuine I did not feel, when talking to them, that they were in despair.... Psychologically they had, most of them at any rate, got over their intense grief; by saying they would never get over it, they were proclaiming their continued affection for the person who had died" *(Death, Grief, and Mourning,* p. 85) .

Sigmund Freud, in a letter to a friend who had lost a son, wrote, "Although we know that after such a loss the acute state of mourning will subside, we also know we shall remain inconsolable and will never find a substitute. No matter what may fill the gap, even if it be filled completely, it neverthe-less remains something else. And actually this is how it should be. It is the only way of perpetuating that love which we do not want to relinquish" (quoted in Bowlby, *Loss,* p. 23).

But Peter Marris points out in *Loss and Change:* "Recovery from grief depends on restoring a sense that the lost attachment can still give meaning to the present, not on finding a substitute" (p. 149).

Page 161
The very purposes and meaning: See Peter Marris, *Loss and Change,* chapters 1 and 2.

Page 162
"It is as if": Sidney Zisook, Stephen R. Shuchter, and Lucy E. Lyons, "Adjustment to Widow-hood," *Biopsychosocial Aspects of Bereavement,* p. 70.

"Includes the evolution": Sidney Zisook and Stephen R. Shuchter, "The Therapeutic Tasks of Grief," *Biopsychosocial Aspects of Bereavement,* p. 181.

"Patterns of thought": John Bowlby, *Loss,* p. 96.

To "retain": Ibid.

Page 163
Think repeatedly: Ibid., p. 250.

"Morbidly introspective": Ibid., p. 68.

"When an adult": Aaron Beck, M.D., *Cognitive Therapy and the Emotional Disorders,* p. 217.

"It is possible": Ibid., p. 235.

Page 164
"One of the mainstays": Stephen R. Shuchter and Sidney Zisook, "A Multidimensional Model of Spousal Bereavement," *Biopsychosocial Aspects of Bereavement,* p. 40.

"The bereaved": Ibid., p. 46.

Page 165
"Biblical faith": Glen W. Davidson, *Understanding Mourning,* p. 46.

"Modified", *"at times"*, *"more appreciative"*: Stephen R. Shuchter and Sidney Zisook, "A Multidimensional Model of Spousal Bereavement," *Biopsychosocial Aspects of Bereavement,* p. 46.

Page 166
A study of widows: See Glick, et. al., *The First Year of Bereavement,* p. 153. I am indebted to Bowlby, *Loss,* p. 101, for first knowledge of this reference.

"At a particular moment": Bowlby, *Loss,* p. 101.

"The first determined movement"; *"Often this is a painful"*: Glick, et. al., *The First Year of Bereavement,* p. 153.

Page 167
"Not only is there": Institute of Medicine, *Bereavement: Results, Consequences, and Care,* p. 54.

"Self-sufficient"; *"headaches, palpitations"*; *"cheerfulness seems"*: Bowlby, *Loss,* p. 153.

Compulsive caretakers: In his book *Loss,* Bowlby discusses compulsive caretaking: "Although the people I have been describing are averse to dwelling on the loss that they themselves . . . have suffered . . . they are none the less apt . . . to concern themselves deeply and often excessively with the welfare of other people. Often they select someone who has had a sad or difficult life, as a rule including a bereavement. The care they bestow may amount almost to an obsession; and it is given whether it is welcomed . . . or not" (p. 156).

Page 168
"Feel none the less"; *"sense of unreality"*: Ibid., p. 160.

"False self ": D. W. Winnicott, "Ego Distortion in Terms of True and False Self," *The Maturational Processes and the Facilitating Environment,* pp. 146, 147. "False self" cited in Bowlby, *Loss,* p. 225.

Brittle and hard; "difficult to live and work with", "little understanding"; "responsible for the breakdown": Bowlby, *Loss,* p. 225.

Page 169
"Only two great": D. H. Lawrence, "Indians and Entertainment," in *D. H. Lawrence and New Mexico,* Keith Sagar, ed., p. 36.

5. Reconstruction

Page 172
"When it's November": The line accurately reads, "Whenever I find myself growing grim about the mouth; whenever it is a damp, drizzly November in my soul; whenever I find myself involuntarily pausing before coffin warehouses, and bringing up the rear of every funeral I meet; and when my hypos [depression] get such an upper hand on me, that it requires a strong moral principle to prevent me from deliberately stepping into the street, and methodically knocking people's hats off—then, I account it high time to get to sea as soon as I can." Herman Melville, *Moby Dick,* W. W. Norton & Company, New York, 1967, p. 12.

"But I want first of all": Anne Morrow Lindbergh, *Gift from the Sea,* p. 23.

Page 182
Lines like these: Lawrence Durrell, *Nunquam,* pp. 20, 280, postface.

Page 186
"Anything is one of a million paths": Carlos Castaneda, *The Teachings of Don Juan: A Yaqui Way of Knowledge,* pp. 106, 107, 160, 185.

Page 187
We need our past: Peter Marris, *Loss and Change,* chapter I.

"Good, bad, or indifferent": Ibid., p. 10.

"A series of interpretations": Ibid., p. 8.

Page 189
Establish a new identity: For an excellent personal account of the difficulties related to establishing a new identity, see Rhoda Tagliacozzo's "The Legacy of Widowhood" in the *New York Times Magazine,* July 31, 1988, p. 12.

Men experience a loss of identity also. Ernest Morgan writes in *Dealing Creatively with Death:* "One aspect of bereavement that I had not anticipated was the loss of identity. With Elizabeth gone I was no longer me! After forty years of sharing on such a broad spectrum of life, I did not have a separate identity. This was not painful, nor did it interfere with my activities, but it was very strange, and several years were required to get over it" (p. 23).

Page 198
"Such disorganization": John Bowlby, *Loss,* p. 246.

"This may be": Beverley Raphael, *The Anatomy of Bereavement,* p. 57.

An autonomous system: I am indebted for the discussion that follows to the pioneering work on emotions and character done by Alexander F. Shand and published in *The Foundations of Character: Being a Study of the Tendencies of the Emotions and Sentiments,* book 2, chapters 1 and 2. About Shand's work, John Bowlby writes in *Loss,* pp. 23, 24: "Shand, drawing for his data on the works of English poets and French prose-writers, not only delineates most of the main features of grief as we now know them but discusses in a systematic way its relation to fear and anger. As a sensitive and perspicacious study his book ranks high and deserves to be better known."

Page 199
"Penetrated throughout": Shand, *The Foundations of Character,* p. 179.

Three distinguishable parts: Ibid., p. 180.

"Better self": Ibid., pp. 56, 57.

"Respect for conscience": Ibid., p. 57.

Page 200
Cognitive model: Aaron Beck, *Cognitive Therapy and the Emotional Disorders,* pp. 52-54.

"Whole matter of arousal": Ibid., p. 54.

"Hot Thoughts/Cool Thoughts": David Burns, *Feeling Good,* pp. 151- 155.

"Daily Record of Dysfunctional Thoughts": Ibid., p. 154.

Page 201
Different kinds of loneliness: Robert S. Weiss, "The Provisions of Social Relationships," *Doing Unto Others,* Zick Rubin, ed., pp. 17-27. I am indebted to Bowlby, *Loss,* pp. 102, 103, for knowledge of this important study.

Page 202
Through marriage: Weiss, "The Provisions of Social Relationships," *Doing Unto Others,* Zick Rubin, ed., p. 23.

Negative types of relationships; "ever-loving"; "someone who is seen"; "is valued": See Beverley Raphael, *The Anatomy of Bereavement,* p. 219.

Page 203
Fill the gap: Ibid., p. 220.

Page 204
Loss of a parent: For fuller discussion of an adult child's loss of a parent, see medical writer Edward Myers's *When Parents Die: A Guide for Adults,* Viking Penguin, 1986; and bereavement authority Katherine Fair Donnelly's *Recovering from the Loss of a Parent,* Dodd, Mead, 1987.

Page 205
"Active interchange"; "hope, fear": John Bowlby, *Loss,* p. 246.

"Little episodes": George H. Pollock, "Mourning and Adaptation," *The International Journal of Psychoanalysis, vol.* XLII, parts 4-5, p. 354.

"Various manifestations": Ibid., p. 352.

"More lasting adaptation": Ibid.

"People who believe": Lily Pincus, *Death and the Family,* p. 122.

Page 206

"The pain experienced": Melanie Klein, "Mourning and Its Relationship to Manic-depressive States," *The International Journal of Psycho-analysis,* vol. XXI, p. 136. 1 am indebted to Pincus, *Death and the Family,* p. 126, for my first exposure to this important research.

"Contradicting drives": Pincus, *Death and the Family,* p. 44.

"All the usual": Ibid., p. 45.

"Becomes unpredictable": Ibid.

"It is not just": Ibid.

Replan our lives: Bowlby states in *Loss* that if the bereaved person chooses not to begin to "replan his life," "the representational models he has of himself and of the world about him remain unchanged" and the individual subsequently finds that "his life is either planned on a false basis or else falls into unplanned disarray" (p. 138).

"A period of ongoing mourning": Beverley Raphael, The Anatomy of Bereavement, p. 57. Also see Pollock, "Mourning and Adaptation," *The International Journal of Psycho-analysis,* vol . XLI I, pare 4-5, p. 352: "As the acute stage of the mourning process progresses, the chronic stage gradually takes over. Here we find various manifestations of adaptive mechanisms attempting to integrate the experience of the loss with reality so that life activities can go on.... Freud has described this chronic stage of the mourning process as the mourning work. This work is a continuation of the process that began more acutely immediately following the loss."

Page 208

Sonnet clxxi, Edna St. Vincent Millay, *Collected Poems,* p. 731.

6. Working Through

Page 226

"Proceed by": Peter Marris, *Loss and Change,* p. 34.

"Grow by": Attributed to Pope Gregory.

Page 233

Loss of a child: Beverley Raphael writes in *The Anatomy of Bereavement* that the loss of a child is difficult to resolve. Studies suggest that "for many mothers [and we can presume other members of the family likewise] something remains; portions of grief are tucked away, appearing from time to time when least expected. They call this 'shadow grief'—a burden that mothers may bear for the rest of their lives. It may intrude on special occasions with a painful memory of the loss, a dull aching reminder that shun out joy for a moment. It is a transient reminder of the loss that comes like a shadow across life" (pp. 266, 267).

Page 238

"Optimism—at least reasonable optimism"; *"Our Expectancies":* "Research Affirms Power of Positive Thinking," Daniel Goleman, the *New York Times,* February 5, 1987, p. 15.

"Forget the whole thing"; *"there is nothing they can do";* *quotations from Martin Seligman:* Ibid.

Page 240
"Practical busy-ness"; "remain meaningless": Peter Marris, *Loss and Change,* p. 34.

"More lastingly damaging"; "Wreck of dead hopes": Ibid.

"A sense of continuity": Ibid.

"Reconstitute the continuities"; "the power to sustain": James Carse, *Death and Existence* pp. 8, 9. For an excellent discussion of the relation of death to life, see Professor Carse's full introduction, pp. 110.

Page 241
"Often the widow's progress": Click, et. al., *The First Year of Bereavement,* p. 154. Cited in Bowlby, *Loss,* p. 98.

Page 242
"That for many": Bowlby, *Loss,* p. 98.

"This process": Lily Pincus, *Death and the Family,* p. 127.

"Can be summoned": Pietro Castelnuovo-Tedesco, "'The Mind As a Stage.' Some Comments on Reminiscence and Internal Objects," *The International Journal of Psycho-analysis,* vol. LIX, part 1, p. 24.

"Is a very powerful": Peter Marris, *Loss and Change,* p. 98.

Page 243
"The central, most urgent task": Ibid., p. 149.

"The family unit": Beverley Raphael, *The Anatomy of Bereavement,* p. 54.

Page 244
Young children's delayed or prolonged grieving: Jane Brody mentions other signs that could mean a child is experiencing unhealthy grieving: "performing poorly in school . . . physical complaints (stomachache, sore or tight throat, loss of appetite, fatigue), anger toward the deceased, anger toward others, adopting the mannerisms or symptoms of the deceased, idealizing the deceased or latching onto a relative or friend as a replacement for the deceased." The *New York Times,* August 12, 1987, p. 18.

Gay community: See Klein and Fletcher, "Gay Grief: An Examination of Its Uniqueness Brought to Light by the AIDS Crisis," in *Journal of Psychosocial Oncology,* vol. 4, no. 3, pp. 15-26.

Page 245
"Their dead and dying friends": Ibid., p. 24.

"The hopes and purposes"; "restoration of faith": Peter Marris, *Loss and Change,* p. 154.

Page 246
"In a situation": Colin Murray Parkes, *Bereavement,* p. 175.

Page 247

"I am committed": In one entry in *Markings* Dag Hammarskjold writes: "It must have been late in September. Or, perhaps, my memory has invented an appropriate weather for the occasion" (p. 29). My memory, too, invented the sentence "I am committed to a life of no return," although that invention occurred immediately upon completing the initial reading of the book. For it was those words, as I invented them, that became a touchstone for me during my own experiences of Working Through. What Mr. Hammarskjold actually wrote was this: "Committed to the future—Even if that only means *'se preparer* a *bien mourir"'* (p. 65) and "There is a point at which everything becomes simple and there is no longer any question of choice, because all you have staked will be lost if you look back. Life's point of no return" (p. 66).

7. Integration

Page 249

Epigraph: From *Partisan Review* essay, "What Literature Means," by Cynthia Ozick.

Page 253

"If my airplane": Lisl Marburg Goodman, *Death and the Creative Life: Conversations with Prominent Artists and Scientists,* p. 79.

Page 254

"In my office": Ibid., p. 80.

"Taking a responsibility"; "Life without death": Ibid., pp. 80-81.

"A creative moment"; "If you ask me": Ibid., pp. 110- 111 , 112, 113.

Page 257

"Chow is now on": Woody Guthrie, *Seeds of Man,* p. 61.

Page 258

"I live on earth": Quoted in "An Obituary for Bucky" by John Pastier, *Arts & Architecture,* Fall 1983.

"My brother collected": From "The Archives: Bucky's Own Thoughts on the Archives," Buckminster Fuller Institute Newsletter, vol. 2, no. 6, p. 1.

Page 259

"I believe": Marguerite Yourcenar, *With Open Eyes,* pp. 201, 205, 259-260.

"Tiou, tiou": French composer Lescuyer, writing in *Langage et Chant des Oiseaux,* reprinted in George Herrick's *Michelangelo's Snowman: A Commonplace Collection,* p. 14.

Page 261

"Mourning-liberation": Term used by George H. Pollock in "Aging or Aged: Development or Pathology," *The Course of Life,* vol. 111, p. 553.

Three states: See Victor Turner and Edith Turner, *Image and Pilgrimage in Christian Culture: Anthropological Perspectives,* p. 2.

"Inwardly transformed"; "betwixt and between": Ibid., p. 249.

"Realm or dimension": Ibid., p. 2.

"To death, to being in the womb": Ibid., p. 249.

Page 262
"Major reformulation": Ibid., p. 3.

"Previous orderings"; "hitherto unprecedented", freedom of thought"; "new experimental models": Ibid., pp. 2, 3.

"Creative outcomes": See George Pollock's "Mourning and Adaptation," *The International Journal of Psycho-analysis, vol.* XLII, pp. 354-355; "The Mourning Process and Creative Organizational Change," Journal *of the American Psychoanalytic Association,* vol. 25, pp. 13-28; "Process and Affect: Mourning and Grief," *The International Journal of Psycho-analysis,* vol. LIX, pp. 267-273.

"New creation", "its energy"; "successor": Pollock, "Process and Affect: Mourning and Grief," p. 270.

Page 268
"Three Children": Poem by James Pounds, Austin, Texas.

Page 271
"There is no permanent": Thomas Berger, *Little Big Man,* p. 433.

Page 276
"Death of a loved one": Beverley Raphael, *The Anatomy of Bereavement,* p. 23.

Page 277
"Bereaved who has never": Lily Pincus, *Death and the Family,* pp. 124- 125.

"If any good"; "Taken to the extreme": Jane E. Brody, "Facing Your Own Mortality," the *New York Times Magazine,* October 9, 1988, pp. 20, 35.

"Four layers": Ernest Becker, *The Denial of Death,* p. 57.

"Thinking and talking": Lily Pincus, *Death and the Family,* p. 250.

Page 278
Heinz Kohut: See Heinz Kohut, M.D., "Forms and Transformations of Narcissism," in *Journal of the American Psychoanalytic Association,* vol. 14, pp. 243-272. All quoted material in this and following five paragraphs is from this source.

Page 280
Time Chronos; *time* Kairos; *"the time within"; "drawn* inside"*: See Peter A. Campbell and Edwin M. McMahan, *Bio-spirituality,* pp. 84-85.

Page 281
"Entelechy": Turner and Turner, *Image and Pilgrimage in Christian Culture,* p. 25.

"A majority": John Bowlby, *Loss,* p. 101.

"There is *no fixed end point"*: Beverley Raphael, The Anatomy *of Bereavement,* p. 47.

"Despite the *popular"*: The Institute of Medicine, Bereavement: *Reactions, Consequences, and Care,* p. 52.

"Sense of release", "has made it clear": Glen Davidson, *Understanding Mourning,* p. 78, p. 16. For a discussion of the time periods of the phases, see chapters 5-8.

Page 282
"One of the most important"; "In general": Sidney Zisook, Stephen R. Shuchter, and Lucy E. Lyons, "Adjustment to Widowhood," *Biopsychosocial Aspects of Bereavement,* p. 52, 71.

Patience and understanding: Frank B. Minirth and Paul D. Meier, in *Happiness Is a Choice* (Baker Book House, 1978, p. 39), write: "Every normal human being. after suffering a significant loss or reversal, goes through all five stages of grief." (Their stages are *denial, anger turned outward, anger turned inward, genuine grief, and resolution.)* "The entire process in a mature individual will take from three to six weeks after a very significant loss such as the death of a mate." Irresponsible statements such as these result in bereaved individuals feeling that they are immature, weak, and deficient when they do not complete their grieving in three to six weeks. I can only suppose that these two men have not studied the complex grieving process in any long-term manner.

So many variables: See Beverley Raphael, *The Anatomy of Bereavement,* pp. 62-64; 221-227, for a discussion of these variables.

Page 283
"Dependent, clinging, ambivalent": Raphael, *The Anatomy of Bereavement,* p. 225.

Page 285
Men and women: Diane Cole writes in *Psychology Today,* vol. 22, no. 12, pp. 60-61, of the differences in the ways men and women mourn.

Phyllis Silverman; "male model"; "learning to break"; "get on with life": Ibid., p. 61.

Page 286
Female model; "you don't break": Ibid.

Education: Speaking of the importance of education, the editors of the Institute of Medicine's *Bereavement: Reactions, Consequences, and Care* write: "Although there are no studies to document the effects of information on the bereavement process, the committee was struck by the widespread view that thorough information of several types can be beneficial and often seems to be lacking.... People need information" (pp. 289-290).

In *Death and the Family,* Lily Pincus says, ". . . education for death is education for life, and should be an underlying feature in all education in schools, universities, and through the media" (p. 250).

Page 287
"The loss through death": Lily Pincus, *Death and the Family,* p. 171.

Page 288
"Each individual": Paul Tournier, *The Adventure of Living,* p. 87.

"The instinct of adventure": Ibid, p. 49.

"Resurgence to resurgence": Ibid., p. 91.

"The greatest of adventures": Ibid., p. 240.

"Working upon"; *"a power of coordinating"*: James Britton, *Prospect and Retrospect,* Gordon Pradl, ed., pp. 83, 91.

"Mysterious way"; "Who knows": Ernest Becker, *The Denial of Death,* pp. 284, 285.

Page 290
"A fire was burning": Poem "Rescue" by William Stafford, published in *The Small Farm,* Spring/Fall, 1979.

Page 292
"The rain": Thomas Merton, *Raids on the Unspeakable,* pp. 9, 10.

DIRECTORY OF RESOURCES

Every grief, of course, is different. What succors one of us when we are mourning does not necessarily succor another. While this individual finds solace in solitary gardening or walks along a creekbank, another is helped most by meeting with a self-help group or talking often with friends. And both the solitary individual and the more gregarious person may choose to seek the support of a professional therapist or counselor.

I have, therefore, attempted to provide an eclectic collection of resources, intending that there be something in the listings appropriate for everyone. The value of what follows, then, will not be found in the specificity of the information, but in the stimulus these suggestions provide for each individual to make her or his own listings.

Books

For those who want to read directly on the subject of loss, the following is a sampling of the many excellent books available on the subject. Many of the books have bibliographies that can lead a reader further.

Becker, Ernest. *The Denial of Death* New York: The Free Press, 1973 (paperback).

Borg, Susan, and Judith Lasker. *When Pregnancy Fails: Families Coping with Miscarriage, Stillbirth, and Infant Death.* New York: Bantam Books, 1988.

Brooks, Anne M. *The Grieving Time: A Year's Account of Recovery from Loss.* New York: Harmony Books, 1989.

Buscaglia, Leo. *The Fall of Freddie the Leaf.* New York: Holt, Rinehart, 1982.

Caine, Lynn. *Widow.* New York: Bantam Books, 1974 (paperback).

Carpenter, Liz. *Getting Better All the Time.* New York: Pocket Books, 1987 (paperback).

Carse, James P. *Death and Existence: A Conceptual History of Human Mortality.* New York: John Wiley & Sons, 1980.

Choron, Jacques. *Death and Western Thought.* New York: Collier Books, 1963 (paperback).

Cousins, Norman. *Anatomy of an Illness As Perceived by the Patient: Reflections on Healing and Regeneration.* New York: W. W. Norton & Company, 1979.

Davidson, Glen W. *Understanding Mourning: A Guide for Those Who Grieve.* Minneapolis, Minn.: Augsburg Publishing House, 1984.

DiGiulio, Robert C. *Beyond Widowhood: From Bereavement to Emergence to Hope.* New York: The Free Press, 1989.

Donnelly, Katherine F. *Recovering from the Loss of a Parent.* New York: Dodd, Mead & Co., 1987.
_____. *Recovering from the Loss of a Sibling.* New York: Dodd, Mead & Co., 1988.

Edelstein, Linda. *Maternal Bereavement: Coping with the Unexpected Death of a Child.* New York: Praeger Publishers, 1984.

Ginsburg, Genevieve D. *To Live Again: Rebuilding Your Life After You've Become a Widow.* Los Angeles: J . P. Tarcher, Inc., 1987.

Goodman, Lisl Marburg. *Death and the Creative Life: Conversations with Prominent Artists and Scientists.* New York: Springer Publishing Company, 1981.

Gordon, Audrey K., and Dennis Klass. *How to Teach Children about Death.* Englewood Cliffs, NJ.: Prentice-Hall, 1979.

Grof, Stanislav, and Joan Halifax. *The Human Encounter with Death.* New York: E. P. Dutton, 1977 (paperback).

Grollman, Earl A. *Talking about Divorce.* Boston: Beacon Press, 1975.

James, John W., and Frank Cherry. *The Grief Recovery Handbook: A Step-by-Step Program for Moving Beyond Loss.* New York: Harper & Row, 1988.

Jewett, Claudia L. *Helping Children Cope with Loss.* Harvard: The Harvard Common Press, 1982 (paperback).

Johnson, Joy, and Marvin Johnson, et. al. *Miscarriage: A Book for Parents Experiencing Fetal Death.* Omaha: Centering Corporation, 1983 (paperback).

Johnson, Joy, and S. M. Johnson. *Children Die, Too.* Omaha: Centering Corporation, 1978 (paperback).

Kast, Verena. *A Time to Mourn: Crowing Through the Grief Process.* Einsiedeln, Switzerland: Daimon Verlag, 1988 (paperback).

Kohn, Jane Burgess, and Willard K. Kohn. *The Widower,* Boston: Beacon Press, 1978.

Krantzler, Mel. *Creative Divorce.* New York: New American Library, 1975 (paperback).

Krauss, Pesach, and Morrie Goldfischer. *Why Me: Coping with Grief, Loss, and Change.* New York: Bantam Books, 1988.

Kubler-Ross, Elisabeth. *Death: The Final Stage of Growth.* Englewood Cliffs, N.J.: Prentice-Hall, 1975 (paperback).

_____. *On Children and Death.* New York: Collier, 1983 (paperback).

Kushner, Harold S. *When Bad Things Happen to Good People.* New York: Avon Books, 1981 (paperback).

Lansky, Vicki. *Divorce Book for Parents: Helping Your Children Cope with Divorce and Its Aftermath.* New York: New American Library, 1989.

LeShan, Eda. *Learning to Say Good-By When a Parent Dies.* New York: Avon, 1988.

Lewis, C. S. *A Grief Observed.* New York: Bantam Books, 1976 (paperback).

Lukas, Christopher, and Henry M. Seiden. *Silent Grief: Living in the Wake of Suicide.* New York: Charles Scribner's Sons, 1987.

Margolis, Otto, et al., eds. *Grief and the Loss of an Adult Child.* New York: Praeger Publishers, 1988.

Meltzer, David. *Death: An Anthology of Ancient Texts, Songs, Prayers, and Stones.* San Francisco: North Point Press, 1984 (paperback).

Moffat, Mary Jane. *In the Midst of Winter: Selections from the Literature of Mourning.* New York: Vintage Books, 1982 (paperback).

Moffatt, Betty Clare. *When Someone You Love Has AIDS: A Book of Hope for Families and Friends.* New York: New American Library, 1986 (paperback).

Morgan, Ernest. *Dealing Creatively with Death.* Jenifer Morgan, editor. Burnsville, N.C.: Celo Press, 1988 (paperback).

Myers, Edward. *When Parents Die: A Guide for Adults.* New York: Penguin Books, 1986 (paperback).

National Institute of Mental Health. *Caring About Kids: Talking to Children about Death.* Rockville, Md.: National Institute of Mental Health (pamphlet).

Nudel, Adele Rice. *Starting Over: Help for Young Widows S Widowers.* New York: Dodd, Mead & Co., 1986.

Rando, Therese A. *Grieving: How to Go on Living When Someone You Love Dies.* Lexington, Mass.: D.C. Heath & Company, 1988.

Robertson, Christina. *A Woman's Guide to Divorce and Decision Making: A Supportive Workbook for Women Facing the Process of Divorce.* New York: Simon and Schuster, 1988 (paperback).

Rollin, Betty. *Last Wish.* New York: Warner Books, 1985 (paperback).

Schaefer, Dan, and Christine Lyons. *How Do We Tell the Children? Helping Children Understand and Cope When Someone Does.* New York: Newmarket Press, 1988 (paperback).

Scherago, Marcia. *Sibling Grief: How Parents Can Help the Child Whose Brother or Sister Has Died.* Redmond, Wash.: Medic Publishing Company 1987 (paperback).

Schiff, Harriet Sarnoff. *Living Through Mourning: Finding Comfort and Hope When a Loved One Has Died.* New York: Viking, 1986.

_____. *The Bereaved Parent.* New York: Crown Publishers, 1977.

Schneider, John. *Stress, Loss,& Grief.* Rockville, Md.: Aspen Publishers, 1984 (paperback).

Siegel, Bernie S. *Love, Medicine Miracles.* New York: Harper & Row Publishers, 1986.

Sontag, Susan. *AIDS and Its Metaphors.* New York: Farrar, Straus & Giroux, 1989.

Stearns, Ann Kaiser. *Coming Back: Rebuilding Lives After Crisis and Loss.* New York: Random House, 1988.

_____. *Living Through Personal Crisis.* New York: Ballantine, 1985 (paperback).

Tatelbaum, Judy. *The Courage to Grieve: Creative Living, Recovery, and Growth Through Grief.* New York: Lippincott & Crowell, 1980.

_____. *You Don't Harc to Suffer: A Handbook for Moving Beyond Life's Crtsis.* New York: Harper & Row, 1989.

Truman, Jill. *Letter to My Husband: Notes about Mourning and Recovery* New York: Viking Penguin, 1987.

Veninga, Robert. *A Gift of Hope: How We Survive Our Tragedies.* New York: Ballantine, 1985 (paperback).

Viorst, Judith. *Necessary Losses.* New York: Simon and Schuster, 1986.

Wallerstein, Judith, and Sandra Blakeslee. *Second Chances: Men, Women, and Children a Decade After Divorce.* New York: Ticknor & Fields, 1989.

Wanderer, Zev, and Tracy Cabot. *Letting Go: A Twelve-Week Personal Action Program to Overcoat a Broken Heart.* New York: Warner Books, 1978 (paperback).

Watson, Elizabeth. *Casts of My Life.* Burnsville, N.C.: Celo Press, 1988.

The books that follow have been written for a professional audience but may be of interest to laypersons as well.

Bowlby, John. *Loss: Sadness and Depression.* New York: Basic Books, 1980.

Glick, Ira O., Weiss, Robert S., and C. Murray Parkes. *The First Year of Bereavement.* New York: John Wiley & Sons, 1974.

Gorer, Geoffrey. *Death, Grief, and Mourning.* Garden City, N.Y.: Doubleday & Co., 1965.

Institute of Medicine, Osterweis, Marian, Solomon, Fredric, and Morris Green, eds. *Bereavement: Reactions, Consequences, and Care.* Washington, D.C.: National Academy Press, 1984.

Marris, Peter. *Loss and Change.* New York: Pantheon Books, 1974.

Parkes, Colin Murray. *Bereavement: Studies of Grief in Adult Life.* New York: Tavistock Publications, 1972.

Pincus, Lily. *Death and the Family: The Importance of Mourning.* New York: Schocken Books, 1974 (paperback).

Raphael, Beverley. *The Anatomy of Bereavement.* New York: Basic Books, 1983 (paperback).

Zisook, Sidney, ed. *Biopsychosocial Aspects of Bereavements* Washington, D.C.: The American Psychiatric Press, Inc., 1987.

Some of the books that were the most important to me when I was grieving did not deal with the subject of loss directly, but with other subjects such as the resiliency of the human spirit, the creativity inherent in every individual, the challenges individuals faced and met as they made real their dreams and visions. Books such as these remind us of what we are capable and, therefore, can often lift us above our sadness and our despair.

Alexander, Christopher. *The Timeless Way of Building.* New York: Oxford University Press, 1979.

Austin, James H. *Chase, Chance, and Creativity: The Lucky Art of Novelty.* New York: Columbia University Press, 1978.

Bakeless, John, ed. *Journals of Lewis and Clark: A New Selection.* New York: New American Library, 1964 (paperback).

Ban Breathnach, Sarah. *Simple Abundance: A Daybook of Comfort and Joy.* New York: Warner Books, 1995.

Bentov, Itzhak. *Stalking the Wild Pendulum: On the Mechanics of Consciousness.* New York: E. P. Dutton, 1977 (paperback).

Bernstein, Leonard. *The Unanswered Question: Six Talks at Harvard.* Cambridge: Harvard University Press, 1976.

Bird, Isabella. *A Lady's Life in the Rocky Mountains.* Norman, Okla.: University of Oklahoma Press, 1960.

Cather, Willa. *Death Comes to the Archbishop.* New York: Vintage Books, 1971 (paperback).

Cheng Nien. *Life and Death in Shanghai.* New York: Penguin Books, 1986 (paperback).

Durreli, Lawrence. *Alexandria Quartet.* New York: E. P. Dutton, 1961 (paperback).

Edwards, Betty. *Drawing on the Right Side of the Brain: A Course in Enhancing Creativity and Artistic Confidence.* Los Angeles: Jeremy P. Tarcher, Inc., 1979.

Fitzgerald, Sally, ed. *The Habit of Being: Letters of Flannery O'Connor.* New York: Random House, 1979 (paperback).

Guthrie, Woody. *Seeds of Man.* New York: E. P. Dutton, 1976.

Kopp, Sheldon. *If You Meet the Buddha on the Road, Kill Him!* New York: Bantam Books, 1972 (paperback).

Lewis, C. S. *The Chronicles of Narnia.* New York: Macmillan, 1983 (paperback).

Lindbergh, Anne Morrow. *Gift from the Sea.* New York: Pantheon Books, 1955.

Lopez, Barry. *Arctic Dreams.* New York: Charles Scribner's Sons, 1986.

Moholy-Nagy, Sibyl. *Native denim in Anonymous Architecture.* New York: Horizon Press, 1957.

Myers, Robert. *Children of Pride: Selected Letters of the Family of the Rev. Dr. Charles Cokock Jones from the years* 1860-1868. New Haven: Yale University Press, 1984.

Nasaw, Jonathan. *West with the Moon.* New York: Franklin Watts, 1987.

Nouwen, Henri J. M. *The Genesee Diary: Report from a Trappist Monastery,* Garden City, N.Y.: Doubleday & Co., 1976.

O'Keefe, Georgia. *Georgia O'Keefe,* New York: Penguin, 1977 (paperback).

Parabola: The Magazine of Myth and Tradition, 656 Broadway, N.Y., N.Y. 10012.

Perkins, David. *The Mind's Best Work* Cambridge: Harvard University Press, 1981.

Ruth and Esther, books of. *The Bible.*

Salzman, Mark. *Iron and Silk.* New York: Random House, 1986 (paperback).

Sarton, May. *House by the Sea: A Journal.* New York: W. W. Norton & Company, 1977.

Sendak, Maurice. *Where the Wild Things Are.* New York: Harper & Row, 1963.

Shonagon, Sei. *The Pillow Book of Sei Shonagon.* Ivan Morris, trans. New York: Columbia University Press, 1967.

Storr, Anthony. *Solitude: A Return to the Self.* New York: The Free Press, 1988.

Tyler, Anne. *The Accidental Tourist.* New York: Berkeley Books, 1985 (paperback).

White, E. B. *Charlotte's Web.* New York: Harper and Brothers, 1952.

Yourcenar, Marguerite. *With Open Eyes: Conversations with Matthieu Galey.* Arthur Goldhammer, trans. Boston: Beacon Press, 1984.

Art

Often during my grieving period, when I was in New York meeting with my publisher, l would go to the Museum of Modern Art to see Monet's water lily paintings. There I would sit, sometimes an hour or more, looking at these paintings, which are so large that they fill whole walls. The colors— pinks and purples and blues—the serenity of the water and the Flowers, the scale of the paintings, all these combined to create in me a feeling of quietness that brought peace to my agitated spirit. Even today, when I'm back in the city, l go pay homage to these beautiful paintings, remembering what they meant to me then.

There was also a painting at the Metropolitan Museum that I went to see again and again— Jules

Bastien-Lepage's *Joan of Arc.* I would stand in front of the canvas, seeing the young woman dressed in her peasant garments, standing among the cabbages in the yard of her parents' cottage. Here was a painting of a flesh-and-blood human being who regardless of the disadvantages under which she lived and acted nevertheless found within herself the capacity to make enormous commitments and show much courage. It wasn't that I *thought* all of this while I was standing there looking at the painting, but I must have *known* it at some level deeper than words. For I was drawn back again and again to look at the painting.

Others who have found solace from art mention other works: Georgia O'Keefe's beautiful flower, shell, and sky paintings; the Dreaming-track paintings of the Australian aboriginals; sandpaintings of the Navajo; the totem poles of the Northwest Indians at New York's Museum of Natural History. The work of one artist in particular has spoken to thousands about the relationship of grief and loss to forgiveness: the awesome Holocaust paintings of Houston artist Alice Cahana.

Whatever one's tastes and preferences in art, there will be some pieces that reach past the pain of loss to touch the depths of one's spirit. To seek out such works for oneself is a worthy activity during bereavement.

Many people who are grieving have also found that painting or drawing themselves, working with clay and other media, making collages, sculpting, have been enormously beneficial as they moved through the grieving process. Check the course offerings of community education programs, as well as the colleges and universities in your locality, to locate activities you would like to engage in. Also, you might choose to work with a trained art therapist who will assist you in using art as an expression of your grieving. For information about how to locate an art therapist in your area, contact The American Art Therapy Association, 1202 Allanson Road, Mundelein, Ill. 60060; (847) 949-6064.

Writing

Keeping a journal is a lifeline for many people as they experience their mourning. The Progoff Journal method, developed by Dr. Ira Progoff, offers a structure that a number of individuals have told me was useful to them as they "wrote through their grieving." You can learn about the Progoff Journal method by reading *At a Journal Workshop* and *The Practice of Process Meditation,* written by Ira Progoff and published by Dialogue House Library in New York. But better yet, attend a Progoff Journal Writing Workshop. To learn dates and locations of these workshops (and to receive information about how to purchase the books above, or other books and tapes related to the Progoff Journal method), write to Dialogue House, 80 East 11th Street, New York, N.Y. 10003; (212) 673-5880.

For those who want to write but not necessarily in a journal format, these books and tapes are excellent.

Baldwin, Christina. *Life's Companion: Journal Writing as a Spiritual Quest.* New York: Bantam Books. 1990 (paperback).

Brande, Dorothea. *Becoming a Writer.* Los Angeles: Jeremy P. Tarcher, Inc., 1934 (paperback).

Cameron, Julia. *The Artist's Way: A Spiritual Path to Higher Creativity.* New York: Jeremy P. Tarcher/Perigee Books. 1992 (paperback).

Cameron, Julia. *The Vein of Gold.* New York: Jeremy P. Tarcher/Perigee Books. 1996.

Metzger, Deena. *Writing for Your Life: A Guide and Companion to the Inner Worlds.* San Francisco: HarperSanFrancisco, *A Division of* HarperCollins*Publishers.* 1992 (paperback).

Neeld, Elizabeth Harper. *Yes! You Can Write.* 1986 (set of six audio cassettes). Available from Nightingale-Conant Corporation, 7300 N. Lehigh Avenue, Chicago, Ill. 60648; (800) 323-5552.

Rico, Gabriele. *Writing the Natural Way.* Los Angeles: Jeremy P. Tarcher, Inc., 1983 (paperback).

Stafford, William. *Writing the Australian Crawl: Views on the Writer's Vocation.* Ann Arbor: University of Michigan Press, 1978 (paperback).

Ueland, Brenda. *If You Want to Write: A Book about Art, Independence and Spirit.* St. Paul, Minn.: Graywolf Press, 1987 (paperback).

Music

Many of the individuals with whom I have talked mentioned particular pieces of music that they turned to again and again during their grieving process. For a young man mourning the loss of his best friend, it was Keith Jarrett's *Koln Concert* and *Arhour Zena*. For an eighty-three-year-old widow whose husband of fifty-four years had recently died, it was Beethoven's C-sharp Minor Quartet, the meditation from Massanet's *Thais,* the "Song to the Evening Star" from Wagner's *Tannhauser,* Liszt's *Liebesträume,* Braga's *Angel's Serenade,* and Beethoven's *Moonlight Sonata.* Others have mentioned the piano music of George Winston, the tapes and albums of Steven Halpern, the sound track of *Chariots of Fire.* The music that I found particularly helpful when I was grieving included JeanMichel Jarre's "Oxygene," Kitaro's "Silk Road," Haydn's symphonies (particularly the 93rd, 94th, and 100th), Mozart's Piano Concerto no. 21 in C, Groffe's *Crand Canyon Suite,* Vivaldi's *The Four Seasons,* Smetana's *The Moldau,* Beethoven's Symphony no. 9, R. Carlos Nakai's *Native American Flute Music,* Puccini's *Madama Butterfly,* Janacek's "Jenufu," and Neil Diamond's *Hot August Night* album. More recently I have learned that these pieces of music have been helpful to those working through the grieving process: the slow movement of the Marcello Oboe Concerto; the slow movement from Rodrigo's *Concierto de Aranjuez;* J. S. Bach's Prelude in E-flat Minor, as arranged for orchestra; Grieg's Holberg Suite, particularly the movement called "Air"; and other Grieg pieces.

Much is now known about the ability of music to affect an individual's sense of well-being; in fact, music therapy has become a mainstream academic study. (New York University, for instance, offers graduate courses in music therapy leading to a master's degree or a doctorate.) A. Watson and N. Drury have written a book called *Healing Music* (Prism Press, 1987), which can be a guide to those who wish to use music to aid them in moving through their grieving.

To learn about music therapy workshops, contact The Bonny Foundation, an Institute for Music-Centered Therapy, at 2020 Simmons Street, Salina, Kans. 67401; (913) 827-1497, for further information about the important role music can play in experiencing one's grieving.

Dance and Other Body Movement Activities

Many bereaved individuals have told me that body work and body movement activities have been some of the most important components of their successful grieving. For some, it was therapeutic massage, Trager body work, or perhaps body movement using the Feldenkrais method. For others, it was dance or low-impact aerobics or yoga. (And for many it was a combination of several of these.)

For information about a Trager practitioner in your area, contact The Trager Institute, 21 Locust Avenue, Mill Valley, Calif. 94941; (415) 388-2688. (You may also want to get a copy of *Trager Mentastics: Movement As a Way to Agelessness,* by Milton Trager, M.D., published by Station Hill Press, Barrytown, N.Y. 12507.)

To learn the names of Feldenkrais teachers in your vicinity, contact The Feldenkrais Guild, 524 Elsworth S.W., Albany, OR 97321; (800) 775-2118.

Lilias Folan has done excellent video and audio tapes for learning and practicing yoga, as well as audio tapes for relaxation. These can be ordered from Rudra Press, 541 Northeast 20th Avenue, Suite 108, Portland, OR 97232-2862; (800) 876-7798. Also, Lilias can be seen teaching yoga in a program called *Lilias, Yoga and You* shown on public television. Check local listings for day and time.

To learn more about dance/movement therapy and/or to obtain the names of registered dance/movement therapists in your community, contact the American Dance Therapy Association, 2000 Century Plaza, Columbia, Md. 21044; (410) 997-4040.

Nature and Outdoor Activities

A beautiful book—*Listening to Nature: How to Deepen Your Awareness of Nature* (written by Joseph Cornell and published by Dawn Publications, 14618 Tyler Foote Rd., Nevada City, Calif. 95959); (916) 478-7540 —has been therapeutic for many people who were engaged in putting their losses into a broader perspective. So have materials such as those published by such organizations as The Sierra Club, 85 Second Street, Second Floor, San Francisco, Calif. 94105, (415) 977-5500; The National Audubon Society, 700 Broadway, New York, N.Y. 10003, (212) 979-3000; and books discussing the Gaia principle, such as James Lovelock's *Gaia: A New Look at Life on Earth* (New York: Oxford University Press, 1987).

Visiting aquariums, walking in redwood forests, hiking in the desert or the mountains, camping, and backpacking are ways many individuals have lifted their spirits when they were in the depths of mourning. Gardening has also been a source of very effective therapy (even looking at seed catalogs and gardening books, many say, helped).

The outdoor programs offered by Outward Bound, 0110 S.W. Bancroft St., Portland, Ore. 97201, (503) 243-1993; the travel expeditions sponsored by such organizations as the American Museum of Natural History, 79th Street at Central Park West, New York, N.Y. 10024, (212) 7695100; and the biking tours offered by many different companies, are just three examples of the kinds of activities many people have found to be valuable as they moved through their grieving process.

Organizations and Self-Help Groups

Below are organizations, clearinghouses, and service groups that exist to provide information and guidance to bereaved individuals.

ACCORD
1941 Bishop's Lane
Suite 202
Louisville, Kentucky 40218
(800) 346-3087

Call the 800 number for information on how to locate the source for these materials in your local area. *In Accord,* a quarterly publication offering assistance for the bereaved in practical as well as emotional matters, is available for $17 per year.

AIDS Project Los Angeles
1313 North Vine Street
Los Angeles, California 90028
(213) 993-2300

Publications and information on AIDS can be obtained from this organization.

Widowed Persons Service
American Association of Retired Persons
601 E Street, N.W.
Washington, D.C. 20049
(202) 434-2277 or (202) 434-2260

An individual need be neither of retirement age nor a member of AARP to benefit from the extremely valuable services offered by this program. More than two hundred local self-help programs throughout the United States are sponsored by the Widowed Persons Service and directed by volunteer widowed individuals who have been trained to assist the bereaved. Bibliographies, pamphlet, and many other resources are available.

Association for Death Education and Counseling
638 Prospect Avenue
Hartford, Connecticut 06105
(860) 586-7503

A professional organization of educators, counselors, medical doctors, nurses, therapists, mental health professionals, clergy, and others specializing in bereavement education and counseling that holds conferences, sponsors research, and offers standards for certification.

Bereavement and Loss Center of New York
Anne Rosberger, Executive Director
170 East 83rd Street, Suite 4P
New York, New York 10028
(212) 879-5655

A private, nonsectarian organization, this center offers professional counseling services for individuals who have suffered loss of various kinds: widows, widowers, parents who have lost children, children who have lost parents, individuals who have lost significant others, and individuals and couples who have experienced prenatal death.

Centering Corporation
1531 North Saddle Creek Road
Omaha, Nebraska 68104
(402) 553-1200

This nonprofit organization is a leader in providing supportive literature for grieving families. Their excellent, economical publications run a wide gamut: grief related to death of children, miscarriage, stillborn deaths, death of siblings, death by suicide, death of grandparents, and much more. These publications are durable and beautifully designed. Filmstrips, a newsletter, and workshops are also part of the corporation's offerings. Catalog of publications available.

The Compassionate Friends
P.O. Box 3696
Oak Brook, Illinois 60522
(630) 990-0010

An international organization or more than six hundred self-help groups throughout the United States that exist to support parents whose children have died. Publications, a newsletter, and many additional services available both through the international office and local chapters. To locate a chapter in your area, call the number listed above.

Mental Health Association of Colorado
6795 East Tennessee Avenue, Suite 425
Denver, Colorado 80224
(303) 377-3040

Offers support, information and referral services for the public and for professionals; a ten week support program; facilitator's program. The institute's *Bereavement Support Group Leadership Manual* (now in its fourth edition) is also available.

National Self-Help Clearinghouse
Room 620N
Graduate School and University Center
City University of New York

25 West 43rd Street
New York, New York 10036
(212) 642-2944

This clearinghouse provides information about self-help groups in all areas of interest. Upon receipt of a self-addressed, stamped envelope, the staff of the clearinghouse will send information about their services and publications.

National Sudden Infant Death Syndrome (SIDS) Foundation
1314 Bedford Avenue, Baltimore, Maryland 21208
(410) 653-8226 (in Maryland)
(800) 221-SIDS (outside Maryland)

An organization of sixty-eight chapters and numerous parent contacts and support groups offering services to families in which a child has died of SIDS. Information about publications, local chapters, and parent contacts available by telephone.

Parents of Murdered Children
100 East Eighth Street
Room B41
Cincinnati, Ohio 45202
(513) 721-5683

A national self-help organization which has local chapters across the United States, Parents of Murdered Children provides resources and support for families who have lost a child as a result of murder.

Parents Without Partners, Inc.
401 North Michigan Avenue
Chicago, Illinois 60611-4267
(800) 637-7974

This organization of mutual support groups (more than eight hundred throughout the United States and Canada) offers educational, social, and family services to single parents and their children. Publications are available for widowed, divorced, and unmarried parents.

International THEOS (They Help Each Other Spiritually) Foundation
322 Boulevard of the Allies
Suite 105
Pittsburgh, Pennsylvania 15222-1919
(412) 471-7779

THEOS is a volunteer network promoting mutual self-help by forming and maintaining local groups; linking individuals for one-to-one support; conducting regional conferences and workshops; publishing material on grief and widowhood; and educating the public on grief and sympathizing.

The Internet

Doing a search on The Internet under the words *grief* and *loss* turns up scores of organizations, materials, and services helpful to grieving individuals. Do not overlook this valuable source of current information.

Church-Sponsored Programs

Beginning Experience is a weekend program designed to help widowed, separated, divorced, and otherwise bereft individuals make a new beginning in life. Participants should be past the initial acute grieving experience and to the point of desiring a new beginning. An interfaith endeavor sponsored by the Catholic church and the Episcopal church, the weekend program, which begins on Friday evening and concludes on Sunday afternoon, is quiet, reflective, and spiritual. For information about Beginning Experience, contact an Episcopal or Catholic church in your area. In addition, many other churches and hospice groups sponsor bereavement and divorce recovery programs on a local level.

In addition, many hospitals, family service agencies, and other local, county, and federal governmental agencies offer programs and services for the bereaved. Ask your doctor, a member of the clergy, or health department personnel for information about such offerings in your local area.

Professional Therapy and Counseling

More and more bereaved individuals are realizing the value of working with someone who understands the grieving process and who can, therefore, serve as a guide through the painful and often treacherous experience. No longer believing that one has to be "sick" or "weak" to engage in the valuable self-care work of therapy and/or counseling, many who are mourning are asking their doctors, associates, priests, rabbis, ministers, family, and friends to recommend a therapist, analyst, or counselor with whom they can work. The *best* person from whom to get a recommendation, of course, is a bereaved individual who has found the work of a particular professional to be helpful and beneficial.

Other sources for learning who is available in your local area include

The International Association for Analytical Psychology
Postfach 115
8042
Zurich, Switzerland
(Ask in your letter for directory listing of the analysts who practice analytical psychology.)

In addition, many major cities in the United States have a center for the study of analytical psychology, for instance, the C. G. Jung Educational Center in Houston, 5200 Montrose, Houston, Tex. 77006, (713) 524-8253; the C. G.Jung Institute of San Francisco, 2040 Gough, San Francisco, Calif. 94109, (415) 771-8055; the C. G. Jung Center of Chicago, 1567 Maple Avenue, Evanston, Ill. 60201, (847) 475-4848; and the C. G. Jung Center in New York, 28 E. 39th Street, New York, N.Y. 10016, (212) 986-5458. If such a center is located in your local area, someone there would be able to tell you how to find and contact an analytical psychology analyst.

You can also learn the names of other medical doctors in your area who provide therapy by contacting

The American Psychiatric Association
1400 K Street, NW
Washington, D.C. 20005
(202) 682-6000

When you call, ask for the telephone number of the district branch of the American Psychiatric Association for your sate. Someone at the district branch will then be able to give you the names of doctors in your local area.

To locate a psychotherapist, contact

The American Psychological Association
1200 17th Street, NW
Washington, D.C. 20036
(202) 955-7600

Ask to be connected to the practice department. Someone there will be able to give you the telephone number of the executive officer of the association serving your state. That person, then, can give you information about therapists in your local area.

Bereaved people with whom I have talked consistently offer one piece of advice about how to evaluate your experience with a counselor, analyst, or therapist. They say this in different words, but the message is the same: Ask yourself if you feel you are "winning" in your commitment to move through the grieving process. If you are "winning," continue the therapy or counseling work. If you are not, find another counselor, analyst, or therapist.

Prayer

Below are resources that provide inspiration for those who wish to find a prayer and quiet time resource during their grieving.

Appleton, George. *The Oxford Book of Prayer.* New York: Oxford University Press, 1985 (paperback).

Ashcroft, Mary Ellen. *The Magdalene Gospel.* New York: Doubleday. 1995.

Brother Lawrence. *The Practice of the Presence of God.* Springdale, PA: Whitaker House, 1982 (paperback).

Castelli, Jim. *How I Pray.* New York: Ballantine Books, 1994 (paperback).

De Caussade, Jean-Pierre. *The Sacrament of the Present Moment.* San Francisco: HarperSanFrancisco, *A Division of* HarperCollins*Publishers,* 1989 (paperback).

Dorsey, Larry, M.D. *Healing Words.* San Francisco: HarperSanFrancisco, *A Division of* HarperCollins*Publishers,* 1993 (paperback).

Doyle, Brendan. *Meditations with Julian of Norwich.* Santa Fe, NM: Bear & Company Publishing, 1983, (paperback).

Dunnam, Maxie. *The Workbook of Living Prayer.* Nashville: The Upper Room, 1974 (paperback).

Foster, Richard J. *Prayer: Finding the Heart's True Home.* San Francisco: HarperSanFrancisco, *A Division of* HarperCollins*Publishers*, 1992.

Judson, Sylvia Shaw. *The Quiet Eye.* Washington, DC: Regnery Gateway, 1982.

Knight, George A. F. *The Daily Study Bible Series, Psalms, Volumes 1 and 2.* Philadelphia: The Westminster Press, 1982 (paperback).

Mother Teresa & Brother Roger. *Seeking the Heart of God, Reflections on Prayer.* San Francisco: HarperSanFrancisco, *A Division of* HarperCollins*Publishers*, 1991.

Nilgiri Press carries books, e.g. *Meditation, The Compassionate Universe, Take Your Time, God Makes the Rivers to Flow*, which thousands of individuals have found valuable in their quiet time. Nilgiri Press, Box 477, Petaluma, CA 94953, (707) 878-2309.

Thurman, Howard. *The Creative Encounter.* Richmond, IN: Friends United Press, 1972 (paperback).

Thurman, Howard. *Inward Journey.* Richmond, IN: Friends United Press, 1971 (paperback).

Tutu, Desmond. *An African Prayer Book.* New York: Doubleday, 1995.

Uhlein, Gabriele. *Meditations with Hildegard of Bingen.* Santa Fe, NM: Bear & Company Publishing, 1983 (paperback).

BIBLIOGRAPHY

Adler, Gerhard. C. G. *Jung Letters, Volume 2: 1951-1961.* Princeton: Princeton University Press 1975.

al-Qusabi, Ghazi. "A Song." *Embassy News,* vol. 4, no. 1 (1980): 20.

Barrett, Wayne, et al. *The Brain: Mystery of Matter and Mind.* New York: Torstar Books, 1984.

Beck, Aaron. *Cognitive Therapy and the Emotional Disorders.* New York: New American Library, 1976 (paperback).

Becker, Ernest. *The Denial of Death.* New York: Macmillan Publishing Company, 1973 (paperback).

Berger, Thomas. *Little Big Man.* New York: Dial Press, 1964.

Bowlby, John. *Loss: Sadness and Depression.* New York: Basic Books, 1980.

Brautigan, Richard. *The Pill Versus the Springhill Mine Disaster.* New York: Dell Publishing Company, 1968 (paperback).

Brody, Jane E. "Facing Your Own Mortality." The *New York Times Magazine* (October 9, 1988): 20.
_____. "The Facts of Death for Children." The *New York Times* (August 12, 1987): 18.

Burns, David. *Feeling Good.* New York: New American Library, 1980 (paperback).

Campbell, Peter A., and Edwin M. McMahon. *Bio-Spirituality.* Chicago: Loyola University Press, 1985.

Carpenter, Liz. *Getting Better All the Time.* New York: Pocket Books, 1987 (paperback).

Carse, James. *Death and Existence: A Conceptual History of Human Mortality.* New York: John Wiley & Sons, 1980.

Castaneda, Carlos. *The Teaching of Don Juan: A Yaqui Way of Knowledge.* New York: Pocket Books, 1968 (paperback).

Castelneuovo-Tedesco, Pietro. "'The Mind as a Stage.' Some Comments on Reminiscence and Internal Objects." *The International Journal of Psycho-analysis,* vol. LIX, part 1 (1978): 20-25.

Cerminara, Gina. *Many Mansions.* New York: New American Library, 1978 (paperback).

Combs, Allan L. "Synchronicity: A Synthesis of Western Thought and Eastern Perspectives." *ReVision, vol.* 5, no. I (1982): 20-27.

Davidson, Glen W. *Understanding Mourning: A Guide for Those Who Grieve.* Minneapolis, Minn.: Augsburg Publishing House, 1984 (paperback).

"Depression." *Newsweek* (May 4, 1987): 48-57.

Dickinson, Emily. *The Complete Poems.* Thomas H. Johnson, ed. Boston: Little Brown & Company, 1960

Durrell, Lawrence. *Numquam.* New York: E. P. Dutton & Co., 1970.

Eliot, T. S. *Four Quartets.* New York: Harcourt, Brace and Company, 1943.

Fried, Martha Nemes, and Morton H. Fried. *Transitions: Four Rituals in Eight Cultures.* New York: W. W. Norton & Company, 1980.

Frost, Robert. *Selected Poems of Robert Frost.* New York: Holt, Rinehart and Winston, 1965.

Gibbons, Reginald, ed. *The Poet's Worst.* Boston: Houghton Mifflin Company, 1979 (paperback).

Glick, Ira. O., Weiss, Robert S., and C. Murray Parkes. *The First Year of Bereavement.* New York: John Wiley & Sons, 1974.

Goleman, Daniel. "Mourning: New Studies Affirm Its Benefits." The *New York Times* (February 5, 1985): 19.
_____. "New Studies Find Many Myths About Mourning." The *New York Times* (August 8, 1989): Cl.
_____. "Research Affirms Power of Positive Thinking." The *New York Times (February* 3, 1987): 15
_____. "Talking to Oneself Is Good Therapy, Doctors Say." The *New York Times* (February 4, 1988): B12.

Goodman, Lisl Marburg. *Death and the Creative Life: Conversations with Prominent Artists and Scientists.* New York: Springer Publishing Company, 1981.

Gorer, Geoffrey. *Death, Grief, and Mourning.* Garden City, N.Y.: Doubleday & Company, 1965.

Greenspan, Stanley, and George Pollock, eds. "Aging or Aged: Development or Pathology." *The Course of Life, Volume III: Adulthood and the Aging Process.* Washington, D.C.: U.S. Government Printing Office, 1980.

Grof, Stanislav, and Joan Halifax. *The Human Encounter with Death.* New York: E. P. Dutton, 1978 (paperback).

Guthrie, Woody. *Seeds of Man.* New York: E. P. Dutton & Co., 1976.

Hall, Nor. *The Moon and the Virgin.* New York: Harper & Row, 1980 (paperback).

Hammarskjold, Dag. *Markings.* Leif Sjoberg and W. H. Auden, trans. New York: Alfred A. Knopf, 1964.

Herrick, George. *Michelangelo's Snowman: A Commonplace Collection.* Ipswich, Mass.: Ipswich Publishers, 1985.

Hunt, Morton. "Sick Thinking." The *New York Times Magazine* (January 3, 1988): 22.

Institute of Medicine, Osterweis, Marian, Fredric Solomon, and Morris Green, eds. *Bereavement: Reactions, Consequences, and Care.* Washington, D.C.: National Academy Press, 1984 (paperback).

Jewett, Claudia L. *Helping Children Cope with Separation and Loss.* Boston: Harvard Common Press, 1982.

Klein, Melanie. "Mourning and Its Relationship to Manic-Depressive States," *The International Journal of Psycho-analysis,* vol. XXI, part 2 (1940): 125-153.

Klein, Sandra Jacoby, and William Fletcher III. "Gay Grief: An Examination of Its Uniqueness Brought to Light by the AIDS Crisis," *Journal of Psychosocial Oncology,* vol. 4, no. 3 (1986): 15-26

Knight, Albert F. "The Death of a Son." The *New York Times Magazine* (June 22, 1986): 34.

Kohut, Heinz. "Forms and Transformations of Narcissism." *Journal of the American Psychoanalytic Association,* vol. 14 (1966): 243-272.

Kubler-Ross, Elisabeth. *Death: The Final Stage of Growth.* Englewood Cliffs, N.J.: Prentice-Hall, 1975 (paperback).

Kutner, Lawrence. "Death Is No Friend, So Take Care When Introducing Him." The *New York Times* (March 10, 1988): 19.

Lathem, Edward Connery, ed. *The Poetry of Robert Frost.* New York: Holt, Rinehart and Winston, 1965.

Lawrence, D. H. "Indians and Entertainment." *D. H. Lawrence and New Mexico,* Keith Sagar, ed. Salt Lake City: Gibbs M. Smith, 1982.

Leer, Frederic. "Running As an Adjunct to Psycho-Therapy." *Social Work* (January 1980): 20-25.

Lindbergh, Anne Morrow. *Gift from the Sea.* New York: Pantheon Books, 1955 (paperback).

Lindemann Erich. *Beyond Grief: Studies in Crisis Intervention.* New York: Jason Aronson, 1979.

Lukas, Christopher, and Henry Seiden. *Silent Grief: Living in the Wake of Suicide.* New York: Macmillan Publishing Company, 1987.

Maddocks, Melvin. "The Words of Jean-Paul Sartre." *The Christian Science Monitor,* vol. 72, no. 103 (1980): 22.

Marris, Peter. *Loss and Change.* New York: Pantheon Books, 1974.

Melville Herman. *Moby Dick.* New York: W. W. Norton & Company, 1967.

Merton Thomas. *Raids on the Unspeakable.* New York: New Directions, 1966.

Millay, Edna St. Vincent. *Collected Poems.* New York: Harper & Brothers, 1956.

Milosz, Czeslaw, ed. *Postwar Polish Poetry.* New York: Doubleday & Company, 1965.

Moffat, Mary Jane, ed. *In the Midst of Winter: Selections from the Literature of Mourning.* New York: Random House, 1982 (paperback).

Morgan, Ernest. *Dealing Creatively with Death: A Manual of Death Education and Simple Burial.* Jenifer Morgan, ed. Burnsville, N.C.: Celo Press, 1988.

Moss, Cynthia. *Elephant Memories: Thirteen Years in the Life of an Elephant Family.* New York: William Morrow, 1988.

Parkes, Colin Murray. *Bereavement: Studies of Grief in Adult Life.* New York: Tavistock Publications, 1972.

Pease, Roland. "Sea Sculpture." The *New York Times* (July 22, 1981): C2.

Perrin, Noel. "Middle-Age Dating." The *New York Times Magazine* (July 6, 1986): 37.

Pincus, Lily. *Death and the Family: The Importance of Mourning.* New York: Schocken Books, 1974.

Pollock, George, and Stanley Greenspan, eds. "Aging or Aged: Development or Pathology." *The Course of Life, Volume III: Adulthood and the Aging Process.* Washington, D.C.: U.S. Government Printing Office, 1980.

Pollock, George H. "Mourning and Adaptation." *The International Journal of Psycho-analysis,* vol. XLII, part 1 (July-October 1961): 1-30.

————. "Anniversary Reactions, Trauma, and Mourning." *The Psychoanalytic Quarterly,* vol. 39, no. 3 (1970): 347-371.

————. "The Mourning Process and Creative Organizational Change." *Journal of the American Psychoanalytic Association,* vol. 25, no. 1 (1977): 3-34.

————. "Process and Affect: Mourning and Grief." *The International Journal of Psycho-analysis,* vol. LIX, parts 2-3 (1978): 255-276.

Pounds, James. "Three Children." Private Collection, Austin, Tex.

Pradl, Gordon, ed. *Prospect and Retrospect: Selected Essays* by James Britton. London: Heinemann Educational Books, 1982.

Raphael, Beverley. *The Anatomy of Bereavement.* New York: Basic Books, 1983 (paperback).

Rilke, Rainer Maria. *Duino Elegies.* Gary Miranda, trans. Portland: Breitenbush Books, 1981.

Rose, Julie. "Mourning a Miscarriage." *Newsweek* (August 3, 1987): 7.

Schneider, John. *Stress, Loss and Grief.* Rockville, Md.: Aspen Systems Corporation, 1984.

Shand, Alexander. *The Foundations of Character: Being a Study of the Tendencies of the Emotions and Sentiments.* London: Macmillan and Co., 1920.

Shuchter, Stephen, and Sidney Zisook. "A Multidimensional Model of Spousal Bereavement." *Biopsychosocial Aspects of Bereavement,* Sidney Zisook, ed. Washington, D.C.: American Psychiatric Press, 1987.

Siegel, Bernie. "How to Improve Your Immune System." *Bottom Line,* vol. 9, no. 18 (1988): 1.

Snyder, Gary. *The Back Country.* New York: New Directions, 1968 (paperback).

————. *The Real Work: Interviews & Talks 1964-1979.* Scott McLean, ed. New York: New Directions, 1980.

Storr, Anthony. *Solitude: A Return to the Self.* New York: The Free Press, 1988.

Teachers Insurance and Annuity Association. "TIAA-CREF Survey Report: Report of Survey of Widowed TIAA-CREF Annuitants." New York: Teachers Insurance and Annuity Association, 1988.

Tournier, Paul. *The Adventure of Living.* New York: Harper & Row, 1965.

Turner, Victor, and Edith Turner. *Image and Pilgrimage in Christian Culture: Anthropological Perspectives.* New York: Columbia University Press, 1978.

van Gennep, Arnold. *The Rites of Passage.* Monika B. Vizedom and Gabrielle L. Caffee, trans. Chicago: University of Chicago Press, 1960.

Weiss, R. S. "The Provisions of Social Relationships." *Doing Unto Others.* Zick Ruben, ed. New York: Prentice-Hall, 1975.

Winnicott, D. W. *The Maturational Processes and the Facilitating Environment.* New York: International Universities Press, 1960.

Yourcenar, Marguerite. *With Open Eyes: Conversations with Matthieu Galey.* Arthur Goldhammer, trans. Boston: Beacon Press, 1984.

Zisook, Sidney, Schuchter, Stephen R., and Lucy E. Lyons. "Adjustment to Widowhood." *Biopsychosocial Aspects of Bereavement.* Sidney Zisook, ed. Washington, D.C.: American Psychiatric Press, Inc., 1987.

Zisook, Sidney, and Stephen R. Schuchter. "The Therapeutic Tasks of Grief." *Biopsychosocial Aspects of Bereavement.* Sidney Zisook, ed. Washington, D.C.: American Psychiatric Press, Inc., 1987

Zisook, Sidney, ed. *Biopsychosocial Aspects of Bereavement.* Washington, D.C.: American Psychiatric Press, Inc., 1987

PERMISSIONS

INDEX

Page numbers in italics refer to notes.

Elizabeth Harper Neeld, PH.D.

Elizabeth Harper Neeld's work celebrates the possibility of a daily sensed connection to the Divine, the courage and resiliency of the human spirit, and the power of story. She is the author of seventeen works, including *From the Plow to the Pulpit; Sister Bernadette: Cowboy Nun From Texas; Yes! You Can Write,* an audio cassette album; and *A Sacred Primer:* The Essential Guide to Quiet Time and Prayer. She also leads spiritual workshops and retreats.

Elizabeth Harper Neeld has been recognized in *Who's Who in America,* Fiftieth Edition; *Who's Who in the World,* Thirteenth Edition; and *Contemporary Authors,* Volume 141 (1994). She lives in Austin Texas, with her husband, Jerele, and two wonderfully idiosyncratic dogs, Dusty and Lacey.

Elizabeth Harper Neeld is available for lectures, retreats, and workshops. Details will be sent upon request. Write Mira Bennett Publishers, 6706 Beauford Drive, Austin, Texas 78750.

See Author Biography on Previous Page

See Order Form on Next Page

Order Form

BOOK
Seven Choices. Third Edition, Revised. Quality Paperback, 364 pages, $14.95

BOOK ON TAPE
Seven Choices. Third Edition, Revised. Abridged and read by the author on audio cassette, approximately three hours playing time, $18.00

POCKET REFERENCE SUPPORT GUIDE
Seven Choices. Carry Anywhere Reference Support Guide. Narratives, descriptions and positive choices for each phase of the grieving process. Sixty-four pages, $4.95

VIDEO
"The Challenge of Grief," a one-hour documentary featuring Elizabeth Neeld and *Seven Choices.* Focuses on the grieving process and AIDS but applicable to all persons experiencing any kind of loss, $19.95

Please send the following:

Seven Choices Paperback	___ copies @ 14.95 each	$_____
Seven Choices Audio Tape	___ copies @ 18.00 each	$_____
Seven Choices Pocket Guide	___ copies @ 4.95 each	$_____
"The Challenge of Grief" Video	___ copies @ 19.95 each	$_____
	Tax	$_____
	Shipping	$_____
	Total	$_____

Sales Tax: Please add 8.25% for items shipped to Texas addresses.
Shipping: $4.00 for the first item and $2.00 for each additional item.

Name: _____
Address: _____
City: _____ State: _____ Zip: _____
Telephone: (____)_____

MAKE CHECKS PAYABLE TO MBI PUBLISHING
Mail to MBI, 6706 Beauford Drive, Austin, Texas 78750

You can also order at www.centerpointpress.com

See Order Form on Next Page

Order Form

BOOK
Seven Choices. Third Edition, Revised. Quality Paperback, 364 pages, $14.95

BOOK ON TAPE
Seven Choices. Third Edition, Revised. Abridged and read by the author on audio cassette, approximately three hours playing time, $18.00

POCKET REFERENCE SUPPORT GUIDE
Seven Choices. Carry Anywhere Reference Support Guide. Narratives, descriptions and positive choices for each phase of the grieving process. Sixty-four pages, $4.95

VIDEO
"The Challenge of Grief," a one-hour documentary featuring Elizabeth Neeld and *Seven Choices.* Focuses on the grieving process and AIDS but applicable to all persons experiencing any kind of loss, $19.95

Please send the following:

Seven Choices Paperback	___ copies @ 14.95 each	$_____
Seven Choices Audio Tape	___ copies @ 18.00 each	$_____
Seven Choices Pocket Guide	___ copies @ 4.95 each	$_____
"The Challenge of Grief" Video	___ copies @ 19.95 each	$_____
	Tax	$_____
	Shipping	$_____
	Total	$_____

Sales Tax: Please add 8.25% for items shipped to Texas addresses.
Shipping: $4.00 for the first item and $2.00 for each additional item.

Name: _____
Address: _____
City: _____ State: _____ Zip: _____
Telephone: (_____)_____

MAKE CHECKS PAYABLE TO MBI PUBLISHING
Mail to MBI, 6706 Beauford Drive, Austin, Texas 78750
You can also order at www.centerpointpress.com